The SAGE
DICTIONARY
of QUALITATIVE
Third Edition INQUIRY

The SAGE DICTIONARY of QUALITATIVE INQUIRY

Third Edition

Thomas A. Schwandt
University of Illinois, Urbana-Champaign

SAGE Publications

Los Angeles • London • New Delhi • Singapore

For information:

Sage Publications, Inc.
2455 Teller Road
Thousand Oaks, California 91320
E-mail: order@sagepub.com

Sage Publications Ltd.
1 Oliver's Yard
55 City Road
London EC1Y 1SP
United Kingdom

Sage Publications India Pvt Ltd
B 1/I 1 Mohan Cooperative Industrial Area
Mathura Road,
New Delhi 110 044
India

Sage Publications Asia-Pacific Pvt. Ltd.
33 Pekin Street #02-01
Far East Square
Singapore 048763

Printed in the United States of America.

Library of Congress Cataloging-in-Publication Data

Schwandt, Thomas A.
The SAGE Dictionary of Qualitative Inquiry / Thomas A. Schwandt.—3rd ed.
    p. cm.
Includes index.
ISBN-13: 978-1-4129-0927-3 (pbk.)

    1. Social sciences—Methodology—Dictionaries. 2. Social sciences—Research—Dictionaries. I. Title.

H61.S4435 2007
300.72—dc22   2006030618

This book is printed on acid-free paper.

    08   09   10   11   10 9 8 7 6 5 4 3 2

Acquiring Editor:	Lisa Cuevas Shaw
Editorial Assistant:	Karen Margrethe Greene
Project Editor:	Astrid Virding
Copyeditor:	Cheryl Rivard
Typesetter:	C&M Digitals (P) Ltd.
Proofreader:	Ellen Brink

CONTENTS

———•◆•———

Conventions   **xvii**
Reader's Guide   **xix**
Preface   **xxvii**
 A Note on Teaching and Learning Qualitative Inquiry
About the Author   **xxxiii**

List of Terms

Abduction   1
Action   1
Action Research   3
Agency (vs. Structure)   4
Analytic Generalization   5
Analytic Induction   6
Analyzing Qualitative Data   6
Antinaturalism   8
Applied Research (*See* Use of Qualitative Inquiry)   8
Appreciative Inquiry   8
Artifact (Artefact)   9
Arts-Based Inquiry   9
Atomism   10
Audience Ethnography   10
Audiotaping   11
Audit Culture/Society   11
Auditing   12
Audit Trail (*See* Auditing)   13
Authenticity   13

Authenticity Criteria   14
Authority   15
Autoethnography   16

Behaviorism   19
Bias   20
Biographical Research   21
Biographical Turn   22
Body   23
Bracketing (Epoché)   24
Bricolage/Bricoleur   24

Careers   27
Case   27
Case Study Research   28
Causal Analysis/Causality   29
Chicago School of Sociology   30
Cinematic Society   31
Coding   32
Cognitivism   33
Collaborative Ethnography   34
Communications Studies   34
Computer-Assisted Data Analysis   35
Confirmability (*See* Trustworthiness Criteria)   36
Conservative Hermeneutics   36
Constant Comparison, Method of   37
Constructivism   37
Content Analysis   41
Context (*See* Contextualism)   41
Context of Discovery/Context of Justification   41
Contextualism   43
Conversation (*See* Dialogue)   44
Conversation Analysis   44
Cooperative Inquiry   45
Covering-Law Model of Explanation   45
Credibility (*See* Trustworthiness Criteria)   46
Crisis of Legitimation   46

Crisis of Representation   48
Criteria   49
Critical Ethnography   50
Critical Hermeneutics   52
Critical Race Theory   53
Critical Social Science   53
Critical Theory   55
Cross-Case Analysis   55
Cultural Anthropology   56
Cultural Relativism   57
Cultural Studies   58
Culture   59

Data   61
Data Collection (*See* Description,
    Generating Data)   61
Data Management, Storage, Retrieval   61
Deconstructionism   62
Deduction (*See* Inference)   64
Deductive-Nomological Explanation
    (*See* Covering-Law Model of Explanation)   64
Dependability (*See* Trustworthiness Criteria)   64
Description   64
Descriptive Statistics   66
Deskwork   67
Dialectic   67
Dialogic Method (*See* Dialogue)   68
Dialogic Text (*See* Dialogism)   68
Dialogism   68
Dialogue   68
Différance (*See* Deconstructionism)   72
Discourse Analysis   72
Discourse Theory   73
Discursive Practice (*See* Discourse
    Analysis, Discourse Theory)   74
Disengagement (*See* Body, Disinterested
    Social Science, Subject-Object Relationship)   74

Disinterested Social Science 74

Documents (*See* Document Analysis) 75

Document Analysis 75

Double Hermeneutic 76

Dramaturgy 76

Dualism 77

Educational Ethnography 79

Embodied (*See* Body) 79

Emergent Design 79

Emic/Etic 81

Emotion 82

Empirical Research (*See* Empiricism) 83

Empiricism 83

Empowerment 85

End of Philosophy 86

Epistemic Criterion (*See* Criteria, Validity) 87

Epistemology 87

Erklärung 89

Essentialism 89

Ethics of Qualitative Inquiry 89

Ethnocentrism 92

Ethnographic Authority (*See* Authority) 93

Ethnographic Methods 93

Ethnographic Naturalism 94

Ethnographic Realism 95

Ethnography 96

Ethnography of Communication 97

Ethnomethodology 97

Evidence 98

Existentialism 99

Experience 100

Experimental Text 102

Explanation 104

External Validity (*See* Generalization) 105

Fact (*See* Description) 107
Fact-Value Distinction 107
Fallibilism 108
Falsification 109
Feminist Epistemologies 110
Feminist Ethics 111
Feminist Ethnography 112
Fidelity to Method/Fidelity to Phenomenon 112
Field 113
Field Journal 115
Field Notes 115
Field Relations 117
Field Studies 118
Fieldwork 118
Focus Groups 119
Foundationalist Epistemologies 120
Frameworks for Qualitative Inquiry 121
Frankfurt School 122
Functionalism 122

Geisteswissenschaften 125
Genealogy 125
Generalization 126
Generating Data 128
Globalization 129
Grand Narrative 129
Grand Theory 130
Grounded Theory Methodology 131

Hermeneutic Circle 133
Hermeneutic Method 135
Hermeneutics 136
Hermeneutics of Suspicion 137
Historicism 138
Historicity 138
Holism 139

Human Action (*See* Action)   140
Hyperreality   140
Hypothetico-Deductive Method   141

Idealism   143
Identity   144
Ideology   145
Idiographic Interpretation   145
Indexicality   146
Inductive Analysis   146
Inductive-Statistical Explanation (*See* Explanation)   147
Inference   147
Informant   148
Informed Consent   149
Inscription   151
Insider/Outsider Perspective   152
Institutional Review Board (IRB)   152
Instrumentalism   154
Instrumental Rationality (*See* Instrumentalism)   155
Intentionalism   155
Intentionality   156
Interest   157
Interpretation   158
Interpretive Anthropology   159
Interpretive Sociology   159
Interpretive Turn   160
Interpretivism   160
Intersubjectivity   161
Intertextuality (*See* Dialogism, Text)   161
Interviewing Logic   161
Interviewing, Types of   163
Interview Society   163

Judgment   167
Justification of a Claim (*See* Evidence)   168

Knowledge   169

Language 173
Language Games 175
Lawlike Generalization 177
Lebenswelt (*See* Lifeworld) 177
Life-History Methodology (*See* Biographical Research) 177
Lifeworld 177
Liminality 179
Literary Turn (in Social Science) 179
Literature Review (*See* Review of Literature) 180
Lived Experience (*See* Experience) 180
Logical Empiricism 180
Logical Positivism 181
Logocentrism (*See* Deconstructionism) 183

Marginal Native (*See* Participant Observation) 185
Materialist Explanation (*See* Explanation) 185
Meaning 185
Meaning Realism (*See* Intentionalism, Objectivism, Realism) 187
Medical Sociology 187
Member Check 187
Memoing 188
Metaethnography 189
Metanarrative (*See* Grand Narrative) 189
Metaphysics 190
Method 190
Methodology 193
Methods of Text Analysis (*See* Textual Analysis, Methods Of) 194
Microethnography 194
Misunderstanding (*See* Understanding) 196
Mixed Methods 196
Modernism/Modernity (*See* Postmodernism, Praxis, Rationalism) 198
Monological (*See* Dialogism, Dialogue) 198
Multiple Realities 198

Naïve Realism (*See* Realism) 201
Narrative 201
Narrative Analysis 202

Narrative Criteria (*See* Verisimilitude)   202
Narrative Ethics   202
Narrative Explanation   203
Narrative Inquiry   203
Narrative Psychology   204
Narrative Realism   204
Native's Point of View   205
Naturalism   205
Naturalistic Inquiry   206
Naturalistic Interpretation of the Social Sciences (*See* Naturalism)   207
Natural Setting (*See* Ethnographic Naturalism, Naturalistic Inquiry)   207
Naturwissenschaften   207
Negative Case   207
Nomothetic Knowledge   208
Nonfoundational Epistemologies   208

Objectivism   209
Objectivist Hermeneutics (*See* Conservative Hermeneutics)   210
Objectivity   210
Observation   211
Ocular Epistemology (*See* Observation)   213
Ontological Hermeneutics (*See* Philosophical Hermeneutics)   213
Ontology (*See* Metaphysics)   213
Oral History   213
Other (The Other, Otherness)   213

Paradigm   217
Paradigmatic Knowledge Claim   218
Participant Observation   219
Participatory Action Research (Par)   221
Peer Debriefing   222
Performance Ethnography (*See* Performance Studies)   222
Performance/Performative/Performativity   222
Performance Studies   224
Phenomenological Sociology   224
Phenomenology   225
Philosophical Hermeneutics   226

Photo-Elicitation, Method of   228
Phronesis (*See* Praxis)   228
Play   228
Pluralism   229
Poiesis (*See* Praxis)   230
Politics of Research   230
Polyphony (*See* Dialogism)   233
Positivism   233
Postempiricism   233
Postmodern Ethnography   234
Postmodern Feminism (*See* Feminist Epistemologies)   235
Postmodernism   235
Postmodern Sensibilities   236
Postpositivism   237
Poststructuralism   237
Practical Rationality/Reason (*See* Praxis,
      Rationality, Technical Rationality)   238
Practical Turn   238
Practice (*See* Praxis)   239
Pragmatism   239
Praxis   240
Prejudice (*See* Bias, Philosophical Hermeneutics)   244
(The) Problem of the Criterion   245
Propositional Knowledge   245
Purposive Sampling (*See* Sampling Logic)   246

Qualitative Evaluation   247
Qualitative Inquiry   247
Qualitative Market Research   249
Qualitative Nursing Research   250
Qualitative Psychology   250
Quantification (*See* Quantitative)   250
Quantitative   250

Radical Hermeneutics (*See* Deconstructionism)   253
Rationalism   253
Rationality   254

Reactivity 255

Realism 256

Realist Tale (*See* Ethnographic Realism) 259

Reciprocity 259

Reductionism 259

Reflexivity 260

Relativism 261

Reliability 262

Representation 263

Representativeness (*See* Sampling Logic) 264

Research as Argument 264

Research Design 265

Respondent (*See* Ethics of Qualitative Inquiry, Informant) 265

Respondent Validation (*See* Member Check) 266

Review of Literature 266

Rhetoric 267

Sample Size (*See* Sampling Logic) 269

Sampling Logic 269

Sampling, Types of 271

Science 271

Scientific Method (*See* Method) 272

Scientism 272

Semiotics 273

Sensitizing Concepts 274

Skepticism 274

Social Anthropology (*See* Cultural Anthropology) 275

Social Constructionism (*See* Constructivism) 275

Sociology of Scientific Knowledge (SSK) 275

Spectator Theory of Knowledge (*See* Observation) 276

Standpoint Epistemologies 276

Statistical Explanation 277

Statistical Generalization 278

Structuralism 278

Subject 279

Subjectivism 279

Subjectivity 280

Subject-Object Relationship   281
Symbolic Interactionism   283

Tacit (Personal) Knowledge   285
Technical Rationality   286
Teleology   287
Text   288
Textual Analysis, Methods of   289
Textual Experimentation   290
Textualism (*See* Text)   291
Textualization (*See* Transcription)   291
Thematic Analysis   291
Theoretical Candor   291
Theoretical Generalization (*See* Generalization)   292
Theoretical Sampling (*See* Grounded
    Theory Methodology, Sampling Logic)   292
Theoretical Saturation (*See* Grounded Theory Methodology)   292
Theory, Types of   292
Theory, Uses of   293
Theory-Laden Observation (*See* Theory-Observation Distinction)   294
Theory-Observation Distinction   294
Theory of Signs (*See* Semiotics)   296
Theory-Practice Relationship (*See* Praxis,
    Use of Qualitative Inquiry)   296
Thick Description   296
Transcription   296
Transferability (*See* Generalization, Trustworthiness Criteria)   297
Triangulation   297
Trustworthiness Criteria   299
Truth   300
Typologies   302

Underdetermination of Theory by Data
    (*See* Theory-Observation Distinction)   303
Understanding   303
Unity of Method (*See* Logical Empiricism, Naturalism)   305
Unity of Sciences (*See* Logical Empiricism, Naturalism)   305

Unobtrusive Data   306
Use of Qualitative Inquiry   306

Validation Hermeneutics (*See* Conservative Hermeneutics)   309
Validity   309
Value-Free Social Science (*See* Disinterested
    Social Science, Fact-Value Distinction)   311
Value Neutrality (*See* Disinterested Social Science,
    Fact-Value Distinction, Politics of Research)   311
Verification   311
Verisimilitude   312
Verstehen   314
Verstehende Sociology (*See* Interpretive Sociology)   317
Visual Research Methods   317
Voice   318

Warranted Assertion   321
Weltanschauung   321
Writing Strategies   322

CONVENTIONS

- Terms are listed alphabetically without regard to hyphens and spaces between words.

- Cross-references are given at the end of each entry and signaled by the bold-faced designation **See also**. Cross-references may direct readers to related or, in some cases, contrasting terms.

- *Italics* are used for foreign words and phrases, for titles of books and journals, and for emphasis.

- Single quotes are used to indicate a novel use of a word or phrase.

- Some entries contain terms or phrases discussed elsewhere in the *Dictionary*. When explanation of another term would be helpful for understanding a particular entry, the term in question appears in ***bold-faced italics***.

READER'S GUIDE

ANALYZING & INTERPRETING
Abduction
Analytic generalization
Analytic induction
Analyzing qualitative data
Careers
Coding
Computer-assisted data analysis
Constant comparison, method of
Content analysis
Conversation analysis
Cross-case analysis
Deduction
Descriptive statistics
Deskwork
Discourse analysis
Document analysis
Generalization
Grounded theory methodology
Idiographic interpretation
Inductive analysis
Inference
Interpretation
Memoing
Metaethnography
Narrative

Narrative analysis
Negative case
Research as argument
Review of literature
Textualization
Textual analysis, methods of
Thematic analysis
Theoretical saturation
Typologies

AUTHORING, WRITING, REPORTING
Authority
Autoethnography
Crisis of legitimation
Crisis of representation
Description
Dialogic text
Dialogism
Ethnographic authority
Ethnographic realism
Experimental text
Literary turn (in social science)
Performance ethnography
Performance studies
Polyphony

Realist tale
Reflexivity
Representation
Review of literature
Rhetoric
Text
Textual experimentation
Textualism
Use of qualitative inquiry
Voice
Writing strategies

CRITERIA & JUSTIFICATION
Auditing
Audit trail
Authenticity criteria
Bias
Confirmability
Context of discovery/context
    of justification
Credibility
Crisis of legitimation
Criteria
Dependability
Epistemic criterion
Ethnocentrism
Evidence
External validity
Fact-value distinction
Falsification
Generalization
Intersubjectivity
Judgment
Justification of a claim
Member check
Narrative criteria
Objectivity

Peer debriefing
Prejudice
(The) Problem of the criterion
Rationality
Reactivity
Reflexivity
Reliability
Respondent validation
Theoretical candor
Transferability
Triangulation
Trustworthiness criteria
Truth
Validity
Value-free social science
Value-neutrality
Verification
Verisimilitude
Warranted assertion

DATA
Artifact (artefact)
Case
Data
Data collection
Data management, storage, retrieval
Description
Documents
Emic/etic
Empirical research
Evidence
Fact
Field journal
Field notes
Generating data
Inscription
Native's point of view

Purposive sampling
Representativeness
Sample size
Sampling logic
Sampling, types of
Theoretical sampling
Theory-observation distinction
Thick description
Transcription
Unobtrusive data

DESIGNING A QUALITATIVE
   STUDY
Bricolage/bricoleur
Biographical turn
Emergent design
Field
Field studies
Interpretive turn
Naturalistic inquiry
Postmodern sensibilities
Practical turn
Research as argument
Research design
Sensitizing concepts
Use of qualitative inquiry

EPISTEMOLOGY
Behaviorism
Body
Bracketing (epoché)
Cognitivism
Constructivism
Cultural relativism
Embodied
Emotion
Empiricism

End of philosophy
Epistemology
Fact-value distinction
Fallibilism
Feminist epistemologies
Foundationalist epistemologies
Instrumentalism
Instrumental rationality
Knowledge
Logical empiricism
Logical positivism
Narrative psychology
Nonfoundational
   epistemologies
Objectivism
Ocular epistemology
Paradigmatic knowledge claim
Phenomenology
Phronesis
Pluralism
Positivism
Postempiricism
Postmodern feminism
Postpositivism
Practical reason/rationality
Pragmatism
Praxis
Propositional knowledge
Rationalism
Rationality
Relativism
Scientism
Skepticism
Social constructionism
Spectator theory of knowledge
Standpoint epistemologies
Subjectivism

Subjectivity
Tacit knowledge
Technical rationality
Truth
Warranted assertion

ETHICS, POLITICS, &
    STANDPOINT
Ethics of qualitative inquiry
Dialectic
Dialogism
Dialogue
Disengagement
Empowerment
Feminist ethics
Field relations
Identity
Informant
Informed consent
Institutional Review Board
Liminality
Monological
Narrative ethics
Objectivity
Other (The Other, Otherness)
Politics of research
Reciprocity
Respondent
Standpoint epistemologies
Subject
Subject-object relationship
Voice

EXPLANATION
Agency (vs. Structure)
Analytic generalization

Causal analysis/causality
Covering-law model of
    explanation
Deductive-nomological
    explanation
Erklärung
Essentialism
Explanation
Functionalism
Genealogy
Holism
Ideology
Inductive-statistical
    explanation
Inference
Lawlike generalization
Materialist explanation
Narrative explanation
Nomothetic knowledge
Poststructuralism
Reductionism
Statistical explanation
Statistical generalization
Structuralism
Teleology
Theoretical generalization

FOUNDATIONAL CONCEPTS
Action
Authenticity
Context
Contextualism
Culture
Double hermeneutic
Ethnographic naturalism
Experience

Fidelity to method/fidelity to
  phenomenon
Geisteswissenschaften
Historicism
Human action
Indexicality
Insider/outsider perspective
Intentionalism
Intentionality
Interpretivism
Language
Language games
Lebenswelt
Lifeworld
Lived experience
Meaning
Multiple realities
Natural setting
Subject-object relationship
Understanding
Verstehen

FRAMEWORKS
Antinaturalism
Critical social science
Disinterested social science
Frameworks for qualitative inquiry
Geisteswissenschaften
Methodology
Naturalism
Naturalistic interpretation of
  the social sciences
Naturwissenschaften
Pluralism
Paradigm
Qualitative inquiry

Quantitative
Science
Unity of method
Unity of science

HERMENEUTICS
Conservative hermeneutics
Critical hermeneutics
Deconstructionism
Dialogue
Double hermeneutic
Hermeneutic circle
Hermeneutic method
Hermeneutics
Hermeneutics of suspicion
Historicity
Intentionality
Interpretation
Language
Misunderstanding
Objectivist hermeneutics
Ontological hermeneutics
Philosophical hermeneutics
Phronesis
Play
Praxis
Prejudice
Qualitative inquiry
Text
Radical hermeneutics
Understanding
Validation hermeneutics
Verstehen

LANGUAGE
Constructivism

Conversation
Deconstructionism
Dialogism
Dialogue
Différance
Discourse theory
Discursive practice
Emic/etic
Indexicality
Intertextuality
Language
Language games
Logocentrism
Poststruturalism
Semiotics
Theory of signs

METHOD
Audiotaping
Biographical research
Conversation
Description
Dialogic method
Dialogue
Ethnographic methods
Fieldwork
Focus groups
Hermeneutic method
Hypothetico-deductive method
Interviewing logic
Interviewing, types of
Life-history methodology
Marginal native
Method
Methodology
Methods of text analysis
Mixed methods

Observation
Oral history
Participant observation
Photo-elicitation, method of
Scientific method
Visual research methods

NATURE OF REALITY
Atomism
Dualism
Essentialism
Experience
Hyperreality
Idealism
Meaning realism
Metaphysics
Naïve realism
Narrative realism
Objectivism
Ontology
Performance/performative/
    performativity
Realism
Subjectivism

SCHOOLS OF THOUGHT
Chicago School of sociology
Frankfurt School
Sociology of scientific
    knowledge

SITES OF PRACTICE
Action research
Appreciative inquiry
Arts-based inquiry
Audience ethnography
Case study research

Collaborative ethnography
Communications studies
Cooperative inquiry
Critical ethnography
Cultural anthropology
Cultural studies
Educational ethnography
Ethnography
Ethnography of communication
Feminist ethnography
Interpretive anthropology
Interpretive sociology
Medical sociology
Microethnography
Narrative inquiry
Participatory action research
Postmodern ethnography
Qualitative evaluation
Qualitative market research
Qualitative nursing research
Qualitative psychology
Social anthropology

SOCIAL THEORY
Atomism
Audit culture/society
Cinematic society
Constructivism
Critical race theory

Dramaturgy
Ethnomethodology
Existentialism
Globalization
Grand narrative
Holism
Interview society
Metanarrative
Modernism/modernity
Phenomenological sociology
Postmodernism
Poststructuralism
Symbolic interactionism
Structuralism

THEORIZING
Analytic generalization
Critical theory
Grand theory
Interest
Research as argument
Theoretical generalization
Theory, types of
Theory, uses of
Theory-observation distinction
Theory-practice relationship
Underdetermination of
    theory by data
Weltanschauung

PREFACE

————•◦•————

Every linguistic experience of the world is experience of the world, not experience of language.

—H.-G. Gadamer, *Truth and Method*,
Trans. J. Weinsheimer & D. G. Marshall,
2nd rev. ed. New York: Crossroads, 1989, p. 546

When you take a word in your mouth, you have not taken up some arbitrary tool which can be thrown in a corner if it doesn't do the job, but you are committed to a line of thought that comes from afar and reaches beyond you.

—H.-G. Gadamer, *Truth and Method*,
Trans. J. Weinsheimer & D. G. Marshall,
2nd rev. ed. New York: Crossroads, 1989, pp. 547–548

This book is a commentary on the meaning of approximately 380 selected words in a research vocabulary—a collection of terms and phrases that partially shape our understanding of the origins, nature, purpose, logic, meaning, conduct, methods, and significance of the practices broadly referred to as qualitative inquiry or qualitative research. The commentary combines explication, explanation, analysis, and, occasionally, criticism and evaluation of this vocabulary. It is written from a particular point of view, thus it is more interpretive than is characteristic of a dictionary. Entries are more like annotations (critical and explanatory remarks) than definitions. I have tried to make these annotations inviting, inclusive of multiple and often contested points of view, and occasionally provocative. My aim has been to interpret terms in such a way that further exploration is stimulated and not foreclosed. The book is intended to stimulate continued examination of the nature and purpose of qualitative inquiry, not to dampen discussion by offering the generally agreed-upon definitions and usage of a word.

As a guidebook for the vocabulary of qualitative inquiry, the *Dictionary* can be particularly useful because concepts acquire different interpretations both within and across the various theoretical perspectives and philosophies—for example, naturalism, interpretivism, social constructionism, feminist theory, phenomenological sociology, philosophical hermeneutics, critical theory, cultural studies, postmodernism, and poststructuralism—that shape the activity of qualitative inquiry. This edition continues to reflect the orientation of the previous editions, namely, to promote investigation of philosophical and methodological assumptions that foreground the practices of qualitative inquiry.

To make it easier for readers to undertake further examination of issues, I added a Reader's Guide to this edition that groups terms into several categories. The categories are not mutually exclusive and exhaustive; they do, however, provide a general sense of clusters of terms that take up similar matters and concerns. This *Dictionary* can be used in a variety of ways. It can be a glossary for the vocabulary of qualitative inquiry in introductory courses on qualitative methods and methodologies or a supplement or complement to texts representative of different theoretical perspectives in courses on the foundations of qualitative inquiry. Some readers have even found it beneficial to read the entire dictionary cover to cover to grasp a sense of what is entailed in thinking about qualitative inquiry.

For a number of reasons, it is becoming exceedingly difficult to catalogue the vocabulary of qualitative inquiry as a distinctive and unique research language. First, investigations into the meaning of social reality informed by a wide variety of often quite different (and in various ways, contradictory) epistemologies, political persuasions, and ethical frameworks all travel under the broad banner of 'qualitative inquiry.' Thus, for example, the significance and meaning of ideas like the politics of research or value neutrality are quite different in studies informed by standpoint epistemologies versus those committed to naturalism. In addition, the notions of meaning and truth bear little resemblance in scientific realism, deconstructionism, and philosophical hermeneutics. Second, the meanings of the very terms that name a theoretical perspective or philosophy are often themselves disputed. Consider, for example, the contested definitions of social constructionism, postmodernism, or post-structuralism. Third, pinning down the vocabulary of qualitative inquiry is also difficult because not all inquiries bearing that label even have the same social object in view. For some, the object of investigation is the meaning of social action itself; for others, it is the accomplishment of that action; some regard their own experience as the proper object; and, for still others, society or human action as an object for analysis gives way to examining what is constructed in the process of communication. Fourth, as the arena of qualitative inquiry continues to expand, embracing new fields of study and new methodologies, it begins to incorporate terms from specialized vocabularies unique to a particular undertaking—for example, grounded theory methodology, conversation and discourse analysis, semiotic analysis, and narrative analysis. Finally, as is readily evident in the various editions of the *Handbook of Qualitative Research*, qualitative inquiry is both a cross-disciplinary and interdisciplinary activity. This means that vocabularies and conceptual meanings from disciplines and fields as diverse as psychology and communication studies, history and sociology, literary studies and philosophy, have become blended into new vocabularies with somewhat different currency and usage.

Of course, none of this means that the language of the practice of qualitative inquiry is indeterminable. Rather, what it suggests is that the language constituting the aim, methods, and significance of the practice is constantly being reinterpreted. This reinterpretation is inevitable given that we are language beings, an idea central to both deconstructionism and philosophical hermeneutics. We are not the ones in charge of language; language is in charge of us. How one makes sense of this characteristic of our being human matters a great deal. On the one hand, one can believe that there is no final, authentic meaning of the words in the language we use; there is always and only an irreducible equivocation and undecidability of meaning in the concepts of the practice of qualitative inquiry (or in any other practice, for that matter). On the other hand, one can hold that the notion of a discoverable, fixed, authentic meaning is mistaken yet maintain that genuine meaning does emerge in the encounter with that which we seek to understand in the event or 'happening' of understanding. In this way of making sense of ourselves, we are conversational partners with other speakers and with texts, partners engaged in a joint search for meaning.

A NOTE ON TEACHING AND
LEARNING QUALITATIVE INQUIRY

Even a cursory glance at the wide-ranging qualitative inquiry literature reveals a field of study with varied and widespread focal points. We read of qualitative research as rooted in the ethnographic traditions of fieldwork sociology and cultural anthropology on the one hand and the emerging perspective of arts-based inquiry on the other; of the influences of methodologies of symbolic interactionism, ethnography, ethnomethodology, standpoint theory, and discourse analysis; of philosophical issues framed by interpretivism, hermeneutics, critical theory, feminist theory, and social constructionism; of the links to postmodern thought, poststructuralism, cultural studies, queer theory, and so on.

One can approach the complicated tasks of teaching and learning the field in view of this dizzying assortment of epistemologies, methodologies, and disciplinary affiliations in at least two ways. One tactic is to seek a kind of reconciliation in which differences, oppositions, and conflicts within the field of study are brought into some sense of order and different ways of thinking are arrayed on a set of key dimensions, issues, or criteria. This approach is evident in sorting, arranging, categorizing, and labeling the complex and diverse activities comprising qualitative inquiry into movements, phases, approaches, paradigms, or traditions. These are efforts to produce a whole surveyable order of things wherein differences, while not necessarily dissolved, are made more coherent, manageable, and hence graspable. As useful as this might be for grasping a sense of the whole, these encyclopedic moves may not be a particularly helpful pedagogical strategy for learning the subject matter.

The 'whole surveyable order' approach to the field sends at least an implicit message that learning qualitative inquiry is a matter of grasping a typology of ways of thinking about qualitative work and then locating oneself as an inquirer somewhere in that systematic classification of approaches, paradigms, or traditions. The subject matter, however, is artificially typologized—one cannot readily identify well-defined professional communities of inquirers that neatly align with so-called paradigms or traditions. In addition, within a given approach, tradition, or paradigm, there is often considerable disagreement on critical issues. We might be better served as teachers and learners if we think of the field of qualitative inquiry less in terms of metaphors suited to typologizing, classifying, sorting, and arranging and more in terms of metaphors that suggest interface, ecology, and relations. These metaphors portray the subject matter in terms of issues, relationships, transactions, and interactions. Issues are unsettled matters about which reasonable people disagree. Relationships may be harmonious or discordant. Interactions may be characterized as agreements, differences, disagreements, oppositions, points of contention, conflicts, and contradictions. Such metaphors suggest that the subject matter of qualitative inquiry is like a dynamic field in which ideas about subjectivity, objectivity, social reality, meaning, understanding, knowing, justification, evidence, and so on are always in play. Accordingly, to teach and to learn qualitative inquiry is to engage this dynamic conversation and to learn how to participate in it with clarity, alacrity, and perspicacity.

We accept the fact that the subject presents itself historically under different aspects at different times or from a different standpoint. We accept that these aspects do not simply cancel one another out as research proceeds, but are like mutually exclusive conditions that exist each by themselves and combine only in us. Our historical consciousness is always filled with a variety of voices in which the echo of the past is to be heard. It is present in the multifariousness of such voices: this constitutes the nature of the tradition in which we want to share and have a part.

—H.-G. Gadamer, *Truth and Method*, Trans. J. Weinsheimer & D. G. Marshall, 2nd rev. ed. New York: Crossroads, 1989, p. 378

ABOUT THE AUTHOR

Thomas A. Schwandt is Professor of Education in the Department of Educational Psychology in the College of Education at the University of Illinois, Urbana-Champaign. He also holds appointments in the Unit for Criticism and Interpretive Theory and the Department of Educational Policy Studies. Previously, he was a faculty member at Indiana University, Bloomington (IU), and a Fellow of the IU Poynter Center for Ethics and American Institutions, a member of the faculty in medical education at the University of Illinois at Chicago, and employed as an evaluator and organizational consultant in the private sector. His papers on qualitative methodology, issues in the philosophy of interpretive social science, and evaluation theory have appeared in a variety of journals and edited books. He is the author of *Evaluation Practice Reconsidered* (Peter Lang, 2002), *Evaluating Holistic Rehabilitation Praxis* (Kommuneforlaget, Oslo, 2004), coeditor (with Katherine Ryan) of *Exploring Evaluator Role and Identity* (Information Age Press, 2002), and coeditor (with Peder Haug) of *Evaluating Educational Reforms: Scandinavian Perspectives* (Information Age Press, 2003).

A

---·◆·---

ABDUCTION   This is a kind of reasoning developed by Charles Sanders Peirce (1839–1914) for the discovery of hypotheses or theories that differs from inductive and deductive inference. In many forms of qualitative inquiry influenced by *grounded theory methodology*, the aim is not to test hypotheses in a deductive fashion, nor to generalize from cases to a wider population (via inductive inference), but to discover or generate theory. Abduction is a way of relating an observation or case to a theory (or vice versa) that results in a plausible interpretation.

See also Inference.

KEY REFERENCES

Danermark, B., Ekström, M., Jacobsen, L., & Karlsson, J. *Explaining Society: Critical Realism in the Social Sciences.* London: Routledge, 2002.
Fann, K. T. *Peirce's Theory of Abduction.* The Hague: Nijhoff, 1970.

ACTION   Qualitative inquirers often refer to their object of study as that of human or social action as opposed to behavior. This language, in part, reflects a distinction between meaningful action and merely reactive behavior introduced by Max Weber (1864–1920) and elaborated by symbolic interactionists like George Herbert Mead (1863–1931). Weber defined sociology as a science concerned with the interpretative understanding of social action, and social action as behavior meaningfully oriented toward the behavior of others. His fourfold typology of social action included instrumentally rational (*zweckrational*), value-rational (*wertrational*), affectual, and traditional action. In addition to Weber,

Parsons, Dewey, Mead, Garfinkel, Giddens, and Habermas, among others, have all elaborated theories of action. For example, Habermas is well known for his sharp criticism of strategic, instrumental, or purposive-rational social action as the guiding *interest* of social inquiry. Habermas builds a case for social inquiry on communicative human action grounded in an emancipatory cognitive interest (versus *zweckrational* grounded in a technical, instrumental cognitive interest). This idea is influential in shaping some qualitative methodologies that draw on the tradition of *critical social science*.

All approaches to qualitative inquiry at least assume some theory of social action. Generally, these theories display one of two general orientations: Either they stress the importance of subjective consciousness (intention) in directing action, or they emphasize the significance of social *praxis* (the enactment or performance of social conduct). The former are varieties of the theory of *intentionalism*—a theory that says that the meaning of an action derives from the intentions of the actor (agent). Hence, the inquirer must adopt some means of making sense of this intention by getting inside the head of the agent, so to speak, or engaging in some kind of psychological reenactment. The latter stress the intentionality of the act itself and argue that to interpret the meaning of an act, the inquirer must connect the act to the wider context of the agent's life, the social setting in which the act is performed, and so on.

The emphasis on action reflects two important ideas: First, behavior is purposive, intentional, and goal directed, not simply a physical response to a stimulus (as claimed, for example, in *behaviorism*). The human agent attaches subjective meaning to her or his behavior. Second, interpreting subjective meaning requires understanding not simply individual beliefs, attitudes, motives, intentions, values, and the like but also intersubjective or shared meanings, values, understandings, and so on that interpenetrate individual thought and action. Thus, the qualitative inquirer assumes that subjectivity is not a matter of individual psychological attributes but is constituted intersubjectively. Charles Taylor argues that a strict neobehaviorist, empiricist account that claims human action can be explained by linking actors' physically observable behaviors to an inventory of individual actors' attitudes, beliefs, and other psychological states is mistaken, for it completely overlooks the notion of intersubjective, shared meanings.

See also Agency, Meaning, Verstehen.

KEY REFERENCES

Cohen, J. "Theories of Action and Praxis," in *The Blackwell Companion to Social Theory,* B. S. Turner, ed. Oxford, UK: Blackwell Publishers, 1996.

Habermas, J. *The Theory of Communicative Action, Vol. 1 Reason and Rationalization of Society.* T. McCarthy, ed. and trans. Boston: Beacon Press, 1981.

Joas, H. *The Creativity of Action.* J. Gaines & P. Keast, trans. Chicago: University of Chicago Press, 1996.

Taylor, C. "Interpretation and the Sciences of Man," *Review of Metaphysics,* 1971, 25, 3–51.

Weber, M. "Basic Sociological Terms," in *Economy and Society.* G. Roth & C. Wittich, trans. New York: Bedminster, 1968.

ACTION RESEARCH   The term was coined by social psychologist Kurt Lewin (1890–1947) in the 1940s to describe a particular kind of research that united the experimental approach of social science with programs of social action to address social problems. Lewin argued that social problems (as opposed to a scientist's own theoretical interests) should serve as the impulse for social research. He developed a model of social inquiry that involved a spiral of interlocking cycles of planning, acting, observing, and reflecting. Although Lewin's approach was well received in organizational research in the 1960s and 1970s, action research has been subject to various criticisms within the social scientific community. Some of these criticisms include that action research is not 'real' research because it does not meet criteria of a valid scientific methodology, that it is little more than refined common sense and not rigorous empirical research, and that it blurs an important distinction that should be maintained between theory and practice. Various forms of action research are alive and well today, however, in the fields of education, organizational and community development, and work life research.

Theories and methodologies of action research are found under a variety of different labels—for example, action inquiry, action science, participatory inquiry, pragmatic action research, collaborative inquiry, *cooperative inquiry,* and participatory action research. For example, building on the work of Lewin and John Dewey (1859–1952), Chris Argyris and Donald Schön (1931–1977) developed a particular form of action research called action science. It seeks to advance basic (or theoretical) knowledge while it simultaneously aims to solve practical problems in organizations and communities. It provides strategies for both problem framing or setting and problem solving and links the two activities in a feedback cycle called "double loop learning." Action scientists work collaboratively with participants to solve problems of practice in particular organizational learning contexts. Reflection and experimentation are encouraged as ongoing processes. Action science employs a variety of methods for generating data including observations, interviews, action experiments, and participant-written cases and accounts.

According to Wilfred Carr and Stephen Kemmis, all action research has the aims of improvement and involvement: Involvement refers to the participation of practitioners in all phases of planning, acting, observing, and reflecting. Improvement is a matter of changing the situation in which a particular social practice takes place, enhancing the understanding that practitioners have of their practice or their capacity to control it, remaking the practice itself, or all of these.

See also Participatory Action Research.

KEY REFERENCES

Argyris, C., Putnam, R., & McClain Smith, D. *Action Science.* San Francisco: Jossey-Bass, 1985.
Carr, W., & Kemmis, S. *Becoming Critical.* London: Falmer, 1986.
Greenwood, D., & Levin, M. *Introduction to Action Research.* Thousand Oaks, CA: Sage, 1998.
Reason, P., & Bradbury, H., eds. *Handbook of Action Research: Participative Inquiry and Practice.* London: Sage, 2001.
Schön, D. *The Reflective Practitioner: How Professionals Think in Action.* New York: Basic Books, 1983.

AGENCY (VS. STRUCTURE) Broadly understood, the term *human agency* signals the capacity of individuals to perceive their situation, reason about it, consciously monitor their action, form motives, and so on. The agency versus structure problem is the sociological version of the philosophical problem of free will versus determinism. In developing social theory, scholars take various positions on the relative weight to be attached to human actions (agency) or external structures or forces. Consider, for example, the difference between functionalist theories that emphasize the social system or the contribution of social institutions to the constitution of society versus *symbolic interactionism* and *ethnomethodology* that place human agency at the core of society. The social theories of Anthony Giddens and Pierre Bourdieu (1930–2002) are examples of attempts to resolve or overcome the tension between structure and agency.

KEY REFERENCES

Baert, P. *Social Theory in the Twentieth Century.* New York: New York University Press, 1998.

Holton, R. J. "Classical Sociological Theory," in *The Blackwell Companion to Social Theory,* B. S. Turner, ed. Oxford, UK: Blackwell, 1996.

ANALYTIC GENERALIZATION   Also called theoretical elaboration, this is a type of *generalization* in which the inquirer attempts to link findings from a particular *case* to a *theory*. (Here theory means something more like a set of theoretical tools, models, or concepts rather than a formalized set of propositions, laws, and generalizations comprising a systematic, unified causal explanation of social phenomena.) A study of some phenomenon in a particular set of circumstances (i.e., a case) is used as evidence to support, contest, refine, or elaborate a theory, model, or concept (note that the case is never regarded as a definitive test of the theory). It appears that this notion is what the interpretive anthropologist Clifford Geertz has in mind when he says it is the job of the ethnographer to make small facts speak to large issues.

Many researchers argue that the findings from qualitative studies of cases or instances of phenomena are most appropriately generalizable to concepts, theoretical propositions, or models and not to universes or populations of cases or instances. Analytic generalization is contrasted with *statistical generalization*.

See also Case Study Research, Generalization.

KEY REFERENCES

Geertz, C. "Thick Description: Toward an Interpretive Theory of Culture," in C. Geertz, ed., *The Interpretation of Culture.* New York: Basic Books, 1973.

Vaughan, D. "Theory Elaboration: The Heuristics of Case Analysis," in C. C. Ragin & H. S. Becker, eds., *What Is a Case?: Exploring the Foundations of Social Inquiry.* Cambridge, UK: Cambridge University Press, 1992.

Yin, R. *Case Study Research,* 2nd ed. Thousand Oaks, CA: Sage, 1994.

ANALYTIC INDUCTION   This is a strategy for analyzing qualitative data based on the assumption that the inquirer should formulate propositions that apply to all instances (or cases) of the problem under analysis. After initial examination of the data, the inquirer develops working hypotheses to explain the data. One example, instance, episode, or case in the data corpus is examined to determine whether the hypothesis fits the facts of that instance. If the hypothesis fits, the inquirer moves to the next instance and again tests for fit. If the hypothesis does not fit the facts, the hypothesis is revised or the phenomenon to be explained is redefined to exclude that instance. An instance that does not fit the hypothesis is called a ***negative case***. The intent here is to use negative instances for continuous refinement of the hypothesis until all instances can be satisfactorily explained.

See also *Analyzing Qualitative Data.*

KEY REFERENCES

Fielding, N. G., ed. *Actions and Structure.* London: Sage, 1988.
Manning, P. K. "Analytic Induction," in *Symbolic Interactionism, vol. 2: Contemporary Issues.* K. Plummer, ed. Brookfield, VT: Edward Elgar, 1991. (Originally published in R. Smith & P. K. Manning, eds., *Qualitative Methods.* Cambridge, MA: Ballinger, 1982)
Silverman, D. *Interpreting Qualitative Data: Methods of Analyzing Talk, Text, and Interaction,* 2nd ed. London: Sage, 2001.

ANALYZING QUALITATIVE DATA   Broadly conceived, this is the activity of making sense of, interpreting, and theorizing data. It is both art and science, and it is undertaken by means of a variety of procedures that facilitate working back and forth between data and ideas. Analysis begins with the processes of organizing, reducing, and describing the data and continues through the activity of drawing conclusions or interpretations from the data, and warranting those interpretations. If data could speak for themselves, analysis would not be necessary.

Some qualitative inquirers place a premium on analysis as a science and stress the fact that analysis should be rigorous, disciplined, systematic, carefully documented, and methodical. To analyze means to break down a whole into its component or constituent parts. Through reassembly of the parts, one comes to understand the integrity of the whole. Thus, the qualitative analyst breaks down the whole corpus of data (field notes, transcriptions, and the like) by categorizing and coding its segments and then tries to establish a pattern for the whole by relating the codes or categories to one another. Having knowledge of the correct application of the right analytic procedures (e.g., **constant comparison method, analytic induction, grounded theory analysis**, and **typological analysis**) figures prominently in this way of thinking about analysis. Other inquirers, although generally no less empirical in their approach to making sense of data, draw a distinction between analysis and interpretation. They emphasize that interpretation is an art of understanding (including representing one's understanding in writing) that is not fully definable in terms of procedure.

Whether viewed as science or art, analysis in qualitative inquiry is recursive and begins almost at the outset of generating data. The inquirer employs a variety of analytic strategies that involve sorting, organizing, and reducing the data to something manageable and then exploring ways to reassemble the data in order to interpret them. Sorting and organizing requires comparing, contrasting, and labeling the data. This initial step is necessary to bring some order to the largely undifferentiated mass of data that the inquirer has generated from observations, interviews, and so on. Sorting can involve making frequency counts of the data, developing categories or typologies to account for all the data, selecting concepts that define relationships among categories, and/or formulating working hypotheses or assertions that explain the data. Choosing concepts, developing typologies, and so on are, in effect, ways of developing an analytic vocabulary by means of which the inquirer fosters the aim of her or his research—that is, to answer questions such as, What is happening? What are people doing? What does it mean to them? How are the realities of everyday life accomplished? How is the social world constituted by its members? Why is it constituted this way rather than that way? The results of data analysis can be presented in tables, graphs, charts, concept maps, and narrative accounts.

See also *Careers, Coding, Computer-Assisted Data Analysis, Emergent Design, Hermeneutic Method, Textual Analysis, Typologies.*

KEY REFERENCES

Bernard, H. R. *Research Methods in Anthropology: Qualitative and Quantitative Approaches,* 2nd ed. Thousand Oaks, CA: Sage, 1994.

Gubrium, J. F., & Holstein, J. A. *The New Language of Qualitative Method.* Oxford, UK: Oxford University Press, 1997.

Miles, M., & Huberman, A. M. *Qualitative Data Analysis: An Expanded Sourcebook,* 2nd ed. Thousand Oaks, CA: Sage, 1994.

Patton, M. Q. *Qualitative Research & Evaluation Methods,* 3rd ed. Thousand Oaks, CA: Sage, 2002.

Wolcott, H. F. *Transforming Qualitative Data: Description, Analysis, and Interpretation.* Thousand Oaks, CA: Sage, 1994.

ANTINATURALISM   This is one of four basic approaches to the study of social phenomena (the others are ***naturalism, pluralism,*** and ***critical social science***). Antinaturalists claim that the study of social phenomena cannot/ should not be undertaken using the same methods of inquiry and with the same goal and modes of explanation that the natural sciences employ to study natural phenomena. For the antinaturalist, there are particular and distinctive features of the social world: (a) The social or human sciences deal with phenomena that are intentional—the meaningful action of individuals—whereas the subject matter of the natural sciences is the behavior of physical phenomena; consequently, (b) social phenomena, unlike natural phenomena, do not admit to causal explanation—the inquirer must attempt to understand (vs. explain) social action by reference to the ways in which humans experience their activities and give meaning to them. Antinaturalists can be found among scholars who embrace ***Verstehen*** approaches, ***phenomenological sociology***, and ***philosophical hermeneutics*** as well as some feminist inquirers.

See also *Action, Authenticity, Explanation, Intentionalism.*

KEY REFERENCES

Outhwaite, W. *Understanding Social Life: The Method Called* Verstehen. London: Allen and Unwin, 1975.

Taylor, C. *Philosophy and the Human Sciences. Philosophical Papers 2.* Cambridge, UK: Cambridge University Press, 1985.

APPLIED RESEARCH   See USE OF QUALITATIVE INQUIRY.

APPRECIATIVE INQUIRY   This is a social constructionist approach to organizational change and development that, rather than focusing on defining and fixing problems, begins by appreciating what is best within an organization, building on existing organizational achievements, strengths, and skills. Developed in the early 1970s at Case Western Reserve University primarily to help corporations sharpen their competitive advantage, appreciative inquiry has now extended into the fields of evaluation and community development. It shares the general philosophy of participatory, collaborative approaches to research and evaluation and commonly makes use of the typical means of generating qualitative data (e.g., observations, interviews, focus groups).

KEY REFERENCES

Preskill, H., & Catsambas, T. T. *Reframing Evaluation Through Appreciative Inquiry.* Thousand Oaks, CA: Sage, 2006.
Watkins, J. M., & Mohr, B. J. *Appreciative Inquiry: Change at the Speed of Imagination.* San Francisco: Jossey-Bass, 2001.

ARTIFACT (ARTEFACT)   Products of human workmanship or handcrafting, for example, a tool, text, work of art, monument, or photograph, are often referred to as artifacts. An artifact is an object that carries meaning about the culture of its creators and users. Understanding and interpreting the composition, historical circumstances, function, purpose, and so on of artifacts are central to the study of material culture.

KEY REFERENCE

Tilley, C. "Ethnography and Material Culture," in P. Atkinson, A. Coffey, S. Delamont, J. Lofland, & L. Lofland, eds., *Handbook of Ethnography.* London: Sage, 2001.

ARTS-BASED INQUIRY   Also known as arts-based educational research (ABER), this is an intellectual and practical development within the broad field of qualitative inquiry that challenges the idea that social inquiry and educational research must conform to norms of science. It reflects multiple interests in the intersection of arts, education, the humanities, and research. This kind of inquiry explores the arts as performance and mode of persuasion, as a means of self-exploration, as a form of pedagogy, and as a mode of representing knowledge. There are strong affinities between this development and ***performance texts****,* poetic representations of data and interpretations, ***autoethnography****,* ethnodrama, and the like.

KEY REFERENCES

Barone, T., & Eisner, E. "Arts-Based Educational Research," in R. M. Jaeger, ed., *Complementary Methods for Research in Education.* Washington, DC: American Educational Research Association, 1997.

Mullen, C. A., & Finley, S., eds. Special Issue: "Arts-Based Approaches to Qualitative Inquiry," *Qualitative Inquiry,* 2003, 9(2).

ATOMISM   Atomism refers to the notion that selves/individuals are self-contained entities each uniquely distinct and separate from others. Also known as ontological atomism, the central atomist claim is that individuals are what they are independently of their relations to others. This idea was perhaps most famously promoted in the political philosophy of Thomas Hobbes (1588– 1679), and it is widely recognized as a cornerstone of Enlightenment thought. This doctrine is challenged by the view of the self as a process rather than an entity— something fluid and changeable that is accomplished and constructed in interaction with others (i.e., dialogically or relationally). Atomism is an individualistic and psychological perspective on the nature of social life that sharply contrasts with the idea of *holism*. This debate is of consequence for qualitative inquiry in several ways. For example, holism is assumed in the sociological perspective that informs much of qualitative inquiry (e.g., ***symbolic interactionism***). Also, criticism of the doctrine of atomistic selves informs the idea of the constructed 'subject' who lies within or behind the person being interviewed or observed.

KEY REFERENCES

Fay, B. *Contemporary Philosophy of Science.* Oxford, UK: Blackwell, 1996.

Holstein, J. A,. & Gubrium, J. F. "Inside Interviewing: New Lenses, New Concerns," in J. A. Holstein & J. F. Gubrium, eds., *Inside Interviewing.* Thousand Oaks, CA: Sage, 2003.

Taylor, C. "The Dialogical Self," in D. R. Hiley, J. Bohman, & R. Schusterman, eds., *The Interpretive Turn.* Ithaca, NY: Harvard University Press, 1991.

Taylor, C. *Sources of the Self.* Cambridge, MA: Harvard University Press, 1992.

AUDIENCE ETHNOGRAPHY   Often used in communications studies and marketing, this is a form of ethnography that explores how audiences produce meaning from media discourses such as television news.

KEY REFERENCES

Alastuutari, P. *Rethinking the Media Audience.* London: Sage, 1999.
Moores, S. *Interpreting Audiences: Ethnography of Media Consumption.* London: Sage, 1993.

AUDIOTAPING Because of the prominent use of interview data in qualitative inquiry, both technological and methodological issues in audio recording and transcribing interviews require close attention. A recording device of any kind is part of the creation of a social context for the interview, and the quality of a transcription is a vital aspect of establishing the dependability of qualitative inquiries.

See also Interviewing Logic, Transcription.

KEY REFERENCES

Bradley, D. "Making and Managing Audio Recordings," in C. Seale, ed., *Researching Society and Culture,* 2nd ed. London: Sage, 2004.
Poland, B. D. "Transcription Quality," in J. A. Holstein & J. F. Gubrium, eds. *Inside Interviewing.* Thousand Oaks, CA: Sage, 2003.

AUDIT CULTURE/SOCIETY The significance of auditing to social theory arises as program and performance auditing practices proliferate in hospitals, schools, universities, social services, and government agencies in contemporary society. An auditing mentality or audit culture is closely associated with neoliberal theories of governance and the ideology of New Public Management (NPM). NPM emphasizes a programmatic restructuring of organizational life and a rationality based on performance standards, accountability, and monitoring. By being submitted to formal audit procedures, the work of organizations is held to be more transparent and accountable. Critics argue that the audit society, audit culture, or the culture of accountability is the latest manifestation of the infiltration of technological, means-end, and instrumental rationality into the forms of everyday life. Auditing is viewed as an example of what Lyotard called the ***performativity*** that is characteristic of modernity—that is, the drive for efficiency, perfection, completion, and measurement that strongly shapes conceptions of knowledge, politics, and ethics. Some scholars argue that auditing (and associated practices such as total quality management, performance indicators, League tables, results-oriented management, and monitoring systems) is not simply a set of techniques but a system of values and goals that becomes inscribed in social practices, thereby influencing the self-understanding of a practice and its role in society. To be audited, an organization (or practice like teaching or providing mental health care) must transform itself into an auditable commodity—auditing thus reshapes in its own image those organizations and practices that are monitored for performance. Others argue that audit culture or society promotes the normative ideal that monitoring systems and accountability ought to replace the complex social-political processes entailed in the design and delivery of social and educational services and the inevitably messy give-and-take of human interactions. Still others contend that the growing influence of an audit culture contributes to the disappearance of the idea of publicness as traditional public service norms of citizenship, representation, equality, accountability, impartiality, openness, responsiveness, and justice are being marginalized or replaced by business norms like competitiveness, efficiency, productivity, profitability, and consumer satisfaction.

KEY REFERENCES

Power, M. *The Audit Society: Rituals of Verification.* Oxford, UK: Oxford University Press, 1997.
Strathern, M. *Audit Cultures: Anthropological Studies in Accountability, Ethics, and the Academy.* London: Routledge, 2000.

AUDITING   This is a procedure whereby an independent, third-party examiner systematically reviews an audit trail maintained by the inquirer. The purpose of the audit is to render a judgment about the *dependability* of procedures employed by the inquirer and the extent to which the conclusions or findings of the study are confirmable. An audit trail is a systematically maintained documentation system. It is an organized collection of materials that includes the data generated in a study; a statement of the theoretical framework that shaped the study at the outset; explanations of concepts, models, and the like that were developed as part of the effort to make sense of the data (often the product of *memoing*); a description of the procedures used to generate data and analyze them; a statement of the findings or conclusions of the investigation; notes about the process of conducting the study; personal notes; and copies of instruments used to guide the generation and analysis of data. The audit trail can serve dual purposes: It can be used by the inquirer as a means of managing record keeping and encouraging reflexivity about procedures, and, as noted above, it can be used by a third-party examiner to attest to the use of dependable procedures and the generation of confirmable findings on the part of the inquirer.

See also Trustworthiness Criteria.

KEY REFERENCES

Lincoln, Y. S., & Guba, E. G. *Naturalistic Inquiry.* Beverly Hills, CA: Sage, 1985.
Schwandt, T. A., & Halpern, E. S. *Linking Auditing and Metaevaluation.* Newbury Park, CA: Sage, 1989.

AUDIT TRAIL   See AUDITING.

AUTHENTICITY   Two senses of this term are part of the lexicon of qualitative inquiry. First, authenticity is regarded as a feature unique to *naturalistic inquiry* (and *ethnographic naturalism*), an approach to inquiry that aims to generate a genuine or true (i.e., 'authentic') understanding of people's experiences. This genuine understanding, also spoken of as seeing the world from the actors' point of view, is achieved through the methods of unstructured interviewing and participant observation. Second, authenticity is a key notion in the German idealist tradition, in the German tradition of phenomenology, and in the philosophical and literary tradition of existentialism. Broadly speaking, key figures in these traditions—for example, Husserl (1859–1938), Heidegger (1889–1976), Nietzsche (1844–1900), Sartre (1905–1980), and Merleau-Ponty (1907–1961)—shared a strong hostility to technological modernity and to the ideology of *scientism*. They argued, although in different ways, that our fundamental (authentic) way of experiencing and engaging the world as human beings is through structures of meaning or significance. For these scholars, human existence is fundamentally different in kind than the being of natural objects studied in the natural sciences. They saw in modernity and scientism a danger to treat human existence or human being as simply another kind of natural 'object' to be studied via the methods of the natural sciences. They feared that this way of thinking led to viewing human existence in objectifying and alienating ways—being was becoming stripped of its unique significance. For example, Sartre argued that regarding the 'self' as a subject for science required adopting the third-person point of view that is disengaged from the experience of self during everyday engaged existence. It is in this context that authenticity refers to a notion of being or existence that is not objectified. An authentic life is a condition of significance; it is emotionally appropriate living, clearly facing up to one's responsibility for what one's life has been and is becoming. The opposites of authenticity are inauthenticity, estrangement, objectification, and alienation, all of which point, in different ways, to a life dehumanized and stripped of responsibility and purpose, to a flight from the fundamental situatedness and embodiedness of self. Living authentically—resisting unthinking conformism, the objectification of existence, and possessive individualism—is often regarded as the central problem of modern social and political life.

See also Experience.

KEY REFERENCES

Cooper, D. E. "Modern European Philosophy," in *The Blackwell Companion to Philosophy,* N. Bunnin & E. P. Tsui-James, eds. Oxford, UK: Blackwell, 1996.
Guignon, C. "Heidegger's 'Authenticity' Revisited," *Review of Metaphysics,* 1984, 38, 321–339.
Taylor, C. *The Ethics of Authenticity.* Cambridge, MA: Harvard University Press, 1991.

AUTHENTICITY CRITERIA   This is a set of *criteria* (and associated procedures) developed by Yvonna Lincoln and Egon Guba for judging the kind of qualitative inquiry that has its origins in a constructivist epistemology. The criteria are as follows:

(a) Fairness—refers to the extent to which respondents' different constructions of concerns and issues and their underlying values are solicited and represented in a balanced, evenhanded way by the inquirer. (Constructions are defined by Lincoln and Guba as the outcomes of various ways that individuals have of making sense of some situation, event, and so on.)

(b) Ontological authenticity—concerned with the extent to which respondents' own constructions are enhanced or made more informed and sophisticated as a result of their having participated in the inquiry.

(c) Educative authenticity—concerned with the extent to which participants in an inquiry develop greater understanding and appreciation of the constructions of others.

(d) Catalytic authenticity—refers to the extent to which action is stimulated and facilitated by the inquiry process.

(e) Tactical authenticity—refers to the extent to which participants in the inquiry are empowered to act.

See also Constructivism, (The) Problem of the Criterion, Trustworthiness Criteria.

KEY REFERENCE

Guba, E. G., & Lincoln, Y. S. *Fourth Generation Evaluation.* Newbury Park, CA: Sage, 1989.

AUTHORITY This notion figures prominently in postmodern and post-structuralist criticisms of *ethnography* wherein it is commonplace to criticize a text's 'call to authority.' This concern about the authority of any ethnographic account is intimately connected to the current *crisis of legitimation* in the human sciences. Critics claim that traditional ethnographers establish their authority through two textual (rhetorical) strategies: First, there is an experiential appeal—the ethnographer claims that he or she was 'there,' in the *'field,'* and thereby acquired firsthand the experience of the other's world, way of life, and so on. Second, the ethnographer as author then suppresses in the act of writing the "I" of the observer. He or she is absent from the text as a genuine author with personal subjectivities, interests, and dispositions and simply impersonally narrates what he or she saw and heard. Taken collectively, these two strategies serve to establish the ethnographer's account as authoritative. In other words, the reader is led to believe that whatever the ethnographer experienced by being in the field, and accordingly reported in the text, would be more or less what any equally well-trained observer would experience and report.

According to postmodern and poststructuralist critics, this bid to establish the authority of the text is closely wedded to the realist assumption that there is a genuine, valid account of the way life 'really is' for those being studied and that this 'real' life can be (relatively) unproblematically captured and represented in the ethnographer's account. Hence, criticism of a text's call to authority is at once a criticism of an ideology of the immediacy of experience and the transparency of representation. For the postmodern ethnographer, there is no such thing as a 'real' account of the way of life of others—all accounts are contested, partial, incomplete, written from some particular standpoint, advance some particular interest, and so on. Any claim that a particular textual account is a valid *representation* (a faithful, accurate rendering) of others' life worlds is nothing more than an effort on the part of the author to persuade the reader that the author's account is authoritative. Thus, traditional concerns with *validity* are replaced by concerns with how a text seeks to legitimate itself—how the authority of the text is established. The postmodern ethnographer seeks to decenter his or her own authority, to render more visible the ways in which the text produces a particular *inscription* of reality, and to disperse or share the authoritativeness of a textual account by featuring more dialogic and polyvocal textual forms.

See also Crisis of Legitimation, Ethnographic Realism, Literary Turn (in Social Science), Representation.

KEY REFERENCES

Clifford, J. "On Ethnographic Authority," *Representations,* 1983, 1(2), 118–146.
Clifford, J., & Marcus, G. E., Eds. *Writing Culture: The Poetics and Politics of Ethnography.* Berkeley: University of California Press, 1986.
Van Maanen, J. *Tales of the Field: On Writing Ethnography.* Chicago: University of Chicago Press, 1988.

AUTOETHNOGRAPHY   Originally defined as the cultural study of one's own people, this term now commonly refers to a particular form of writing that seeks to unite ethnographic (looking outward at a world beyond one's own) and autobiographical (gazing inward for a story of one's self) intentions. The aim in composing an autoethnographic account is to keep both the subject (knower) and object (that which is being examined) in simultaneous view. It is commonly claimed that the striking stories that frequently comprise autoethnography are intended to illustrate and evoke rather than to state or make a claim, and that the author of such a text aims to invite readers into the text to relive the experience rather than to interpret or analyze what the author is saying.

See also Experience, Narrative, Writing Strategies.

KEY REFERENCES

Ellis, C. "Evocative Autoethnography: Writing Emotionally About Our Lives," in *Representation and the Text: Re-Framing the Narrative Voice,* W. G. Tierney & Y. S. Lincoln, eds. Albany: SUNY Press, 1997.

Ellis, C., & Bochner, A. P. "Autoethnography, Personal Narrative, Reflexivity: Researcher as Subject," in *Handbook of Qualitative Research,* 2nd ed., N. K. Denzin & Y. S. Lincoln, eds. Thousand Oaks, CA: Sage, 2000.

Hayano, D. M. "Autoethnography," *Human Organization,* 1979, 38, 99–104.

Reed-Danahay, D. *Auto/ethnography: Rewriting the Self and the Social.* Oxford, UK: Berg, 1997.

B

BEHAVIORISM   As a sociopsychological theory, scientific or methodological behaviorism is the view that the only truly scientific investigation is that which limits itself to behavioral data—that is, that which can be measured and observed, especially patterns of physical responses to environmental stimuli. The theory emphasizes determinable and invariant principles of human conduct and social behavior. It is strongly deterministic: Behaviors are associated in *lawlike* ways with environmental stimuli and reinforcements. It is also reductionistic in that it holds that there is no need to invent complex mental constructs to explain why behavior happens. While the theory is most often associated with behavioral and educational psychology, it is also evident in research traditions in other fields, particularly in political science. As a philosophical doctrine, behaviorism figured prominently in the thinking of *logical positivism*. Also spoken of as the doctrine of physicalism, philosophical behaviorism meant that the mental states of individuals (their intentions, beliefs, etc.) and indeed all that is considered social are ultimately explainable in terms of physical, that is, behavioral, expressions.

See also Action, Reductionism.

KEY REFERENCES

Ayer, A. J., ed. *Logical Positivism.* Glencoe, IL: Free Press, 1959.
Slife, B., & Williams, R. N. *What's Behind the Research? Discovering Hidden Assumptions in the Behavioral Sciences.* Thousand Oaks, CA: Sage, 1995.
Taylor, C. *The Explanation of Behaviour.* London: Routledge & Kegan Paul, 1964.

BIAS Two senses of this term figure prominently in criticisms of qualitative inquiry. In the first sense, readily found in dictionaries, bias denotes a tendency in inquirers that prevents unprejudiced consideration or judgment. For example, the tendency to rely on a particular informant or to cross the line between rapport and friendship in dealing with informants, respondents, or participants can lead to the prejudicial drawing of inferences or generalizing from nontypical or nonrepresentative persons or events. Also, the tendency to be unaware of how one's interactions in a field site threaten, disrupt, create, or sustain patterns of social interaction might result in a prejudicial account of social behavior in the site. In the second sense, bias means individual preferences, predispositions, or predilections that prevent neutrality and objectivity. This sense of the term *bias* is evident when an inquirer is criticized for taking the side of or advocating for a particular group of informants (and the inquirer is thus thought to be incapable of rendering a neutral account of the social action); for imposing a priori a theoretical framework or interpretation on the data; or when it appears as though the researcher uses data to confirm a hypothesis or belief held before the study was undertaken.

Although biases of these kinds are a problem for all methodologies for social investigation, they are thought to be particularly acute in forms of qualitative inquiry that rely on fieldwork because the latter is admittedly an intensely personal experience. *Fieldwork* requires the active, sustained, and long-term involvement of the inquirer with respondents and the cultivation of empathy with and attachment to the people one studies in order to gain access to their own understandings of their life ways. Hence, bias resulting from over-reliance on accessible or key informants and/or selective attention to dramatic events or statements, the biasing effects of the presence of the inquirer in the site of investigation, and biases stemming from the effects of the respondents and the site on the inquirer can be particularly difficult problems in fieldwork.

It is beyond dispute that sound inquiry practice requires critical reflection on one's actions and predispositions and awareness of the potential both of being deceived and of deceiving one's self. However, the extent to which bias is believed to be a problem in qualitative studies is related to assumptions about objective *method*. A significant subset of qualitative inquiry is wedded to a conception of method as a device for setting aside or controlling bias. The devotion to method as holding the key to sound inquiry is predicated on the assumption that we need some means of removing our tendencies as everyday human beings to be biased or prejudiced in our investigations of social life so that we may come to have genuine, legitimate, objective knowledge. Since

Descartes, at least, social science (and philosophy) has been obsessed with this understanding and pursuit of a strong sense of method.

In light of this understanding of method, bias or prejudice is always defined negatively as something that interferes with, prevents, or inhibits having true, genuine knowledge. However, it is precisely this understanding of method and prejudice that is severely criticized by advocates of *philosophical hermeneutics*. For example, Hans-Georg Gadamer's (1900–2002) critique of the Cartesian notion of method as providing a sure path to knowledge is based in large part on a rehabilitation of the word "prejudice." Building on the work of Martin Heidegger (1889–1976), Gadamer argued that prejudice ('prejudgment') can be neither eliminated nor set aside, for it is an inescapable condition of being and knowing. In fact, our understanding of our selves and our world depends upon having prejudgment. What we must do in order to achieve understanding is to reflect on prejudice (prejudgment) and distinguish enabling from disabling prejudice.

See also Objectivity, Reflexivity, Subjectivity.

KEY REFERENCES

Gadamer, H.-G. *Truth and Method,* 2nd rev. ed. J. Weinsheimer & D. G. Marshall, trans. New York: Crossroad, 1989.
LeCompte, M. D., & Preissle, J. *Ethnography and Qualitative Design in Educational Research,* 2nd ed. New York: Academic Press, 1993.

BIOGRAPHICAL RESEARCH   Like the term *ethnography,* biography refers to both a product and a process. It is an account (in writing, film, etc.) of an individual's life and the activity of composing that account. Biographical research is an assembly of procedures for generating and interpreting the stories or narratives of individual's lives. Biographies, life histories, and the biographical method are often used in qualitative research, especially given the growing interest in *narrative* methodologies.

The biographical method, also spoken of as life-history methodology, is a generic term for a variety of approaches to qualitative study that focus on the generation, analysis, and presentation of the data of a life history (the unfolding of an individual's experiences over time), life story, personal experience narrative, autobiography, and biography. Data can be generated from interviews as well as from personal documents (letters, journals, diaries, etc.). The methodology assumes that social *action* can best be understood from the accounts and perspectives of the people involved, and thus the focus is on an individual subjective definition and experience of life. However, because most qualitative inquirers assume that the subjective world of experience is at once intersubjectively constituted, life-history approaches seek to interrelate the private and the public, the personal and the social. Private, personal, biographic, subjective perspectives are linked to meanings, definitions, concepts, and practices that are historical, structural, public, and social.

Biographical methods take up a number of interrelated methodological, philosophical, and epistemological concerns surrounding what constitutes a biography (e.g., Is it a retelling or an active production of a consistent understanding of a life?), subjectivity, life course, *experience,* and how to best describe, interpret, and write a life-history text. Diverse methodologies are influenced by assumptions from critical theory of society, phenomenological, hermeneutic, semiotic, and poststructural perspectives.

See also Interviewing Logic, Narrative Analysis.

KEY REFERENCES

Berteaux, D., ed. *Biography and Society: The Life-History Approach in the Social Sciences.* London: Sage, 1981.
Chamberlayne, P., Bornat, J., & Wengraf, T., eds. *The Turn to Biographical Methods in Social Science.* London: Routledge, 2000.
Denzin, N. K. *Interpretive Biography.* Thousand Oaks, CA: Sage, 1989.
Weymann, A., & Heinz, W. R., eds. *Biography and Society.* Weinheim, Germany: Beltz, 1995.

BIOGRAPHICAL TURN   This is a phrase identified several years ago signifying the growing use of biographical research methods in the social sciences to account for both individual actions and social and cultural changes. This effort to unite social theory with biographical experience is sometimes also referred to as *narrative analysis.*

KEY REFERENCES

Chamberlayne, P., Bornat, J., & Wengraf, T., eds. *The Turn to Biographical Methods in Social Science.* London: Routledge, 2000.
Daiute, C., & Lightfoot, C., eds. *Narrative Analysis: Studying the Development of Individuals in Society.* Thousand Oaks, CA: Sage, 2004.

BODY   In the history of *epistemology* at least since Descartes, the ideal epistemic agent (the one who engages in knowing, i.e., the knower or subject) is an individual, disengaged, disembodied mind. This conception is captured in the familiar binary oppositions: mind-body, reason-desire, and mental-manual. The mind or the purely mental is associated with reason, rationality, and knowledge. The body or the purely physical is associated with emotions, desires, passions, personal involvement, and commitments.

Two twentieth-century strands of thought are largely responsible for restoring a concern with the body (and all its associations) to our thinking about epistemology. One strand emanates from the work of the French phenomenologist Maurice Merleau-Ponty (1908–1961) along with the feminist scholarship of Luce Irigaray, Gayatri Spivak, Judith Butler, Naomi Schor, Hèlene Cixous, and many others. Here, the central idea is that the lived body is not an object in the world distinct from the knowing subject. Rather, we experience the world as embodied subjects; the body itself is the original knowing 'subject.' Merleau-Ponty explained that our agency is essentially embodied and that the lived body is the center of our actions and desires that we never fully grasp or control by personal decision. This idea of embodied agency also occupies a central place in Charles Taylor's *philosophical hermeneutics*. Feminist scholars have argued that the lived body is not an ahistorical, biologically given, acultural object but is represented and used in specific ways in particular cultures. Hence, the lived body is crucial to understanding woman's social and psychical existence. A second strand of thought is associated with the work of Nietzsche (1844–1900), Deleuze (1925–1995), and Foucault (1926–1984). Here, the body is regarded as a social site or surface on which law, morality, and values are inscribed. Foucault's work has been particularly influential in shaping the sociology of the body.

See also Intentionality.

KEY REFERENCES

Butler, J. *Gender Trouble: Feminism and the Subversion of Identity.* New York: Routledge, 1990.

Grosz, E. *Volatile Bodies: Toward a Corporeal Feminism.* Bloomington: Indiana University Press, 1994.

Merleau-Ponty, M. *Phenomenology of Perception,* C. Morris, trans. London: Routledge & Kegan Paul, 1962. (Originally published in 1945)

Schatzki, T., & Natter, W., eds. *The Social and Political Body*. New York: Guilford Press, 1996.

Taylor, C. *Philosophical Arguments*. Cambridge, MA: Harvard University Press, 1995.

Turner, B. *Regulating Bodies: Essays in Medical Sociology*. London: Routledge, 1992.

BRACKETING (EPOCHÉ)   The term originates in Husserl's (1859–1938) phenomenology (*The Idea of Phenomenology,* posthumously published in 1950, English trans. W. P. Alston & G. Nakhnikian, 1964), which was strongly opposed to philosophical *realism*—the doctrine claiming that an external world exists independent of one's knowledge of it. Husserl argued that the everyday assumption of the independent existence of what is perceived and thought about (what he called "the natural attitude") should be suspended, so that one could investigate what is perceived and thought about without that assumption. In other words, one ought to suspend judgment about the existence of the world and 'bracket' or set aside existential assumptions made in everyday life and in the sciences. By performing such a reduction or bracketing, it becomes possible to focus on the intrinsic nature or *phenomenology* of conscious acts such as perceiving or remembering. The *phenomenological sociology* of Alfred Schutz (1899–1956) developed this idea of setting aside or bracketing everyday assumptions in order to concentrate on the phenomenology of the experience of the everyday world, that is, on *how* that experience is constituted. Schutz's work, in turn, influenced the development of *ethnomethodology*. Ethnomethodologists bracket, set aside, or suspend commonsense assumptions about social reality in order to understand *how* it is that actors experience their world as real, concrete, factual, and objective—in short, to understand how the taken-for-granted features of social life are accomplished.

See also Lifeworld.

KEY REFERENCES

Garfinkel, H. *Studies in Ethnomethodology*. Englewood Cliffs, NJ: Prentice-Hall, 1967.

Gubrium, J. F., & Holstein, J. A. *The New Language of Qualitative Method*. Oxford, UK: Oxford University Press, 1997.

BRICOLAGE/BRICOLEUR   Even a cursory glance at the ever growing editions of *The Handbook of Qualitative Research* (3rd ed., Sage, 2005) will reveal that qualitative inquiry comprises a variety of methodological and philosophical ideas drawn from traditions of interpretivism, phenomenology, hermeneutics, ethnomethodology, ethnography, semiotics, cultural studies, feminism, and critical theory, to name but a few. Given this diversity in intellectual origins, strategies, methods, and practices, it becomes difficult to define in any precise way who the qualitative inquirer is and what it is that he or she does. Of late, some scholars in qualitative inquiry have found the terms *qualitative researcher* and *qualitative research* inadequate descriptors of what they believe to be the manifold ***identity*** and ***practice*** of the qualitative inquirer and have substituted the terms *bricolage* and *bricoleur* as alternatives. For example, Norman Denzin and Yvonna Lincoln (*The Handbook of Qualitative Research,* Sage, 1994, p. 2) describe the multiple methodologies used in qualitative inquiry as *bricolage* and the qualitative inquirer as *bricoleur,* one who is "adept at performing a large number of diverse tasks, ranging from interviewing to observing, to interpreting personal and historical documents, to intensive self-reflection and introspection . . . [and one who] reads widely and is knowledgeable about the many interpretive paradigms (feminism, Marxism, cultural studies, constructivism) that can be brought to any particular problem." As a *bricoleur,* the qualitative inquirer is capable of donning multiple identities—researcher, scientist, artist, critic, performer—and engaging in different kinds of *bricolage* that consist of particular configurations of (or ways of relating) various fragments of inherited methodologies, methods, empirical materials, perspectives, understandings, ways of presentation, situated responsiveness, and so on into a coherent, reasoned approach to a research situation and problem. The *bricolage* appears to vary depending upon one's allegiance to different notions of interpretation, understanding, representation, and so on drawn from various intellectual and practice traditions.

The terms are traceable to Lévi-Strauss, who, in seeking to define the savage mind, defined a *bricoleur* as "someone who works with his hands and uses devious means." He sharply contrasted the *bricoleur* and the engineer. The *bricoleur* draws on a heterogeneous collection of inherited odds and ends kept at hand on the chance they might someday prove useful for some project. What the *bricoleur* produces is *bricolage*—a kind of pieced-together (in contrast to algorithmically guided) yet structured solution to a problem. (Jacques Derrida [*Writing and Difference,* A. Bass, trans., University of Chicago Press, 1978, p. 285] criticized this binary distinction, arguing that "if one calls *bricolage* the necessity of borrowing one's concepts from the text of a heritage which is more or less coherent or ruined, it must be said that every discourse is *bricoleur.*")

The mixing of methodologies, discourses, substantive theories, and the like that *bricolage* signifies can be read in a variety of ways. Some might see it as a sign of methodological and theoretical impurity in the field of qualitative inquiry—a symptom of a pathology that must be diagnosed, explained, and somehow remedied. Others might read *bricolage* as a kind of necessary and productive insecurity about confining qualitative inquiry to disciplinary boundaries. And still others may view *bricolage* as a way of signaling that the object of qualitative inquiry as well as the practice itself is relational and processual (a network of interlocking discourses) rather than fixed and formal.

KEY REFERENCES

Denzin, N. K, & Lincoln, Y. S. "Introduction: The Discipline and Practice of Qualitative Research," *The Handbook of Qualitative Research,* 2nd ed., Thousand Oaks, CA: Sage, 2000.

Hammersley, M. "Teaching Qualitative Method: Craft, Profession, or Bricolage?" in C. Seale, ed., *Researching Society and Culture,* 2nd ed. London: Sage, 2004.

Lévi-Strauss, C. *The Savage Mind.* Chicago: University of Chicago Press, 1966.

Weinstein, D., & Weinstein, M. A. "Georg Simmel: Sociological Flaneur Bricoleur," *Theory Culture and Society,* 1991, 8, 151–168.

C

CAREERS This is a device often used for organizing and analyzing qualitative data that helps explain how individuals progress through social settings
or experiences. Erving Goffman's (1922–1982) examination of the moral
career of the mental patient—the series of progressive changes occurring in
the patient's self-concept/identity as he or she moves through a sequence of
positions, roles, and lifestyles—and Howard Becker's use of the idea of a
deviant career to understand how people come to be marijuana users are classic examples.

KEY REFERENCES

Becker, H. *Outsiders: Studies in the Sociology of Deviance*. New York: Free Press, 1963.
Goffman, E. *Asylums: Essays on the Social Situation of Mental Patients and Other
    Inmates*. New York: Doubleday, 1961.

CASE The terms *case* and *unit of analysis* are often used interchangeably in
social research, yet to a qualitative inquirer, the term 'case' means something
more than just "*n* of 1." In the sociological and anthropological literature,
a case is typically regarded as a specific and bounded (in time and place)
instance of a phenomenon selected for study. The phenomenon of interest may
be a person, process, event, group, organization, and so on. Empirical cases are
routinely used in the study of law, business, and medicine. Cases are generally
characterized on the one hand by their concreteness and circumstantial speci-
ficity and on the other by their theoretical interest or generalizability. There
is disagreement as to whether the case is an empirical unit ('out there' to be

discovered and observed) or a theoretical construct that serves the interest of the investigator. Hence, the sociologist Howard Becker advises that instead of asking, "What is a case?" inquirers should continually ask themselves, "What is this a case *of*?"

See also Case Study Research, Generalization.

KEY REFERENCE

Ragin, C. C., & Becker, H. S. *What Is a Case? Exploring the Foundations of Social Inquiry.* Cambridge, UK: Cambridge University Press, 1992.

CASE STUDY RESEARCH   This is a strategy for doing social inquiry, although what constitutes the strategy is a matter of some debate. One useful way of thinking of this approach to inquiry is in terms of the distinction between case study and variable study: In case study, the *case* itself is at center stage, not variables. Robert Yin argues that a case study strategy is preferred when the inquirer seeks answers to how or why questions, when the inquirer has little control over events being studied, when the object of study is a contemporary phenomenon in a real-life context, when boundaries between the phenomenon and the context are not clear, and when it is desirable to use multiple sources of evidence. Robert Stake emphasizes that the foremost concern of case study research is to generate knowledge of the particular. He favors case studies that aim to discern and pursue understanding of issues intrinsic to the case itself. However, he acknowledges that cases can be chosen and studied because they are thought to be instrumentally useful in furthering understanding of a particular problem, issue, concept, and so on. Both Stake and Yin argue that case studies can be used for theoretical elaboration or *analytic generalization*.

See also Cross-Case Analysis.

KEY REFERENCES

Flyvbjerg, B. "Five Misunderstandings about Case-Study Research," in C. Seale, G. Gobo, J. F. Gubrium, & D. Silverman, eds., *Qualitative Research Practice.* London: Sage, 2004.

Hamel, J., with Dufour, S. & Fortin, D. *Case Study Methods.* Newbury Park, CA: Sage, 1993.

Stake, R. *The Art of Case Study Research.* Thousand Oaks, CA: Sage, 1995.

Yin, R. *Case Study Research: Design and Methods,* 3rd ed. Thousand Oaks, CA: Sage, 2002.

CAUSAL ANALYSIS/CAUSALITY   Causation is intimately related to *explanation;* asking for an explanation of an event is often to ask *why* it happened. For many social scientists, deterministic (universal) and statistical (probabilistic) causal laws are thought to play a pivotal role in defining what constitutes a legitimate explanation of social phenomena. Although causal relations are important in social inquiry, exactly how to define a causal relationship is one of the most difficult topics in epistemology and the philosophy of science. There is little general agreement on how to establish causation. Some philosophers and social scientists argue that cause means an underlying *lawlike* mechanism that accounts for the regular observed association of events. Others support an inductive model of causation: A statement of a cause summarizes the regular association of events of type C with events of type E. Still others claim that a cause is best defined as a necessary and sufficient condition for the occurrence of an event. In addition, there is a long-standing debate in social science between analysis and narration. Many social scientists believe that it is only by means of causal analysis that a genuine explanatory account can be had. Others argue that telling a story is sufficient; in other words, narratives explain.

Experimental designs, specifically randomized controlled trials, are generally regarded as the most appropriate means for causal investigations. Although these designs, when executed properly, are powerful tools, there are other means that, at least in principle, are capable of establishing causal claims (e.g., time series designs, regression-discontinuity designs, forensic methods, and case studies).

From the fact that qualitative inquiry as a whole eschews experimental designs, one cannot conclude that the study of cause is unimportant in all qualitative work. For example, the strategy of *analytic induction* was developed as a nonexperimental method suitable for establishing causal accounts using qualitative data. Moreover, there are many varieties of qualitative inquiry that aim to develop causal accounts of social phenomena using structural, functional, and materialist explanations. Some defenders of qualitative work have argued that qualitative inquiry is somehow more attuned to the idea of multiple, probabilistic causes of events than so-called quantitative approaches to the social sciences. However, this claim is suspect because quantitative studies in the social sciences rely heavily on statistical (i.e., probabilistic) explanations involving multiple causes and do not always assume a deterministic view of causality. Some scholars claim that a concern with causality in qualitative inquiry was characteristic of its 'modernist phase' that has now ended. That will no doubt come as news to many qualitative inquirers still concerned with causal questions.

To understand the importance (or lack thereof) that the study of causal relations plays in qualitative inquiry, we must consider the doctrine of *naturalism*. Defenders of naturalism in social science argue that the goal of social inquiry is to create causal explanations of human behavior (however it may be that cause is defined). Phenomenological and hermeneutic approaches to qualitative inquiry reject causal explanation as the proper goal of the human sciences. They argue that we can only understand or interpret human *action;* we cannot give a causal explanation of it. Some feminist researchers share in this rejection of naturalism. Also, postmodern approaches to social inquiry aim to deconstruct all language of cause and effect.

See also *Explanation.*

KEY REFERENCES

Abbott, A. *Methods of Discovery: Heuristics for the Social Sciences.* New York: W. W. Norton & Company, 2004.

Denzin, N. K, & Lincoln, Y. S. "Introduction: The Discipline and Practice of Qualitative Research," *The Handbook of Qualitative Research,* 2nd ed. Thousand Oaks, CA: Sage, 2000.

Little, D. *Varieties of Social Explanation.* Boulder, CO: Westview Press, 1991.

Ragin, C. C. *The Comparative Method: Moving Beyond Qualitative and Quantitative Strategies.* Berkeley: University of California Press, 1987.

Scriven, M. "Causation," in S. Mathison, ed., *Encyclopedia of Evaluation.* Thousand Oaks, CA: Sage, 2005.

CHICAGO SCHOOL OF SOCIOLOGY   The Chicago School or tradition of sociology developed in the period from about 1920–1940 in the Department of Social Science and Anthropology at the University of Chicago and is associated with the work of Robert Park (1864–1944), W. I. Thomas (1863–1947),

Ernest Burgess (1886–1966), Everett C. Hughes (1898–1983), and their students. It is generally recognized as the primary source of sociological fieldwork. Park introduced the sociology of Georg Simmel (1858–1918) to the sociologists of the Chicago School; other important influences on their work included the pragmatism of G. H. Mead (1863–1931) and John Dewey (1859–1952), the *symbolic interactionism* of Herbert Blumer (1900–1987), and interactions with socioanthropologist colleagues at Chicago. Chicago sociologists practiced a rich variety of ethnographic fieldwork including life histories; community studies; studies of medical education; occupational studies; urban ethnographies of 'deviant' subcultures including taxi dancers, hobos, and gang members (reflecting Park's advice to students to explore and document the subcultures of the city of Chicago); and studies combining a focus on the nature of work, professional identity, role, and status that developed from the intellectual direction provided by Hughes. The tradition figures prominently not simply in the history of fieldwork but in the professional identity of contemporary sociologists: "Although now well dispersed, the Chicago School still represents a sort of mythical Eden to many contemporary sociologists who locate their personal pedigree and purpose in the profession by tracing back their lineage on the family tree planted in Chicago" (J. Van Maanen, *Tales of the Field,* University of Chicago Press, 1988, p. 20).

KEY REFERENCES

Bulmer, M. *The Chicago School of Sociology.* Chicago: University of Chicago Press, 1984.

Hammersley, M. *The Dilemma of Qualitative Method: Herbert Blumer and the Chicago Tradition.* London: Routledge, 1989.

CINEMATIC SOCIETY This is a particular way of conceptualizing lived human experience that is studied in qualitative inquiry. The central idea is that the experience we take as an object of study is already mediated by mass-media images. The 'real' as it is visually experienced is a staged and socially constructed production. The inquirer has no direct access to a firsthand world of 'real' experiences; he or she can only study its representations or images of the real.

See also Experience, Hyperreality.

KEY REFERENCES

Denzin, N. K. *The Cinematic Society: The Voyeur's Gaze.* Thousand Oaks, CA: Sage, 1995.
Hall, S., Hobson, S., Lowe, A., & Willis, P., eds. *Culture, Media, and Language.*
    London: Routledge, 1992.

CODING   To begin the process of analyzing the large volume of data generated in the form of transcripts, field notes, photographs, and the like, the
qualitative inquirer often engages in the activity of coding. Coding is a procedure that disaggregates the data, breaks them down into manageable segments,
and identifies or names those segments. Although it is impossible to identify
and name without at least an implicit conceptual structure, coding is often
classified as relatively descriptive or analytical/explanatory depending on the
degree of interpretation involved. Coding requires constantly comparing and
contrasting various successive segments of the data and subsequently categorizing them. Coding can be accomplished in at least three different ways that
can be combined:

   1. An a priori, content-specific scheme is first developed from careful
study of the problem or topic under investigation and the theoretical interests
that drive the inquiry. The codes are derived directly by the social inquirer
from the language of the problem area or theoretical field. Data are then examined and sorted into this scheme.
   An a priori, non-content-specific scheme is developed and data are sorted
into the scheme. Non-content-specific schemes are ways of accounting for the
data by sorting them into a typology. The typology may be based on commonsense reasoning (e.g., type of event, time of occurrence, participants
involved, reactions of participants, physical setting) or derived from the
assumptions of a particular methodological framework like symbolic interactionism (e.g., practices, episodes, encounters, roles, relationships).

   2. A grounded, a posteriori, inductive, context-sensitive scheme. This
scheme may also begin with a simple typology, but here analysts (a) work with
the actual language of respondents to generate the codes or categories and
(b) work back and forth between the data segments and the codes or categories
to refine the meaning of categories as they proceed through the data.

Depending on the approach taken, the process of coding can yield either a fully labeled (coded) set of data that can be retrieved and manipulated for further analysis or new data documents (e.g., analytical memos, graphic displays) used in further analysis. Qualitative data can be coded for the purpose of generating theories and concepts as well as for testing hypotheses.

Perhaps the three most troublesome tendencies to be aware of in coding are (1) the tendency to code largely at the descriptive level rather than to code for the purposes of explaining or developing an understanding of 'what's going on here'; (2) the tendency to think of coding as a mechanical, straightforward, algorithmic process thereby ignoring the prior conceptualization and theoretical understandings that are involved; and (3) the tendency to regard codes or categories as 'fixed' or unchanging labels thereby ignoring their organic, dynamic character.

See also *Analyzing Qualitative Data; Careers; Computer-Assisted Data Analysis; Content Analysis; Grounded Theory Methodology; Memoing; Textual Analysis; Methods of, Thematic Analysis; Typologies.*

KEY REFERENCES

Lofland, J., & Lofland, L. H. *Analyzing Social Settings,* 3rd ed. Belmont, CA: Wadsworth, 1995.

Miles, M. B., & Huberman, A. M. *Qualitative Data Analysis,* 2nd ed. Thousand Oaks, CA: Sage, 1994.

Strauss, A. *Qualitative Analysis for Social Scientists.* Cambridge, UK: Cambridge University Press, 1987.

COGNITIVISM This is a broad critique of the behaviorists' strict insistence on studying the observable behavior of humans (and animals). Cognitivism makes active mental processes (e.g., attention, memory, and information processing) the primary object of study and views knowledge as symbolic, mental constructions in the minds of individuals. Although cognitivist studies broaden the perspective on the study of human experience beyond the narrow objectivism of *behaviorism,* they share with behaviorism an underlying acceptance of *logical positivism.* Qualitative studies in psychology are likely to turn instead to ideas from *phenomenology* and *existentialism.*

See also *Qualitative Psychology.*

KEY REFERENCES

Ashworth, P. D. *Psychology and Human Nature.* Hove, NY: Psychology Press, 2000.
Potter, J., & Wetherell, M. *Discourse and Social Psychology: Beyond Attitudes and Behaviour.* London: Sage, 1987.

COLLABORATIVE ETHNOGRAPHY   Collaboration, in the sense of working together to accomplish something, is characteristic of ethnographic work in general. Ethnographers, as a matter of course in carrying out fieldwork, engage others and seek out their cooperation and collaboration in learning about a culture. However, the term *collaborative ethnography* means something more than this usual and customary arrangement. It refers to doing ethnography that deliberately and explicitly emphasizes collaboration in every aspect of the ethnographic undertaking including conceptualizing the project, conducting fieldwork, and writing up the ethnography. This approach to ethnography was specifically recommended to the American Anthropological Association (2002) through a report of a task force that examined the responsibilities of doing anthropology of indigenous peoples: "The El Dorado Task Force insists that the anthropology of indigenous peoples and related communities must move toward 'collaborative' models in which anthropological research is not merely combined with advocacy, but inherently advocative in that research is, from the outset, aimed at material, symbolic, and political benefits for the research population, as its members have helped to define these." Critical social science, feminist, and postmodern approaches to anthropology inquiry all influence this way of thinking of ethnographic work.

KEY REFERENCES

American Anthropological Association. "El Dorado Task Force Papers." Washington, DC: American Anthropological Association, 2002.
Lassiter, L. E. *The Chicago Guide to Collaborative Ethnography.* Chicago: University of Chicago Press, 2005.
Marcus, G. E. "From Rapport Under Erasure to Theaters of Complicit Reflexivity," *Qualitative Inquiry,* 2001, 7(4), 519–528.

COMMUNICATIONS STUDIES   Also called media studies, this is an academic field that examines all aspects of communication (e.g., interpersonal, intrapersonal, intercultural, telecommunication, advertising, marketing, and film), information theory, rhetoric, and other aspects of communication theory broadly conceived. It embraces (although not exclusively) the use of various qualitative inquiries including *performance studies, cultural studies, and critical ethnography.*

KEY REFERENCE

Lindlof, T. R., & Taylor, B. C. *Qualitative Communication Research Methods,* 2nd ed. Thousand Oaks, CA: Sage, 2002.

COMPUTER-ASSISTED DATA ANALYSIS   This is a growing subfield of a larger movement concerned with technological innovation in qualitative inquiry. New audio recording devices, laptop computers, portable high-quality video cameras, and software for data analysis and visual imaging are making possible new procedures for generating and analyzing qualitative data. The introduction of computer software for facilitating qualitative data analysis coincides with and is partially responsible for the concern about developing rigorous, systematic methods of processing data. Software tools are used for recording, storing, indexing, cross-indexing, coding, sorting, and so on. They facilitate the management of large volumes of data and enable the analyst to locate, label (categorize or code), cross-reference, and compile various combinations of segments of textual data.

In some discussions of software tools for data analysis, the implicit assumption often seems to be that because computer-managed analysis is by definition more algorithmic, systematic, and rigorous, it is, therefore, better. However, while computer-assisted tools make qualitative inquiry a different practice, 'different' is not synonymous with 'better.' One need not be a neo-Luddite to be concerned about how the introduction of these tools contributes to the definition of the discursive practice called qualitative inquiry. As Neil Postman (*Technopoly,* Vintage, 1993) reminds us, embedded in every tool is an ideological bias, a predisposition to construct the world to which the tool will be applied as one thing rather than another. While developers and frequent users of qualitative analysis tools may customarily reflect on these embedded predispositions, it is not entirely clear that the causal user does. The operations made possible by software are not neutral tools; rather, they structure the undertaking of qualitative inquiry. John Seidel, the developer of ETHNO-GRAPH™, notes that the following dangers accompany the benefits of software tools: (a) an infatuation with the volume of data one can deal with leading to sacrificing resolution for scope; (b) a reification of the relationship between researcher and data wherein the researcher assumes that data are 'things out there' that can in a relatively simple and straightforward manner be discovered, identified, collected, counted, and sorted thereby ignoring the fact that data are artifacts of complex processes of identifying, naming, indexing, and coding that, in turn, are shaped by theoretical and methodological assumptions; and (c) a distancing of the researcher from the data.

See also Field Notes.

KEY REFERENCES

Fielding, N. G., & Lee, R. M. *Computer Analysis and Qualitative Research.* London: Sage, 1998.

Kelle, U. "Computer-Assisted Qualitative Data Analysis," in C. Seale, G. Gobo, J. F. Gubrium, & D. Silverman, eds., *Qualitative Research Practice.* London: Sage, 2004.

Seidel, J. "Method and Madness in the Application of Computer Technology to Qualitative Data Analysis," in N. G. Fielding & R. M. Lee, eds., *Using Computers in Qualitative Research.* Thousand Oaks, CA: Sage, 1991.

Weitzman, E., & Miles, M. B. *Computer Programs for Qualitative Data Analysis: A Software Sourcebook.* Thousand Oaks, CA: Sage, 1995.

CONFIRMABILITY   See TRUSTWORTHINESS CRITERIA.

CONSERVATIVE HERMENEUTICS   Also called validation or objectivist *hermeneutics,* this theory of interpretation defines hermeneutics as a method for the validation of the meaning embedded in a text. Its principal advocates are the Italian legal historian Emilio Betti and the American professor of literature E. D. Hirsch. Both Betti and Hirsch argue that an author's intended meaning of a text is a fixed, determinate entity or object that can be depicted or portrayed accurately. This meaning is the external reference point against which competing interpretations of a text are judged to be valid or invalid. In this version of hermeneutics, *method* plays a key role in helping prevent the misinterpretation of a text—that is, the danger of reading something into the text because of the interpreter's own bias or standpoint. Method is regarded as a means of stepping outside the *hermeneutic circle* in order to achieve historical objectivity and validity in interpretation. This kind of hermeneutics contrasts sharply with *critical hermeneutics, philosophical hermeneutics,* and *deconstructionism.*

KEY REFERENCES

Betti, E. "Hermeneutics as the General Methodology of the *Geisteswissenschaften,*" in J. Bleicher, ed., *Contemporary Hermeneutics.* London: Routledge & Kegan Paul, 1980.

Gallagher, S. *Hermeneutics and Education.* Albany: SUNY Press, 1992.

Hirsch, E. D. *The Aims of Interpretation.* Chicago: University of Chicago Press, 1976.

Hirsch, E. D. *Validity in Interpretation.* New Haven, CT: Yale University Press, 1973.

CONSTANT COMPARISON, METHOD OF In this method for *analyzing qualitative data,* devised by Barney Glaser and Anselm Strauss, data in the form of field notes, observations, interviews, and the like are coded inductively, and then each segment of the data is taken in turn and (a) compared to one or more categories to determine its relevance and (b) compared with other segments of data similarly categorized. As segments are compared, new analytic categories as well as new relationships between categories may be discovered. It is through this method that categories and their properties are identified and integrated and the emerging grounded theory is delimited.

See also Abduction, Coding, Grounded Theory Methodology.

KEY REFERENCES

Glaser, B. "The Constant Comparative Method of Qualitative Analysis," in G. J. McCall & J. L. Simons, eds., *Issues in Participant Observation.* Reading, MA: Addison-Wesley, 1969.

Glaser, B., & Strauss, A. *The Discovery of Grounded Theory.* Chicago: Aldine, 1967.

Strauss, A.L., & Corbin, J. *Basics of Qualitative Research,* 2nd ed. Thousand Oaks, CA: Sage, 1990.

CONSTRUCTIVISM This is a particularly elusive term with different meanings depending on the discourse in which it is used. For example, constructivism in mathematics and logic, or the ideas of construct and construct validity that play a central role in the methodologies of experimental psychology and psychometrics, bears little resemblance to the notions of constructivism readily found in the contemporary literature in the social sciences. Also, the latter generally have very little to do with everyday, garden-variety constructivism, which is the belief that the mind is active in the construction of knowledge. Most of us would agree that knowing is not passive—a simple imprinting of sense data on the mind—but active; that is, the mind does something with these impressions, at the very least forms abstractions or concepts. In this sense, constructivism means that human beings do not find or discover knowledge so much as construct or make it. We invent concepts, models, and schemes to make sense of experience, and we continually test and modify these constructions in the light of new experience. Furthermore, there is an inevitable historical and sociocultural dimension to this construction. We do not construct our interpretations in isolation but, rather, against a backdrop of shared understandings, practices, language, and so forth. This ordinary sense of constructionism holds that all knowledge claims and their evaluation take place within a conceptual framework through which the world is described and explained. Everyday constructivism thus opposes a *naïve realism* and strict *empiricism* that assume the possibility of some kind of unmediated, direct grasp of the empirical world and that knowledge (i.e., the mind) simply reflects or mirrors what is 'out there.'

Notions of constructivism encountered in the social sciences generally go far beyond this ordinary sense of constructing. There are two broad strands of constructivist thought. One strand, known as radical constructivism or psychological constructivism, focuses more on the individual knower and acts of cognition, and its most well-known advocate is Ernst von Glasersfeld. The central idea in radical constructivism is that human knowledge cannot consist in accurate representation or faithful copying of an external reality, that is, of a reality that is nonphenomenal (existing apart from the knower's experiences). Knowledge is redefined procedurally—as an unending series of processes of inner construction. The reliability of constructions is determined instrumentally in terms of their evolutionary viability. (Radical constructivism claims a debt to the genetic *epistemology* of Jean Piaget [1896–1980]. Although Piaget is perhaps better known for his work in developmental psychology, he did considerable work in theory of knowledge. He rejected both *empiricism* and *rationalism* and, like Kant [1724–1804], held that knowledge of the world is mediated by cognitive structures. However, unlike Kant, Piaget did not consider these structures to be given a priori but rather viewed them as the products of a process of construction resulting from the interaction of mind and environment [see his *Introduction à l'epistemologie génétique,* 3 vols., 1950; *The Origins of Intelligence in Children,* Norton, 1952].)

A second strand of constructivism focuses more on social process and interaction and is generally known as social constructionism. Social constructionism has some affinity to theories of **symbolic interactionism** and **ethnomethodology** that emphasize the actor's definition of the situation; that seek to understand how social actors recognize, produce, and reproduce social actions and how they come to share an intersubjective understanding of specific life circumstances. The classic work in this area is Peter Berger and Thomas Luckmann's *The Social Construction of Reality* (Doubleday, 1966).

Ian Hacking argues that social constructivist arguments generally arise as follows: Scholars claim that some particular X (childhood, gender, poverty, frailty, disability, etc.) is taken for granted or appears to be inevitable. They argue that X need not be at all as it is at present; it is not determined by the nature of things, nor is it inevitable. They aim to undermine the idea that X has an 'essence.' Diana Fuss, for example, claims that

> What is at stake for the constructionist are systems of representations, social and material practices, laws of discourses, and ideological effects. In short, constructionists are concerned above all with the production and organization of differences, and they therefore reject the idea that any essential or natural givens precede the process of social determination. (p. 3)

The constructivist seeks to explain how human beings interpret or construct some X in specific linguistic, social, and historical contexts. In addition, many constructivists hold that X is something that should be severely criticized, changed, or overthrown.

In making sense of constructivism, it is important to distinguish just what is being constructed. Again, Hacking is helpful here in explaining that three broad types of things are said to be socially constructed (imagine substituting one of the following for X in the paragraph above): (1) items or objects that are in the world in a commonsensical meaning of the phrase—for example, states (childhood), practices (domestic abuse), conditions (health), actions (labeling something criminal or deviant), behavior (attention deficit disorder), experiences (of being disabled), relations (gender); (2) ideas—including conceptions, beliefs, theories, attitudes toward; and (3) facts, truth, reality, knowledge, in sum, everything.

There are both weak and strong versions of social constructionism, depending on their respective views regarding the social construction of everything. Both versions share the view that our concepts, theories, ideas, and so forth do not chart, map, or straightforwardly represent or mirror reality. However, the weak variety would not hold that *every* object, idea, and so forth in the world, and indeed *every* aspect of the world (i.e., every thing in itself) is a social construct. Instead of this kind of universal constructivism, weak constructivism might focus on how our experience of some particular object or idea, our classifications of same, and our interest in same are socially constructed. This is a roundabout way of saying that weak social constructionism does not deny reality in the ordinary commonplace sense of that term. For example, one might write a social history of the notion of disability, schizophrenia, altruism, mental illness, family, domestic violence, gender, childhood, and so forth revealing how each is culturally produced or unmasking each as an ideology, and still maintain that it is real. Strong social constructivists do appear to deny any **ontology** of the real whatsoever. Gergen, for example, argues that "one must be suspicious of all attempts to establish *fundamental* ontologies—incorrigible inventories of *the real*" (p. 75; emphasis in the original). Taken literally, that may well mean that everything in the world and about the world is nothing but a sociolinguistic product of historically situated interactions, a kind of linguistic or semantic **idealism**. Moreover, many strong social constructionists endorse radical perspectivalism, a doctrine that claims that our experience, thought, and speech about reality and/or reality itself are a function of the particular conceptual scheme or framework (e.g., culture, form of life, language game, paradigm) in which we live and that different conceptual schemes yield incommensurable understandings of experience and reality.

See also Description, Essentialism, Fallibilism, Realism.

KEY REFERENCES

Collin, F. *Social Reality.* London: Routledge, 1997.

Fuss, D. *Essentially Speaking: Feminism, Nature, and Difference.* New York: Routledge, 1989.

Gergen, K. J. *Realities and Relationships: Soundings in Social Construction.* Cambridge, MA: Harvard University Press, 1994.

Hacking, I. *The Social Construction of What?* Cambridge, MA: Harvard University Press, 1999.

Phillips, D. C., ed. *Constructivism in Education: Opinions and Second Opinions on Controversial Issues.* National Society for the Study of Education 99th Yearbook, Vol. 1. Chicago: University of Chicago Press, 2000.

Potter, J. *Representing Reality: Discourse, Rhetoric, and Social Construction.* London: Sage, 1996.

Sarbin, T. R., & Kitsue, J. I., eds. *Constructing the Social.* Thousand Oaks, CA: Sage, 1994.

von Glasersfeld, E. *Radical Constructivism: A Way of Knowing and Learning.* London: Falmer, 1995.

CONTENT ANALYSIS   This is a generic name for a variety of means of *textual analysis* that involve comparing, contrasting, and categorizing a corpus of data in order to test hypotheses. The analysis usually, but not always, relies on some statistical procedures for drawing samples and establishing intercoder reliability. The central steps to this procedure include (a) creating a set of codes, (b) systematically applying those codes to some set of textual data, (c) establishing the interrater reliability of coders when more than one coder is employed, (d) creating a matrix of variables from the texts and codes, and (e) analyzing the matrix by means of some univariate, bivariate, or multivariate statistical procedure. The data to be coded may be cultural artifacts (texts of various kinds, documents, records, billboards, television shows, films, advertisements, etc.) or events. Although classic context analysis emphasizes systematic, objective, quantitative description of content derived from researcher-developed categories, contemporary forms of content analysis include both numeric and interpretive means of analyzing data.

See also *Analyzing Qualitative Data, Coding.*

KEY REFERENCES

Neuendorf, K. A. *The Content Analysis Guidebook.* Thousand Oaks, CA: Sage, 2002.

Reinharz, S. *Feminist Methods in Social Research.* Oxford, UK: Oxford University Press, 1992. (See the chapter on content analysis.)

Weber, R. P. *Basic Content Analysis,* 2nd ed. Thousand Oaks, CA: Sage, 1990.

CONTEXT   See **CONTEXTUALISM.**

CONTEXT OF DISCOVERY/CONTEXT OF JUSTIFICATION   The philosophy of *logical positivism* was based on a strict *empiricism* that relied only on perception and induction in the formation of scientific claims. *Theory* and theoretical terms were nothing more than a language that functioned as a filing system for organizing data and hypotheses. Moreover, the starting points for scientific discovery—that is, the theoretical interests and dispositions of inquirers—were largely regarded as irrelevant to the task of developing justifiable scientific claims. The philosophy of *logical empiricism* reintroduced the ideas of discovery and theoretical dispositions as relevant features of the picture of scientific claim making. It did so, however, in a way so as not to subvert the primary importance of empirical testing. Logical empiricists argued that there is indeed a process of intellectual discovery and theoretical speculation that produces new ideas and hypotheses. In this process, known as the context of discovery, the imagination, intellectual interests, values, dispositions, and theoretical inclinations of individual scientists, as well as institutional commitments and values influencing the scientist's choices, are all relevant matters. These extrascientific ('external') concerns, however, are completely irrelevant (and must be eliminated) once the scientist embarks upon the process of the epistemological validation of a hypothesis. This ('internal') process—known as the context of justification—is governed by epistemic concerns and procedures. It is here that a scientific claim is checked, tested, and critically evaluated.

This sharp distinction between two contexts was first introduced in 1938 by Hans Reichenbach (1891–1953) and was featured in both Karl Popper's (1902–1994) and Ernest Nagel's (1901–1985) philosophies of science. The distinction met with sharp criticism from philosophers who argued that a complete understanding of the epistemology of science could only be had by recognizing science as a social enterprise and by considering the interrelationships between the dynamics of theory development, the acceptance and rejection of theories, the choice of which experiments to perform to test a theory, and so on.

Despite the rather thoroughgoing criticism of this doctrine, it continues to serve as a key methodological principle in the philosophy of *naturalism*. Defenders of naturalism generally argue that epistemological concerns are primary and that it is important to distinguish between ideology (or history or sociology) and epistemology when discussing the testing and growth of scientific knowledge. According to this view, emotions, interests, ideologies, and values have a bearing on or influence the problems one addresses and the hypotheses one develops but are irrelevant to cognitive assessment of those problems and hypotheses. Moreover, the spirit of the doctrine is evident in other contemporary efforts to come to terms with the relationship between a normative philosophy of science (the traditional concerns of epistemology) and an empirical sociology of knowledge. For example, some feminists argue that a distinction between the two contexts cannot be maintained, and defenders of the Strong Programme in the *Sociology of Scientific Knowledge* appear to collapse the distinction and argue that knowledge is whatever we take it to be.

See also Fact-Value Distinction, Tacit (Personal) Knowledge.

KEY REFERENCES

Hollis, M. *The Philosophy of Social Science: An Introduction.* Cambridge, UK: Cambridge University Press, 1994.

Reichenbach, H. *Experience and Prediction.* Chicago: University of Chicago Press, 1938.

CONTEXTUALISM   Several senses of this term play an important role in current thinking about qualitative inquiry. In one sense, contextualism refers to a humanistic theory that explains the kinds of beings that we are. This theory holds that human nature is specified and made intelligible only by the particular context (i.e., symbolic systems) in which it is found. Clifford Geertz's views of human nature in his *The Interpretation of Cultures* (Basic Books, 1971) reflect this theory. In a second sense, contextualism refers to the nature of interpretations. Hermeneutic contextualism is the view that interpretations are always context bound; that is, they always take place within some background of beliefs and practices (culture, form of life, language game, or tradition) that is never at once and completely capable of articulation. Moreover, interpretations are context bound in the sense that a specific situation determines the form and direction of an interpretation. A third sense of context as formative is related to the second. In *cultural studies,* context or contextualism indicates not simply an empirical environment given beforehand against which some *action* is to be understood. Context is not simply a background of influences and determinants of meaning, identity, speech, and so forth that is detachable from those human actions. Nor is context simply the set of interrelated conditions in which something occurs or exists. Rather, context is produced in the social practice of asking questions about meaning, identity, speech, and so on.

See also Indexicality.

KEY REFERENCES

Grossberg, L. *Bringing It All Back Home: Essays on Cultural Studies.* Durham, NC: Duke University Press, 1997.

Holstein, J. A., & Gubrium, J. F. "Context: Working It Up, Down, and Across," in C. Seale, G. Gobo, J. F. Gubrium, & D. Silverman, eds., *Qualitative Research Practice.* London: Sage, 2004.

Hoy, D. R., Bohman, J. F., & Shusterman, R., eds. *The Interpretive Turn: Philosophy, Science, Culture.* Ithaca, NY: Cornell University Press, 1991.

CONVERSATION   See DIALOGUE.

CONVERSATION ANALYSIS   This methodology for *textual analysis* arose out of *ethnomethodology*. It is concerned specifically with examining the structure of talk itself in order to reveal how speakers produce orderly social interaction. The methodology requires the detailed analysis of precisely prepared transcripts. Like ethnomethodology, conversation analysis rejects referential theories of language use that assume that words have meaning by standing for things and that an utterance (or sentence) means what it does because its parts refer to or correspond to elements of an actual or possible state of affairs. Because utterances 'stand for' in this way, in this theory of language use, one is primarily concerned with the quality of that 'standing for'—that is, the extent to which the utterance is accurate, truthful, distorted, and so on. In contrast, conversation analysis assumes a pragmatic theory of language use in which the meaning of an utterance is the role it plays in a particular social practice. On this view, words and sentences 'do things'—they perform actions like inviting, rebuking, complaining, complimenting, and so on—they do not simply (or even) refer (see J. L. Austin, *How to Do Things with Words,* Oxford University Press, 1962). The conversation analyst is interested in understanding the many things that utterances can do and how they do what they do in particular social practices.

See also Language.

KEY REFERENCES

Have, P. T. *Doing Conversational Analysis: A Practical Guide.* London: Sage, 1999.

Heritage, J. "Explanations as Accounts: A Conversation Analytic Perspective," in *Analyzing Everyday Explanation: A Casebook of Methods,* C. Antaki, ed. London: Sage, 1988.

Rapley, T. "Analyzing Conversation," in C. Seale, ed., *Researching Society and Culture,* 2nd ed. London: Sage, 2004.

Sacks, H. *Lectures on Conversation,* vols. I and II. G. Jefferson, ed. Oxford, UK: Blackwell, 1992.

Silverman, D. *Harvey Sacks: Social Science and Conversation Analysis.* Cambridge, UK: Polity, 1998.

COOPERATIVE INQUIRY   This form of participatory qualitative research arose out of criticisms of traditional research practices in which the researcher is in control of all aspects of the inquiry and the subjects or participants as data sources merely provide information. In cooperative inquiry, the relationship between researchers and subjects/participants is bilateral and they work together as coresearchers and cosubjects designing, managing, and drawing conclusions from the research. The developers of this approach characterize it as research *with* people rather than *on* people and oriented toward helping those involved in the inquiry to understand their world, develop new and creative ways of looking at things, and learn how to act to change the things they want to change.

See also Action Research.

KEY REFERENCES

Heron, J. *Co-operative Inquiry: Research Into the Human Condition.* London: Sage, 1999.

Heron, J., & Reason, P. "The Practice of Co-operative Inquiry: Research 'With' Rather Than 'On' People," in P. Reason & H. Bradbury, eds., *Handbook of Action Research.* London: Sage, 2001.

Reason, P. *Human Inquiry in Action.* London: Sage, 1998.

COVERING-LAW MODEL OF EXPLANATION   The most influential, although not universally accepted, view of what constitutes *the* logic of *explanation* in the social sciences or an adequate social *scientific* explanation is the covering-law model. This model explains an event/action by subsuming (covering) it under one or more general causal laws. This model has two forms: In the case where laws are deterministic (universal), a deductive-nomological (i.e., *lawlike*) explanation is possible. This takes the following form:

$L_1, L_2, L_3, \ldots L_n$ (Testable causal laws)

$C_1, C_2, C_3, \ldots C_n$ (Testable statements of background conditions)

E   (Statement of the event, action to be explained)

In circumstances where laws are statistical (probabilistic), explanation takes an inductive-statistical form:

$L_1, L_2, L_3, \ldots L_n$ (Testable statistical laws)

$C_1, C_2, C_3, \ldots C_n$ (Testable statements of background conditions)

E   (Statement of the event, action to be explained)

In the former, the laws and conditions deductively entail the event or action to be explained by showing why it was necessary under the circumstances. In the latter, laws and conditions help show only why the event or action was probable (not necessary).

Much controversy surrounds the issue of whether the covering-law model in general is the most appropriate definition of social scientific explanation and what constitutes a legitimate form of an inductive-statistical explanation. Nonetheless, for defenders of *logical empiricism,* this is a generally accepted account of what constitutes theoretical explanation. On this view, the goal of social science is to develop social *theory*—a unified causal explanation that ties together laws, generalizations, hypotheses, and so on. Other models or accounts of explanation (functional, structural, materialist) are also popular in social science, but there is significant debate about whether these models are more or less variations on the kind of causal explanation defended in the covering-law model or simply poor substitutes.

KEY REFERENCE

Little, D. *Varieties of Social Explanation.* Boulder, CO: Westview Press, 1991.

CREDIBILITY   **See TRUSTWORTHINESS CRITERIA.**

CRISIS OF LEGITIMATION   This phrase is shorthand for a set of issues that arise from questioning the *authority* of the interpretive *text* characteristic of *postmodernism* and *poststructuralism*. Authority here refers to the claim a text makes to be an accurate, true, complete account of experience, meaning, a way of life, and so forth. Traditionally, these kinds of concerns about the authority of an account are considered to be epistemological matters. In other words, an account is judged in terms of the validity, accuracy, and truthfulness of its claims. Hence, the ability of a text to persuade, sway, influence, or command an audience's attention depends, for the most part, on the extent to which the claims made in a text are accurate, warranted, and so forth. In other words, in this perspective, the quality of evidence and argument presented to warrant a claim are more important than the rhetoric and style of presentation.

Postmodernist thought regards these traditional concerns with validity as vacuous. It does so because it argues as follows: (a) The notion of validity rests on the assumption that a textual account is capable of faithfully representing some set of experiences in 'the world-out-there'; (b) various rules and procedures are employed to judge the validity of this act of representation—for example, respondent validation, triangulation, internal coherence, careful fit to theory; (c) there is no such thing as a 'real' world of experience out there, however, only various textual constructions that create experience and in the process transform it; (d) hence, the rules and procedures employed to establish the validity of a text or to provide a warrant for claims made in a text are, in actuality, only devices employed by the author of a particular text to assert some kind of power over the reader by persuading the reader that the particular text in question is authoritative or legitimate; (e) because there can be no such thing as a valid and authoritative account, there can only be various kinds of accounts that, via a variety of different means (e.g., appeals to evidence, standpoint, involvement, subjectivity, emotionality, feeling, participation, and so on) seek to persuade readers of their legitimacy; and (f) hence, validity is replaced by notions of authority and legitimation, and rhetorical and political issues trump traditional epistemological concerns.

To the extent that this argument itself accurately captures the state of affairs in interpretive work, there would be no real crisis. There would simply be debate about the merits of various ways of persuading readers of the legitimacy of an account. But a genuine crisis does in fact arise, because despite this turn away from epistemology and toward rhetoric and politics, the core problem of criteria remains, namely, on what basis are we to discriminate between better and worse accounts? When legitimation becomes a matter of exercising authority and power, the question naturally arises, what are legitimate and illegitimate means of exercising power?

See also *Crisis of Representation, Experience, (The) Problem of the Criterion, Rhetoric.*

KEY REFERENCE

Denzin, N. K. *Interpretive Ethnography: Ethnographic Practices for the 21st Century.* Thousand Oaks, CA: Sage, 1997.

CRISIS OF REPRESENTATION   This phrase was coined by George Marcus and Michael Fischer to refer specifically to the uncertainty within the human sciences about adequate means of describing social reality. This crisis arises from the (noncontroversial) claim that no interpretive account can ever directly or completely capture lived *experience*. Broadly conceived, the crisis is part of a more general set of ideas across the human sciences that challenge long-standing beliefs about the role of encompassing, generalizing (theoretical, methodological, and political) frameworks that guide empirical research within a discipline. Symptoms of the crisis include the borrowing of ideas and methods across disciplines (e.g., social sciences to literature, literature to philosophy, philosophy to social science), questioning the dominance of post–WW II frameworks and theories that guided inquiry (e.g., Parsonian sociology, Marxism, French structuralism), and the general turn away from developing theoretical models of social and natural order to debates about epistemology, method, forms of representation, and the like. Although fore-shadowed and shaped in the antipositivist writing of German scholars in the late nineteenth and early twentieth centuries, these are the sets of ideas that, over the past three or four decades, have come to characterize the postmodern condition of the social sciences (and related conditions in literature, philosophy, arts, architecture, and so on).

Within the crisis, both radically skeptical and optimistic voices are discernible. Radical skeptics insist that what we are faced with are only texts— that is, particular *inscriptions* that create different accounts of lived experience. There is no direct, unmediated link between the inscriptions of any particular *text* and the 'real' world of experience. There are no real-world referents (no such thing as 'experience' as an object) to which the language of descriptive and explanatory accounts of human *action* can be mapped and against which it can be judged. Moreover, all attempts to describe and explain are always, at best, incomplete, reductive, and insufficient and, at worst, misleading, perverse, fraudulent, and deceptive. Texts (accounts, representations, interpretations) refer only to other texts; the language of representation is only rhetoric. More optimistic responses acknowledge the importance of examining the rhetoric of representation but are not willing to concede that the dilemma of representation dissolves the responsibility of the social scientist to describe and explain the social world.

See also Crisis of Legitimation, Grand Theory, Postmodernism, Representation, Rhetoric.

KEY REFERENCES

Atkinson, P. *The Ethnographic Imagination.* London: Routledge, 1990.
Gubrium, J., & Holstein, J. *The New Language of Qualitative Method.* Oxford, UK: Blackwell, 1997.
Marcus, C., & Fischer, M. *Anthropology as Cultural Critique.* Chicago: University of Chicago Press, 1986.

CRITERIA   Criteria are standards, benchmarks, norms, and, in some cases, regulative ideals that guide judgments about the goodness, quality, validity, truthfulness, and so forth of competing claims (or methodologies, theories, interpretations, etc.). A criterion is distinguishable from various procedures employed to achieve the criterion. For example, the validity of a claim is a criterion; demonstrating that that criterion is met might involve using procedures such as analytic induction, member checking, and triangulation.

Criteria that have been proposed for judging the processes and products of social inquiry include truth, relevance, validity, credibility, plausibility, generalizability, social action, and social transformation, among others. Some of these criteria are epistemic (i.e., concerned with justifying knowledge claims as true, accurate, correct), others are political (i.e., concerned with warranting the power, use, and effects of knowledge claims or the inquiry process more generally); still others are moral or ethical standards (i.e., concerned with the right conduct of the inquirer and the inquiry process in general).

Traditionally, criteria are an essential feature of *epistemology*—they are standards by means of which one distinguishes genuine, objective knowledge from mere belief. Charles Taylor explains that the quest for a set of externally defined standard(s)—criteria—against which competing methodologies, values, theories, claims, conjectures, and so forth are independently weighed is based on the assumption that rational arbitration of differences *requires* such standards. In other words, it is absolutely necessary to have criteria, for without them it would be impossible to determine whether one is behaving rationally. Criteria are considered to be decisive considerations that both parties to a dispute about competing claims must accept. Taylor is highly critical of this conception of criteria central to foundationalist epistemologies. He defends an alternative view of practical rationality and a form of argument that evaluates transitions from one interpretation to another.

Poststructuralist and postmodernist approaches to qualitative inquiry are also shaping the way we conceive of criteria. Given the growing influence of narrative approaches and experimental texts in qualitative inquiry, it is becoming more common to find discussions of rhetorical and aesthetic criteria replacing discussions of epistemic criteria. Other scholars argue that epistemological criteria cannot be neatly decoupled from political and critical agendas and ethical concerns. Some scholars in qualitative inquiry have little patience for discussing criteria within different epistemological frameworks and theoretical perspectives and prefer to focus on the craft of using various methodological procedures for producing 'quality' work.

See also *Authenticity Criteria, Fact-Value Distinction, Knowledge, (The) Problem of the Criterion, Rationality, Trustworthiness Criteria, Validity, Verisimilitude.*

KEY REFERENCES

Hammersley, M. *Reading Ethnographic Research: A Critical Guide.* London: Longman, 1990.
Richardson, L., ed. "Special Focus: Introduction—Assessing Alternative Modes of Qualitative and Ethnographic Research: How Do We Judge? Who Judges?" *Qualitative Inquiry,* 2000, 6(2), 251–291.
Seale, C. F. *The Quality of Qualitative Research.* London: Sage, 1999.
Smith, J. K. *After the Demise of Empiricism: The Problem of Judging Social and Educational Inquiry.* Norwood, NJ: Ablex, 1993.
Taylor, C. *Philosophical Arguments.* Cambridge, MA: Harvard University Press, 1995.

CRITICAL ETHNOGRAPHY *Critical* ethnographic studies of social practices and cultural institutions specifically aim to criticize the taken-for-granted social, economic, cultural, and political assumptions and concepts (e.g., family, work, self, agency, power, conflict, race, class, and gender) of Western, liberal, middle-class, industrialist, capitalist societies. Critical ethnographies are focused, theorized studies of specific social institutions or practices that aim to change awareness and/or life itself. They may engage in ideology critique or demystification, showing, for example, interests hidden behind, or vested in, cultural meanings and practices or revealing forms of domination or power. They may employ the technique of juxtaposing Western practice against the 'other' practice in order to probe and make problematic understandings assumed in each. Theoretical sources for critique are multiple and include ideas drawn from cultural Marxism, critical theory of the Frankfurt School, praxis theory, cultural studies, feminist studies, racialized and queer epistemologies, and the broad postmodern critique of advanced capitalist societies. Some examples of the rich variety of studies informed by these different and sometimes overlapping theoretical frameworks include Paul Willis's *Learning to Labour* (Columbia University Press, 1981); Peter McLaren's *Schooling as a Ritual Performance* (Rowman & Littlefield, 1999); Jean Comaroff's *Body of Power, Spirit of Resistance: The Culture and History of a South African People* (University of Chicago Press, 1985); Michael Taussig's *Shaminism, Colonialism and the Wild Man* (University of Chicago Press, 1991); Michelle Fine and Lois Weiss's *The Unknown City* (Beacon Press, 1999); and Kathleen Stewart's *A Space on the Side of the Road* (Princeton University Press, 1996). While difficult to characterize in terms of a single set of features, critical ethnographies in the main are marked by several shared dispositions: a disavowal of the model of ethnographer as detached, neutral participant observer; a focus on specific practices and institutions more so than holistic portraits of an entire culture; an emancipatory versus a solely descriptive intent; and a self-referential form of reflexivity that aims to criticize the ethnographer's own production of an account. This last feature may perhaps be the most telling for what constitutes a *critical* ethnographic investigation. Critical social science, in general, aims to integrate theory and practice in such a way that individuals and groups become aware of the contradictions and distortions in their belief systems and social practices and are motivated to change those beliefs and practices. A critical theoretical approach to social investigation links hermeneutic (interpretive) and explanatory interests to normative concerns. However, this approach is never innocent; it is never merely a theory 'about' the world. Because critical social scientists assume that their very ways of theorizing the world constitute the ways we access the world (theories provide the categories through which we think about and experience the world), they interrogate (and frequently disrupt and decenter) their way of theorizing by means of reflexive critique.

See also Critical Social Science.

KEY REFERENCES

Carspecken, P. F. "The Hidden History of Praxis Theory Within Critical Ethnography and the Criticalism/Postmodernism Problematic," in Y. Zou & E. T. Trueba, eds., *Ethnography and Schools*. Lanham, MD: Rowman & Littlefield, 2002.

Kincheloe, J., & McLaren, P. L. "Rethinking Critical Theory and Qualitative Research," in N. K. Denzin & Y. S. Lincoln, eds., *Handbook of Qualitative Research,* 2nd ed. Thousand Oaks, CA: Sage, 2000.

Levinson, B., Foley, D., & Holland, D., eds. *The Cultural Production of the Educated Person: Critical Ethnographies of Schooling and Local Practice.* Albany: State University of New York Press, 1996.

Marcus, G. E. *Ethnography Through Thick and Thin.* Princeton, NJ: Princeton University Press, 1988.

Marcus, G. E., & Fischer, M. M. J. *Anthropology as Cultural Critique.* Chicago: University of Chicago Press, 1986.

CRITICAL HERMENEUTICS   Also known as depth hermeneutics, this version of *hermeneutics* is explained by Karl Otto-Apel and Jürgen Habermas as well as other critical theorists. It is characterized by several general ideas. First, it is highly skeptical about given meanings and interpretations. It is suspicious of claims to truth and knowledge and seeks to demystify those claims by engaging in a critique of ideologies that distort understanding and communication. Second, it is emphatically normative; that is, its critiques of meanings and practices are undertaken for the purposes of transforming society and emancipating individuals from false consciousness such that undistorted communication and nonideological understandings can be realized. Finally, it is materialist—it is concerned not simply with the relationship between language, meaning, and understanding but with concrete, empirical economic, social, organizational, and political conditions and practices that shape human beings as knowers and as social agents. Critical hermeneutics often draws on psychoanalysis as a model for the hermeneutic task integrating both causal explanation and interpretive self-understanding.

See also Critical Social Science, Critical Theory.

KEY REFERENCES

Habermas, J. *Knowledge and Human Interests.* J. J. Shapiro, trans. Boston: Beacon Press, 1971.

Kögler, H. H. *The Power of Dialogue: Critical Hermeneutics After Gadamer and Foucault.* P. Henrickson, trans. Cambridge: MIT Press, 1996.

CRITICAL RACE THEORY This is a theoretical and methodological framework with roots in legal studies, political theory, philosophy, anthropology, and sociology connecting research, policy, and race. It begins from the assumption that race and racism are at the very center of social and institutional life and uses stories, narrative inquiries, and other forms of both quantitative and qualitative study, to challenge existing assumptions about the social construction of race in society. There is no single set of principles to which all critical race theorists subscribe. They are, however, united around two central interests—understanding how an establishment of white supremacy and its subordination of people of color has been created and is perpetuated and undoing the relationship that exists between law and racial power.

KEY REFERENCES

Crenshaw, K., Gotanda, N., Peller, G, & Thomas, K., eds. *Critical Race Theory: Key Writings That Formed the Movement.* New York: New Press, 1995.
Delgado, R., & Stefancic, J., eds. *Critical Race Theory,* 2nd ed. Philadelphia: Temple University Press, 1999.
Lopez, G. R., & Parker, L., eds. *Interrogating Racism in Qualitative Research Methodology.* New York: Peter Lang, 2003.
Tate, W. F. "Critical Race Theory," *Review of Research in Education,* 1996, 22, 201–247.

CRITICAL SOCIAL SCIENCE Generally, this is the research program undertaken by a variety of social theorists that are strongly influenced by ***critical theory***. Critical theory of society, in turn, can be characterized as a blend of practical philosophy and explanatory social science, sharing and radically reforming the intentions of both. Practical philosophy is concerned with the specifics of ethical and political life (***praxis***) and the actions that must be undertaken to achieve the good life; explanatory social science produces scientific knowledge of the general causes of social ***action***. Critical social science is characterized by several general themes. First, its aim, broadly conceived, is to integrate theory and practice in such a way that individuals and groups become aware of the contradictions and distortions in their belief systems and social practices and are then inspired to change those beliefs and practices. Its method here is immanent critique, which challenges belief systems and social relations not by comparing them to some set of external standards but by showing that these practices do not measure up to their own standards and are internally inconsistent, hypocritical, incoherent, and hence comprise a false consciousness. Second, critical social science is thus practical and normative and not merely descriptive and explanatory. Third, it is foregrounded in a critique of instrumental, technical reason. Critical theorists (among other social theorists) argue that this kind of means-end reasoning is pervasive; it informs the traditional empirical-analytic sciences and dominates not only societal processes and cultural meaning but also the dynamics of personality formation. Critical social scientists argue that instrumental reason aims to eliminate crises, conflict, and critique. Although founded in the Enlightenment bid to liberate people from myth, ignorance, and oppression, the rationalization of social and individual life by means of instrumental reason actually works to suppress the very self-transformative, self-reflexive, critical, liberating impulses on which it was founded. Critical inquiry supports a kind of reasoning that is practical, moral, and ethically and politically informed. Fourth, to retain or recapture the Enlightenment belief in the power of human reason to affect individual and social transformation, critical social science argues that a form of inquiry is needed that fosters enlightened self-knowledge and effective social-political action. The logic of critical social inquiry requires linking hermeneutic and explanatory social scientific interests to normative concerns. This feature of critical social science marks it as distinctly different from social science characterized by *naturalism* and *antinaturalism*. Finally, critical social science is self-reflexive. To prevent a critical theory of society from becoming yet another self-serving ideology, the theory must account for its own conditions of possibility and its transformative effects. It rejects the idea of *disinterested social science* and emphasizes attending to the cultural and historical conditions on which the theorist's own intellectual activity depends.

See also Frankfurt School, Interest.

KEY REFERENCES

Calhoun, C. "Social Theory and the Public Sphere," in B. S. Turner, ed., *The Blackwell Companion to Social Theory.* Oxford, UK: Blackwell, 1996.

Comstock, D. E. "A Method for Critical Research," in M. Martin & L. C. McIntyre, eds., *Readings in the Philosophy of Social Science.* Cambridge: MIT Press, 1994.

Fay, B. *Critical Social Science.* Ithaca, NY: Cornell University Press, 1987.

Fay, B., & Moon, J. D. "What Would an Adequate Philosophy of Social Science Look Like?" in M. Martin & L. C. McIntyre, eds., *Readings in the Philosophy of Social Science,* Cambridge: MIT Press, 1994.

CRITICAL THEORY Critical theory refers both to a way of theorizing and to the product of that theorizing. It is distinguishable from the traditional empiricist way of thinking about theorizing and theory in the following ways: First, it is a way of submitting the very 'givenness' or taken-for-granted character of the social world (its concepts, understandings, cultural categories, etc.) to critical reconsideration and is thus part of the self-reflective public discourse of a democratic society. Traditional theory fails to recognize that theory itself constitutes the way we access the world; that theory provides the categories through which we think about and experience the world. Second, it regards theory as intimately related to *praxis*. In the empiricist tradition, the theorist does not regard her or his activity of theorizing as part of social practice. Rather, the theorist is disinterested and views theorizing as an activity that takes place alongside all the other activities that comprise social life but has no immediately clear connection to those activities. In a separate step, that is not part of the theorist's work, theory must be applied to practice. In sharp contrast, critical theorizing is 'interested' and simultaneously empirical and normative. Third, it is a kind of theory that employs the method of immanent critique, working from within categories of existing thought in order to radicalize those categories, reveal their internal contradictions and shortcomings, and demonstrate their unrecognized possibilities.

See also Frankfurt School; Theory, Types of.

KEY REFERENCES

Bernstein, R. J. *The Restructuring of Social and Political Theory.* Philadelphia: University of Pennsylvania Press, 1976.

Calhoun, C. "Social Theory and the Public Sphere," in B. S. Turner, ed., *The Blackwell Companion to Social Theory.* Oxford, UK: Blackwell, 1996.

Horkheimer, M. *Critical Theory,* trans. M. J. O'Connell. New York: Continuum, 1972. (Original German text published 1937)

CROSS-CASE ANALYSIS (also called comparative case method or comparative analysis) A study can include the examination of one case or a collection of cases in order to learn something about a concept, theory, social process, and so on. Cross-case or comparative approaches include functional analysis as first developed by Durkheim (1858–1917), Marx's (1818–1883) theory of modes of production in societies, and Weber's (1864–1920) methods of historical comparison using ideal types; contemporary methods of quasi-experimentation using multivariate statistical analysis (e.g., T. D. Cook and D. Campbell, *Quasi-Experimentation: Design and Analysis Issues for Field Settings,* Rand McNally, 1979); and *metaethnography.* In cross-case analysis, two central issues are the rationale for the selection of multiple cases in a single study and the procedures for analyzing data across the cases.

Robert Yin advises that the choice of single or multiple cases is a design decision. Cases are rarely if ever chosen as a sample of some universe of cases. Rather, a single-case design is chosen because the case is thought to be critical to the elaboration or test of a theory, extreme, unique, or unusually revelatory. The choice of multiple-case designs (permitting cross-case analysis) follows what Yin calls a replication rather than a sampling logic: Additional cases are chosen for study because such cases are expected to yield similar information or findings or contrary but predictable findings. Robert Stake agrees that cases are not chosen for *representativeness.* He defines instrumental case study as strategy whereby a case is studied because it can shed light on a particular pre-given issue, concept, or problem. When several cases are chosen within a single study to achieve this aim, each is thought to be useful in that regard. The result is what he calls a collective case study.

See also Case Study Research; Coding; Sampling; Types of.

KEY REFERENCES

Miles, M., & Huberman, A. M. *Qualitative Data Analysis,* 2nd ed. Thousand Oaks, CA: Sage, 1994.
Ragin, C. C. *The Comparative Method: Moving Beyond Qualitative and Quantitative Strategies.* Berkeley: University of California Press, 1987.
Stake, R. E. *The Art of Case Study Research.* Thousand Oaks, CA: Sage, 1995.
Yin, R. *Case Study Research,* rev. ed. Thousand Oaks, CA: Sage, 1989.

CULTURAL ANTHROPOLOGY Also known as social or sociocultural anthropology, in the twentieth century in both American and British traditions (the latter usually referred to as British Social Anthropology), this became a primary locale of *ethnography* and myriad examinations of its purpose, ethics, and methods that inform much of the discussion of qualitative inquiry in other fields and disciplines.

See also Culture.

KEY REFERENCES

Ember, C. E., & Ember, M. *Cultural Anthropology,* 11th ed. New York: Prentice Hall, 2003.

Marcus, G. E., & Fischer, M. M. J. *Anthropology as Cultural Critique,* 2nd ed. Chicago: University of Chicago Press, 1999.

Monaghan, J., & Just, P. *Social and Cultural Anthropology: A Very Short Introduction.* Oxford, UK: Oxford University Press, 2000.

Spradley, J., & McCurdy, D.W., eds. *Conformity and Conflict: Readings in Cultural Anthropology,* 11th ed. New York: Allyn & Bacon, 2002.

CULTURAL RELATIVISM In the 1920s and 1930s in the United States, cultural relativism was a set of methodological principles that both enabled and justified the study of cultural diversity by anthropologists. The principles encompassed respect for different conceptions of what it meant to behave rationally in different societies, endorsed the view that cultures are comprised of different systems of values, and supported the notion that firsthand observation rather than simply conjecture undertaken from the comfort of one's own library was necessary to understand the ways in which cultures organized their respective ways of life. **(See also NATIVE'S POINT OF VIEW.)** In the 1950s, this set of methodological principles often came to be interpreted as a normative doctrine. As such, it led to widespread concern that anthropology was at least implicitly claiming that all cultural value systems were equal, thus making comparative moral judgments impossible. Moreover, the focus on documenting widespread cultural diversity seemed to argue against the possibility of any meaningful generalization about human societies and values, thereby casting doubt on anthropology as a genuine science. With the appearance of interpretive anthropology in the late 1960s and early 1970s, the idea of cultural relativism as method was resurrected as a rationale for engaging in *ethnography*. Marcus and Fischer claim that contemporary *interpretive anthropology* once again embodies a reinvigorated methodological principle (but not the doctrine) of cultural relativism. In their view, it is precisely because it has resurrected and strengthened this notion that the practice of ethnography is capable of "challenging all those views of reality in social thought which prematurely overlook or reduce cultural diversity for the sake of the capacity to generalize or to affirm universal values, usually from the still-privileged vantage point of global homogenization, emanating from the West" (p. 33).

See also Cultural Studies, Other (The Other, Otherness), Relativism.

KEY REFERENCES

Geertz, C. "Anti Anti-relativism," *American Anthropologist,* 1984, 86(2), 263–277.
Marcus, C., & Fischer, M. *Anthropology as Cultural Critique.* Chicago: University of Chicago Press, 1986.
Rosaldo, R. "On Headhunters and Soldiers: Separating Cultural and Ethical Relativism," *Issues in Ethics,* 2000, 11(1), 1–9.

CULTURAL STUDIES   This is a diverse field devoted to the study of *culture,* yet the particular practices of cultural study differ not only in terms of contexts in which these studies unfold (e.g., British cultural studies, Australian cultural studies, U.S. cultural studies, African cultural studies, and Pacific cultural studies) but also in methods employed (e.g., participant observation, various means of textual analysis, and statistical survey techniques), the frameworks that give rise to particular foci for a study (e.g., postcolonial relations, semiotics, gender studies, media studies), and social theories that provide it with substantive concerns (e.g., critical race theory, neo-Marxism, feminist social theory, communications theory, and poststructuralism). All cultural studies appear to share a view that culture is both language and practice in use. Culture is that shifting, contested, conflictual site of the meanings, values, norms, beliefs, actions, and so on that make up the stuff of everyday life for some social group. Cultural studies aim to examine the internal organization of those meanings, values, norms, and so on; how they relate to one another; and, hence, how certain objects and events in a culture acquire particular meaning(s). Cultural studies are also characterized by the simultaneous affirmation of culture and the attempt to deconstruct and criticize culture. In other words, these studies seek to understand how notions like *identity,* social group, community, and place become constituted as same through shared language and practice, but at the same time, these studies seriously question these very ideas as kinds of imaginary social unities that provide an explanatory basis.

KEY REFERENCES

Grossberg, L., Nelson, C., & Treichler, P. A., eds. *Cultural Studies.* New York: Routledge, 1992.
Morley, D., & Chen, K. H., eds. *Stuart Hall: Critical Dialogues in Cultural Studies.* New York: Routledge, 1996.

Rodman, G. "Subject to Debate: (Mis)reading Cultural Studies," *Journal of Communication Inquiry,* 1997, 21(2), 58–69.

CULTURE   What constitutes culture and how it is best described and interpreted are matters of much debate. A recent publication listed over 300 definitions from a wide variety of disciplines. There is little overall consensus on its precise meaning, although there is general agreement that culture (a) is not an objectified, self-enclosed, coherent thing or object and (b) is not something that is learned by observing and documenting but something that is inferred; culture is portrayed, written, or inscribed in the acts of representation of the inquirer. In ***ethnography,*** culture is used as an analytic rather than a descriptive term. In other words, the term does not describe a set of traits of a group but refers instead to a form or pattern abstracted from observed behavior. Presently, that pattern is most often spoken of as an ideational system—that is, a kind of knowledge and understanding that members of a given group share. Yet it is not clear whether this abstraction is an ideal type, norm, mean, and so on. Culture can be framed in terms of meaning, symbolism, language, and discourse drawing respectively on phenomenology, cultural anthropology, structuralism, semiotics, ***cultural studies,*** and critical theory. It can also be viewed through functionalist, dramaturgical, Weberian, Durkheimian, Marxist, and poststructural perspectives.

See also *Field.*

KEY REFERENCES

Alexander, J. C., & Seidman, S., eds. *Culture and Society: Contemporary Debates.* Cambridge, UK: Cambridge University Press, 1990.

Baldwin, J. R., Faulkner, S. L., Hecht, M. L., & Lindsley, S. L., eds. *Redefining Culture: Perspectives Across the Disciplines.* Mahwah, NJ: Lawrence Erlbaum, 2006.

Rosaldo, R. "Whose Cultural Studies? Cultural Studies and the Disciplines," in P. Gibian, ed., *Mass Culture and Everyday Life.* New York: Routledge, 1997.

Wuthnow, R., et al., eds. *Cultural Analysis.* London: Routledge & Kegan Paul, 1984.

D

— ◦◦◦ —

DATA   Recorded observations, in textual or numeric form, are called data. (A single observation is a datum.) Observations here include (literally) direct observation, interviews, surveys, paper-and-pencil instruments such as tests, field notes, and so on. Data may be either structured or unstructured. For example, open-ended interviews, field notes, focus groups, as well as historical archives (of records, diaries, manuscripts, newspaper clippings, and so on) all yield unstructured data, whereas questionnaires and multiple-choice tests produce structured data. Data are also understood as the *evidence* a researcher generates in a study.

See also Description, Generating Data, Unobtrusive Data.

KEY REFERENCE

Marsh, C. *Exploring Data: An Introduction to Data Analysis for Social Scientists.* Cambridge, UK: Polity Press, 1988.

DATA COLLECTION   See DESCRIPTION, GENERATING DATA.

DATA MANAGEMENT, STORAGE, RETRIEVAL   Simply stated, fieldwork generates lots of 'stuff' (more technically, the data corpus or the data log), and the longer one is engaged in field study, the more stuff one accumulates—tapes of interviews, audiotape transcripts, field notes, personal notes, notes on readings, photographs, and copies of documents. An absolutely essential task for any fieldworker is designing a system for organizing, cataloging, and indexing these materials in the data log that makes it possible to retrieve them efficiently, duplicate them, and use them for different tasks. The system one designs will, in turn, affect the way one conceptualizes the process of analyzing the data.

KEY REFERENCE

Miles, M., & Huberman, A. M. *Qualitative Data Analysis,* 2nd ed. Thousand Oaks, CA: Sage, 1994.

DECONSTRUCTIONISM   This is the kind of *hermeneutics* practiced in *poststructuralism,* also called radical hermeneutics and the *hermeneutics of suspicion.* The term *Destrucktion* was originally explained by Martin Heidegger (1889–1976), although Jacques Derrida's (1930–2004) term *deconstruction* is the most often cited source. Derrida strongly objects to what he calls *logocentrism* or the logocentric bias of Western thought. Terms conceived as naturally referring to something are called logi (from the Greek *logos,* which can mean 'word,' 'speech,' or 'reason'). Any account (explanation) of the world that presupposes such terms is logocentric. Derrida claims that all of Western thought assumes that there can be an authoritative, universal language that can disclose what is real, true, right, and beautiful. Western thought seeks to establish through language an order of truth and reality that will stand as an authoritative basis for judging truth-falsity, reality-illusion, right-wrong, and so on. Moreover, Western thought makes use of a set of binary oppositions or dualisms—for example, speech-writing, meaning-form, presence-absence, mind-body, masculine-feminine, nature-culture—in its efforts to establish an order of truth and reality.

Derrida developed his critique of the logocentric bias of Western thought by drawing on the work of the French structural linguist Ferdinand de Saussure (1857–1913). Saussure argued that the sense or meaning of a word (sign) is determined only by its relations to and differences from other words in a network of language. Derrida concluded that there is no interior language of thought and intention such that the sense and referent of a term (sign) is determined by its nature. In other words, there is no such thing as an object, idea, or concept present to the mind of the speaker that gives a particular word its sense or meaning. Thus, the meaning or sense of a word can never be fully present to the mind. Rather, the meaning of a word is only intelligible in terms of its relations in an infinite network of other words in a language. Words (signs) only signify other words (signs). Derrida argued that once we recognize the logocentricity of all accounts of the natural and social world, then language is only an endless play of signifiers with indeterminate meaning, and thought and intention are merely wordlike and have no intrinsic connection to some referent.

Deconstructionism is a kind of internal critique that reveals that the meaning of words only occurs in relations of sameness and difference. The act of deconstruction takes place within the terms that have shaped the text; it does not stand outside of the text but unfolds within the position being discussed in the text itself. The deconstruction of a text reveals that language is only a network of signs and their *différance* (an amalgam of the French terms for difference and deferral). According to Derrida, for everything affirmed in a text (e.g., authorship, meaning, man, and truth), there is an 'other' that contrasts with it. This 'other' is thought to be absent but in fact it is contained in that which is affirmed as a deferred or different meaning. Deconstruction is the process whereby these deferred and different meanings are revealed to be operating as invisible dimensions of ever unfolding schemes of meanings. This *play* of meaning within a web or network of language means that meaning can never be fixed, single, and unambiguous. The aim of deconstruction is not to decode a *text* to somehow reveal its meaning or truth but to displace or unsettle taken-for-granted concepts like the unity of the text, the meaning or message of the text, or the authorship of the text. As Pauline Rosenau (1992) explains, deconstructionism

> involves demystifying a text, tearing it apart to reveal its internal hierarchies and its presuppositions [e.g., author-text; object-subject]. It lays out the flaws and the latent metaphysical structures of a text [e.g., unity, identity, meaning, authorship]. A deconstructive reading of a text seeks to discover its ambivalence, blindness, logocentricity . . . [it] examines what is left out of a text, what is unnamed, what is excluded, and what is concealed. (p. 120)

Deconstruction is not undertaken for the purposes of revealing errors or showing various different interpretations, for that would assume that there is *a* truth, meaning, or sense to be revealed. In this respect, deconstructionism departs from *philosophical hermeneutics,* which holds that there is a meaning to be constructed in the engagement of the interpreter with the text (see, e.g., the dispute between Derrida and Gadamer in D. P. Michelfelder and R. E. Palmer, eds., *Dialogue and Deconstruction: The Gadamer-Derrida Exchange,* SUNY Press, 1989). Deconstructionism shares with ***critical hermeneutics*** a suspicion of what purports to be the truth and thus seeks to unmask this erroneous assumption. But unlike critical hermeneutics, radical hermeneutics or deconstructionism holds out little hope for achieving emancipation from ideologically distorted meanings. For the deconstructionist, there is nothing more to interpretations than the endless plays of different signifiers (words) with ambiguous, conflicting meanings.

See also *Dualism, Hermeneutics of Suspicion, Play, Semiotics.*

KEY REFERENCES

Caputo, J. D. *Radical Hermeneutics: Repetition, Deconstruction and the Hermeneutic Project.* Bloomington: Indiana University Press, 1987.
Cooper, D. E. "Modern European Philosophy," in N. Bunnin & E. P. Tsui-James, eds., *The Blackwell Companion to Philosophy.* Oxford, UK: Blackwell, 1996.
Culler, J. *On Deconstruction: Theory and Criticism After Structuralism.* Ithaca, NY: Cornell University Press, 1982.
Denzin, N. K. "Postmodernism and Deconstructionism," in D. R. Dickens & A. Fontana, eds., *Postmodernism and Social Theory.* New York: Guilford Press, 1994.
Derrida, J. *Positions.* Chicago: University of Chicago Press, 1981.
Derrida, J. *Writing and Difference.* London: Routledge & Kegan Paul, 1987.
Rosenau, P. *Post-Modernism and the Social Sciences.* Princeton, NJ: Princeton University Press, 1992.
Siedman, S. *Contested Knowledge: Social Theory in the Postmodern Era,* 2nd ed. Oxford, UK: Blackwell, 1998.

DEDUCTION   See INFERENCE.

DEDUCTIVE-NOMOLOGICAL EXPLANATION   See COVERING-LAW MODEL OF EXPLANATION.

DEPENDABILITY   See TRUSTWORTHINESS CRITERIA.

DESCRIPTION   A description is an act of giving an account of that which we perceive. We can perceive objects and events, and we can perceive facts about those objects and events. For example, I can see an object, say, airplane lights in the night sky, without in fact knowing *that* they are airplane lights. I might be mistaken; what I take as airplane lights may in fact be stars. In other words, one can give a descriptive account of an object or event without knowing in fact that that is what one is seeing. When we speak of description as the empirical basis for interpretive work, what we are usually concerned about is not the perception of objects or events per se but the perception of facts about them. Descriptions in interpretive work are factual claims about what we perceive, for example, *that* this person that I am observing is teaching. In other words, description is not simply an account of what I see (or hear) but a claim *that* this is in fact the case.

What complicates the description of factual perception is that seeing facts is relative to the conceptual resources, background knowledge, language, and so on of the observer. For example, I cannot give a description of the factual perception of the event of teaching unless I have a concept of teaching and a way of classifying it among the various kinds of acts that humans engage in. That the description of factual perception is relative to some conceptual scheme does not necessarily mean that believing is seeing, for there still are objects and events that we perceive. Rather, what it signifies is that factual descriptions are not just states of affairs in the world that present themselves to us in some unmediated way. (That is why it is more appropriate to say that we generate or construct factual descriptions, not simply 'collect' data.) That factual descriptions depend on conceptual schemes means that such descriptions are 'theory-laden' and that there is no such thing as pure description or 'raw' data. The knowledge that all description is theory-laden is generally accepted. Simply carving up the field of social action by deciding what to observe and what not to observe requires some foreknowledge of what is and is not important to attend to.

Careful, detailed factual description of people, objects, and *action* is said to be the empirical basis or foundation of ethnography and qualitative inquiry more generally. At least two different kinds of conceptual schemes figure prominently in the factual descriptions employed in qualitative studies. One is description of events and actions (*what* people are doing) achieved through participant observation and typically reported in the actors' own words. This kind of description is the foundation of *ethnographic naturalism* and *interpretivism.* The other kind of descriptive scheme, characteristic of *ethnomethodology,* is more concerned with *how* (not what) people do what they do. Instead of a kind of description that takes the reader to the setting and reveals who the actors are, what they are doing, and so forth, this second kind of description treats what is 'there' in interaction of actors as not simply evident to observation but constructed through social interaction. Description thus focuses on social processes, on how social life is constituted in interaction.

Both of these conceptual schemes for describing the perception of facts are challenged in postmodern and poststructuralist critiques of qualitative work. This challenge unfolds, roughly, as follows: (a) Description is typically regarded as distinct from interpretation. Description is thought to be a matter of the correct representation of the 'real' lived experience of actors. This 'real' experience is thought to be something that exists 'out there' in the world, outside of any effort to recreate it and represent it in a textual account. (b) There is no such thing as 'real' experience conceived outside of its textual recreation, however. (c) Hence, the distinction between description as primary and interpretation as secondary collapses. All description is a form of interpretation—representations exist only in textual creation. The worlds (actions, events) that we study are created through the texts that we write. (d) Thus, the notion that description of factual perception (through whatever conceptual scheme) constitutes an empirical grounding or foundation for the representations that characterize interpretive work is chimerical.

See also Representation, Thick Description.

KEY REFERENCES

Fay, B. *Contemporary Philosophy of Social Science.* Oxford, UK: Blackwell, 1996.
Gubrium, J., & Holstein, J. *The New Language of Qualitative Method.* Oxford, UK: Blackwell, 1997.
Wolcott, W. *Transforming Qualitative Data: Description, Analysis, and Interpretation.* Thousand Oaks, CA: Sage, 1994.

DESCRIPTIVE STATISTICS   These are mathematical techniques used for the purposes of organizing, displaying, and summarizing a set of numerical data. They include measures of central tendency (mean, median, and mode) and measures of variability (standard deviation). It is not at all uncommon for field studies to report the results of community or group surveys using descriptive statistics.

KEY REFERENCE

Bernard, H. R. *Social Research Methods: Qualitative and Quantitative Approaches.* Thousand Oaks, CA: Sage, 2000.

DESKWORK This phrase indicates the task and activities of a phase of qualitative work that takes place after one has completed *fieldwork*. It refers to the activities of organizing, sense making, analyzing, and interpreting of field notes and the writing up of the study.

KEY REFERENCE

Van Maanen, J. *Tales of the Field: On Writing Ethnography.* Chicago: University of Chicago Press, 1988.

DIALECTIC The Greek word *dialegein* means 'to argue' or 'converse' and *dialectic* is interpreted somewhat differently in Socratic, Platonic, Aristotelian, Hegelian, and Marxist thought. One common use is Socratic—dialectic refers to a conversational, question and answer, and refutational form of argument. Some scholars, however, see an important distinction between dialectic defined in this way and conversation or *dialogue*. They argue that in a genuine conversation or dialogue, two parties embrace their uniqueness, recognize their differences, and do not necessarily seek agreement or unanimity. Whereas in a dialectic exchange, points of view remain disembodied and hypothetical, logic is the arbiter of conflicting points of view, and the goal is a unified point of view.

Another common use derives from Hegel's and Marx's use of the term to describe a three-stage process of social change—thesis (an idea or set of ideas accepted by most people), antithesis (introduction of a new idea or set of ideas contrary to the first causing the thesis and antithesis to be debated), and synthesis (the two sets of ideas are synthesized to produce a new idea or set of ideas that then becomes the commonly accepted thesis once again). Dialectic in this sense refers to a process of conflict and resolution, but it does not imply progress or improvement. Changing ideas about the nature, purpose, and means of qualitative inquiry in the past thirty years might best be characterized as a dialectic movement rather than as a development in stages or phases that implies the replacement of old ideas with new and better ones.

See also Dialogue.

KEY REFERENCES

Baxter, L. A., & Montgomery, B. M. *Relating: Dialogues and Dialectics.* New York: Guilford, 1996.

Friedman, M. "Martin Buber's 'Narrow Ridge' and the Human Sciences," in
    M. Friedman, ed., *Martin Buber and the Human Sciences.* Albany: State
    University of New York Press, 1996.

DIALOGIC METHOD   See DIALOGUE.

DIALOGIC TEXT   See DIALOGISM.

DIALOGISM   Mikhail Bakhtin (1895–1975) introduced this term to
describe a particular genre of the novel, one that featured multiple, interactive
voices, styles, and points of view (also called a *polyphony* of valid voices),
none of which assumed any particular priority. A dialogic text stands in sharp
contract to a *monologic* text that depends on the centrality of a single authoritative voice. Dialogism also signifies that a text carries on a continual dialogue
with other texts (***intertextuality***). Common use of the term now extends beyond
this initial formulation such that dialogism is roughly equivalent to a multivo-
cal text of any kind (including ethnographies and other reports of qualitative
inquiry).

See also Dialogue, Text.

KEY REFERENCES

Bahktin, M. *The Dialogical Imagination: Four Essays by M. M. Bakhtin,* M. Holquist,
    ed., M. Holquist & C. Emerson, trans. Austin: University of Texas Press, 1981.
Holquist, M. *Dialogism.* London: Routledge, 2002.

DIALOGUE   According to Douglas Walton (1989), a dialogue (an exchange
of speech acts between partners in a turn-taking fashion aimed at a shared
goal) can take several forms that serve different purposes:

   (1) In an *information-seeking dialogue,* one party has the goal of finding
information that the other party is believed to possess. This kind of dialogue
transpires when inquirers use interviews of various kinds to elicit information
from respondents or informants.

(2) In an *inquiry dialogue,* the primary aim is to determine the facts relevant to a claim. This dialogue begins with an initial position that lacks a certain degree of knowledge, which must be overcome. Thus, the inquiry seeks out proof of, or more likely a warrant for, the initial position based on available evidence and reasoning. A version of this kind of dialogue is employed in research when an inquirer tests a developing claim, assertion, or working hypothesis. The dialogue with respondents or participants, as the case may be, becomes a means of seeking evidence to support (and to refute) the developing notion.

(3) In a *negotiation dialogue,* the primary goal of each party is to advance its self-interest, and the primary method is to bargain. Dialogues of this kind involving trade-offs and concessions may characterize, in part, an action researcher's exchange with participants in deciding on a focus or objective for a study that is satisfactory to both parties.

(4) In an *action-seeking dialogue,* one party seeks to bring about a specific course of action by the other party. The dialogue might involve a question-answer exchange in which one party asks for further explication, justification, or clarification of the action. The method employed might be one issuing imperatives or seeking more to persuade gently or to convince. (Readers who have teenage children are probably quite familiar with action-seeking dialogues.) In participatory and collaborative forms of qualitative inquiry, this kind of dialogue might unfold between a researcher and participants (or between coresearchers and coparticipants) around matters of focusing an inquiry, generating and analyzing data, and so on.

(5) A critical discussion, also called an *argumentative or persuasion dialogue,* arises from a difference of opinion or an issue to be resolved that has (at least) two sides. The basic goal is to prove a thesis in order to resolve a dispute or issue over whether the action in question has value. The primary obligation in such a dialogue is a burden of proof. Each party to a dialogue seeks to prove its thesis by some combination of internal proof (substantiating one's position by inference from the other parties' concessions) and external proof (appeals to scientific evidence or expert opinion/sources).

Of course, these types of dialogue are not necessarily mutually exclusive. A particular dialogic encounter could well include, for example, elements of both an information-seeking dialogue and an action-seeking dialogue. These types are offered as a heuristic based on the primary goal of any given conversation.

Argumentative or persuasion dialogues frame conversation, discussion, and deliberation as procedures or means (ideal forms of procedural rationality) to develop defensible (although always corrigible) conclusions. These dialogues have a number of both positive and negative rules (or prohibitions). For example, parties to the dialogue ought to abide by, for example, (a) rules of relevance (do not wander too far off the point), (b) cooperativeness (answer questions that have been asked; accept characterizations of one's position if they are accurate), and (c) informativeness (tailor one's presentation to what other parties to the dialogue know or do not know). A successful persuasion dialogue also depends on abiding by other requirements including not shifting the agenda at issue; always making a serious effort to defend a commitment when challenged; not failing to reply appropriately to questions; always being willing to clarify, define, or justify the meaning or definition of some significant term, and so on (Walton, 1989).

In Western thought, these kinds of persuasion dialogues or critical discussions are generally regarded as the ideal or normative model of a 'good' dialogue because they are built upon standard rules—a (informal) logic of argumentation—that establish how critical discussion should take place. Hence, in the literature on arguments, there is extensive treatment of what comprises valid arguments, what role appeals to emotion and authority play in argumentation, and how to identify logical errors, biases, and fallacies. This conception of logical argumentation, persuasion, or critical discussion lies at the heart of what in Western thought is assumed to be reasonable and rational behavior. Moreover, this kind of dialogue is regarded as central to democratic forms of government. Nussbaum's (1997) claims are illustrative of many others to this effect:

> The case for preferring democracy to other forms of government is weakened when one conceives of democratic choice as simply the clash of opposing interests. It is very much strengthened by conceiving of it in a more Socratic way, as the expression of a deliberative judgment about the overall good. . . . Logical analysis is at the heart of democratic political culture. When we do wrong to one another politically, bad argument is often one cause. . . . Logical analysis dissipates confusions. It unmasks prejudice that masquerades as reason. Doing without it would mean forfeiting one of the most powerful tools we have to attack abuses of political power. Although logic will not get us to love one another, it may get us to stop pretending that we have rational arguments for our refusals of sympathy. (pp. 27, 36)

All of the types of dialogue discussed above relate in a broad way to the idea of dialogue as a tool of reason. Dialogue is regarded as an instrument, method, means, or procedure to achieve some end; it is a matter of how we are to proceed rationally in the exchange of messages for the purposes of gaining information, bringing some state of affairs to pass, reaching agreement, settling a dispute, and so on. This way of thinking about dialogue is not without its critics who claim, for example, that skills in argumentation are culture bound and thus may preclude the participation of some individuals and groups; that the norms typically governing such dialogues (turn taking, responding directly to a statement made, cooperativeness, and so on) are also culture bound and often function to exclude those with different senses and styles of participation; that dialogues in which parties discuss their experiences may be more helpful than those which are structured as arguments; and that so-called objective value judgments said to emerge from dialogue are often no more than an expression of the will of the powerful.

Another way of thinking about dialogue—found in the work of Mikhail Bakhtin (1895–1975), Charles Taylor, and Hans-Georg Gadamer (1900–2002), for example—considers dialogue in a substantive rather than a procedural way. In other words, dialogue is an existential condition, so to speak, that signifies how human beings exist in some ethical or moral space and how their identity is formed. (The distinction between a procedural and a substantive conceptualization of dialogue is neither absolute nor dichotomous; procedural and substantive considerations may overlap.) Understood in a substantive way, dialogue signifies a particular way of being. Here, dialogue refers to a kind of ethics (and/or moral ontology) of relation, a way of understanding the self, a way we are as human beings in the world. (*Ethics* here does not refer to a code of professional conduct but to our ethical or moral orientation as human beings.) A strong and articulate defense of this idea can be found in the work of Charles Taylor, who argues for the fundamentally dialogical character of human life and is strongly critical of what he calls the disengaged first-person-singular (or monological) self. Martin Buber's (1878–1965) notion of an I–Thou relation also speaks to the idea that being is fundamentally relational (i.e., dialogic). To say that human life is fundamentally dialogical in character is to say that our identities as individuals are "formed in dialogue with others, in agreement or struggle with their recognition of us. . . . My discovering my identity doesn't mean that I work it out in isolation but that I negotiate it through dialogue, partly overt, partly internalized, with others" (Taylor, 1992, pp. 45–46, 47).

Closely related is the concept of dialogue as an event of understanding that arises in the tradition of *philosophical hermeneutics*. At the heart of this notion lies the idea that understanding happens to us (understanding is something like an unending interpretative undertaking, something never 'finished'); it is something we participate in as historical beings (versus an activity over which we have complete and objective personal control). The key to realizing a genuine event of understanding is that it is through dialogue with an other that we allow the other to speak to us. This means that we do not simply debate our view versus their view (thereby simply reproducing, restating, and continuing to argue for our current understandings) but that each party to the event of understanding genuinely risks her or his own self-understanding and thereby is open to the possibility of a mutually evolved new and different understanding. Finally, dialogue can be understood as a form of *play*.

See also *Interviewing Logic, Play, Rationality, Understanding.*

KEY REFERENCES

Burbules, N. *Dialogue in Teaching: Theory and Practice.* New York: Teachers College Press, 1993.

Jodalen, H., & Vetlesen, A. J. *Closeness: An Ethics.* Oslo: Scandinavian University Press, 1997.

Nussbaum, M. C. *Cultivating Humanity: A Classical Defense of Reform in Liberal Education.* Cambridge, MA: Harvard University Press, 1997.

Taylor, C. "The Dialogical Self," in D. R. Hiley, J. F. Bohman, & R. Shusterman, eds., *The Interpretive Turn.* Ithaca, NY: Cornell University Press, 1991.

Taylor, C. *The Ethics of Authenticity.* Cambridge, MA: Harvard University Press, 1992.

Taylor, C. *The Sources of the Self.* Cambridge, MA: Harvard University Press, 1989.

Van Eemeren, F. H., Grootendorst, R., Blair, J. A., & Willard, C. A., eds. *Argumentation: Perspectives and Approaches.* Dordrecht: Foris, 1987.

Walton, D. *Informal Logic.* Cambridge, UK: Cambridge University Press, 1989.

DIFFÉRANCE   See DECONSTRUCTIONISM.

DISCOURSE ANALYSIS   The study of *discourse*—understood broadly as an examination of language in use or the study of actually occurring language ('texts') in specific communicative contexts—is central to the kinds of analyses undertaken in *ethnomethodology, conversation analysis,* and *poststructuralism.* Discourse analysis is one of the many procedures employed in *textual analysis.* It is a general term covering a variety of approaches to the analysis of recorded talk; sometimes used interchangeably with conversation analysis, it is distinguishable by its more strict focus on the content of talk than on its linguistic organization. Discourse analysis is an interdisciplinary approach drawing on insights from ethnomethodology, sociolinguistics, cognitive psychology, communication studies, and ordinary language philosophy. It is principally concerned with the analysis of the process of communication itself.

Discourse, however, has a somewhat different meaning when used in conversational analysis and ethnomethodology than in Foucauldian discourse analysis. In the former, discourse takes up the structure of talk itself in specific kinds of practices and refers to the processes whereby speakers methodically construct their worlds of meaning. It is concerned with *how,* for example, speakers accomplish ('do') intimacy, lying, trust, description of the real, and so forth. In Foucault's (1926–1984) work, the term 'discourse' refers more broadly to systems of thought that construct subjects and their worlds. For Foucault, discourses are practices (composed of ideas, ideologies, attitudes, courses of action, terms of reference) that systematically constitute the subjects and objects of which they speak.

See also Genealogy.

KEY REFERENCES

Foucault, M. *The Archaeology of Knowledge.* New York: Pantheon, 1972.

Hepburn, A., & Potter, J. "Discourse Analaytic Practice," in C. Seale, G. Gobo, J. F. Gubrium, & D. Silverman, eds., *Qualitative Research Practice.* London: Sage, 2004.

Phillips, N., & Hardy, C. *Discourse Analysis: Investigating Processes of Social Construction.* Thousand Oaks, CA: Sage, 2002.

Potter, J. "Discourse Analysis as a Way of Analyzing Naturally Occurring Talk," in D. Silverman, ed., *Qualitative Research: Theory, Method, and Practice.* London: Sage, 1997.

Potter, J. *Representing Reality: Discourse, Rhetoric and Social Construction.* London: Sage, 1996.

Potter, J., & Wetherell, M. "Discourse Analysis," in J. A. Smith, R. Harré, & L. Langenhove, eds., *Rethinking Methods in Psychology.* London: Sage, 1995.

Schiffrin, D. *Approaches to Discourse.* Oxford, UK: Blackwell, 1994.

DISCOURSE THEORY Postmodern discourse theory defines all social phenomena as structured semiotically by codes and rules and therefore amenable to linguistic analysis using semiotic concepts, for example, sign, expression, content, interpretant, codes, and so forth. This is another way of saying that meaning is not given but socially constructed. Discourse theory addresses the means (ideological, material, institutional, relational) whereby discourses are constituted, operate, conflict, and so on. This theory challenges and often encompasses previous semiotic theories.

See also *Poststructuralism, Semiotics.*

KEY REFERENCE

Best, S., & Kellner, D. *Postmodern Theory.* New York: Guilford Press, 1991.

DISCURSIVE PRACTICE   See DISCOURSE ANALYSIS, DISCOURSE THEORY.

DISENGAGEMENT   See BODY, DISINTERESTED SOCIAL SCIENCE, SUBJECT-OBJECT RELATIONSHIP.

DISINTERESTED SOCIAL SCIENCE   Western social science generally endorses the idea that social scientists as scientists should adopt the *theoretical attitude*—that is, scientific contemplation at a distance. As the creator of theory, the social scientist ought to be a disinterested observer of the sociopolitical world and, in that sense, disengaged from society. Social scientists should study the workings of society dispassionately and aim only at developing and testing theoretical explanations of the way the world is. In this way of thinking, the activity of theorizing social and political life as traditionally conceived lies outside the rest of the activity of social life. Judgments about the way the sociopolitical world ought to be should be left to others to decide. The enterprise of social science and the individual social scientist should be value free—that is, neutral with respect to decisions about how we should live or act as humans in society. Social science can be relevant to decisions about values but only by empirically demonstrating consequences of different means to various ends or by describing and explaining the values and norms held by members of a society. This attitude or posture does not mean that science has no values whatsoever: The scientific enterprise upholds the values of dispassionate, objective, and critical investigation of scientific claims and the idea of scientifically informed (but neutral with respect to social norms) policy making.

This separation of empirical explanatory theory from normative concerns (as well as a sharp distinction between the 'is' and the 'ought,' or between scientific claims about social phenomena and practical-moral discourse, or the heterogeneity of facts and values) in the work of the social inquirer is challenged by a variety of different philosophies of social inquiry including *participatory action research,* some feminist methodologies, *critical social science,* and some versions of *philosophical hermeneutics.*

See also Critical Theory, *Fact-Value Distinction.*

KEY REFERENCES

Bernstein, R. J. *The Restructuring of Social and Political Theory.* Philadelphia: University of Pennsylvania Press, 1976.
Root, M. *Philosophy of Social Science.* Oxford, UK: Blackwell, 1993.

DOCUMENTS   See DOCUMENT ANALYSIS.

DOCUMENT ANALYSIS   This term refers broadly to various procedures involved in analyzing and interpreting data generated from the examination of documents and records relevant to a particular study. These sources of data can include public records (e.g., political and judicial reports, government documents, media accounts, television scripts, yearbooks, and minutes of meetings), private documents (e.g., medical histories, letters, diaries, school records, personal journals, and memoirs), interview transcripts and transcripts prepared from video records, and photographs. The literature on document analysis also addresses a variety of issues concerning obtaining access to records and documents and examining their authenticity.

See also Textual Analysis, Methods of.

KEY REFERENCES

Mason, J. *Qualitative Researching.* London: Sage, 1996.
Plummer, K. *Documents of Life: An Introduction to the Problems and Literature of a Humanistic Method.* London: Allen and Unwin, 1983.

Prior, L. "Documents," in C. Seale, G. Gobo, J. F. Gubrium, & D. Silverman, eds., *Qualitative Research Practice.* London: Sage, 2004.

Scott, J. *A Matter of Record: Documentary Sources in Social Research.* Cambridge, UK: Polity, 1990.

DOUBLE HERMENEUTIC   This term was coined by the social theorist Anthony Giddens, who argues that the double hermeneutic characterizes the social sciences and serves to distinguish them from the natural sciences. The social scientist studies social phenomena (i.e., human actions of various kinds) that (unlike the objects studied in natural science) are already constituted as meaningful. Humans are concept-using beings whose concepts of their action help constitute what those actions are and what they mean. Hence, the first task of the social inquirer is to understand the concepts of the social actors that are the object of study. That is, the inquirer must first get to know the world of the actors, what they already know and have to know to 'go on' with their daily social activity. From this first-level understanding, social inquirers construct second-order concepts and theories to explain what social actors are doing. Yet these second-order concepts of the social scientist can, in turn, actually become first-order concepts as they are appropriated and interpreted by social actors. In other words, the concepts and theories of the social inquirer can circulate in and out of the very social world that those concepts were first invented to analyze and explain. Social scientific theory and concepts, unlike those in natural science, can actually alter the way society behaves. There is thus a double process of interpretation.

KEY REFERENCE

Giddens, A. *The Constitution of Society: Outline of a Theory of Structuration.* Berkeley: University of California Press, 1984.

DRAMATURGY   The sociologist Erving Goffman (1922–1982) pioneered the analysis of the interactional order of social life (what people do when they are in the presence of others) via the metaphor of theater. He employed a variety of dramaturgical terms (e.g., performance, impression management, face-work, front-stage and back-stage behavior) that have become part of the vocabulary of social analysis. In postmodern social theory, this metaphor of life as theater becomes reality, society *is* theater.

See also *Performance/Performative/Performativity, Play.*

KEY REFERENCES

Branaman, A. "Goffman's Social Theory," in C. Lemert & A. Branaman, eds., *The Goffman Reader.* Oxford, UK: Blackwell, 1997.
Denzin, N. K. *Images of Postmodern Society.* Thousand Oaks, CA: Sage, 1991.
Goffman, E. *The Presentation of Self in Everyday Life.* Garden City, NJ: Doubleday, 1957.

DUALISM This is the doctrine that reality consists of two separable parts (e.g., the distinction between appearance and reality), and it is accompanied by binary thinking commonly expressed in the distinctions valid versus invalid, good or bad, right or wrong, true or false. It is generally acknowledged that dualism and binary thinking characterize all aspects of Western thought. The list of dualisms that figure prominently in the history of Western thought is virtually endless—fact-value, mind-body, experience-reason, sacred-profane, being-nothingness, means-end, objective-subjective, reason-emotion, objectivism-relativism, analytic-synthetic, explanation-understanding. The poststructuralist philosophy of ***deconstructionism*** championed by Jacques Derrida (1930–2004) is intimately concerned with unmasking the operation of this binary thinking in Western metaphysics. However, Derrida's work is not the first to call our attention to the problems associated with such thinking. Scholarship in the tradition of American pragmatism, including John Dewey's (1859–1952) philosophy of instrumentalism, which drew on the work of Charles Sanders Peirce (1839–1914), the criticisms of logical positivism delivered by W. V. O. Quine (1908–2000), and the contemporary pragmatic stance taken in the work of Richard Bernstein, all aim to overcome the problems of modern philosophy brought on by binary thinking.

KEY REFERENCES

Bernstein, R. J. *Beyond Objectivism and Relativism: Science, Hermeneutics, and Praxis.* Philadelphia: University of Pennsylvania Press, 1983.
Derrida, J. *Writing and Difference.* London: Routledge, 1978.
Dewey, J. *The Quest for Certainty.* New York: Minton, Balch, 1929.

E

EDUCATIONAL ETHNOGRAPHY   One of the areas in which qualitative work, broadly conceived, is practiced, educational *ethnography* encompasses *participation observation* research and *field studies* in and on educational institutions and settings. The roots of this work stem largely from the tradition of cultural anthropology in the United States and fieldwork sociology in Britain.

KEY REFERENCES

Delamont, S., & Atkinson, P. *Fighting Familiarity: Essays on Education and Ethnography.* Cresskill, NJ: Hampton Press, 1995.

Gordon, T., Holland, J., & Lahelma, E. "Ethnographic Research in Educational Settings," in P. Atkinson, A. Coffey, S. Delamont, J. Lofland, & L. Lofland, eds., *Handbook of Ethnography.* London: Sage, 2001.

Hammersley, M. *Classroom Ethnography: Empirical and Methodological Essays.* Milton Keynes: Open University Press, 1990.

Spindler, G., ed. *Doing the Ethnography of Schooling: Educational Anthropology in Action.* New York: Holt, Rinehart & Winston, 1982.

EMBODIED   See BODY.

EMERGENT DESIGN   Fieldworkers routinely adjust their inquiry plans and strategies in response to what they are learning as their study unfolds. For example, a fieldworker may (a) discover documents of particular importance that she was not aware existed, (b) come across particular respondents who need to be interviewed when this was not anticipated, (c) identify and cultivate a relationship with a key informant where that may have been thought impossible, (d) decide after a study is already under way to conduct a community survey to gather a broader picture of an issue, and/or (e) realize that a particular aspect of a social setting is more relevant to understanding some phenomenon than was initially imagined. By both allowing for and anticipating changes in strategies, procedures, questions to be asked, ways of generating data, and so on, the fieldworker seeks to make her or his plans (i.e., design) *attuned* and *responsive* to the circumstances of the particular study.

This characteristic of planning and conducting a field study is often referred to as *emergent design*. If we use the strict sense of the word *emergent* (i.e., arising unexpectedly), it would be reasonable to say that the fieldworker does encounter emergent issues and/or emergent circumstances that call for a response, and, hence, the plan for fieldwork ought to flexible and adaptive. As a modifier for the term *design,* however, the term *emergent* can mistakenly suggest that the design itself arises unexpectedly or that the fieldworker has no design or plan at all at the outset of the study. This kind of complete laissez-faire attitude of seeing 'what happens' is ill advised. The fieldworker seeks to portray and understand some problem, event, or issue and should have given careful thought in advance of undertaking the fieldwork how that understanding can best be developed and how claims made about the meaning, cause, or accomplishment of human action can be warranted.

It may be more appropriate to talk of emergent *analysis* in qualitative studies. This signals the fact that the design and process of fieldwork is less linear and more circular in nature. The relevant contrast is between those studies that have hypotheses, measures, and means of analysis all clearly spelled out in advance and studies in which hypotheses and analysis emerge from the interaction of the kinds of questions asked and the kinds of data generated. For example, the plans for a quasi-experimental study would be worked out in detail in advance of actually conducting the study (from precise specification of hypotheses, through selection of groups, to specification of variables, choice and pretesting of measures, specification of procedures for the statistical analysis of data, etc.). The means of analysis are specified in advance so that a priori hypotheses can be correctly tested. Preparation for a field study is somewhat different. A field study would be theoretically structured at the outset: The researcher would decide how to specify (name, identify) the social action (e.g., teaching, negotiating, giving care, and bargaining) or entities (e.g., group, community) to be investigated, develop questions about the phenomenon (e.g., *What* happens? *How* does it happen? *Why* does it happen? and

What does it mean?) that focus the research and give it purpose, and have thought about the kinds of data sources and procedures that would generate relevant evidence. Yet the actual analysis would be less like a prespecified process of testing and verification and more like discovery. Analysis unfolds in an iterative fashion through the interaction of the processes of generating data, examining preliminary focusing questions, and considering theoretical assumptions. Analysis thus becomes a process of elaborating a version of or perspective on the phenomenon in question, revising that version or perspective as additional data are generated and new questions are asked, elaborating another version, revising that version or perspective, and so on. *Memoing* and analytic *coding* are means of undertaking this iterative and emergent analysis.

See also *Fidelity to Method/Fidelity to Phenomenon, Grounded Theory Methodology, Research Design, Sensitizing Concepts.*

KEY REFERENCES

Flick, U. *An Introduction to Qualitative Research.* London: Sage, 1998.
Lincoln, Y. S., & Guba, E. G. *Naturalistic Inquiry.* Beverly Hills, CA: Sage, 1985.
Lofland, J., & Lofland, L. H. *Analyzing Social Settings: A Guide to Qualitative Observation and Analysis,* 3rd ed. Belmont, CA: Wadsworth, 1995.
Mason, J. *Qualitative Researching.* London: Sage, 1996.

EMIC/ETIC   Originating in linguistics (phonemic vs. phonetic), a distinction between emic and etic cultural categories was once popular in cognitive anthropology. Emic terms were indigenous—specific to a language or culture—whereas etic terms were developed by the social inquirer and used to describe and compare sociocultural systems. Etic terms were used by cognitive anthropology and other formalist approaches to ethnography as something like a codebook of concepts facilitating cross-cultural comparisons. This absolute distinction has been severely criticized on the grounds that there are no purely etic categories unbound to some specific context. Interest in distinguishing inside from outside perspectives remains, although it is now recognized that these distinctions are relative. The terms *emic* and *etic* are still occasionally used more broadly: *Emic* is used to refer to first-order concepts—the local language, concepts, or ways of expression used by members in a particular group or setting to name their experience. *Etic* is used to refer to second-order concepts—the social scientific language used by the scientist to refer to the same phenomena. *Emic* may also be used to refer to the processes of cataloging, description, and categorization, and *etic*, to indicate the process of explanation.

Clifford Geertz (1983, p. 57) introduced the concepts *experience-near* and *experience-distant* as a refinement of the emic-etic distinction. An experience-near concept is one that a respondent or informant "might naturally and effortlessly use to define what he [sic] or his fellows see, feel, think, imagine, and . . . which he would readily understand when similarly applied by others"; an experience-distant concept is one "that specialists of one sort or another . . . employ to forward their scientific, philosophical, or practical aims." Geertz explained that both kinds of concepts are necessary in ethnographic analysis because "confinement to experience-near concepts leaves the ethnographer awash in immediacies, as well as entangled in vernacular. Confinement to experience-distant ones leaves him [sic] stranded in abstractions and smothered in jargon" (p. 57). Geertz uses these concepts to defend the methodology of participant observation as a *dialectic* of experience and interpretation. He stresses the importance of grasping insiders' perspectives through experience-near concepts while simultaneously illuminating their connection to experience-distant concepts.

See also Native's Point of View.

KEY REFERENCES

Geertz, C. *Local Knowledge.* New York: Basic Books, 1983.
Harris, M. "History and Significance of the Emic/Etic Distinction," *Annual Review of Anthropology,* 1976, 5, 329–350.

EMOTION   At least three aspects of this notion figure prominently in the broad field of qualitative inquiry. First, some feminist scholars argue that Western epistemology has tended to emphasize reason at the expense of emotion, regarding reason as the indispensable faculty for acquiring knowledge. Instead of viewing emotion as something that should be controlled and excluded by strict application of *method*, these scholars argue for restoring emotion (and other ways of knowing with the body) to our epistemological models. Second, in addition to the notion of emotion figuring prominently in arguments for reuniting reasoning and feeling, the sociological investigation of emotionality as a process and intersubjective accomplishment is one particular kind of qualitative study. Third, the interest in *autoethnography* and *performance ethnography* and related efforts to create a poetics of experience (versus traditional modes of representation) reflects a specific concern with portraying the subjective, emotional experiences of the inquirer and evoking readers' emotional responses to the text.

See also Body, Existentialism, Subjectivity.

KEY REFERENCES

Denzin, N. K. *On Understanding Emotion.* San Francisco: Jossey-Bass, 1984.

Ellis, C. "Emotional Sociology," *Studies in Symbolic Interaction, Vol. 12.* Greenwich, CT: JAI Press, 1991.

Ellis, C. "Sociological Introspection and Emotional Experience," *Symbolic Interaction,* 1991, 14, 23–50.

Ellis, C., & Flaherty, M. G, eds. *Investigating Subjectivity.* Newbury Park, CA: Sage, 1992.

Jaggar, A. M. "Love and Knowledge: Emotion in Feminist Epistemology," in A. Garry & M. Pearsall, eds., *Women, Knowledge, and Reality: Explorations in Feminist Philosophy.* Boston: Unwin & Hyman, 1989.

EMPIRICAL RESEARCH   See EMPIRICISM.

EMPIRICISM   This is the name for a family of epistemological theories that generally accept the premise that knowledge begins with sense experience. Empiricism is often contrasted with *rationalism,* which holds that reason is the primary way of acquiring knowledge, and with *pragmatism,* which holds that action, not just any kind of experience, is both the source and test of all knowledge. The two main schools of empiricist epistemology are naïve (also called classic, radical, strict, or vulgar) empiricism and *logical empiricism*. The former is the empiricism of Bacon (1561–1626), Hume (1711–1776), and the logical positivists of the Vienna Circle. It holds that all knowledge is experiential and that knowledge claims can be justified only by appeal to the evidence of the senses (experience, observation, experiment). Strict empiricism relies exclusively on perception and induction in building knowledge claims and eschews any important role whatsoever for concepts and theories. (The latter are simply a convenient way—a filing system, if you will—of organizing observations.) The relationship between theory and data in strict empiricism is shown in Figure E.1a. The strict empiricist believes that data in the form of sense perceptions, observations (or observation statements), comprise the bedrock or foundation of all knowledge claims. Observations are often referred to as brute data, indicating that they are accessible to all competent observers and elemental in nature (i.e., require no further interpretation). (Note: Strict empiricists do *not* argue that knowledge is somehow 'given' in the brute data of experience, such that the inquirer is merely a spectator or passive recording device. On the contrary, these empiricists engage in lively debate concerning how concepts and theories [i.e., explanations, predictions] that we construct are to be related to the data of observation.)

The strict empiricism of logical positivist philosophy was strongly challenged by historians and philosophers of science called the **Weltanschauung** analysts (e.g., Thomas Kuhn, Stephen Toulmin, Norwood Hanson, Michael Polanyi), who argued that the worldviews (*Weltanschauungen*) of scientists— their prior knowledge, historical circumstances, beliefs, concepts, and so on— played a critical role in the testing and justification of scientific claims. Logical empiricism is, in part, a response to these criticisms. It is a more moderate variety of empiricism that continues to accord an important place to empirical observation, but it also allows for an active role played by concepts and theories in what constitutes valid knowledge. The relationship between theory and data in logical empiricism is shown in Figure E.1b.

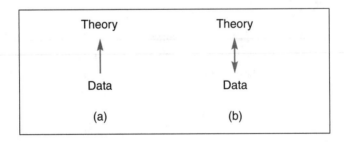

Figure E.1   Relationship Between Theory and Data in (a) Logical Positivism and
(b) Logical Empiricism

Criticism of both varieties of empiricism is central to what is often called the **interpretive turn** in the human sciences. This turn is marked by the belief that all knowledge claims are interpretations, and that there is nothing to appeal to in judging an interpretation but other interpretations. In other words, empirical data (the data of observation and experience) cannot provide any special basis or foundation for knowledge claims that is somehow free of interpretation.

All forms of qualitative inquiry are empirical research to the extent that they deal in the data of *experience*. Many kinds of claims and assertions made in case study, ethnography, life history, oral history, and the like are often based on the *evidence* of observations—both those of the inquirer and the reports of people studied. When a qualitative inquirer makes a claim (assertion, statement, working hypothesis, etc.) about an event, object, process, person, or so on and offers as evidence or warrant for that claim its relationship to experience (something the inquirer or respondents saw or heard), then that inquirer is engaging in empirical inquiry. To say that qualitative inquiry is empirical research, however, is not to say that it rests on the philosophy of empiricism. Qualitative inquiry deals in empirical matters but is informed by a variety of different epistemologies including logical empiricism, pragmatism, phenomenology, social constructionism, poststructuralism, and feminism.

See also Epistemology, Postempiricism, Theory-Observation Distinction.

KEY REFERENCES

Hollis, M. *The Philosophy of Social Science: An Introduction.* Cambridge, UK: Cambridge University Press, 1994.

Taylor, C. "Interpretation and the Sciences of Man," *Review of Metaphysics,* 1971, 24, 3–51. (Reprinted in C. Taylor, *Philosophical Papers 2. Philosophy and the Human Sciences.* Cambridge, UK: Cambridge University Press, 1985)

EMPOWERMENT   Some forms of *critical ethnography,* action research, participatory, collaborative, and *cooperative inquiry* are specifically concerned with inequities of power and privilege (between researchers and respondents and among various kinds of respondents). These kinds of inquiries are motivated by criticisms of prevailing practices of power (e.g., who controls knowledge, whose definitions of problems and solutions dominate discussion, what role experts play, and who has power to speak) and aim to be inclusive, empowering, and emancipatory. Empowerment here can mean doing research in such a way that it produces knowledge and action directly useful to a group of people; it can also mean consciousness raising—that is, helping groups of people, through processes of constructing and using their own knowledge, to see through the ways in which established structures, institutions, and individuals monopolize the production and use of knowledge for their own purposes. In the context of active or interactional interviewing, empowerment refers to efforts to regard the respondent more fully and actively as an equal partner in an interview conversation and to establish a space in which the respondent's own story can be told and heard.

KEY REFERENCES

Fals Borda, O., & Rahman, M. A., eds. *Action and Knowledge: Breaking the Monopoly with Participatory Action Research.* New York: Intermediate Technology Publications/Apex Press, 1991.

Holstein, J. A., & Gubrium, J. F. "Inside Interviewing: New Lenses, New Concerns," in J. A. Holstein & J. F. Gubrium, eds., *Inside Interviewing: New Lenses, New Concerns.* Thousand Oaks, CA: Sage, 2003.

Mishler, E. G. *Research Interviewing: Context and Narrative.* Cambridge, MA: Harvard University Press, 1986.

Reason, P., & Bradbury, H. "Inquiry and Participation in Search of a World Worthy of Human Aspiration," in P. Reason & H. Bradbury, eds., *Handbook of Action Research.* London: Sage, 2001.

END OF PHILOSOPHY   The work of Friedrich Nietzsche (1844–1900) is looked to particularly by poststructuralists as having heralded the death of traditional philosophical concerns with clarifying the meaning of truth, reality, morality, virtue, and the like. The existentialist and phenomenological philosophy of fellow German philosopher Martin Heidegger (1889–1976) is also sometimes appealed to in the same way. Following in the wake of and building on the insights of these and other pronouncements of the death of philosophy are a variety of postphilosophical positions (e.g., *feminist theories, poststructuralism, critical theory, philosophical hermeneutics,* postanalytic philosophy, neopragmatism) taken up by Sandra Harding, Nancy Fraser, Nancy Harstock, Allison Jaggar, Jacques Derrida, Michel Foucault, Hans-Georg Gadamer, Jürgen Habermas, Jean-François Lyotard, Alasdair MacIntyre, Hilary Putnam, Richard Rorty, and Charles Taylor, to name but a few.

Whether we use the phrase after philosophy, end of philosophy, postanalytic philosophy, or postphilosophy matters less than understanding the nature of the turmoil. This period is characterized by various criticisms of notions that form the core of the Enlightenment tradition: the necessity and universality of reason; the autonomous, disengaged, atomistic, sovereign, rational subject; knowledge as representation; the separation of philosophy from rhetoric and poetics; and so on. The period is marked by mergers of philosophy with other disciplines, including anthropology, literary theory, history of science, and political theory. The debates comprising this period have influenced the way social science philosophers and social scientists define the nature and aim of social inquiry; the authority, role, identity, and expertise of the inquirer; the epistemological status of claims to represent social reality; and so on. Of course, claims that traditional philosophy has come to an end have met with resistance. Thus, the contemporary scene in the broad field of qualitative inquiry is philosophically complex and has moved well beyond the tired debate of quantitative versus qualitative methods into far more interesting (and complicated) matters of the epistemology, ethics, and politics of inquiry.

See also Epistemology, Knowledge.

KEY REFERENCES

Baynes, K., Bohman, J., & McCarthy, T., eds. *After Philosophy: End or Transformation?* Cambridge: MIT Press, 1987.
Rajchman, J., & West, C., eds. *Post-Analytic Philosophy.* New York: Columbia University Press, 1985.

EPISTEMIC CRITERION   See CRITERIA, VALIDITY.

EPISTEMOLOGY   This is the study of the nature of knowledge and justification. There are many theories of epistemology. For example, empiricist epistemology argues that knowledge is derived from sense experience. Genuine, legitimate knowledge consists of beliefs that can be justified by observation. Rationalist epistemology argues that reason is the sure path to knowledge. Rationalists may claim that sense experiences are an effect of external causes; that a priori ideas (concepts, theories, etc.) provide a structure for making sense of experience; and/or that reason provides a kind of certainty that the senses cannot provide.

Rather than conceiving of the differences between so-called qualitative and quantitative inquiry in terms of tools and methods, students of qualitative inquiry might be better served by examining the differences (and similarities) among epistemologies for qualitative inquiry—for example, the epistemologies of empiricism and hermeneutics or empiricist and feminist epistemologies. Epistemologies provide much of the justification for particular methodologies (i.e., the aim, function, and assumptions of method).

Many criticisms are directed at what is sometimes called the epistemological project or philosophy as epistemology. There are two significantly different strands of criticism here that share the same diagnosis but issue in different remedies, so to speak. The diagnosis is that both rationalist and empiricist epistemologies are foundationalist; that is, they seek permanent, indisputable criteria for knowledge—one finds it in reason, the other in sense experience. These epistemologies are also characterized by their interest in an autonomous, detached subject (knower) and a preoccupation with establishing correspondence between ideal and object, concept and observation. The quest for certainty characteristic of these epistemologies not only has been found wanting but is thought to be a futile and dysfunctional search.

Postempiricist, hermeneutic, feminist, poststructuralist, pragmatist, and critical social science approaches to social inquiry all generally accept (and have in various ways made) this diagnosis. Yet two different responses result. One response is pragmatic and fallibilistic. It holds that knowledge is by definition uncertain and that the best we can do is make a stand on the basis of (admittedly fallible) human judgment that requires the use of both reason and evidence. This response abandons epistemology with a capital "E"—the search for the foundations or essences of knowledge—but retains the idea of epistemology with a lowercase "e"—reflection of various kinds about what it means to know. The other response is one of radical *skepticism* or epistemological nihilism. It holds that diverse realities, plural constructions, the absence of certainty, intertextuality, shifting identities of subjects, and the like all add up to the undecidability of all interpretation. No one interpretation, and no single judgment are decidedly better than any other. This response abandons the entire idea of epistemology or assumes what might be called "epistemological impossibilism" (M. Calinescu, *Five Faces of Modernity,* Duke University Press, 1987).

See also End of Philosophy, Fallibilism, Knowledge, Objectivism, Pluralism, Pragmatism.

KEY REFERENCES

Bohman, J. *New Philosophy of Social Science: Problems of Indeterminacy.* Cambridge: MIT Press, 1991.

Grayling, A. C. "Epistemology," in N. Bunnin & E. P. Tsui-James, eds., *The Blackwell Companion to Social Theory.* Oxford, UK: Blackwell, 1996.
Hollis, M. "Philosophy of Social Science," in N. Bunnin & E. P. Tsui-James, eds., *The Blackwell Companion to Philosophy.* Oxford, UK: Blackwell, 1996.

ERKLÄRUNG   This is the German term for *explanation.*

See also *Explanation,* Verstehen.

ESSENTIALISM   This is a metaphysical doctrine that holds that objects have essences—that is, intrinsic identifying or characterizing properties that constitute their real, true nature. Some feminists, for example, argue that there are essential features of men's and women's biology, identity, and gender. For other feminists, essentialism is their foil. They claim that plurality, otherness, difference, and heterogeneity characterize our understanding of notions like subject, man, woman, gender, self, family, intelligence, and anxiety.

See also *Constructivism.*

KEY REFERENCES

Fuss, D. *Essentially Speaking: Feminism, Nature, and Difference.* New York: Routledge, 1989.
Stein, E. "Conclusion: The Essentials of Constructionism and the Construction of Essentialism," in E. Stein, ed., *Forms of Desire: Sexual Orientation and the Social Constructionist Controversy.* New York: Garland, 1992.

ETHICS OF QUALITATIVE INQUIRY   In the widest sense, the subject matter of ethics is the justification of human actions, especially as those actions affect others. The subject matter of ethics includes various ethical systems or theories and means of ethical reasoning. Ethical theories include, for example, deontological ethics (based on concepts of duty or what it is right to do); consequentialist ethics (based on the idea of achieving some good state of affairs); and virtue ethics (based on the qualities of character necessary to live well). Approaches to ethical reasoning include applied ethics, which is often modeled on a deductive model of practical reasoning; *narrative ethics,* which emphasizes the importance of personal identity, the virtues of character, and the individual and collective stories in which those virtues are made intelligible; and casuistry—an approach to ethical reasoning that attempts to steer a course between these two approaches.

Addressing ethical issues in social research typically requires taking into account considerations beyond those of ethical theories and models of ethical reasoning. When social researchers consider the reasons for their own and others' actions during the conduct of research, assess the validity of those reasons, and reform their actions against the backdrop of some systematic and thoughtful account of human responsibility, they must, of necessity, recognize that ethics, epistemology, and politics are intertwined. In other words, inquirers cannot rightly understand their ethics—mores, habits, obligations, and modes of thought that shape and define their interactions as social scientists with others—without simultaneously thinking through what constitutes legitimate, warranted knowledge of social life, as well as what comprises their political commitments and responsibilities as inquirers into the nature and meaning of human affairs.

This does not necessarily mean that, given different understandings of the ethics-epistemology-politics nexus, different ethical principles (e.g., *informed consent;* avoidance of deception, avoidance of harm/risk; treating others always as ends, never as means; and no breaches of promise or confidence) are involved. Rather, it suggests that special attention must be paid to the means of addressing ethical and political issues (and styles of reasoning) that are associated with various ways in which we envision and enact the relationship between researcher and researched. The following are ways of thinking about that relationship in qualitative studies (Elliott, 1988):

1. Researcher as detached, objective, outside expert; researched as subjects, data sources, respondents.

2. Researcher as marginal participant (participant-observer); researched as informants.

3. Researcher as facilitator (helping the researched activate their own capacities for self-observation, critique, advocacy), critic, advocate, change agent, adversary to the established and powerful; researched as coresearchers, coparticipants, collaborators.

In the relationship identified in 1 above (and all that it entails epistemologically and politically), it is commonplace to conceive of the ethical obligations of researcher to researched in terms of a contract—a written agreement between the two parties. The contract explains the purpose of the research, the anticipated duration and extent of subjects' involvement, the procedures to be employed by the researcher, assurances of confidentiality, the potential risks/benefits to subjects, and a means whereby subjects can gain further information from the investigator. The terms of the contract include that it is voluntary on the part of the subjects, specifies the form (if any) of compensation for participation, entails no penalty for a subject's withdrawal from a study, and so forth. This contractual model of ethics is one most often assumed in the workings of *institutional review boards (IRBs)* in universities.

In general, all features of a contractual conceptualization of ethics are entailed in the ethical and political relations between researcher and researched as characterized in 2 and 3 above. In these latter two ways of framing human relations in research, however, several special obligations arise due to the fact that these relationships are characterized by considerably extended personal exchanges, substantial dealings between the researcher and those he or she studies, and different research agendas. Moreover, because these substantial exchanges, relations, and agendas are dynamic and subject to change over time, they require of the researcher a heightened capacity to anticipate potential ethical dilemmas and demand a special kind of normative attention in the course of fieldwork. In the view of the ethicist William F. May, these special ethical obligations might better be understood in terms of a covenantal (as opposed to a contractual) ethic—an exchange of promises, an agreement that shapes the future between two parties, an ethic that is responsive and reciprocal in character. May explains:

> The duties of fieldworkers to their host populations—duties to respect confidences, to communicate to them the aims of the research, to protect anonymity, to safeguard rights, interests and sensitivities, to give fair return for services rendered, to anticipate the consequences of publication, to share the results of research with affected parties, and to be sensitive to the diversity of values and interests of those studied—all these duties rest on a deeper footing than a contract, on a lower pedestal than philanthropy [that pretends to a wholly gratuitous altruism], and on a more concrete foundation than Kant's universal principle of respect. (pp. 367–368)

The notion of a covenantal ethic signals the particularly weighty moral responsibility entailed in qualitative studies, the need for moral/ethical awareness—special vigilance or alertness to circumstances that demand attention, and the ever present need to be prepared, through adequate ethical training, to address such circumstances in morally responsible ways.

See also Field Relations, Fieldwork, Institutional Review Board (IRB), Other *(The Other, Otherness), Politics of Research, Reciprocity.*

KEY REFERENCES

Bulmer, M., ed. *Social Research Ethics.* New York: Macmillan, 1982.

Elliott, J. "Educational Research and Outsider-Insider Relations," *Qualitative Studies in Education,* 1988, 1(2), 155–166.

Gubrium, J. F., & Silverman, D., eds. *The Politics of Field Research.* Newbury Park, CA: Sage, 1989.

May, W. F. "Doing Ethics: The Bearing of Ethical Theories on Fieldwork," *Social Problems,* 1980, 27(3), 358–370.

Murphy, E., & Dingwall, R. "The Ethics of Ethnography," in P. Atkinson, A. Coffey, S. Delamont, J. Lofland, & L. Lofland, eds., *Handbook of Ethnography.* London: Sage, 2001.

Ryen, A. "Ethical Issues," in C. Seale, G. Gobo, J. F. Gubrium, & D. Silverman, eds., *Qualitative Research Practice.* London: Sage, 2004.

ETHNOCENTRISM   This is a form of *prejudice*—a predisposition or preconception—that has both a weak and a strong interpretation. A weak interpretation of ethnocentrism means that we always see the world through our own self-understandings (i.e., the understandings of 'our' group, community, culture, etc.). A strong version adds the condition that our own self-understandings are superior, and that we expect the self-understandings of others to converge with ours. *Postmodern ethnography*, in general, argues that practically the entire practice of cultural anthropology is located in a long history of Western colonialism and the spread of Western culture and thus is guilty of being ethnocentric in the strong sense noted above.

Viewed more broadly, across the entire spectrum of qualitative studies, worries about ethnocentrism figure prominently in the *interpretive turn* in the human sciences as follows: If all efforts to understand others are always interpretations made only against the backdrop of the interpreter's way of life, culture, and so forth, are not all such interpretations inevitably ethnocentric? There are several different responses to this question. Richard Rorty, for example, claims that indeed all efforts to understand others are always made by "our own lights" and that we ought to be frank about that. Clifford Geertz acknowledges that interpretations cannot be anything but an attempt to portray one way of life in the categories of another but is highly critical of Rorty's "easy comforts of merely being ourselves." Geertz argues that the inescapable ethnocentricity (in a weak sense) of interpretations need not lead to radical *skepticism* or *relativism;* in fact, it considerably increases the moral responsibilities of the interpreter to give an accurate and responsible portrayal of others' ways of life. David Couzens Hoy, Charles Taylor, and James Bohman also accept the weak sense of ethnocentrism noted above and, like Geertz, argue that it does not necessarily entail radical interpretive skepticism. All three argue (although in very different ways) that it is possible to engage in normative criticism of different ways of life or social practices, despite the fact that we always see the world through our own self-understandings. Both Hoy and Taylor adopt the view that "we understand *ourselves* differently as a result of encountering others who have a different self-understanding themselves."

See also Other *(The Other, Otherness).*

KEY REFERENCES

Bohman, J. *New Philosophy of Social Science.* Cambridge: MIT Press, 1991.

Geertz, C. "The Uses of Diversity," *Michigan Quarterly Review,* 1986, 23, 105–123.

Hoy, D. C. "Is Hermeneutics Ethnocentric?" in D. R. Hiley, J. F. Bohman, & R. Shusterman, eds., *The Interpretive Turn.* Ithaca, NY: Cornell University Press, 1991.

Rorty, R. "Solidarity or Objectivity" and "On Ethnocentrism: A Reply to Clifford Geertz," in R. Rorty, *Objectivity, Relativism, and Truth. Philosophical Papers Vol. 1.* Cambridge, UK: Cambridge University Press, 1991.

Taylor, C. "Understanding and Ethnocentricity," in *Philosophy and the Human Sciences. Philosophical Papers 2.* Cambridge, UK: Cambridge University Press, 1985.

ETHNOGRAPHIC AUTHORITY   See AUTHORITY.

ETHNOGRAPHIC METHODS   This is the collection of methods for generating and analyzing qualitative data that are grounded in a commitment to firsthand experience and examination of some particular social or cultural phenomena. The primary method is participant observation, but related methods include forms of interviewing; collection and analysis of various kinds of documents, visual materials, and *artifacts;* photography; collection of oral histories; and so on. This extensive collection of methods is often referred to more generically as qualitative research methods.

See also Ethnography.

KEY REFERENCE

Schensul, J., & LeCompte, M. D., eds. *Ethnographer's Toolkit.* 7 vols. Walnut Creek, CA: AltaMira Press, 1999.

ETHNOGRAPHIC NATURALISM   Various interpretations of this doctrine, also called social realism, foreground some of the practices of qualitative inquiry. A strong interpretation of the doctrine means the inquirer must capture the 'authentic,' 'true,' or real nature of social phenomena and that this is best accomplished by 'being there' in the 'natural' setting where such phenomena occur. A weak interpretation means respect for or attention to the nature of phenomenon under study. Further, both weak and strong versions share the idea of fidelity to phenomenon and reject the idea of fidelity to methodological principles. In other words, the primary commitment of the social inquirer should be to remain true to the nature of the phenomenon under study rather than to honor a particular conception of scientific method. Ethnographic naturalism typically finds its expression in *ethnographic realism*. Defenders of postmodern approaches to ethnographic work (e.g., in sociology, Norman Denzin, Patricia Clough; in anthropology, Stephen Tyler) take strong exception to this doctrine.

See also Ethnographic Realism, Experience, Fidelity to Method/Fidelity to Phenomenon, Field, Naturalistic Inquiry, Representation.

KEY REFERENCES

Denzin, N. K. *The Research Act,* 3rd ed. Englewood Cliffs, NJ: Prentice-Hall, 1989.
Gubrium, J., & Holstein, J. *The New Language of Qualitative Method.* Oxford, UK: Blackwell, 1997.
Hammersley, M. *What's Wrong With Ethnography?* London: Routledge, 1992.
Lofland, J., & Lofland, L. H. *Analyzing Social Settings,* 3rd ed. Belmont, CA: Wadsworth, 1995.
Matza, D. *Becoming Deviant.* Englewood Cliffs, NJ: Prentice-Hall, 1969.

ETHNOGRAPHIC REALISM The genre of ethnographic writing that reflects the assumptions of ethnographic naturalism is called ethnographic realism. If *ethnography* is both process and product, then traditionally its process of *participant observation* is built on the doctrine of *ethnographic naturalism* and its product reflects the practice of ethnographic realism. The genre is composed of a number of literary conventions that contribute to the construction of a representational text, that is, a text that claims to represent literally the ways of life, attitudes, practices, beliefs, and so on of those studied. John Van Mannen identifies the following four conventions as characteristic of these texts or what he calls "realist tales": First, the experience of the researcher serves as a source of authority, but the author is virtually completely absent from most segments of the text. Van Maanen notes that "Ironically, by taking the 'I' (observer) out of the ethnographic report, the narrator's authority is apparently enhanced, and audience worries over personal subjectivity become moot." Second, a documentary style is employed to focus on the mundane details of everyday life revealing the powers of observation of the inquirer. This catalog of observations is often presented via standard anthropological or sociological categories that typically are used to divide the complex field of others' ways of life into something manageable (e.g., family life, work life, social networks, customs, beliefs, rituals, and kinship patterns). Details within these categories are not randomly arranged but accumulate systematically and redundantly to demonstrate something important about respondents' lived *experience* from the fieldworker's point of view. Third, the native's (respondent's) point of view is painstakingly produced through extensive, closely edited quotations to convey that what is presented is not the fieldworker's view but authentic and representative remarks of respondents. Finally, there is a marked absence of reflection on whether the fieldworker got it right, a tendency toward a no-nonsense approach to presenting representations and accounts. Van Maanen calls this the attitude of "interpretive omnipotence" on the part of the author.

Postmodern ethnography (in both sociology and anthropology) has arisen largely as a challenge to the doctrine of ethnographic realism and the production of realist texts. In a variety of ways it questions the notion that fieldwork texts can be direct, matter-of-fact accounts of others' experience unclouded by how the fieldworker produced the product. It experiments with other textual forms that reflect the social dynamics of fieldworker-respondent relations as interlocutory, dialogical, collaborative, and cocreative of understanding the lives of others.

See also Authority, Experimental Text, Literary Turn (in Social Science), Representation.

KEY REFERENCES

Denzin, N. K. *Interpretive Ethnography: Ethnographic Practices for the 21st Century.* Thousand Oaks, CA: Sage, 1997.
Van Maanen, J. *Tales of the Field.* Chicago: University of Chicago Press, 1988.

ETHNOGRAPHY   The methodology born in cultural anthropology, ethnography is a particular kind of qualitative inquiry distinguishable from case study research, descriptive studies, naturalistic inquiry, and so forth by the fact that it is the process and product of describing and interpreting cultural behavior. Cultural anthropology, broadly conceived as a practice, includes both ethnography, which is regarded as the activity of describing a culture, and ethnology, which is the historical-geographical study of peoples or cultures that involves classifications, comparisons, and explanations of cultural differences. Although there is considerable disagreement in the meaning of the term *culture*, both anthropological and sociological definitions of ethnography stress the centrality of culture as the analytic concept that informs the doing of ethnography.

What ethnography has in common with several other kinds of qualitative inquiries is its emphasis on firsthand *field study*. Thus, ethnography is often (perhaps wrongly) used as a synonym for fieldwork and its characteristics of prolonged time in the *field*, generation of descriptive data, development of rapport and empathy with respondents, the use of multiple data sources, the making of *field notes*, and so forth. Although many kinds of qualitative inquirers may engage in fieldwork (i.e., use ethnographic methods), not all do ethnographic fieldwork (i.e., do ethnography).

Ethnography unites both process and product, *fieldwork* and written text. Fieldwork, undertaken as *participant observation*, is the process by which the ethnographer comes to know a culture; the ethnographic text is how culture is portrayed. There is general agreement that culture itself is not visible or tangible but is constructed by the act of ethnographic writing. Hence, understanding what it means to 'write' culture (i.e., literal *representation*, *inscription*, *transcription*, *textualization*, cultural translation) is a critical concern in ethnography.

See also Interpretive Anthropology.

KEY REFERENCES

Atkinson, P., Coffey, A., Delamont, S., Lofland, J., & Lofland, L., eds. *Handbook of Ethnography.* London: Sage, 2001.

Bryman, A. E. *Ethnography.* 4 vols. London: Sage, 2001.

Van Maanen, J. *Tales of the Field.* Chicago: University of Chicago Press, 1988.

Wolcott, H. "On Ethnographic Intent," in G. Spindler & L. Spindler, eds., *Interpretive Ethnography of Education: At Home and Abroad.* Hillsdale, NJ: Lawrence Erlbaum Associates, 1987.

ETHNOGRAPHY OF COMMUNICATION This broad arena comprises ethnographic studies that are primarily focused on the problems, possibilities, and processes of communication, sociolinguistics, people's use of language and narrative, language acquisition, language habits, and/or the performative aspects of language.

KEY REFERENCES

Gumperz, J., & Hynes, D., eds. *Directions in Sociolinguistics: The Ethnography of Communication.* New York: Blackwell, 1972.

Keating, E. "The Ethnography of Communication," in P. Atkinson, A. Coffey, S. Delamont, J. Lofland, & L. Lofland, eds., *Handbook of Ethnography.* London: Sage, 2001.

Saville-Troike, M. *The Ethnography of Communication: An Introduction.* Oxford, UK: Blackwell, 2003.

ETHNOMETHODOLOGY This term was coined by Harold Garfinkel, who formed a new school of sociology around this approach. Garfinkel drew, in part, on the resources of the ***phenomenological sociology*** of Alfred Schutz (1899–1956) to fashion an approach to the study of social life that opposed mainstream sociology, including the functionalist sociology of Garfinkel's teacher, Talcott Parsons (1902–1979). Garfinkel objected to the idea that the normal course for human intentions and actions is set by social rules and norms that exist prior to intention and action. He claimed that mainstream sociology treated human actors as "judgmental dopes" who passively carried out prescribed actions on the basis of internalized social norms. Social action, in his view, was not to be explained by appeal to such rules or norms or by examination of actors' subjective beliefs or intentions. Rather, the sociologist was to look to *how* actors do things and *what* they do, examining the methods, procedures, and organization of social action.

Ethnomethodology is thus interested in how people accomplish the interactions we take for granted in everyday life, for example, promising, trusting, agreeing, negotiating, and so on. It is the study of social action as the product and achievement of knowledgeable and reflective social actors. It focuses on the ways that various aspects of the *life world* are produced, experienced, or accomplished interactionally and discursively. As a methodology for studying social life, ethnomethodology is committed to *bracketing* the researcher's own sense of the way encounters are socially structured or accomplished in order to describe how members in a specific setting or parties to an interaction themselves accomplish a sense of structure.

Broadly conceived, ethnomethodology covers the cognitive sociology of Aaron Cicourel, constitutive ethnography, and more recent forms of the approach known as *conversation analysis*.

See also Discourse Analysis, Language.

KEY REFERENCES

Atkinson, J. M., & Heritage, J., eds. *Structures of Social Action.* Cambridge, UK: Cambridge University Press, 1984.

Baert, P. *Social Theory in the Twentieth Century.* New York: New York University Press, 1998.

Garfinkel, H. *Studies in Ethnomethodology.* Englewood Cliffs, NJ: Prentice-Hall, 1967.

Heritage, J. "Ethnomethodology," in A. Giddens & J. Turner, eds., *Social Theory Today.* Stanford, CA: Stanford University Press, 1987.

Mehan, H., & Wood, H. *The Reality of Ethnomethodology.* New York: Wiley, 1975.

Pollner, M., & Emerson, R. M., "Ethnomethodology and Ethnography," in P. Atkinson, A. Coffey, S. Delamont, J. Lofland, & L. Lofland, eds., *Handbook of Ethnography.* London: Sage, 2001.

EVIDENCE   This is information that bears on determining the validity (truth, falsity, accuracy, etc.) of a claim or what an inquirer, in part, provides to warrant a claim. Sources of evidence include the senses, reason, and testimony of others. Types of evidence appealed to in qualitative inquiry include various kinds of written texts (e.g., transcripts), verbal records, visual records, cultural artifacts, and observer accounts. Different qualitative methodologies rely on different types of evidence to support their claims.

Evidence is essential to justification, and justification takes the form of an argument about the merit(s) of a given claim. It is generally accepted that no evidence is conclusive or unassailable (and hence, no argument is foolproof). Thus, evidence itself must often be judged for its credibility, and that typically means examining its source and the procedures by which it was produced. When we speak of rules of evidence in different practices (e.g., social inquiry, legal proceedings, medical diagnosis, psychiatric treatment), we are generally concerned with different means or procedures whereby evidence is judged to be credible in that particular practice.

There are a number of strategies for linking evidence (facts, data) to claims (provisional conclusions), but each way of making that *inference* has serious flaws. *Induction* is the strategy of piling up evidence of specific instances or cases and then inferring a general conclusion. *Confirmation* entails showing that the evidence supports the claim. *Testability/falsifiability* is a strategy used to demonstrate that the evidence does not necessarily contradict the claim (and thereby enhances the likelihood that the claim is true).

Some forms of postmodern qualitative inquiry argue that the account prepared by the inquirer is not to be judged as an argument based on evidence, but more like a poem or novel. In other words, the inquirer's account of lived *experience* is not intended to represent that experience but to evoke some particular feelings, attitudes, or dispositions in the reader of the account. Of course, arguments based on evidence come into play here as well. First, we would judge the claim that "accounts should evoke, not represent" based on the arguments and evidence for such a claim. Also, we would judge whether any particular evocative account does the job of 'evoking' well by arguing whether or not it does so by appeal to evidence for good poetry or quality novels.

See also Data, Empiricism, Validity.

KEY REFERENCES

Hammersley, M. *Reading Ethnographic Research.* London: Longman, 1990.
Weston, A. *A Rulebook for Arguments,* 2nd ed. Indianapolis, IN: Hackett, 1992.

EXISTENTIALISM   This post–World War II philosophical and literary movement that unfolded primarily in France in the work of Sartre (1905–1980), Simone de Beauvoir (1905–1986), and Merleau-Ponty (1907–1961), among others, combined the focus of *phenomenology* on the 'intentional' character of human existence with a radical insistence on individual *authenticity*. Its particular relevance for qualitative inquiry lies in the work of the existential sociologists of the 1970s and their successors. Existential sociology strongly objected to traditional cognitive sociology claiming that the latter was overly rational both in its approach to understanding social life and its portrayal of the conduct of social life. It argued that traditional sociology was strongly wedded to a sharp divide between the experiencing subject (the inquirer) and the object (social life) to be understood. Existential sociology claimed that inquirers were part of the phenomenon they seek to understand, and, therefore, it promoted a return to the direct, lived experience of the individual fieldworker as the source of knowledge about the social world. Contemporary versions of this kind of sociology, evident in *autoethnography* and related practices, are critical of earlier forms for not incorporating a concern for emotionality, subjectivity, and the lived experience of the fieldworker into the field of representation itself. Postmodern 'existentialist' inquirers seek to collapse completely the distinction between the inquirer's experience and the 'field' of social action that he or she witnesses. They argue that no neat distinction can be drawn between the 'inquirer's' experience and the 'other's' world; there is only the inquirer's *inscription* or representation.

See also Experience, Intentionality.

KEY REFERENCES

Douglas, J. D., & Johnson, J. M., eds. *Existential Sociology.* Cambridge, UK: Cambridge University Press, 1977.
Ellis, C., & Flaherty, M. G., eds. *Investigating Subjectivity: Research on Lived Experience.* Newbury Park, CA: Sage, 1992.
Kotarba, J. A., & Fontana, A., eds. *The Existential Self in Society.* Chicago: University of Chicago Press, 1987.

EXPERIENCE   Qualitative inquiry deals with human lived experience. It is the *lifeworld* as it is lived, felt, undergone, made sense of, and accomplished by human beings that is the object of study. From the perspective of *ethnographic naturalism,* authentic experience is what inquirers aim to capture in their accounts. By using the right methods to observe and probe, the inquirer can reveal, describe, and map the lived experience of others (their interactions, intentions, the meanings they attach to their actions, etc.) and, subsequently, present it as it was actually lived or undergone by particular actors in particular circumstances. In this way of thinking, experience is distinguishable from its representation. Inquirers are capable of accomplishing this feat because they learn to operate on the border between lived experience and its representation (hence, the notions of inquirer as marginal native and participant observer). The inquirer's own lived experience (as an eyewitness, participant observer) functions as a means of access to the experience of others. Often, the inquirer's own experience becomes part of the recounting or representation of the experience of others in, for example, what Van Maanen (1988) has called confessional and impressionist tales.

Many postmodern and poststructuralist approaches to qualitative inquiry object strongly to the assumption that the inquirer can operate on some imaginary border between the experience of others and its representation. They do not necessarily deny that there is a world of lived experience, but they argue that it is impossible to represent such experience as it is 'actually' lived. This is so because language and speech create experience; hence, the very idea of having access to one's own experience as some kind of unmediated, direct lived 'happening' is chimerical because that very experience is itself discursively determined. Moreover, inquirers add another layer, so to speak, to such discursive constitution of experience because through their very acts of researching and writing, they continuously create and transform the experience they seek to describe and map. Thus, there are can only be inscriptions or retellings of experience.

In the phenomenological tradition, which is the source of ideas for both **philosophical hermeneutics** and **deconstructionism**, the notion of experience is defined quite differently than in the empirical sciences (including many versions of qualitative inquiry). In the empirical sciences, there is a nearly exclusive preoccupation with the *epistemological* role of experience. The concern with validated knowledge leads to a standardization of experience, and to a scientific conception of experience as an object, something that one might eventually validate as knowledge. In other words, knowledge and experience are distinguished. Experience itself is objectified as we take a third-person perspective toward our experience. In that way, experience becomes the world 'out there' that serves as the tribunal for testing and validating knowledge claims. In a similar way, the acts of understanding (knowing) and applying knowledge are separated. Knowledge is a product that the knower comes to possess about experience. In a separate step, this knowledge can then, if one chooses, be applied.

Particularly in the work of Gadamer (1900–2002), this scientific or empirical view of experience is found wanting because it strips experience of its *historicity*—its processual and dynamic character. In this tradition, experience is not a Baconian repository of sense data or a tribunal against which one tests a knowledge claim, nor is it something that is perfected and replaced by knowledge. Rather, experience has a processual, historical character; it is anticipatory and open. There is a knowing *within* experience. Gadamer explores these different senses of experience using the two German words for the notion: *Erlebnis* denotes experience as something one has, an event or adventure connected with a subject; it permits a plural 'experiences' that can be repeated by anyone. *Erfahrung* refers to experience as something one undergoes so that subjectivity is drawn into an 'event' of meaning; experience so understood is integrative, unfolding, dynamic, and hence singular. Several different, although not necessarily incompatible, ways of conceiving of lived human experience as an object of study in qualitative inquiries are shown in Figure E.2.

See also Crisis of Representation, Inscription, Representation.

KEY REFERENCES

Bruner, E. M. "Experience and Its Expressions," in *The Anthropology of Experience,* V. M. Turner & E. M. Bruner, eds. Urbana: University of Illinois Press, 1986.

Denzin, N. K. "Representing Lived Experience in Ethnographic Texts," *Studies in Symbolic Interaction, Vol. 12.* Greenwich, CT: JAI Press, 1991.

Gubrium, J., & Holstein, J. *The New Language of Qualitative Method.* Oxford, UK: Blackwell, 1997.

Risser, J. *Hermeneutics and the Voice of the Other: Re-reading Gadamer's Philosophical Hermeneutics.* Albany: SUNY Press, 1997.

Van Maanen, J. *Tales of the Field.* Chicago: University of Chicago Press, 1988.

EXPERIMENTAL TEXT   This is a generic term for forms of writing qualitative studies that employ different literary and artistic genres (e.g., poems, stories, and performances). It also signals a comingling of journalistic, fictional, factual, and ethnographic accounts. Various forms of textual experimentation are often undertaken in an explicit bid to decenter the political and interpretive authority of the inquirer. *Testimonio,* for example, is both a research strategy and a form of textual presentation that has some affinity to both the novel and the autobiography yet challenges those genres by giving voice to a previously anonymous and voiceless other.

See also Autoethnography, Performance/Performative/Performativity.

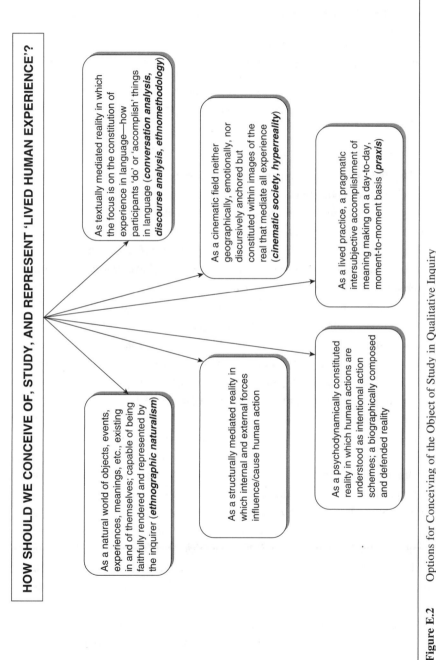

HOW SHOULD WE CONCEIVE OF, STUDY, AND REPRESENT 'LIVED HUMAN EXPERIENCE'?

As a natural world of objects, events, experiences, meanings, etc., existing in and of themselves; capable of being faithfully rendered and represented by the inquirer (***ethnographic naturalism***)

As textually mediated reality in which the focus is on the constitution of experience in language—how participants 'do' or 'accomplish' things in language (***conversation analysis, discourse analysis, ethnomethodology***)

As a structurally mediated reality in which internal and external forces influence/cause human action

As a cinematic field neither geographically, emotionally, nor discursively anchored but constituted within images of the real that mediate all experience (***cinematic society, hyperreality***)

As a psychodynamically constituted reality in which human actions are understood as intentional action schemes; a biographically composed and defended reality

As a lived practice, a pragmatic intersubjective accomplishment of meaning making on a day-to-day, moment-to-moment basis (***praxis***)

Figure E.2   Options for Conceiving of the Object of Study in Qualitative Inquiry

103

KEY REFERENCES

Beverly, J. "Testimonio, Subalternity, and Narrative Authority," in N. K. Denzin & Y. S. Lincoln, eds., *Handbook for Qualitative Research,* 2nd ed., Thousand Oaks, CA: Sage, 2000.

Brady, I. *Anthropological Poetics.* Savage, MD: Rowman & Littlefield, 1991.

Clifford, J., & Marcus, G. E. *Writing Culture: The Poetics and Politics of Ethnography.* Berkeley: University of California Press, 1986.

Denzin, N. K. *Interpretive Ethnography: Ethnographic Practices for the 21st Century.* Thousand Oaks, CA: Sage, 1997.

EXPLANATION   In commonsense usage, to explain something is to make it intelligible or understandable. However, usually, when we ask for an explanation, we are asking for an account of *why* something happened. Qualitative inquiry is often concerned not simply with what human actions mean but why they occur. Explanations of action take a variety of different forms. Perhaps the most common form is the ***covering-law model of explanation,*** but other efforts to explain human ***action*** include (a) Peter Winch's (1926–1997) model of social action as meaningful, rule-governed behavior, (b) functional explanations that account for social action in terms of the beneficial consequences that action has for the well-being or continuation of the larger social system, (c) materialist explanations that construe human action (e.g., a social institution, political arrangement, particular social practice, group attitude, and ideology) in terms of the relation of that action to the material environment or culture of a society or group (topography, climate, social arrangements, technological factors, etc.), (d) Foucault's ***genealogy,*** which aims to explain how subjects are constituted through discursive practices, (e) Habermas's theory of communicative action, (f) the efforts of ***ethnomethodology*** to explain actions in terms of their formal properties (i.e., *how* actors do things and what is being done), and (g) historicist or ***narrative explanation.***

One of the fundamental disputes in the broad field of qualitative inquiry centers on the issue of *nomological* versus historicist (i.e., narrative) accounts of human action. This dispute is often characterized as the quarrel between defenders of explanation (***Erklärung***) as the proper aim of the human sciences and those defending understanding (***Verstehen***) as the proper aim. Nomological explanations of the kind found in the natural sciences are characterized by their generality, universality, and atemporality. Defenders of ***Verstehen*** argue that if explanation means this natural science model of nomological, causal explanation, then explanation is not possible in the human sciences; because human action is intentional and meaningful, it cannot be 'explained' in terms of general laws. In their view, human action can be 'interpreted' only by (a) developing an understanding of its constitutive intersubjective meanings, (b) exploring the various forms that meaningful social action assumes (e.g., ritual, practice, rule-following, drama), (c) fashioning linguistic accounts showing how language is constitutive of action, or (d) describing some particular, temporal, circumstantial sequence of events that led up to the action to be accounted for (there is no implication that these events *always* lead to the action in question or that the events are subject to some lawful pattern).

See also Causal Analysis/Causality; Intentionalism; Nomothetic Knowledge; Theory, Types of.

KEY REFERENCES

Bohman, J. *New Philosophy of Social Science.* Cambridge: MIT Press, 1991.
Little, D. *Varieties of Social Explanation: An Introduction to the Philosophy of Social Science.* Boulder, CO: Westview Press, 1991.
Fay, B. *Contemporary Philosophy of Social Science.* Oxford, UK: Blackwell, 1996.

EXTERNAL VALIDITY   See GENERALIZATION.

F

FACT   See DESCRIPTION.

FACT-VALUE DISTINCTION   This is the notion that we should not confuse claims about how things are (facts) with claims about how things should be (values). The empiricist David Hume (1711–1776) is well known for his arguments that one cannot derive statements of value (the 'ought') from statements of fact (the 'is'). Influenced in part by Hume, the logical positivists argued that statements of value are not subject to reason because they are only expressions of preferences, attitudes, feelings, or assertions of will. Because they are claims of this kind, values are always subject to endless argument, and unlike claims of fact (or mathematics and logic), they can never be verified or falsified. Hence, value claims are not really knowledge claims at all and should not be allowed to intrude in the assessment of the truth or falsity of a scientific claim. (This is known as the emotivist theory of values or the doctrine of the radical undecidability of values.) This way of thinking about values, namely, that they are not subject to rational debate and cannot be justified and decided upon in the same manner as facts, is particularly troublesome. For if this is so, the determination of alternate courses of action in social policy or assessments of the merit of different social and educational interventions cannot be subject to warranted argument and rational deliberation.

The principle of value neutrality in social science is derived, in part, from this understanding of the fact-value distinction. Max Weber (1864–1920) is generally regarded as responsible for introducing the idea that the social scientist should be value neutral. That is, scientists should limit investigation to scientific explanation (i.e., the facts of the matter) and exclude their own political and moral (i.e., value or normative) judgments. This principle is often misunderstood. On the one hand, scientists *do* hold a set of 'internal' (discipli-nary and epistemic) values in high regard. These epistemic values include public criticism (objectivity), consistency, testability, truth, fruitfulness, scope, reliability, and so on. Of course, as the history of the development of scientific method shows, this set of values is not fixed once and for all but is itself debat-able and changes over time. Nonetheless, it is in terms of this set of epistemic values, or **criteria,** that the truth or falsity (or warrantability) of claims (i.e., 'the facts of the matter') is settled. On the other hand, the work of the scien-tist is, without a doubt, also subject to influence by 'external' or 'extrascien-tific' values including institutional and personal social, political, and moral values. According to the principle of value neutrality, these 'external' values should not be allowed to intrude in determining the truth or falsity of scientific claims. The inquirer should keep unconditionally separate the establishment of empirical fact and her or his own moral and political values. Stated somewhat differently, an inquirer should never confuse description and explanation with criticism and evaluation. The fact-value distinction is thus preserved.

Depending on one's point of view, this principle is either a dogma to be overcome or a regulative ideal to be upheld. For defenders of **naturalism,** value neutrality is an important methodological principle and the cornerstone of objectivity. For critical theorists and many feminist inquirers, among others, value neutrality must be exorcised to make way for a union of explanation and criticism in social theory.

See also *Context of Discovery/Context of Justification, Disinterested Social Science.*

KEY REFERENCES

House, E. R., & Howe, K. R. *Values in Evaluation and Social Research.* Thousand Oaks, CA: Sage, 1999.

Phillips, D. C. *The Expanded Social Scientist's Bestiary.* Savage, MD: Rowman & Littlefield, 2000.

Root, M. *Philosophy of Social Science.* Oxford, UK: Blackwell, 1993.

Weber, M. *The Methodology of the Social Sciences.* E. Shils & H. Finch, ed. and trans. New York: Free Press, 1968.

FALLIBILISM   This is the doctrine that knowledge and beliefs are inherently uncertain, never irrefutable, or beyond dispute. It is an epistemological stance that cautions against arrogance in the holding of cherished beliefs. Fallibilism is a statement about our epistemological limitations, not about the nature of the world per se. In other words, it is not a claim that the world is unknowable or that there is no world to be known; it simply means that our knowledge of that world is of a kind that is never certain. Fallibilists claim that we are content with our current (reasonably well-warranted) knowledge claims until some evidence comes along to challenge them and possibly causes us to revise or abandon them. The notion stands midway between dogmatism (the idea that we hold our beliefs to be true unquestionably and in the absence of any certainty) and radical *skepticism* (the idea that knowledge of any kind is impossible). The idea of a fallibilist epistemology was explained by Charles Sanders Peirce (1839–1914) as part of his detailed critique of Cartesian epistemology. It is also a key notion in Karl Popper's (1902–1994) philosophy of science.

See also *Falsification, Nonfoundational Epistemologies, Postempiricism, Pragmatism.*

KEY REFERENCE

Fay, B. *Contemporary Philosophy of Social Science.* Oxford, UK: Blackwell, 1996.

FALSIFICATION   Karl Popper (1902–1994) advanced the principle of falsification (or falsifiability) as a means of demarcating science from nonscience. He argued that the claims made by science are always, at least in principle, capable of being shown to be incorrect (i.e., falsified), while the claims of nonscientific pursuits are not. If a scientific claim withstands attempts to falsify it, it is then considered corroborated but not confirmed or verified. Popper was a fallibilist who strongly defended the (now widely accepted) view that scientific claims are never proved or conclusively justified. He believed that the growth of scientific knowledge is best characterized as a process of conjecture and refutation, as shown in Figure F.1. In philosophy of science, falsification has been criticized as an untenable explanation for the growth of scientific knowledge, but it continues to serve as a practicable research principle in many forms of research. For example, the idea of seeking negative cases or disconfirming (versus supporting) evidence for hypotheses in qualitative studies reflects this principle. The principle is also a key notion in the methodology for the human sciences defended in *naturalism.*

Problem identification

↘

Tentative solutions (conjectures)

↘

Error elimination through the testing of conjectures (refutation)

↘

Further conjectures

↘

Further refutations, and so on

Figure F.1   A Popperian View of the Growth of Scientific Knowledge

KEY REFERENCES

Fay, B. *Contemporary Philosophy of Social Science.* Oxford, UK: Blackwell, 1996.
Phillips, D. C. *The Expanded Social Scientist's Bestiary.* Lanham, MD: Rowman & Littlefield, 2000.
Popper, K. *Conjectures and Refutations,* 2nd ed. New York: Basic Books, 1965.

FEMINIST EPISTEMOLOGIES   There is no single feminist epistemology. Discussions of epistemology by feminists simultaneously exhibit a wide range of ideas including criticism of both traditional epistemology (*rationalism* and *empiricism*), arguments that reason and objectivity are gendered concepts, tension with *postmodernism,* and alliances with ideas of *critical social science* and *participatory action research.* Three strands of feminist epistemology have been identified, although there is great variance within each:

1. Feminist *empiricism:* A defense of experiential or observational data as the only legitimate basis for the testing of hypotheses and theory. Feminist empiricists argue that these kinds of data about women's experiences are traditionally missing from medical, psychological, and sociological theory. They seek to rectify this situation by producing empirically more accurate pictures of social reality. However, feminist empiricism does not accept without question the methodological assumptions (e.g., detached objectivity, neutrality, and so forth) associated with empiricist epistemology.

2. Feminist *standpoint epistemologies:* Inquiry ought to begin in and be tested against the lived sociopolitical experiences of women because women have a more complete and less distorted vision of real social relations unavailable to men insofar as they benefit from the exploitation of women. These epistemologies often draw on Marxist and neo-Marxist analyses of class domination and the division of labor in society.

3. Feminist *postmodernism:* This is a catchall phrase for an incredibly rich variety of perspectives that in one sense 'come after' the first two epistemologies noted above. Postmodern epistemologies are in part characterized by debates between standpoint perspectives and defenders of *deconstructionism* and postmodern notions like the suspicion of all universalizing claims, the rejection of truth as an oppressive illusion, and the relativizing of experience to local micropolitics. Some scholars see postmodernism and feminist theory as incompatible; others believe that insights of postmodernism—particularly its concerns with linking knowledge and power; its preoccupation with concrete, particular sites of struggles against oppression; its opening up of discourse to multiple voices; its critique of objectivity—actually serve to strengthen feminist epistemology.

KEY REFERENCES

Alcoff, L., & Potter, E., eds. *Feminist Epistemologies.* New York: Routledge, 1993.
Antony, L. M., & Witt, C., eds. *A Mind of One's Own: Feminist Essays on Reason and Objectivity.* Boulder, CO: Westview Press, 1993.
Harding, S., & Hintikka, M. B., eds. *Discovering Reality: Feminist Perspectives on Epistemology, Metaphysics, Methodology, and Philosophy of Science.* Dordrecht: D. Reidel, 1983.
Nicholson, L. J., ed. *Feminism/Postmodernism.* New York: Routledge, 1990.

FEMINIST ETHICS   Feminist approaches to ethics (and to philosophy more generally) are distinguishable by their explicit criticism of male biases in the topics, issues, interests, theories, and modes of argument that characterize traditional Western ethics. Feminists have developed a number of women-centered approaches to ethics (e.g., feminine, maternal, and lesbian) that aim to revalue women's moral experience by attending specifically to women's moral agency and their interests, rights, and practices. Virtually all of these approaches are critical of traditional ethical theories and practices for overvaluing masculine traits of autonomy, independence, mind, and reason as well as for thinking too little of traits such as interdependence, community, body, connection, and emotion. Likewise, these approaches express strong dissatisfaction with ways of moral reasoning that are primarily preoccupied with rules and principles of universality and impartiality while neglecting the moral import of principles of relationship, empathy, and particularity.

KEY REFERENCES

Card, C., ed. *Feminist Ethics.* Lawrence: University of Kansas Press, 1991.

Frazer, E., Hornsby, J., & Lovibond, S., eds. *Ethics: A Feminist Reader.* Oxford, UK: Blackwell, 1992.

Held, V. *Justice and Care: Essential Readings in Feminist Ethics.* Boulder, CO: Westview Press, 1995.

Jagger, A. *Living With Contradictions: Controversies in Feminist Social Ethics.* Boulder, CO: Westview Press, 1994.

Noddings, N. *Caring: A Feminine Approach to Ethics and Moral Education,* 2nd ed. Berkeley: University of California Press, 2003.

Walker, M. *Moral Understandings: A Feminist Study in Ethics.* New York: Routledge, 1998.

FEMINIST ETHNOGRAPHY   Just as there is no single feminist episte-mology, there is no single conception of feminist ethnography. What makes ethnography feminist is that it is a form of research undertaken by feminists in the fields of cultural anthropology, sociology, education, cultural studies, nursing, and so forth.

KEY REFERENCES

Bell, D., Caplan, C., & Karin, W. J., et al., eds. *Gendered Fields: Women, Men, and Ethnography.* London: Routledge, 1993.

Reinharz, S. *Feminist Methods in Social Research.* Oxford, UK: Oxford University Press, 1992.

Skeggs, B. "Feminist Ethnography," in P. Atkinson, A. Coffey, S. Delamont, J. Lofland, & L. Lofland, eds., *Handbook of Ethnography.* London: Sage, 2001.

FIDELITY TO METHOD/FIDELITY TO PHENOMENON   This is another way of expressing the principle of *ethnographic naturalism*. This notion is said to distinguish qualitative field studies from the kinds of experimental studies conducted by psychologists. The claim is that qualitative studies are based on the presupposition of being faithful, in the first instance, to the phenomenon under investigation: The social world must be understood as it is in its 'natural' state. One should not attempt to structure or arrange the world of lived experience to meet some prior commitment to the requirements of scientific method (i.e., fidelity or faithfulness to methodological principles).

See also Emergent Design, Naturalistic Inquiry.

KEY REFERENCE

Diesing, P. *Patterns of Discovery in the Social Sciences*. New York: Aldine, 1971.

FIELD   Traditionally, the field is the physical place or site where one goes to do *fieldwork*. For anthropologists, this has often been some foreign land with arrival on-site dutifully noted in what is called an arrival tale in the report of the fieldwork. More generally, it is where your colleagues say you are when you are doing your research: "Where's Mary?" "She's in the field." The notion of 'field' as a place or situation where some particular social *action* transpires whether or not the inquirer is present sets the notion apart from the idea of an 'artificial' setting (i.e., a laboratory experiment) where some set of circumstances is especially contrived by the inquirer. (However, the laboratory setting itself can be the 'field' in which one studies the behavior of scientists, for example.) Thus, the notion of the field is in part tied to the doctrine of *ethnographic naturalism*.

The notion of what constitutes 'being in the field' is currently under a great deal of reexamination. Traditionally, this notion meant being physically displaced from some comfortable familiar setting (i.e., the university) to some exotic, linguistically, and physically challenging remote place where one conducted a study. This traditional conception is less applicable as more and more fieldworkers undertake studies in nearby locales, including occasionally the fieldworker's own work setting. More significantly, the idea of the field as a place 'out there' in which one studies is being challenged by claims such as the following: "The field is not so much a place as it is a particular relation between oneself and others, involving a difficult combination of commitment and disengagement, relationship and separation" (R. Lederman, "Pretexts for

Ethnography: On Reading Fieldnotes," in R. Sanjek, ed., *Fieldnotes,* Cornell University Press, 1990, p. 88); "The 'field' is not an entity 'out there' that awaits discovery and exploration by the intrepid explorer. The field is not merely reported in the texts of fieldwork: it is constituted by our writing and reading" (P. Atkinson, *The Ethnographic Imagination,* Routledge, 1992, p. 8). Other criticisms are directed at the notion of the field as a single site. Ethnographers point to the fact that globalization interpenetrates and structures our notions of culture, politics, economy, and subjectivity. The particular site in which one studies sociocultural phenomena is thus perhaps to be understood only in terms of connections, parallels, and contrasts among multiple, interrelated sites. Some qualitative inquirers influenced by poststructuralist thought offer a more radical critique. They argue that the concept of the field (events, actions, contexts) as locatable in time and place ought to be replaced by the idea of a field as a multiplicity of images and reproductions characteristic of a *cinematic society.* In such a society, life is theater and the field is a staged social production. Hence, the traditional analytic vocabulary in which words like 'the field,' 'being in the field,' 'field notes,' 'field journal,' and so on are used to frame the object and process of study is no longer applicable. One is no longer studying something real in a real field but rather images of the real *(see hyperreality).*

See also Participant Observation.

KEY REFERENCES

Burawoy, M., Blum, J. A., George, S., Gille, Z., Gowan, T., Haney, L., Klawiter, M., Lopez, S. H., Ó Riain, S., & Thayer, M. *Global Ethnography: Forces, Connections, and Imaginations in a Postmodern World.* Berkeley: University of California Press, 2000.

Denzin, N. K. *Images of Postmodern Society.* London: Sage, 1991.

Gubrium, J. F., & Holstein, J. A. *The New Language of Qualitative Method.* Oxford, UK: Oxford University Press, 1997.

Gupta, A., & Ferguson, J., eds. *Anthropological Locations: Boundaries and Grounds of Field Science.* Berkeley: University of California Press, 1997.

Marcus, G. E. *Critical Anthropology Now: Unexpected Contents, Shifting Constituencies, Changing Agendas.* Santa Fe, NM: School of American Research Press, 1999.

Marcus, G. E. *Ethnography Through Thick and Thin.* Princeton, NJ: Princeton University Press, 1998.

FIELD JOURNAL   The field journal is a bound notebook that the field-worker carries into the *field* and in which is recorded observational notes, personal notes, sketches, ideas, lists of terms, and so on. In this journal are recorded what are often called jottings or jotted notes—phrases, key words, quotes, and so on—which are later used as memory aids in the writing up of full *field notes*. What exactly is contained in the field journal is a matter of research purpose, individual style, and need.

KEY REFERENCES

Lofland, J., & Lofland, L. H. *Analyzing Social Settings: A Guide to Qualitative Observation and Analysis*, 3rd ed. Belmont, CA: Wadsworth, 1995.
Sanjek, R., ed. *Fieldnotes: The Makings of Anthropology*. Ithaca, NY: Cornell University Press, 1990.

FIELD NOTES   Field notes are a kind of *evidence* on which inquirers base claims about meaning and understanding. There is no standard definition of field notes, their form, or content, however. Some fieldworkers define field notes as 'raw' data or material—notes made in the *field* based on observations and conversations, rough diagrams and charts, lists of terms, and so on. Others contrast field notes with data, defining field notes more along the lines of daily entries made in a *field journal* to record thoughts, impressions, initial ideas, working hypotheses, issues to pursue, and so on. For some, field notes include all those things collected in the course of *fieldwork*—the fieldwork journal, transcripts of conversations and interviews, photographs, audiotapes and video-tapes, copies of documents, and artifacts. Others exclude some of these as not belonging to field notes proper. This wide variation in defining field notes is attributable to the fact that these kinds of notes are very much prepared for an audience of one—the fieldworker—and thus are individualistic and personal and reflective of the unique ways individual fieldworkers conduct fieldwork. Common wisdom also holds that the written product of fieldwork—the ethnography, case study, and so on—is based on field notes. But that is only partially correct, for fieldworkers come back from the field with both field notes (however defined) and 'headnotes'—the former written down, the latter continually evolving and changing. Written reports of fieldwork are a product of both of these kinds of notes.

Approaches to qualitative inquiry that place a premium on systematic, rigorous methods of generating and analyzing data will define field notes as carefully prepared archives of data and documentation. Figure F.2 displays the traditional way of understanding the relationship of field notes to the finished product of field research.

Written report of fieldwork

↑

Analysis and interpretation

↑

Field notes

(Complete verbatim transcriptions, photographs, fully written field notes)

↑

Fieldwork

(Gaining access, building rapport, participant observation, interviewing)

Figure F.2   Traditional Conception of the Place of Field Notes

In this scheme, field notes are regarded as the 'real' data on which the finished product rests. Data are tangible objects to be entered into files and records that can be manipulated and coded in various ways. (The logic of computer-assisted analysis of qualitative data seems to rest on this way of thinking about field notes.) Therefore, these notes are distinguished from headnotes and from a record of reactions or a chronology of ideas found in a fieldwork journal. In this portrayal, field-note data are analogous to data in the form of responses to a survey or the results of the application of a psychometric measure. In sum, on a scientific conception of doing qualitative work, field notes are linked to the production of the final report in something resembling a building-block model. Scientific analysis of qualitative data assumes that resulting interpretations or understandings of human action are capable of being found in or traced to discrete segments of data in the form of written notes on observations, typed transcripts, parts of documents, and so on.

The definition of field notes and their relationship to fieldwork activity and written reports of fieldwork, however, are far more complex and problematic for several reasons. First, field notes have a dynamic character: What one knows and records early on in fieldwork will be different than what one knows and records later. Second, preparing field notes requires interpretive and textualizing practices. In other words, the making of field notes is itself an interpretive practice, not merely a kind of recording. Third, while field notes, broadly conceived, may indeed be the data that preserve the insights and understandings of fieldworkers forthcoming from their close and longtime encounter with that which they seek to understand, those field notes 'become' the final written report through complex processes of translation.

See also *Analyzing Qualitative Data, Inscription, Thick Description, Transcription.*

KEY REFERENCES

Emerson, R. M., Fretz, R. I., & Shaw, L. L. *Writing Ethnographic Fieldnotes.* Chicago: University of Chicago Press, 1995.
Sanjek, R., ed. *Fieldnotes: The Makings of Anthropology.* Ithaca, NY: Cornell University Press, 1990.

FIELD RELATIONS   This is a shorthand way of referring to the complex set of logistical, procedural, ethical, and political dimensions of relating to informants, gatekeepers, respondents, and others in the *field* in which one studies. Included here are the responsibilities entailed in gaining access to settings, people, and documents; establishing and maintaining trust; negotiating a particular role in the setting; and departing the field. Confessional tales included in fieldwork reports often focus on some aspect of field relations as well as on the trials and tribulations of fieldwork more generally.

See also *Ethics of Qualitative Inquiry, Fieldwork, Participant Observation, Reciprocity.*

KEY REFERENCES

Punch, M. *The Politics and Ethics of Fieldwork.* Beverly Hills, CA: Sage, 1986.
Shaffir, W. B., & Stebbins, R. A., eds. *Experiencing Fieldwork: An Inside View of Qualitative Research.* Newbury Park, CA: Sage, 1991.
Van Maanen, J. *Tales of the Field.* Chicago: University of Chicago Press, 1988.

FIELD STUDIES   This is a generic designation for all forms of social science research (e.g., *case study research* and *ethnography*) that involve direct, first-hand observation in naturally occurring situations or events and that rely principally on techniques of *participant observation* and *interviewing*. Field studies can involve the generation of both numeric and nonnumeric data. Not all qualitative studies are necessarily field studies because a qualitative inquirer could use existing texts, documents, or cultural artifacts as the data for analysis.

See also Field, Fieldwork.

KEY REFERENCE

Lofland, J., & Lofland, L. H. *Analyzing Social Settings: A Guide to Qualitative Observation and Analysis,* 3rd ed. Belmont, CA: Wadsworth, 1995.

FIELDWORK   This term refers to all those activities that one engages in while in the *field* including watching, listening, conversing, recording, interpreting, dealing with logistics, facing ethical and political dilemmas, and so on. It is an intensely personal and social process requiring both physical and intellectual stamina, political acumen, and moral sensitivity. *Participant observation* has traditionally been thought of as the *methodology* employed in fieldwork, but interview studies (including life-history work and oral history), case studies of various kinds, and coparticipative inquiries like *action research* all entail some aspects of fieldwork as well. In the literature, the fieldwork process is often reconstructed into phases (e.g., gaining entry, negotiating access, maintaining *field relations,* collecting and analyzing data, and exiting the field) in order to address in some manageable way all the various skills, knowledge, and attitudes entangled in fieldwork activity. In practice, however, fieldwork rarely unfolds in any neatly linear fashion.

Fieldwork is often discussed more as a set of tool skills rather than a way of being in the world in relation to others. This is due, in part, to connotations associated with the term 'field*work*' coupled with the lingering legacy of *logical empiricism* that stresses the importance of *method* in defining scientific inquiry. In other words, fieldwork is traditionally defined as a particular kind of labor or work one engages in to produce results. This labor requires means-end knowledge—a set of procedural or tool skills (a kind of technical knowledge) used to solve the puzzle of understanding human action. This is not to deny that there is extensive literature on field relations and fieldwork ethics. But this literature is also often presented as a tool-like knowledge—a set of guidelines, procedures, and obligations entailed in the epistemologically responsible and ethically correct use of data-gathering and analysis tools. The notion of fieldwork as a tool skill set seems to be particularly prominent in the applied fields where the discovery of qualitative inquiry is more recent (e.g., health professions, social services administration, and telecommunications).

A reconceptualization of what fieldwork is and what fieldwork knowledge consists of, however, is at least suggested in ideas from *social constructionism, pragmatism, critical social science,* and *philosophical hermeneutics.* This different way of thinking does not mean abandoning notions of technical competence in skills of watching, listening, conversing, and recording. Rather, the shift in thinking about fieldwork means situating those concerns within a different framework for knowledge and a different mode of the inquirer's engagement with the social world. When fieldwork is defined as *praxis* requiring a kind of practical-moral knowledge, emphasis shifts from a tool skill set to exploring the following ideas: (a) the fieldworker's way of being in the world, (b) the difference between wisdom and knowledge, (c) the moral and epistemological commitments to dialogue that fieldwork entails, (d) the kind of knowledge of other people it requires, (e) the incoherence, ambiguity, and contradictoriness of experience, and (f) fieldwork as a kind of communicative action or practical discourse.

See also Ethics of Qualitative Inquiry, Participant Observation.

KEY REFERENCES

Wolcott, H. F. *The Art of Fieldwork.* Walnut Creek, CA: AltaMira Press, 1995.
Wolf, D. L., ed. *Feminist Dilemmas in Fieldwork.* Boulder, CO: Westview, 1996.

FOCUS GROUPS   Focus group interviews or discussions bring together a group of people to discuss a particular topic or range of issues and are commonly found in media and communication studies, evaluation research, and organizational research. Focus groups are used both as a stand-alone method of generating data and in combination with other methods. Their successful use requires careful planning (including strategies for recruiting participants, logistics of recording data, and so on), thoughtfully prepared questions (with special attention paid to phrasing and sequencing), skillful moderation of the discussion, and thorough analysis of the data.

KEY REFERENCES

Kruger, R. A., & Casey, M. A. *Focus Groups: A Practical Guide for Applied Research,* 3rd ed. Thousand Oaks, CA: Sage, 2000.

Macnaghten, P., & Myers, G. "Focus Groups," in C. Seale, G. Gobo, J. F. Gubrium, & D. Silverman, eds., *Qualitative Research Practice.* London: Sage, 2004.

Tonkiss, F. "Using Focus Groups," in C. Seale, ed., *Researching Society and Culture,* 2nd ed. London: Sage, 2004.

FOUNDATIONALIST EPISTEMOLOGIES These epistemologies assume the possibility and necessity of the *ultimate* grounding of knowledge claims. To be considered genuine, legitimate, and trustworthy, knowledge must rest on foundations that require no further justification or interpretation. *Rationalism* and *empiricism* are foundationalist epistemologies. *Logical positivism* initially endorsed foundationalism (by attempting to establish that statements about sense perception were the foundation for all empirically meaningful claims) but eventually moved to a nonfoundationalist epistemology under the influence of Otto Neurath (1882–1945).

The term *objectivism* is often used as a synonym for *foundationalist epistemologies*. For example, Richard J. Bernstein defines objectivism as

> the base conviction that there is or must be some permanent, ahistorical matrix or framework to which we can ultimately appeal in determining the nature of rationality, knowledge, truth, reality, goodness, or rightness. An objectivist claims that there is (or must be) such a matrix and that the primary task of the philosopher is to discover what it is. (p. 8)

He argues that many scholars believe that the only alternatives to objectivism are *relativism* or radical *skepticism,* and he offers a fallibilistic *pragmatism* as a middle way.

See also Fallibilism, Nonfoundational Epistemologies.

KEY REFERENCES

Bernstein, R. J. *Beyond Objectivism and Relativism: Science, Hermeneutics, and Praxis.* Philadelphia: University of Pennsylvania Press, 1983.

Grayling, A. C. "Epistemology," in *The Blackwell Companion to Philosophy,* N. Bunnin & E. P. Tsui-James, eds. Oxford, UK: Blackwell, 1996.

Rorty, R. *Philosophy and the Mirror of Nature.* Princeton, NJ: Princeton University Press, 1979.

FRAMEWORKS FOR QUALITATIVE INQUIRY   A framework, for present purposes, is a configuration of an interrelated set of assumptions, concepts, values, and practices that comprise a way of viewing reality. A considerable amount of the literature in qualitative inquiry is given to identifying what comprises its unique framework (or set of frameworks). Interpretive paradigms (positivist/postpositivist, constructivist, feminist, ethnic, Marxist, cultural studies, queer theory), methodologies (qualitative versus quantitative), social theories (symbolic interactionism, ethnomethodology) and 'traditions' (biography, phenomenology, grounded theory, ethnography, case study) have been put forth as candidates for frameworks. The editors of the *Handbook of Qualitative Research* have organized the history of qualitative inquiry into a framework composed of a series of historical moments or phases. Some scholars argue that seeking frameworks in such grand schemes based on foundational methodological or epistemological principles and paradigms is misguided and that we are better served by thinking of qualitative inquiry in terms of actual social practices of research. Others argue that frameworks are more or less subject matter or field specific—for example, ethnography of communication, ethnography of health and medicine, educational ethnography, qualitative nursing research, qualitative psychology, and so forth.

KEY REFERENCES

Creswell, J. *Qualitative Inquiry and Research Design: Choosing Among Five Traditions.* Thousand Oaks, CA: Sage, 1997.

Denzin, N. K., & Lincoln, Y. S. "Introduction: The Discipline and Practice of Qualitative Research," in N. K. Denzin & Y. S. Lincoln, eds., *Handbook of Qualitative Research,* 3rd ed. Thousand Oaks, CA: Sage, 2005.

Seale, C. "History of Qualitative Methods," in C. Seale, ed., *Researching Society and Culture.* London: Sage, 2004.

Seale, C., Gobo, G., Gubrium, J. F., & Silverman, D. "Introduction: Inside Qualitative Research," in C. Seale, G. Gobo, J. F. Gubrium, & D. Silverman, eds., *Qualitative Research Practice.* London: Sage, 2004.

Travers, M. *Qualitative Research Through Case Studies.* London: Sage, 2001.

FRANKFURT SCHOOL   This is the name given to members of the Marxist-oriented *Institut für Sozialforschung* (Institute for Social Research) founded in 1923 in Frankfurt, Germany. Since most of the Institute's members were Marxists and Jews, the institute was forced into exile by the Nazis. In 1934, it formally moved to Columbia University. In this institute, a blend of explanatory social research, normative critique, and philosophical reflection divorced from the positivist and materialist inclinations of orthodox Marxism emerged that came to be called a critical theory of society by its members in the mid-1930s. Its most influential director was Max Horkheimer (1895–1973), and its first generation included the social theorists T. W. Adorno (1903–1969), Herbert Marcuse (1898–1979), Walter Benjamin (1892–1940), and Erich Fromm (1900–1980), among others. Jürgen Habermas, a student of both Adorno and Horkheimer, is perhaps the most widely known member of the second generation of critical theorists to emerge from the Institute after its return to Germany in 1950.

See also Critical Social Science.

KEY REFERENCES

Benhabib, S. *Critique, Norm, and Utopia: A Study of the Foundations of Critical Theory.* New York: Columbia University Press, 1986.
Bronner, S. E., & Kellner, D. K., eds. *Critical Theory and Society.* New York: Routledge, 1989.
Hoy, D. C., & McCarthy, T. *Critical Theory.* Oxford, UK: Blackwell, 1994.

FUNCTIONALISM   Functionalist theories or models aim to explain human behavior (e.g., rituals, customs, and ceremonies) and sociocultural institutions (e.g., family, church, and state) in terms of the functions they perform in a particular group, society, culture, or community. In sociology, functionalism is most often associated with the work of Émile Durkheim (1858–1917) and Talcott Parsons (1902–1979) and in anthropology with the work of Bronislaw Malinowski (1884–1942). A variation called structural functionalism was developed by the anthropologist Alfred Radcliffe-Brown (1881–1995), who distinguished between *structure* (a network of social relations and institutions comprising the permanent framework of society) and *function* (the way in which these relations and institutions contributed to the stable functioning of society). Functionalist explanations are also found in political science and systems theory. A common criticism of these kinds of explanations is that they assume stability and harmonious function of aspects of a society or culture and thus fail to address conflict.

See also Explanation.

KEY REFERENCES

Baert, P. *Social Theory in the 20th Century.* New York: New York University Press, 1998.
Giddens, A. *Studies in Social and Political Theory.* New York: Basic Books, 1997.

G

———◆·◆·◆———

GEISTESWISSENSCHAFTÉN   A German term usually translated as 'human sciences.'

See also *Science,* Verstehen.

GENEALOGY   This notion originates with Nietzsche (1844–1900), who insisted upon the interpretive character of all human thought. Nietzsche claimed that a particular kind of historical inquiry he called genealogical inquiry—an examination of the conditions under which various ways of interpreting and evaluating ourselves have arisen—was a valuable means of reevaluating interpretations of human life. Genealogical inquiry is thus a way of explaining our selves to ourselves. Drawing on the work of Nietzsche, Foucault's (1926–1984) later work (e.g., *Discipline and Punish,* and the three-volume *History of Sexuality*) employed a genealogical approach to understanding how we have been constituted as subjects in various systems of thought and bodies of knowledge that are intimately connected to systems of social control, domination, and, more broadly, the exercise of power. Moreover, Foucault strongly emphasized that these relations of power and knowledge that constitute social relations operate regardless of any particular individual's subjective awareness or intentions. The subject is constituted as a particular kind of subject through these discourses of power and knowledge. The purpose of engaging in genealogical inquiry is to disturb the taken-for-granted and allegedly self-evident character of our interpretations of 'subjects' as, for example, men, women, boys, girls, criminals, adolescents, and so on. Baert (1998) captures the notion of genealogical inquiry as follows:

The genealogist goes back in time to show that at some point radically new meanings were allocated to concepts. He or she then demonstrates that the emergence of these new meanings was due to power struggles or contingency. The new meanings were subsequently transmitted across generations, and so became part of the culture. These meanings gradually came to be experienced by people as self-evident, necessary, innocuous (if not honorable and consistent). Foucault's genealogy . . . aims at demonstrating that these meanings are neither obvious, necessary, harmless, honorable, [n]or coherent. (p. 123)

KEY REFERENCES

Baert, P. *Social Theory for the Twentieth Century.* New York: New York University Press, 1998.

Foucault, M. *Discipline and Punish: The Birth of the Prison.* London: Allen Lane, 1977.

Foucault, M. "Nietzsche, Genealogy, History," in *Language, Counter-memory, Practice,* D. F. Bouchard, ed. Ithaca, NY: Cornell University Press, 1977.

Geuss, R. "Nietzsche and Genealogy," *European Journal of Philosophy,* 1994, 2(3), 274–292.

GENERALIZATION   A generalization is a broad, encompassing statement or proposition made by drawing an inference from observation of the particular. Generalization is an act of reasoning from the observed to the unobserved, from a specific instance to all instances believed to be like the instance in question. Theories are thus generalizations for they explain some phenomenon across a variety of specific instances or cases of that phenomenon. Generalization or generalizability (also called *external validity*) is traditionally held to be one of the ***criteria*** for social scientific inquiry.

Broadly interpreted, generalization refers to the wider relevance or resonance of one's inquiry beyond the specific context in which it was conducted. Generalization is the process involved in moving from the specification of patterns, relations, processes, conditions, and meanings discerned in the data generated in the study of some particular event, person, institution, group, and so forth to a more general and abstract understanding of these aspects of human experience. This process is either *empirical-statistical* or *theoretical-analytic* reflecting two different logics of sampling. *Empirical generalizations* are made by first carefully selecting a representative sample from a population of interest and then, by means of a statistical inference, calculating the probability that findings based on the sample are characteristic of the population. This is the least commonly used approach to generalization in qualitative studies. *Theoretical or analytical generalizations* do not rely on the logic of representative sampling. Rather, the selection of groups, units, cases, and so forth to study is made on the basis of their relevance to the theoretical account or explanation that the inquirer is developing. In other words, the criterion used to select cases from which one will generalize is not their representativeness. Rather, the criterion for deciding what cases to select for study is the extent to which they contribute to supporting and refuting the argument or explanation being developed by the inquirer.

The most well-developed version of this notion of theoretical elaboration or **analytic generalization** is discussed in **grounded theory methodology**, but it also is found in efforts to use qualitative studies to reconstruct social theory by means of the extended case method. Theoretical elaboration is also the notion underlying Clifford Geertz's efforts to connect the microscopic or situation-specific character of ethnography to more general understandings. Geertz (1983, p. 23) notes, "The important thing about the anthropologist's findings is their complex specificness, their circumstantiality." Specific cases, however, provide the context-specific material that makes it possible to think "realistically and concretely about" social scientific concepts and theories (e.g., modernization, stratification, legitimacy, integration, conflict, charisma, and structure) and to work "creatively and imaginatively with them."

There are several other positions on the desirability, possibility, and process of generalization within the broad field of qualitative inquiry. Robert Stake (1995), for example, defends the importance of what he calls *naturalistic generalizations*—conclusions that both inquirer and reader arrive at through engagement in life or through vicarious experience—in contrast to formal, propositional generalizations. He argues that inquirers ought to assist readers in making naturalistic generalizations by developing interpretive accounts that are personal, narrative in structure, and richly detailed.

Yvonna Lincoln and Egon Guba (1985) maintain that generalization is unrealizable, but, in a manner similar to Stake, they claim that extrapolation or **transferability** of findings from one specific **case** to another is possible. In their view, case-to-case transfer, an activity that is the responsibility of the reader of research, can be accomplished if the inquirer provides sufficient detail about the circumstances of the situation or case that was studied so that readers can engage in reasonable but modest speculation about whether findings are applicable to other cases with similar circumstances. Transferability, like theoretical elaboration, is a way to deal with the apparent paradox of qualitative work: its avowed focus on the particular and its simultaneous refusal to deny any interest whatsoever in the general.

Likewise, Norman Denzin (1989) has promoted an affirmative postmodern approach to generalizing in interpretive studies. He holds the view that contextual, multi-voiced, interactional, and interpretive texts contribute to theoretical understanding by illuminating interpretive theories already at work in the connections that frame the stories that are told. The inquirer engages in generalizing by making vivid and critical examinations of the connections between unique, uncommon lived experiences and the commonality of groups, social relationships, and culturally constructed images that partially define those experiences.

On the other hand, the impossibility and undesirability of any and all attempts to generalize is characteristic of some radical postmodernist approaches to qualitative study. These approaches are opposed to *theory* of any kind and look instead to the uniqueness of events and perspectives. They take an antitheoretical and antigeneralizing interest in the contingent and specific circumstances of everyday life events; they emphasize local narratives, local knowledge.

See also Cross-Case Analysis, Inference, Sampling Logic.

KEY REFERENCES

Burawoy, M. "Reconstructing Social Theories," and "The Extended Case Method," in *Ethnography Unbound: Power and Resistance in the Modern Metropolis,* M. Burawoy, et al., eds. Berkeley: University of California Press, 1991.
Denzin, N. *Interpretive Interactionism.* Thousand Oaks, CA: Sage, 1989.
Flick, U. *An Introduction to Qualitative Research.* London: Sage, 1998.
Geertz, C. "Thick Description: Towards an Interpretive Theory of Culture," in C. Geertz, *The Interpretation of Cultures.* New York: Basic Books, 1983.
Lincoln, Y. S., & Guba, E. G. *Naturalistic Inquiry.* Beverly Hills, CA: Sage, 1985.
Seale, C. F. *The Quality of Qualitative Research.* London: Sage, 1999.
Stake, R. *The Art of Case Study Research.* Thousand Oaks, CA: Sage, 1995.

GENERATING DATA   It is a common mistake to think that data are somehow simply 'out there' and thus discovered and collected (i.e., gathered) like picking grapes from the vine. On the contrary, what constitutes data depends upon one's inquiry purposes and the questions one seeks to answer. Data are generated or constructed within conceptual schemes and by various means that are deemed appropriate to serving particular purposes and answering particular questions.

See also Description, Theory-Observation Distinction.

KEY REFERENCE

Mason, J. *Qualitative Researching.* London: Sage, 1996.

GLOBALIZATION   This notoriously elusive term broadly refers to world-wide changes in economic, technological, and political processes, and in communications and technology that increasingly impact social life within and across nations and societies. Disagreements about the nature and extent of that impact—for example, whether it (a) fosters homogenization of societies or celebrates multiculturalism, cultural exchange, and access to cultural diversity, (b) primarily reflects a corporatist agenda and benefits only the elite in society and thus must be countered by an antiglobalizing movement to address the claims of the world's poor and working classes, (c) displaces the role of nations in global politics and supplants their authority with the rule of quasi-government agencies such as the World Bank and the International Monetary Fund, (d) is primarily a market-oriented phenomenon, or (e) can genuinely contribute to the growth of world democracy—fuel the debates over the meaning of globalization and, consequently, the way the term is employed in qualitative studies.

KEY REFERENCES

Appaduri, A. *Modernity at Large: Cultural Dimensions of Globalization.* Minneapolis: University of Minnesota Press, 1996.

Cohen, R., & Kennedy, P. *Global Sociology.* New York: New York University Press, 2000.

Hall, S. "The Global, the Local, and the Return of Ethnicity," in C. Lemert, ed., *Social Theory: The Multicultural and Classical Readings.* Boulder, CO: Westview Press, 1991.

Held, D., McGrew, A., Goldblatt, D., & Perraton, J. *The Global Transformations Website.* Available at www.polity.co.uk/global/

GRAND NARRATIVE   Also called a master narrative or metanarrative, the term figures prominently in Jean-François Lyotard's (1924–1998) explanation of what the condition of postmodernity means. Lyotard claimed that modern science is characterized by the pursuit of absolute standards, grand theory, and universal categories. Moreover, the legitimation of science as a practice, as well as various other modern social and political practices, relied on metanarratives. Two prominent examples of the latter are the Enlightenment narrative of human progress through the advancement of scientific knowledge and the Marxist narrative of the triumph of socialism through class conflict and the revolution of the proletariat. For Lyotard, postmodernity meant the decline of the legitimating power of these grand narratives and the turn toward the acceptance of all knowledge as incomplete, tentative, local, perspectival, and resistant to all forms of unification.

See also Grand Theory, Postmodernism.

KEY REFERENCE

Lyotard, J.-F. *The Postmodern Condition: A Report on Knowledge.* Minneapolis: University of Minnesota Press, 1984.

GRAND THEORY   In the social sciences, grand theory refers to those efforts devoted to abstract, analytical theory building. It stands in contrast to empiricist approaches that emphasize that knowledge of society is best acquired by accumulating empirical generalizations through improvements in methodology as well as scientific approaches that encourage the development of lawlike propositions and axiomatic theory. The work of Talcott Parsons (1902–1979) stands as an exemplar of grand theory in sociology. The period from roughly 1950–1970 in sociology was characterized by strong criticism of this kind of Parsonian theorizing from various viewpoints including Robert Merton's (1910–2003) defense of middle-range theory, Barney Glaser and Anselm Strauss's (1916–1996) arguments for grounded theory, and C. Wright Mills (1916–1962) and Alvin Gouldner's (1920–1980) criticisms of abstract theory as a retreat from social action and practical reality. Grand theory experienced a resurgence in sociology in the late 1970s and early 1980s as represented, for example, in the structuration theory of Anthony Giddens, Jürgen Habermas's theory of communicative action, and Niklas Luhmann's system theory. More generally, there is a significant part of social theory that today is given to more speculative, less empirical, less scientific, and more all-encompassing social theorizing. These efforts are met by criticisms on the one hand from empiricists who are suspicious of any efforts to explain society that are seemingly 'merely philosophical' and on the other hand from post-modernist and poststructuralists who are deeply suspicious of all forms of grand theory and argue for the necessarily fragmented and incomplete character of all forms of knowledge.

See also Postmodernism.

KEY REFERENCE

Skinner, Q., ed. *The Return of Grand Theory in the Human Sciences.* Cambridge, UK: Cambridge University Press, 1985.

GROUNDED THEORY METHODOLOGY   This term is often used in a nonspecific way to refer to any approach to developing theoretical ideas (concepts, models, formal theories) that begins with data. But grounded theory methodology is a specific, highly developed, rigorous set of procedures for producing formal, substantive theory of social phenomena. This approach to the analysis of qualitative data simultaneously employs techniques of induction, deduction, and verification to develop theory. Experience with data generates insights, hypotheses, and generative questions that are pursued through further data generation. As tentative answers to questions are developed and concepts are constructed, these constructions are verified through further data collection.

Grounded theory methodology requires a concept-indicator model of analysis that, in turn, employs the method of ***constant comparison***. Empirical indicators from the data (actions and events observed, recorded, or described in documents in the words of interviewees and respondents) are compared looking for similarities and differences. From this process, the analyst identifies underlying uniformities in the indicators and produces a coded category or concept. Concepts are compared with more empirical indicators and with each other to sharpen the definition of the concept and to define its properties. Theories are formed from proposing plausible relationships among concepts and sets of concepts. Tentative theories or theoretical propositions are further explored through additional instances of data. The testing of the emergent theory is guided by theoretical sampling. Theoretical sampling means that the sampling of additional incidents, events, activities, populations, and so on is directed by the evolving theoretical constructs. Comparisons between the explanatory adequacy of the theoretical constructs and these additional empirical indicators go on continuously until theoretical saturation is reached (i.e., additional analysis no longer contributes to anything new about a concept). In this way, the resulting theory is considered conceptually dense and grounded in the data.

KEY REFERENCES

Glaser, B., & Strauss, A. *The Discovery of Grounded Theory.* Chicago: Aldine, 1967.

Strauss, A. *Qualitative Analysis for Social Scientists.* Cambridge, UK: Cambridge University Press, 1987.

Strauss, A., & Corbin, J. *Basics of Qualitative Research: Techniques and Procedures for Developing Grounded Theory,* 2nd ed. Thousand Oaks, CA: Sage, 1998.

H

HERMENEUTIC CIRCLE   There are two different interpretations of this notion—one is methodological, the other ontological. As first developed in ancient rhetoric and then elaborated by Friedrich Schleiermacher (1768–1834) in nineteenth-century *hermeneutics,* this notion refers to the nature and means of interpreting a text. The circle signified a methodological process or condition of understanding, namely, that coming to understand the meaning of the whole of a text and coming to understand its parts were always interdependent activities. Construing the meaning of the whole meant making sense of the parts, and grasping the meaning of the parts depended on having some sense of the whole. This conception of the circle is shown in Figure H.1.

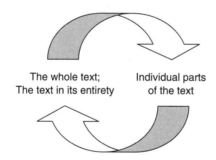

The whole text;   Individual parts
The text in its entirety   of the text

Figure H.1   The Hermeneutic Circle as Method of Interpretation

For Schleiermacher, and for current versions of *conservative hermeneutics,* the hermeneutic circle indicates a necessary condition of interpretation, but the circularity of the process is only temporary—eventually the interpreter can come to something approximating a complete and correct understanding of the meaning of a text in which whole and parts are related in perfect harmony. Said somewhat differently, the interpreter can, in time, get outside of or escape the hermeneutic circle in discovering the 'true' meaning of the text.

In the work of Martin Heidegger (1889–1976) and Hans-Georg Gadamer (1900–2002), the notion of the hermeneutic circle is given a stronger, more radical, and ontological interpretation. In their work, the circularity of interpretation is not simply a methodological principle but an essential feature of all knowledge and understanding. In other words, the fact that every interpretation relies on other interpretations, and so on, points to the finite and situated character of all understanding. The hermeneutic circle thus signifies the universality of hermeneutics—interpretation is a ubiquitous and inescapable feature of all human efforts to understand; there is no special evidence, method, experience, or meaning that is independent of interpretation or more basic to it such that one can escape the hermeneutic circle. Moreover, all efforts to interpret (to understand) always take place within some background (e.g., historical tradition, web of belief, and practice) that cannot be transcended. In this sense, we always 'belong' to history. The image of the hermeneutic circle is thus transformed into a picture of how the interpreter is bound to a tradition and history on the one hand and to the particular object of interpretation on the other. The notion is best captured in Figure H.2 (adapted from S. Gallagher, *Hermeneutics and Education,* SUNY Press, 1992, p. 106).

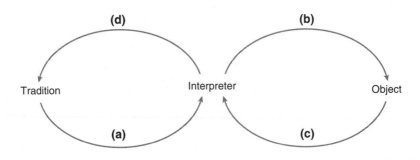

Figure H.2   The Hermeneutic Circle in Philosophical Hermeneutics

Gallagher explains that the anterior operation of tradition (a) as a forestructure of understanding both conditions and suggests the foreconceptions ('prior knowledge,' if you will) (b) that the inquirer brings to interpret the object (a text or another human being). The feedback from the reading of the text (or from another human being's response in a conversation) motivates a new projection of meaning (interpretation). The relations (b) and (c) represent the hermeneutic circle. The relationship signified by (d) indicates that in the process of interpreting, the inquirer's relation to a particular tradition can change; foreconceptions (prior understandings) can be challenged and modified, and so on. The fact that there is no escaping the hermeneutic circle (no escaping the fact that we belong to history and to tradition) reveals its ontological character, that is, we are 'interpretive' beings.

See also *Hermeneutic Method, Philosophical Hermeneutics.*

KEY REFERENCES

Hiley, D. R., Bohman, J. F., & Shusterman, R., eds. *The Interpretive Turn: Philosophy, Science, Culture.* Ithaca, NY: Cornell University Press, 1991.

Taylor, C. "Interpretation and the Sciences of Man," in C. Taylor, *Philosophy and the Human Sciences, Philosophical Papers 2.* Cambridge, UK: Cambridge University Press, 1985. (Originally published in *Review of Metaphysics,* 1971, 25, 3–51)

HERMENEUTIC METHOD   Where the act of interpreting an utterance, text, or action is defined as a kind of exegesis (a clarification and subsequent explication of meaning that at first appears strange and puzzling), we imagine it to be a kind of critical analysis or explanation using the method of the ***hermeneutic circle***. The ***method*** involves playing the strange and unfamiliar parts of an action, text, or utterance off against the integrity of the action, narrative, or utterance as whole until the meaning of the strange passages and the meaning of the whole are worked out or accounted for. (Thus, for example, to understand the meaning of the first few lines of a poem, I must have a grasp of the overall meaning of the poem, and vice versa.) In this process of applying the hermeneutic method, the interpreter's self-understanding and sociohistorical location neither affects nor is affected by the effort to interpret the meaning of the text or utterance. In fact, in applying the method, the interpreter abides by a set of procedural rules that help ensure that the interpreter's historical situation does not distort the bid to uncover the actual meaning embedded in the text, act, or utterance, thereby helping to ensure the objectivity of the interpretation.

When we speak of ***Verstehen*** as the 'method' of the human sciences, it is this conception of hermeneutic method that is operative. In other words, defenders of *Verstehen* as method argue that because human action is intentional, it requires a special method to be understood (a method different from the method of explanation characteristic of the natural sciences). This idea that understanding proceeds by and is the result of the application of method—in this case, the hermeneutic method that is most appropriate to making sense of intentional speech or action—is repudiated in *philosophical hermeneutics* and *deconstructionism.*

See also Hermeneutic Circle, Intentionalism.

KEY REFERENCES

Gallagher, S. *Hermeneutics and Education.* Albany: SUNY Press, 1992.
Kerdeman, D. "Hermeneutics and Education: Understanding, Control, and Agency," *Educational Theory,* 1996, 48(2), 241–266.

HERMENEUTICS   This term refers generally to the art, theory, and philosophy of interpreting the meaning of an object (a *text,* a work of art, social *action,* the utterances of another speaker, etc.). However, there are several varieties of hermeneutics behind which lay complex theoretical disputes. Friedrich Schleiermacher (1768–1834), who is generally recognized as a creator of modern hermeneutic theory, defined hermeneutics as the art of understanding practiced in reading classical, biblical, and legal texts. At the beginning of the twentieth century, Wilhelm Dilthey (1833–1911) extended the idea of hermeneutics to the epistemology and methodology of the human sciences. From Dilthey onward to the contemporary human sciences, hermeneutics has meant the theory of interpretation as a particular methodology. This interpretation, however, was challenged by Martin Heidegger (1889–1976), who understood hermeneutics to be the existential-phenomenological analysis of the constitution of *Dasein* ('existence' or being in the world'). He argued that hermeneutics ('understanding') is a fundamental concept of *ontology,* that is, a basic characteristic of human existence. Hans-Georg Gadamer (1900–2002) developed Heidegger's ideas of hermeneutics (or 'understanding') as a primary and universal way of our being in the world and argued for hermeneutics as a kind of practical philosophy. Furthermore, because understanding is viewed as a linguistic event, Gadamer explored the centrality of language and dialogue to understanding. Inspired by both Heidegger and Nietzsche (1844–1900),

Jacques Derrida (1930–2004) and colleagues practiced a form of radical or deconstructionist hermeneutics. Also, drawing on insights from Marx (1818–1883), Freud (1856–1939), and ideas of the **Frankfurt School**, Jürgen Habermas in his early work developed a theory of critical or depth hermeneutics. Along with the tradition of **Verstehende sociology**, the German tradition of hermeneutical thought serves as the major source of ideas for qualitative inquiry.

See also Conservative Hermeneutics, Critical Hermeneutics, Deconstructionism, Hermeneutics of Suspicion, Philosophical Hermeneutics.

KEY REFERENCES

Bleicher, J. *Contemporary Hermeneutics: Hermeneutics as Method, Philosophy and Critique.* London: Routledge & Kegan Paul, 1980.
Grondin, J. *Sources of Hermeneutics.* Albany: SUNY Press, 1995.
Hekman, S. *Hermeneutics and the Sociology of Knowledge.* Notre Dame, IN: University of Notre Dame Press, 1986.
Palmer, R. *Hermeneutics: Interpretation Theory in Schleiermacher, Dilthey, Heidegger, and Gadamer.* Evanston, IL: Northwestern University Press, 1969.

HERMENEUTICS OF SUSPICION   This term was coined by French philosopher Paul Ricoeur (1913–2005) to characterize the hermeneutical philosophy of the more radical followers of Nietzsche (1844–1900), principally Derrida (1930–2004) and Foucault (1926–1984). Also called radical or deconstructionist hermeneutics, this philosophy is profoundly suspicious of whatever purports to be the truth; it argues that all interpretations are false and there is no escape from false consciousness. Its goal is to deconstruct—decipher, decode, or unmask—the reality or truth of the meaning of all notions or ideas that we take for granted and show these meanings to be entirely contingent and relative. Jürgen Habermas's **critical hermeneutics** shares this view to the extent that it seeks to unmask false consciousness. Yet, because Habermas trusts in language and dialogue and holds out hope for the restoration of meaning and institutions, he also shares something with the **philosophical hermeneutics** of Gadamer and what is called the hermeneutics of trust.

See also Deconstructionism.

KEY REFERENCES

Caputo, J. *More Radical Hermeneutics: On Not Knowing Who We Are.* Bloomington: Indiana University Press, 2000.

Caputo, J. *Radical Hermeneutics: Repetition, Deconstruction, and the Hermeneutic Project.* Bloomington: Indiana University Press, 1987.

Michelfelder, D. P., & Palmer, R. E., eds. *Dialogue and Deconstruction: The Gadamer-Derrida Encounter.* Albany: SUNY Press, 1989.

HISTORICISM This doctrine figured prominently in nineteenth-century German thought, most notably in the work of Wilhelm Dilthey (1833–1911), and is foundational to the development of *antinaturalism* and hence to much current thinking about qualitative inquiry. It is the view that we are historical beings or that there is an inescapably historical character to all of human existence such that all knowledge and understanding is inevitably interpretive, particular, perspectival, and contextual. As an epistemological doctrine, historicism developed in opposition to nomologicalism, which is the view that knowledge of society should be expressible in general laws offering universal, atemporal explanation.

Some confusion surrounds the use of the term that is attributable in large part to the fact that Karl Popper (1902–1994) (*The Poverty of Historicism,* 1957) used the term to mean just the opposite of what is defined above. Popper argued that to be historicist meant to believe that history has a pattern, that that pattern can be captured in historical laws, and that the task of the social scientist is to discover these laws, for they can be used to direct social action and policy. Popper was extremely critical of the view that there is a process of development working its way out through history.

See also Narrative Explanation.

KEY REFERENCES

Fay, B. *Contemporary Philosophy of Social Science.* Oxford, UK: Blackwell, 1996.

Henderson, D. K. *Interpretation and Explanation in the Human Sciences.* Albany: SUNY Press, 1993.

HISTORICITY (Also historicality or *Geschichtlichkeit*) This notion figures prominently in phenomenological and hermeneutic traditions. It refers to a fundamental or essential feature of human existence, namely, that we are not merely *in* history but *belong* to history. History (or tradition), in other words, is not something external to us, objective, or past; rather, it is a dynamic force that enters into all efforts to understand. Thus, our history (or tradition) is not something that can be overcome by a method that would make objective knowledge possible in the human sciences. The historical character of our being is not a limitation or restriction on our ability to know but the very condition or principle of understanding. Taken to its extreme, the notion of historicity is equivalent to radical relativism or universal perspectivism.

See also Hermeneutic Circle, Historicism, Philosophical Hermeneutics.

KEY REFERENCES

Gadamer, H.-G. *Truth and Method,* 2nd rev. ed., J. Weinsheimer & D. G. Marshall, trans. New York: Crossroad, 1989.

Grondin, J. *Introduction to Philosophical Hermeneutics*, J. Weinsheimer, trans. New Haven, CT: Yale University Press, 1994.

HOLISM A long-standing dispute in the social sciences concerns the proper level or means of explanation of social phenomena. Holism (also called methodological or metaphysical holism) is the view that explanation of social phenomena must proceed at the macroscopic level in terms of social 'wholes' (e.g., classes, groups, communities, societies, and states) and their properties. It assumes that the actions of individuals are a function of the place of these individuals within some social whole or system of meaning. Two prominent examples of explanations of social phenomena reflecting metaphysical holism are structuralism and Foucault's archaeology; in psychology, the Gestalt doctrine is an example of holistic explanation with respect to psychological phenomena. Holism denies that it is possible to reduce explanation of the 'whole' in question to more fundamental parts. Critics of holism call it metaphysical because they claim that social wholes like societies, groups, and states are unobservable and hence nonempirical.

Holism is opposed to methodological individualism (also called explanatory reductionism). This doctrine holds that the basic units of social life are self-directing individuals and that explanation of social phenomena must focus on the decisions, attitudes, actions, and so on of individuals. This view assumes that social wholes are reducible to, and capable of explanation in terms of, the activities of individuals that comprise those wholes.

It is often said that defenders of qualitative inquiry endorse holism and oppose efforts at reductionism. In this argument, however, the term 'holism' seems to be used as a synonym for *contextualism*—that is, the view that the meaning of particular language and human *action* can be understood only in the specific context in which it unfolds.

See also Reductionism.

KEY REFERENCES

Martin, M., & McIntyre, L. C., eds. *Readings in the Philosophy of Social Science.* Cambridge: MIT Press, 1994.

Phillips, D. C. *Holistic Thought in Social Science.* Stanford, CA: Stanford University Press, 1976.

HUMAN ACTION   See ACTION.

HYPERREALITY   This is a term coined by Jean Baudrillard to describe the condition of life in postmodernity. He argued that we live in an era of simulation brought on by technologies of information processing, media, and cybernetic control systems. These technologies implode the once-taken-for-granted boundary between image/simulation and reality such that the very ground of the 'real' disappears. Models and simulations begin to replace 'real' life. Distinctions between what is 'real' and 'unreal' begin to blur, and 'hyperreal' signals that the real becomes artificially reproduced as real. Thus, the hyperreal is not unreal or surreal but more real than real! Hyperreality refers to the condition wherein models of the real replace the real as real. For example, when models of an ideal home, an ideal relationship, or an ideal physical body as portrayed in various media become determinant of a 'real' home, relationship, or body, the boundary between hyperreality and everyday life blurs and eventually disappears. Simulations come to constitute reality itself. The notion figures prominently in discussions in poststructuralist interpretive ethnography of what it means to represent social life in written accounts (see, e.g., N. K. Denzin, *Interpretive Ethnography: Ethnographic Practices for the 21st Century,* Sage, 1997).

See also Cinematic Society.

KEY REFERENCES

Baudrillard, J. *Simulations.* New York: Semiotext(e), 1983.
Best, S., & Kellner, D. *Postmodern Theory.* New York: Guilford, 1991.

HYPOTHETICO-DEDUCTIVE METHOD   The *covering-law model of explanation* holds that human behavior is explained when the inquirer has discovered the relevant generalizations that 'cover' the case to be explained. This model of explanation uses the hypothetico-deductive method to form hypotheses, deduce implications, and test those hypotheses against experience. The steps in the ideal version of the method are: (1) Theory provides the definitions, assumptions, and hypotheses about human behavior; (2) predictions about behavior are logically deduced from theory; (3) those predictions are then tested through a process of empirical observation; (4) based on the results of observations, the inquirer concludes either that the theory is consistent with the facts (i.e., it explains the behavior) or the theory is inconsistent with the facts; (5) if experimental results and theory are consistent, no further work is needed; however, if they are inconsistent, then the theory must either be discarded in favor of a better theory or modified to accommodate the newly required facts. For defenders of the antinaturalist stance of *interpretivism,* this method of explanation is regarded as inappropriate for making sense of human *action.* Interpretivists claim that action cannot be explained but must be understood, hence they argue that the method of *Verstehen* must be used in the human sciences.

KEY REFERENCE

Hollis, M. *The Philosophy of Social Science.* Cambridge, UK: Cambridge University
    Press, 1994.

I

---•◦◆◦•---

IDEALISM This philosophical doctrine holds that the world (reality, real objects) does not exist independently of minds. Idealist explanations of sociocultural and historical phenomena give priority to mental phenomena and thus contrast with materialist explanations that give primacy to material/physical phenomena and processes. Idealism stands in opposition both to *realism,* which defines the world (objects of knowledge) as a real structure that exists independently of our experience with it, our knowledge of it, and the conditions that allow us access to it, and to strict or direct *empiricism,* which claims that the objects of knowledge are simply observable atomistic events. An idealist does not necessarily hold that the natural and social worlds are unreal or nonexistent, but that there is no unmediated access to such worlds—that is, no direct understanding of the world. The world is always interpreted through mind. As is the case with any philosophical notion with a long history, idealism is a complicated view with many varieties. It is a philosophy that tries to say something about what lies behind or beyond experience, and in that sense, early-nineteenth-century German idealism (J. G. Fichte [1762–1814], F. W. J. Schelling [1775–1854], G. W. F. Hegel [1770–1831], all building on Immanuel Kant's [1724–1804] transcendental idealism) served as the fertile ground for the late-nineteenth- and early-twentieth-century reaction to *logical positivism's* insistence on a strict empiricism. The spirit of idealism—its recognition of the importance of mind, life, emotion, and so forth—is a wellspring of qualitative inquiry, although not all so-called qualitative inquirers are necessarily philosophical idealists.

KEY REFERENCES

Bunge, M. *Finding Philosophy in Social Science.* New Haven, CT: Yale University Press, 1996.

Robinson, H. "Berkeley," in *The Blackwell Companion to Philosophy,* N. Bunnin & E. P. Tsui-James, eds. Oxford, UK: Blackwell, 1996.

IDENTITY There is a long psychological and sociological tradition of examining this concept of sameness and unity of self amid change and diversity. The concept has received special attention from about the 1950s onward as notions of the loss of meaning in modern society and the accompanying search for identity began to collide with feminist, postmodernist, and cultural studies and their various examinations of the composition of the subject and the politics of identity. At present, both the terms *identity* and *self* are widely discussed as projects or accomplishments rather than in terms of essences, substances, or categories. It is common to see examinations of an individual's multiple identities that are not simply attributable to individual intention or to classification in terms of familiar categories of race, class, and gender but, rather, the outcome of some collective practical activity or the result of the social construction of a moral-political order. Identities or various 'subject-positions' in society are thought to be constituted in the complex social interaction of language, gesture, bodily significations, desires, intents, and so forth. Identities are simultaneously epiphenomenal (derivative)—in that they are socially bestowed, sustained, or transformed—and phenomenal (material). Whether identities or subject-positions are capable of integration, endure, or have some kind of 'natural' basis behind or beneath them is widely debated. Some postmodernists argue that individuals are 'sites' for competing cultural interpretations of the subject or self and thus are very skeptical of notions such as *an* identity, *a* subject, or *a* self. On this view, identity (or the self) is always fragmented, never integrated, never fixed, always being remade.

KEY REFERENCES

Bauman, Z. *Life in Fragments: Essays in Postmodern Morality.* Oxford, UK: Blackwell, 1995.

Butler, J. *Gender Trouble: Feminism and the Subversion of Identity.* New York: Routledge, 1990.

Lasch, S., & Friedman, J., eds. *Modernity and Identity.* Oxford, UK: Blackwell, 1992.

IDEOLOGY   Although the term has been employed in many ways, one common usage is to refer to a set of social, political, and moral values, and attitudes, outlooks, and beliefs that shape a social group's interpretation of its behavior and its world. Following a usage established by Karl Marx (1818–1883), to label an outlook as ideological typically is to criticize it for obscuring or distorting the truth. Hence, ideologies must be unmasked or disclosed as Dorothy Smith (1990, pp. 42–43) explains: "ideological practices ensure that the determinations of our everyday, experienced world remain mysterious by preventing us from making them problems for inquiry." She urges social inquirers to think ideologically, by which she means "to think in situationally determined modes since ideology deprives us of access to, hence critique of, the social relational substructure of our experience."

KEY REFERENCES

Burbules, N. C. "Forms of Ideology-Critique: A Pedagogical Perspective," in P. L. McLaren & J. M. Giarelli, eds., *Critical Theory and Educational Research.* Albany: SUNY Press, 1995.

Smith, D. *The Conceptual Practices of Power.* Boston: Northeastern University Press, 1990.

Thompson, J. B. *Studies in the Theory of Ideology.* Cambridge, UK: Polity Press, 1984.

IDIOGRAPHIC INTERPRETATION   The German philosopher Wilhelm Windelband (1848–1915) developed the notion that the human or historical sciences aimed at idiographic explanation—a concern with particular instances or sociohistorically situated individual events—whereas the natural sciences were concerned with nomothetic (*lawlike*) explanation—the study of individual events for the purpose of forming general laws. The production of idiographic knowledge served the aims (values, interests) of human self-understanding and self-affirmation, while the pursuit of nomothetic knowledge served the aim of the mastery of nature. Windelband argued that any event could be studied either way (in other words, he did not posit a fundamental difference in the phenomena of the natural and human sciences), but that what distinguished human science was its concern with the method of idiographic interpretation.

This distinction between the individualizing approach of the human sciences and the generalizing approach of the natural sciences is preserved in the methodological traditions of biography, ethnography, and case study.

Robert Stake's (1995) argument for the importance of what he calls 'intrinsic case study'—studying a case because the case itself is of primary interest—is a current restatement of this idea.

KEY REFERENCES

Polkinghorne, D. *Methodology for the Human Sciences.* Albany: SUNY Press, 1983.
Stake, R. *The Art of Case Study Research.* Thousand Oaks, CA: Sage, 1995.

INDEXICALITY   This is a central notion in ***ethnomethodology;*** however, many versions of qualitative inquiry assume that language and action are indexical, which means that the meaning of language or action is dependent upon (i.e., 'indexed to') the context in which it arises. The notion of indexical meanings or expressions challenges the idea that interpretive inquirers merely represent what they hear and see—that is, simply observe and record speech and action. If meanings of speech and action are indexical, then interpreters must somehow come to understand and eventually portray the context in which meanings are situated. This notion of indexicality is apparent in Clifford Geertz's claim that the ethnographer's task is to "inscribe" (write down) social discourse, but that what he or she writes down is not the event of speaking itself (i.e., the language and actions that comprise the discourse) but the "said" of speaking—the meaning of the event, not the event as event. Writing about that context, about situated use, or about what Geertz refers to as the thought, gist, or content of speaking and acting is an act of interpretation, not mere representation.

See also *Contextualism, Description, Inscription, Language, Language Games, Representation.*

KEY REFERENCES

Garfinkel, H. *Studies in Ethnomethodology.* Englewood Cliffs, NJ: Prentice-Hall, 1967.
Geertz, C. "Thick Description: Toward and Interpretive Theory of Culture," in Geertz,
      The Interpretation of Cultures. New York: Basic Books, 1973.
Heritage, J. C. *Garfinkel and Ethnomethodology.* Cambridge, UK: Polity Press, 1984.

INDUCTIVE ANALYSIS   It is commonly said that qualitative studies are distinguishable by their commitment to inductive analysis, which usually is defined as working from the data of specific cases to a more general conclusion. This understanding of inductive analysis, however, is by no means unique to qualitative work—much of probability theory and statistics is part of this logic of induction. There is something of a half-truth in the claim that qualitative studies are inductive. Qualitative analysis often does indeed begin with the data of specific cases, but that simply means that its efforts at analysis are grounded in data and not speculative or abstract. Qualitative analysis often (but not always) seeks to construct hypotheses by mucking around for ideas and hunches in the data rather than deriving those hypotheses in the first instance from established theory. However, typically, qualitative analyses employ some combination of inductive and deductive analyses. The claim that qualitative studies are inductive may actually be a way of saying that they reject the *hypothetico-deductive method* of the natural sciences.

See also Abduction, Explanation, Inference.

KEY REFERENCE

Strauss, A. *Qualitative Analysis for Social Scientists.* Cambridge, UK: Cambridge University Press, 1987.

INDUCTIVE-STATISTICAL EXPLANATION   See EXPLANATION.

INFERENCE   To make an inference is to draw a conclusion from particular premises. Three kinds of rules or procedures for making inferences are *deductive, inductive,* and *abductive.* In deduction, the conclusion must follow from the premises (in other words, it is logically impossible for the conclusion to be false if the premises are true). A common principle of deductive inference (or a legitimate deductive argument) employed in social science is modus tollens, which takes the following form:

Modus Tollens

Premise 1: If *p*, then *q*

Premise 2: Not *q*

Inference: Therefore, not *p*.

Inductive inferences (and arguments) are more typical in social scientific inquiry. One kind of inductive inference relies on the principle of enumeration to reach a general conclusion about a group or class of individuals or events from observations of a specific set of individuals or events. The inference-making process is something like this: I have observed a suitable number of As under a reasonably wide variety of circumstances and have seen that they are Bs; hence, I infer that *all* As are Bs. In other words, I generalize the conclusion derived from my sample of As to all As. (Of course, the potential threat to the integrity of the inference here is how to determine what constitutes a suitable number of observations and a reasonably wide variety of circumstances.) A second kind of inductive inference is a statistical argument, which also depends upon the principle of enumeration but in which the conclusion is stated in probabilistic terms like "most," "many," "rarely," "some," and so on rather than "all" or "always."

An abductive inference (or abductive reasoning) is also called an inference to the best explanation. Imagine that you are examining a set of evidence and have devised a number of possible hypotheses that might explain the evidence. Inference to the best explanation is selecting that one hypothesis that provides the best explanation of the available evidence. The kind of inference making that takes place here assumes that inquiry is a kind of puzzle that requires speculation and best guesses. Abductive inference is explained by C. S. Peirce (1839–1914), but it also bears some similarity to Karl Popper's (1902–1994) conception of science as a process of conjectures and refutations.

See also Abduction, Generalization, Validity.

KEY REFERENCE

Polkinghorne, D. *Methodology for the Human Sciences.* Albany: SUNY Press, 1983.

INFORMANT   This is one of several terms—including *participant, subject, actor, respondent, collaborator, interviewee,* and *the observed*—used to identify the individuals that a researcher studies. Each term implies a different kind of ethical, political, and pedagogical relationship between the researcher and those he or she studies. Anthropological and sociological fieldworkers often make use of informants. Informants are knowledgeable insiders and assist the fieldworker in gaining and maintaining access, developing an insider's understanding (or learning the actor's point of view), and checking emerging understandings. They act as a *fieldwork* assistant, debriefer, and guide and often provide the fieldworker with information on what he or she cannot experience.

A researcher-informant relationship reflects the assumption that the fieldworker is in a position of learning about a culture or group, and the informant serves as a special kind of teacher, guide, and facilitator. This relationship and role is often cultivated by the fieldworker; an informant is identified, selected, and trained to the role. Informants often become the confidant and trusted advisor of the fieldworker, developing a special bond of trust. While rapport characterizes the fieldworker's relationship with most participants in a given study, friendship is more likely with informants.

The growing interest in the politics of fieldwork and the purpose of studying others' ways of life is causing reexamination of the forms of the researcher-researched relationship in several ways. First, although not denying that participants in a particular social setting have their own special perspectives on the action in that setting, postmodern ethnographers are questioning whether the idea of informant is not yet another way to objectify the Other or to use the Other as an extension of the imperialist gaze of the ethnographer. Second, some advocates of participatory approaches to research aim to recast all parties to a study as coparticipants rather than classify them as respondents, informants, researchers, and so on. This is more than a semantic distinction; it signals a democratic impulse underlying the inquiry and a different goal of the inquiry process. Third, some feminist researchers, particularly those committed to action research and participatory inquiry, argue for identification with those one studies and for putting the researcher 'on the same plane' as the respondent.

KEY REFERENCES:

Dean, J. P., Eichorn, R. L., & Dean, L. R. "Fruitful Informants for Intensive Interviewing," in *An Introduction to Social Research,* 2nd ed., J. T. Doby, ed. New York: Appleton-Century-Crofts, 1967.
Wolcott, H. *The Art of Fieldwork.* Walnut Creek, CA: AltaMira Press, 1995.

INFORMED CONSENT Informed consent—the notion that research subjects have the right to know they are being researched, the right to be fully informed about the nature and purpose of the research, the right to know the

risks and benefits of their participation, and the right to withdraw from participation at any time—is one of the standard ethical requirements of all social
research. The idea of obtaining informed consent reflects the moral principle
of respect for persons—that is, treating them as ends, not as means. Many
Institutional Review Boards require that all social researchers obtain a form
of written informed consent. Often this requirement reflects assumptions of a
fairly structured clinical model of research—that is, a clear hypothesis about
some intervention is being tested, the relationship between the researcher and
the research subjects is clearly bounded, procedures involved can be clearly
specified, and actual risks and benefits of the research can be (relatively speaking) described in some detail. (Whether subjects in clinical and biomedical
studies actually are fully capable of making sense of the research or fully
understand the risks entailed by their participation is another matter.) This way
of thinking of the requirement of informed consent as the clear specification
of risks presents some particularly knotty problems for ethnographic
researchers whose research is not nearly as structured, and who often find it
difficult, therefore, to clearly specify risks to participants in advance. In addition, the risks and benefits that participants typically encounter with a fieldworker are, as Bosk and DeVries (2004, p. 253) note,

> often not so different from those of normal interaction with a stranger who
> will become a close acquaintance, an everyday feature of a lifeworld, and
> then disappear, after observing intimate moments, exploring deep feelings,
> and asking embarrassing questions. There is the risk inherent in any fleeting
> human relationship—the risk of bruised feelings that come from being used,
> the loss when a fixture in a social world disappears, or the hurt of realizing
> that however differently it felt at the moment, one was used as a means to an
> end. The risk is magnified by a certain unavoidable deception in every ethno-
> graphic investigation, a certain pretense that comes from trying to have both
> researcher and informant forget that what is going on is not a normal, natural
> exchange but research—not just everyday life as it naturally occurs but work,
> a job, a project—"No really, I'm interested in what you have to say, think,
> feel, and believe for more than my own narrow instrumental academic
> purposes." (p. 253)

In addition to this difficulty in identifying and specifying risks, many
ethnographers, and qualitative researchers using ethnographic methods in field
studies, work across the Northern and Southern Hemispheres, in oral cultures,
or in specific social settings where experiences with a signed consent contract

might be quite alien (and alienating), and where consent may be viewed as a token of Western bureaucratic systems. Finally, field studies often involve observation conducted in public settings—shopping malls, town halls, and board meetings, for example—where obtaining written informed consent in advance from all participants in the setting is difficult, to say the least. None of this means that the requirement for informed consent ought to be abandoned, but that making practical arrangements to honor this ethical principle in qualitative inquiry often requires considerable ingenuity and careful thought.

See also Ethics of Qualitative Inquiry.

KEY REFERENCES

Bosk, C. L., & DeVries, R. G. "Bureaucracies of Mass Deception: Institutional Review Boards and the Ethics of Ethnographic Research," *Annals, AAPSS,* 595 (September 2004), 249–263.

Ryen, A. "Ethical Issues," in C. Seale, G. Gobo, J. F. Gubrium, & D. Silverman, eds., *Qualitative Research Practice.* London: Sage, 2004.

INSCRIPTION   Literally, this term means to "write down," but its connotations in contemporary fieldwork are more profound and suggest that writing down what one sees and hears is not so simple or innocent an act. Clifford Geertz was among the first to challenge the idea that a fieldworker merely observes and records. He argued that the correct answer to the question "What does the ethnographer do?" is "He or she writes." *Postmodern ethnography,* however, challenges the centrality of inscription as the origin of realistic description in fieldwork. Inscription signals that writing down (and this includes photographing, videotaping, or audiotaping) is far from mere mechanical recording. The act of writing requires prior focus, selection, and interpretation. Further, inscription signals an interruption in the fieldworker's attention to the flow of social discourse (speech and action). The fieldworker as participant-observer turns away from that discourse to make a note (mental or written, long field note or scratch note). Hence, inscription is not some orderly process of data 'gathering' but an act of selective attention, a particular kind of practice whereby data are generated, undertaken in the midst of other activity.

See also Description, Field Notes, Representation, Thick Description, Transcription.

KEY REFERENCE

Clifford, J. "Notes on (Field)notes," in R. Sanjek, ed., *Fieldnotes: The Makings of Anthropology.* Ithaca, NY: Cornell University Press, 1990.

INSIDER/OUTSIDER PERSPECTIVE   This is one way of thinking about the difference in the *epistemology* of *interpretivism* versus *naturalism* or the difference between *understanding* and *explanation.* An internalist or insider perspective holds that knowledge of the social world must start from the insider or social actor's account of what social life means. To know the world of human *action* is to understand the subjective meanings of that action to the actors. In contrast, an externalist or outsider perspective argues that knowledge of the social world consists in causal explanations of human behavior. The social world (much like the natural world) can (and should) be viewed with a spectator's detachment. In fact, the externalist argues that this kind of outside objective stance is necessary to develop explanations (much like the explanations fashioned in the natural sciences) that are grounded in either empirical regularities or in underlying causes, mechanisms, and necessities (scientific *realism*).

See also Intentionalism, Subject-Object Relationship.

KEY REFERENCE

Smith, J. K. *The Nature of Social and Educational Inquiry: Empiricism Versus Interpretation.* Norwood, NJ: Ablex, 1989.

INSTITUTIONAL REVIEW BOARD (IRB)   For more than thirty years, the federal government in the United States has had in place rules and mechanisms for protecting the rights of subjects involved in social and biomedical research. In 1974, the U.S. Congress authorized the formation of the National Commission for the Protection of Human Subjects of Biomedical and Behavioral Research and charged it to identify the basic ethical principles that underlie the conduct of research with human beings. In 1979, the commission issued *The Belmont Report: Ethical Principles and Guidelines for the Protection of Human Subjects,* which held that three basic ethical principles underlie all human research—beneficence, respect for persons, and justice. Beginning in 1991, federal regulations, known as the "Common Rule" (formally titled "Protection of Human Subjects"—part 46 Tile 45 of the Code of Federal Regulations), reflecting these principles, were adopted by sixteen federal agencies involved in commissioning federally funded research (including the National Institutes of Health, the National Science Foundation, the Department of Education, the Department of Agriculture, the Department of Health and Human Services, and the Department of Defense). The Common Rule defines research as "a systematic investigation, including research development, testing and evaluation, designed to develop or contribute to generalizable knowledge," and a "human subject" as "a living individual about whom an investigator (whether professional or student) conducting research obtains (1) data through intervention or interaction with the individual, or (2) identifiable private information" (the terms *intervention, interaction,* and *private information* are further defined in the Common Rule). Research institutions (universities, hospitals, private research organizations) must comply with the Common Rule if their investigators are to be eligible to receive funding from one of these agencies. To ensure compliance, the rules require that these institutions must establish an IRB (also known as a Research Ethics Committee) that is vested with the authority to review, require modification, and approve or disapprove research subject to the Common Rule. The IRB's principal role is to determine the risks to subjects involved in the research under review; whether, if appropriate, potential or real benefits outweigh risks; and whether researchers obtained the full, ***informed consent*** of research subjects. For the most part, the Common Rule was directed at medical and psychological studies that involved the greatest risk to human participants. (A similar set of principles and regulations governing the ethical conduct of research is in place in Canada.)

While there has always been analysis and criticism of the ways in which ethical issues are best addressed through various means of conducting human subjects research, as well as assessment of the manner in which IRBs function (see, for example, the journal *IRB: Ethics & Human Research* published by the Hastings Center and the online *IRB Forum* at www.irb.forum.org), beginning approximately around the turn of the century, this criticism reached a new peak with the publication of several influential studies and papers in social science journals. The consensus of these studies was that IRBs were taking a highly conservative approach to the application of the Common Rule, interpreting the principles in a manner most fitting high-risk biomedical clinical research and inappropriately extending that way of thinking to all of the human sciences (including journalism, oral history, ethnographic studies in various fields, other kinds of 'qualitative studies,' and so on). Furthermore, criticisms were directed at IRBs for failing to display considered judgment of how different kinds of research procedures required different ways of making sense of informed consent as well as the risks and benefits of research and the vulnerability of research participants. Qualitative researchers, of all stripes, felt particularly vulnerable and under attack, and calls for the reformation of the ways in which IRBs go about the business of vetting various forms of social research for ethical adequacy have mounted.

See also Ethics of Qualitative Inquiry.

KEY REFERENCES

American Association of University Professors. *Protecting Human Beings: Institutional Review Boards and Social Science Research. Academe,* 2001, 87(3), 55–67.

Bosk, C. L., & DeVries, R. G. "Bureaucracies of Mass Deception: Institutional Review Boards and the Ethics of Ethnographic Research," *Annals, AAPSS,* 595 (September 2004), 249–263.

Canella, G. S., & Lincoln, Y. S., eds. Special Issue: "Dangerous Discourses II: Comprehending and Countering the Redeployment of Discourses (and Resources) in the Generation of Liberatory Inquiry," *Qualitative Inquiry,* 2004, 10(2), 165–309.

Center for Advanced Study. "Improving the System for Protecting Human Subjects: Counteracting IRB 'Mission Creep'." Champaign: College of Law, University of Illinois at Urbana-Champaign. Available at www.cas.uiuc.edu/documents/whitepaper.pdf

Haggerty, K. D. "Ethics Creep: Governing Social Science Research in the Name of Ethics," *Qualitative Sociology,* 2004, 27, 391–414.

Sieber, J. E., Plattner, S., & Rubin, P. "How (Not) to Regulate Social and Behavioral Research," *Professional Ethics Report,* 2002, (15)2, 1–4.

INSTRUMENTALISM   At least three senses of this term are found in the literature on the foundations of qualitative inquiry. First, in the philosophy of science, instrumentalism is an antirealist view of theories and theoretical terms. The logical positivists were instrumentalists (and, not, as is often claimed, realists). They regarded theories and concepts as nothing more than tools, devices, or instruments allowing scientists to move from a set of obser-vation statements to another set of predicted observations. In this sense, logical positivists privileged observation statements over theoretical terms or reduced the latter to the former. Second, a critique of instrumentalism or instrumental rationality as a defining interest of the empirical-analytic sciences figures prominently in the work of critical theorists, postmodernists, poststructuralists, feminists, and contemporary writers on philosophical hermeneutics. Here, the term means something like means-end thinking and is associated with *scientism* and technicism. The argument is that empirical-analytic sciences serve an interest in the prediction and instrumental control of nature. When this interest is extended to the social or human sciences, it results in the manipulation of social relations, the attempt to transform what are essentially moral-political matters into technical problems to be solved, the support of dominant political and social classes and their agendas, and the impoverishment of democratic political discussion. Third, in the pragmatic epistemology of John Dewey (1859–1952), instrumentalism signifies that the truth (warranted assertability) of all concepts and actions resides in the extent to which they function successfully to direct, integrate, and control our interactions with the social and natural world.

See also Pragmatism.

KEY REFERENCES

Fay, B. *Social Theory and Political Practice.* London: Allen and Unwin, 1975.
Thayer, H. S. *Meaning and Action: A Critical History of Pragmatism,* 2nd ed. Indianapolis, IN: Hackett, 1981.

INSTRUMENTAL RATIONALITY   See INSTRUMENTALISM

INTENTIONALISM   All qualitative inquiry at least implicitly assumes that human action is intentional—that is, it reflects the motives, beliefs, attitudes, desires, and so on of actors. Intentionalism is the name for the doctrine that understanding the meaning of human action requires understanding intentions. This doctrine assumes that meaning is a kind of fixed entity or object independent of the inquirer that *resides or is located within* action and is discoverable (hence, the doctrine is often called meaning realism). To understand intentions, the inquirer has two related options. The first is to discover the intentions of the actor, by getting inside the actor's head, so to speak, to discern motives, beliefs, attitudes, and so on. The second is to attempt to discover the intention in the act itself by locating it within some network of actions, language, or practices that give the act its meaning. Intentionalism is one version of *antinaturalism,* but its view of meaning is radically at odds with the conception of meaning found in *philosophical hermeneutics.*

See also Action, Explanation, Interpretivism, Meaning.

KEY REFERENCES

Fay, B. *Contemporary Philosophy of Social Science.* Oxford, UK: Blackwell, 1996.
Roth, P. A. *Meaning and Method in the Social Sciences: A Case for Methodological Pluralism.* Ithaca, NY: Cornell University Press, 1987.

INTENTIONALITY   Originating in Scholastic philosophy, but coming to prominence in the work of the nineteenth-century German philosopher Franz Brentano (1838–1917), intentionality is a central principle of all phenomeno-logical approaches to human inquiry. Its meaning derives from the Latin root *intendo* (to aim at or to extend toward); thus, it does not refer to intentions in the ordinary sense of doing something on purpose. Rather, intentionality signifies a state of engagement with the world; our consciousness or mental states are always 'about' something. It stands in sharp contrast to a Cartesian conception of human agency, which holds that the individual mind, consciousness, or being (human existence) faces a pregiven world on which it 'operates,' so to speak. The agent or knowing subject is distinct from the object to be known. Individual consciousness takes on a project of theoretical contemplation of this pregiven world.

Intentionality is the view that individual consciousness or individual historical being is already 'there' before individual awareness of same. In other words, consciousness or being is part of the pregiven *lifeworld*—consciousness or being is *already engaged* (i.e., historical, temporal, and social). Thus, intentionality stresses the fundamental interaction of mind and world, subject and object. Although we can distinguish subject from object, intentionality means that our experiences of the natural and social world are not a separate sphere of subjective reality that stands in contrast to the sphere of objective reality of the world 'out there.' 'Being' and experience are already in the world, subject and object are always united.

Intentionality calls our attention to the fact that as humans, we are in the first instance (i.e., fundamentally, essentially) beings who are engaged with the world. We are related to the world we experience and live in through structures of meaning and significance. This way of understanding our being or agency as humans stands in sharp contrast to the everyday and scientific assumption that we can experience and engage in the social and natural worlds 'in themselves.' But this kind of objectifying stance of disengagement, this view of our agency as subjects standing over and against the world we experience, is secondary or derivative. We are first and foremost engaged beings, hence the expression *being in the world*. Scholars in the phenomenological tradition (including, among others, Merleau-Ponty, Husserl, Heidegger, Gadamer, and Taylor) argue in various ways that the modern ascendance of the objectifying stance of science (*scientism*) has led to our losing sight of the way in which we as humans are fundamentally engaged with the world, and this in turn has led us to feel alienated from both self and world.

See also *Body, Philosophical Hermeneutics, Subject-Object Relationship.*

KEY REFERENCES

Cooper, D. "Modern European Philosophy," in *The Blackwell Companion to Philosophy,* N. Bunnin & E. P. Tsui-James, eds. Oxford, UK: Blackwell, 1996.
Crotty, M. *The Foundations of Social Research.* London: Sage, 1998.
Taylor, C. *Philosophical Arguments.* Cambridge, MA: Harvard University Press, 1995.

INTEREST   This notion plays an important role in Habermas's critical theory of society. To Habermas, interests are not individual preferences but cognitive or knowledge-constitutive ideas, which means that they determine what counts as knowledge. These interests are also defined as basic or fundamental. In other words, they are not just part of a way of knowing the world (an ***epistemology***) but are also rooted in human nature or particular aspects of social life. Habermas described three primary cognitive interests—technical, practical, and emancipatory—and identified each with a different form of social science. The technical interest requires the isolation of objects and events in order to examine them empirically and form theoretical explanations of them. The empirical-analytic disciplines are informed by this technical interest as well as by a conception of social life as purposive-rational or instrumental action (or simply, work, i.e., the ways in which we manipulate and control our world in order to survive and thrive in it). ***Nomothetic knowledge*** is essential to this conception. The practical interest is concerned with developing intersubjective understanding and agreement on values, meanings, and practices. The historical-hermeneutic disciplines are guided by this interest as well as by the assumption that human life is characterized by interaction or communicative action through which we establish consensual norms for behavior and mutual understanding of intentions and obligations. The emancipatory interest is an effort to provide an account of the genesis of meanings, values, and practices and how they are reflections of changing social structures. Critically oriented social sciences are grounded in this interest as well as in the assumption that reflection about interests is central to social life. Reflection requires free, open communication as well as the material conditions that permit this kind of communication in order to determine how our meanings, practices, and values may be ideologically frozen or distorted. Habermas regarded the emancipatory interest as the most basic interest.

See also *Critical Social Science; Theory, Types of.*

KEY REFERENCE

Habermas, J. *Knowledge and Human Interests,* J. J. Shapiro, trans. Boston: Beacon Press, 1971.

INTERPRETATION   This is the act of clarifying, explicating, or explaining the meaning of some phenomenon. The claims of both the natural and human or social sciences are interpretations in this sense. However, the terms ***interpretivism,*** *interpretive* (or *interpretative*) *social science,* and the ***interpretive turn*** carry a somewhat narrower or more specific meaning. These terms all signal a fundamental difference between the two sciences: The natural sciences explain the behavior of natural phenomena in terms of causes; the human sciences interpret or understand the meaning of social ***action***. In these terms, the notion of interpretation refers to ways of conceiving of the aim and method of the human sciences as informed by the traditions of ***hermeneutics*** and ***Verstehende sociology***.

KEY REFERENCE

Rabinow, P., & Sullivan, W. M., eds. *Interpretive Social Science: A Second Look.* Berkeley: University of California Press, 1987.

INTERPRETIVE ANTHROPOLOGY   This term describes a number of developments in concepts of culture and the method of ethnography that transpired in the late 1960s and early 1970s in anthropology. Interpretive anthropologists understand culture not in terms of social structures and behaviors but in terms of meanings, symbols, and ideas. They view ethnography as a method whereby culture can be read and interpreted as *text* and its meaning(s) inscribed in the accounts prepared by the ethnographer. Interpretive anthropology (or interpretive ethnography) is sometimes contrasted with critical anthropology (or *critical ethnography*)—the former focused on uncovering systems of meaning constructed by human agents, the latter focused on how those meaning systems came to exist and how they function to serve particular interests.

KEY REFERENCES

Geertz, C. *The Interpretation of Cultures.* New York: Basic books, 1973.

Geertz, C. *Local Knowledge: Further Essays in Interpretive Anthropology.* New York: Basic Books, 1983.

Marcus, G. E., & Clifford, M. M. J. *Anthropology as Cultural Critique.* Chicago: University of Chicago Press, 1986.

INTERPRETIVE SOCIOLOGY   Also referred to as *interpretivism* (and *Verstehende* Sociology), this is a shorthand way of referring to several social theories (e.g., *symbolic interactionism, phenomenological sociology, ethnomethodology*) that assign a central place to the method of *Verstehen.* These approaches are also often called *hermeneutic* because they accept the premise that interpretation or understanding is the fundamental way that human beings participate in the world. However, the hermeneutic tradition that traces its roots to Hans-Georg Gadamer (1900–2002) and is developed by Charles Taylor, Jürgen Habermas, Anthony Giddens, Paul Ricoeur (1913–2005), and others is actually critical of interpretive sociology. Criticisms center on two ideas: First, interpretive sociology confines itself largely to the study of subjective meanings, the meanings that reside within individual actors. The hermeneutic tradition argues that this approach ignores the more general underlying structures of intersubjective meanings. Second, apologists for hermeneutical approaches argue that interpretive sociology retains a subject-object dichotomy and an objectivist conception of *method*.

See also Interpretivism.

KEY REFERENCES

Giddens, A. *New Rules of Sociological Method,* 2nd ed. Stanford, CA: Stanford University Press, 1993.

Habermas, J. *On the Logic of the Social Sciences,* S. W. Nicholsen & J. A. Stark, trans. Cambridge: MIT Press, 1988.

Schwandt, T. A. "Three Epistemological Stances for Qualitative Inquiry: Interpretivism, Hermeneutics, and Social Constructionism," in N. K. Denzin & Y. S. Lincoln, eds., *The Handbook of Qualitative Research,* 2nd ed. Thousand Oaks, CA: Sage, 2000.

INTERPRETIVE TURN   This is a term designating a widespread interest in the epistemological, political, and moral aspects of the nature, origin, and justification of interpretations across several disciplines including philosophy, literary criticism, cultural anthropology, jurisprudence, and sociology. It also includes the study of interpretations as an activity in the natural sciences.

KEY REFERENCES

Hiley, D. R., Bohman, J. F., & Shusterman, R., eds. *The Interpretive Turn: Philosophy, Science, Culture.* Ithaca, NY: Cornell University Press, 1991.

Mitchell, W. J. T., ed. *The Politics of Interpretation.* Chicago: University of Chicago Press, 1982.

INTERPRETIVISM   (Or the interpretivist tradition) This term is occasionally used as a synonym for all qualitative inquiry, blurring important distinctions in intellectual traditions. More accurately, the term denotes those approaches to studying social life that accord a central place to **Verstehen** as a method of the human sciences, that assume that the meaning of human action is inherent in that action, and that the task of the inquirer is to unearth that meaning.

See also Ethnographic Naturalism, Intentionalism, Interpretive Sociology, Meaning, Naturalistic Inquiry.

KEY REFERENCE

Giddens, A. *New Rules of Sociological Method,* 2nd ed. Stanford, CA: Stanford University Press, 1993.

INTERSUBJECTIVITY   Literally, this means occurring between or among (or accessible to) two or more separate subjects or conscious minds. Thus, intersubjective criticism and agreement are regarded as one means of establishing the *objectivity* of a claim.

For many qualitative inquirers, the term signifies the character or nature of the *lifeworld* and the social constitution of the self. The everyday world is made up of our individual interpretations of experience, behavior, action, meaning, and so forth. These interpretations, however, are not simply subjective (i.e., the perspectives of individual subjects), and we could not understand shared or common interpretations by somehow summing up or averaging the interpretations of all subjects. Our interpretive schemes, our ways of making meaning of experience, are essentially intersubjective, socially constituted through symbolic interaction. Hence, intersubjectivity lies at the heart of subjectivity as well as objectivity.

See also Action, Meaning.

KEY REFERENCES

Mead, G. H. *Selected Writings,* A. J. Reck, ed. New York: Bobbs-Merrill, 1964.
Taylor, C. "Interpretation and the Sciences of Man," in C. Taylor, *Philosophy and the Human Sciences, Philosophical Papers 2.* Cambridge, UK: Cambridge University Press, 1985. (Originally published in *Review of Metaphysics,* 1971, 25, 3–51)

INTERTEXTUALITY   See DIALOGISM, TEXT.

INTERVIEWING LOGIC   Behind every interview there is a working model or logic informing one's understanding of the parties to an interview and the interview process. The conventional model or logic regards the interview process as a means of gaining direct access to an interviewee's experience. The interview is a behavioral event—that is, verbal behavior, a verbal exchange, or pattern of verbal interaction. The interviewee is regarded as a passive vessel of answers for the kind of factual and experiential questions put to her or him by the interviewer. Using the logic of stimulus-response (question and answer), the interviewer aims to ask the right questions so as to elicit responses in the form of authentic feelings and meanings of the interviewee. The interviewer follows procedures for questioning and behaving in such a way that he or she does not contaminate the process or bias the interviewee and prevent the outpouring of accurate, authentic accounts from the interviewee. The interviewer must remain neutral in the interview process—that is, he or she must not shape the information that is being extracted from the vessel of answers. The interview situation itself is regarded as an event that is isolated from cultural and situational norms and frameworks of meaning that typically shape all kinds of encounters between individuals in society.

An alternative model or logic regards interviewing as a particular kind of discursive, narrative, or linguistic event or practice unfolding in a specific sociopolitical context. In this event, interviewer and respondent are regarded as agents active in the coconstruction of the content of the interview (hence, the interview is referred to as the *active* interview). What transpires in the interview is the dynamic, purposeful shaping of stories and experiences on the part of the interviewee. As Holstein & Gubrium (2003, p. 14) explain, "the active respondent can hardly 'spoil' what he or she is, in effect, subjectively constructing in the interview process. Rather, the active subject pieces experiences together before, during, and after occupying the respondent role. The subject is always making meaning, regardless of whether he or she is actually being interviewed." Similarly, the interviewer's behavior is not considered in terms of contamination or bias; rather, that behavior is unavoidably part of the communicative event in which the interviewee's meaning is assembled in its narration. Framing interviews in this way requires not simply attending to *what* was said by each party in the interview but also to *how* the joint meaning-making process unfolds.

See also Interviewing, Types of.

KEY REFERENCES

Gubrium, J. F., & Holstein, J. A. "Inside Interviewing: New lenses, New Concerns," in J. F. Gubrium & J. A. Holstein, eds., *Inside Interviewing: New Lenses, New Concerns.* Thousand Oaks, CA: Sage, 2003.

Holstein, J. A., & Gubrium, J. F. *The Active Interview.* Thousand Oaks, CA: Sage, 1995.

Kvale, S. *InterViews: An Introduction to Qualitative Research Interviewing.* Thousand Oaks, CA: Sage, 1996.

Mishler, E. *Research Interviewing: Context and Narrative.* Cambridge, MA: Harvard University Press, 1986.

INTERVIEWING, TYPES OF   It is commonplace to classify interviews as either structured (closed, forced-choice responses) or unstructured (open-ended responses). The latter category is then further subdivided into informal conversational interviews, the interview guide approach, and the standardized open-ended interview. An alternative classification probes more deeply into the rationale for unstructured and structured approaches and organizes interviews in terms of the kind of research task involved and the kind of knowledge sought, as shown in Table I.1 (based on Silverman, 2001, pp. 86–98). The typical in-depth, semistructured, or unstructured interview aims to elicit stories of experience. The *active* interview is framed as an interactional encounter. Note that ***oral history*** interviews do not fit neatly in this classification. They are something of a hybrid between fact-finding and elicitation of stories and memories of experience.

See also *Interviewing Logic.*

KEY REFERENCES

Patton, M. Q. *Qualitative Research & Evaluation Methods,* 3rd ed. Thousand Oaks, CA: Sage, 2002 (Chapter 7, "Qualitative Interviewing").

Silverman, D. *Interpreting Qualitative Data: Methods for Analysing Talk, Text, and Interaction,* 2nd ed. London: Sage, 2001.

INTERVIEW SOCIETY   This term coined by David Silverman (1993) signifies that we live in a society in which interviews seem central to making sense of our lives. In such a society, selves and identities are constructed through interviews. The popularity and use of the interview form—in talk shows, news interviews, celebrity profiles, film, and so on—leads us to expect that persons, if properly asked, will reveal their innermost lives, their authentic selves, to the expert interviewer (as journalist, priest, detective, psychoanalyst, or researcher). Silverman argues that an interview society is characterized by

Table I.1   Types of Interviews

Interview Type	Influences	Type of Knowledge Sought	Research Task
Fact-finding	Empiricism Logical empiricism Logical positivism	Facts about behaviors and attitudes; beliefs; feelings and motives; standards of action (what the respondent thinks should or could be done in a specific situation); present and past behaviors; conscious reasons	Generate factual data—data that are valid independent of research setting and researcher behavior
Elicitation of stories of experience	Ethnographic naturalism Intentionalism Naturalistic inquiry	Authentic accounts of lived (subjective), inner experience including emotions, feelings, etc.	Generate 'in-depth' data that are the product of the empathetic relationship between interviewee and interviewer as peers, companions, conversational partners, etc.
Interactional encounter	Ethnomethodolgy Social constructionism	Interviewee's responses are not simply representations of the world, but in part constitute the world they describe	Combined focus on both the form (*how* did meaning making happen) and the content (*what* was said) of the interview

three conditions: First, there must be a sense that the self is the proper object of narration—a belief in the idea that subjectivity informs. Every individual has the potential to be a respondent and has something meaningful to offer when interviewed. Second, there must be an information-gathering apparatus—a "technology of the confessional"—that serves as a practical means to secure the product of the interview (i.e., the 'confession'). Third, interviewing as a mass technology must be readily available and recognizably in place in society, such that just about everyone knows what it takes to be an interviewer or interviewee.

KEY REFERENCES

Atkinson, P., & Silverman, D. "Kundera's *Immortality:* The Interview Society and the Invention of the Self," *Qualitative Inquiry,* 1997, 3(3), 304–325.

Gubrium, J. F., & Holstein, J.,A. "From the Individual Interview to the Interview Society," in J.,F. Gubrium & J.,A. Holstein, eds., *Postmodern Interviewing.* Thousand Oaks, CA: Sage, 2003.

Silverman, D. *Interpreting Qualitative Data: Methods for Analysing Talk, Text, and Interaction.* London: Sage, 1993.

Silverman, D. *Qualitative Research: Theory, Method, and Practice.* London: Sage, 1997.

J

JUDGMENT A judgment is a considered, deliberate opinion based on good reasons. As a means of reaching a decision or resolving disagreements, judgment is often contrasted with alogrithmic, technical, rule-bound, or procedural decision making. Judgment is also distinguished from the expression of mere opinion or taste. Judgment requires an ability to unite general principles, standing commitments, and established conventions or rules with the specifics of the situation at hand. Knowing how to make good judgments is essential in every aspect of being a researcher.

A common mistake in the education of inquirers is that of confusing the development of methodological prowess in the form of knowledge of procedures and technique with the ability to make good judgments. Two examples should suffice to make the point: A researcher can be adept at procedures for the statistical design and analysis of quasi-experiments, but no amount of procedural knowledge will help that researcher determine which rival hypotheses are most important to consider in a given research situation and what is the best way to rule them out. Likewise, a fieldworker can have a thorough grasp of all the principles involved in conducting a 'good' interview—including design of the interview, knowledge of appropriate interviewer behaviors, and knowledge of the ethical principles of informed consent, confidentiality, and protecting the rights of informants—but be incapable of offering good reasons for a sound judgment in response to the question, "How will you approach the interview with Bob on Monday?"

See also Praxis.

KEY REFERENCES

Barber, B. *The Conquest of Politics.* Princeton, NJ: Princeton University Press, 1988.
Bernstein, R. J. *Beyond Objectivism and Relativism: Science, Hermeneutics, and Praxis.* Philadelphia: University of Pennsylvania Press, 1983.
Larmore, C. E. *Patterns of Moral Complexity.* Cambridge, UK: Cambridge University Press, 1987.

JUSTIFICATION OF A CLAIM   See EVIDENCE.

K

———⊷◆⊶———

KNOWLEDGE   One of the primary reasons that the field of qualitative inquiry is so diverse and broad is that it is a site in which metatheoretical debates about the nature of knowledge and its production are being played out. Although it is most likely that the majority of practitioners of the various kinds of qualitative inquiry do not actively entertain or engage in these debates, the issues nonetheless foreground their work. In the brouhaha that often surrounds efforts to label this view or that as postpositivist, constructionist, empiricist, postmodernist, interpretivist, feminist, poststructuralist, and so forth, it is easy to lose sight of the fact that all of these perspectives are struggling with a set of issues concerning the nature of knowledge and its justification. These issues can very roughly be captured as follows: (a) What is knowledge? Is knowledge the search for foundations, or is it about dismantling taken-for-granted foundations? Is it characterized by a quest for certainty or by acceptance of fundamental fallibility? Are knowledge, values, and politics inevitably intertwined, or ought they be kept separate? (b) Who is the 'knower'—a single, solitary, disengaged critically reflective mind; an engaged, embodied, dialogical self? (c) What are we attempting to know in the human sciences—meanings, processes, accomplishments, causes, structures, or forces? (d) How do we generate knowledge—via method, intuition, reason, sensory experience? (e) What is the scope of a claim to know—general, universal, atemporal or particular, individual, and temporal? (f) What form should knowledge take—discursive, narrative, practical, tacit, propositional?

At one time or another in the history of our thinking about the form and function of knowledge, strong arguments have been assembled for all of the possible answers to the questions listed above. Despite these different ways of thinking, however, there is something of working consensus in

Anglo-American thought about what knowledge is. What is being played out in the arena of qualitative inquiry is a set of manifold criticisms of the following most fundamental assumptions concerning knowledge across the disciplines, as explained by Elizabeth Grosz (1993):

1. The centrality and neutrality of *method* to the production of knowledge: Methods, procedures, and techniques used to generate socially legitimate knowledge are assumed to be transparent and neutral instruments or intellectual tools that contribute to the growth of knowledge but do not constitute the object of knowledge. Any contribution or influence that these tools might have on what it is that we seek to know can be calculated and distinguished from the object of knowledge. These tools are not integral to our understanding of what knowledge is but only convenient for it, thus they do not distort, manipulate, or constrain (in ways beyond calculation) that which we seek to know.

2. The scope and limits of knowledge are set by boundaries within and between the disciplines of the human and natural sciences: For example, psychology deals with the 'interior' of subjects, sociology with the 'exterior'; philosophy deals with the universal, history with the particular. Grosz claims that "although the boundaries are not *immutable,* enabling some cross-fertilization between disciplines, nevertheless each defines and is defined by both a mainstream or core and a periphery or margins. These margins and the *spaces between disciplines* are unable to be theorized in the terms of the core—that is, within the discipline itself" (p. 190).

3. Shared assumptions about the *criteria* according to which knowledge is judged to be valid or true: These criteria include clarity, precision, the capacity to be verified or falsified, parsimony, communicability, translatability, and so forth. Grosz argues, "underlying these [criteria] is a belief that the object of investigation, whether a text, human behavior, or social interactions, exists independently of knowledge of it, presuming a 'reality' resistant to false or invalid methods, misinterpretation, or misrepresentation" (p. 191).

4. The presumption that knowledge is atemporal and transgeographic: Even though knowledge is produced at specific times and in specific places, the genesis of knowledge is considered irrelevant to its nature: "Knowledges do not carry the index of their origins" (p. 191).

5. The presumption that genuine knowledge is neither personal or idiosyncratic: "The knowing subject who produces knowledge is, as it were, bracketed off from the knowledges thus produced" (p. 191).

See also Epistemology, Paradigmatic Knowledge Claim.

KEY REFERENCE

Grosz, E. "Bodies and Knowledge: Feminism and the Crisis of Reason," in L. Alcoff & E. Potter, eds., *Feminist Epistemologies.* New York: Routledge, 1993.

L

LANGUAGE Underlying virtually all contemporary versions of qualitative inquiry is the belief that language is central to understanding meaning and being. This belief, in turn, rests on an important distinction between two different families of language theories. One family is variously called empiricist, representational, referential, designative, descriptive, or the picture theory of language; the other family includes theories of the pragmatics of language, the 'use' theory of language, and the expressivist-constitutive theory of language.

The picture theory of language assumes that the mind contains concepts and ideas that presumably represent an external reality (the ways things are). Knowledge consists in having ideas that reliably and accurately represent reality. The words in our language are given meaning by being attached to (depicting) the things being represented via our ideas that represent them. In other words, the way things are shapes the way we (perceive and) conceive them, and this, in turn, is expressed in the language we use. Thus, the meaning of words and sentences is explained by the way they depict or represent the world. In this theory, language is an instrument or tool at our disposal by which we gain objective knowledge of the world. Because the picture theory of language is primarily about how language represents the world, two kinds of concerns dominate. The first is understanding the syntactical relations of language, its logical structure; the second is defining the semantic relations of a language, the way in which words are linked with observations.

In pragmatic and expressivist-constitutive views of language, the relationship of language to the world is reversed. These theories assume that our language shapes what we see and how we see it, and those things shaped by language constitute reality. [Note: One must be careful here in making sense of the notion of 'constitutes.' A radical interpretation of this notion, found in some versions of *social constructionism* and *poststructuralism,* is linguistic idealism—the thesis that there is nothing more to reality than our symbolic interpretations or that reality is a product of our linguistic practices. A more moderate interpretation concedes that indeed there is a language-independent reality but that our awareness and understanding of that reality are mediated by interpretation and language. In other words, there is no direct, language-free cognition.] On these views, language is a range of activities in which we express and realize a certain way of making sense of and being in the world. The meaning of words and sentences cannot be simply explained by their ability to designate or depict something. Rather, the meaning of words and sentences is also explained by their relation to other words and sentences as well as how they are used.

Two different kinds of concerns (often, but not always, interrelated) are characteristic of this family of theories. The first is a practical interest— understanding the different ways in which words and sentences are used to accomplish something (e.g., to give an order, to tell a joke, to make a description). This interest is readily apparent in the centrality of the notion of *index- icality* in *ethnomethodology* and *conversation analysis.* It also underlies those versions of *social constructionism* concerned with the way in which meaning is generated in language. The second is an ontological and phenomenological interest—understanding how it is that language constitutes being. Here, language is not regarded as a tool at our disposal but as itself constituting a framework in which we have purposes, behaviors, meanings, and so forth. Notions like 'we are language beings' or 'language does not belong to us, we belong to language' stem from this interest. This interest in 'linguisticality' (in the idea that language constitutes being) stands in opposition to a central doctrine in modern versions of humanism that underlie empiricist epistemology, namely, the autonomous, self-actualizing, atomistic self. In this doctrine, knowledge and meaning arise within the subject, the individual knower. Human *agency* is decidedly 'monological.' In the expressivist-constitutive view, however, language is a background or framework that we belong to, not a practice we partake in, or a tool that we as individual knowing agents choose to use. Thus, human agency is engaged and 'dialogical'; we are always already participating in practices and understandings that are not located in me or in you as individuals but in the common spaces between us. The linguistic (or discursive) nature of being figures prominently, albeit in quite different ways, in the *genealogy* of Foucault, Heidegger's existential *phenomenology,* Gadamer and Taylor's *philosophical hermeneutics,* and Derrida's *deconstructionism.*

See also Discourse Analysis, Language Games, Meaning, Semiotics.

KEY REFERENCES

Shapiro, M. J. *Language and Political Understanding: The Politics of Discursive Practices.* New Haven, CT: Yale University Press, 1981.
Taylor, C. *Philosophical Arguments.* Cambridge, MA: Harvard University Press, 1995.

LANGUAGE GAMES This notion originates in Ludwig Wittgenstein's (1889–1951) later writings, particularly his *Philosophical Investigations* (1952). Here, in an apparent rejection of his earlier views, Wittgenstein advanced the notion that words and sentences do not have meanings because they designate, refer to, or depict reality. Rather, words and sentences acquire their meanings because they are used in some rule-governed, self-contained practice like a game. As examples of language games, Wittgenstein mentioned giving orders and obeying them, describing the appearance of an object, forming and testing a hypothesis, reporting an event, and making a joke or telling a joke. Thus, the notion of language games as forms of life (combinations of intentions, motivations, speech, action, interests, and so on) was used to direct attention away from language as designation to language as activity.

The picture theory of language and its concern with what and how terms designate or represent was a principal preoccupation in Wittgenstein's earlier work and a central concern of the philosophy of logical positivism. Thus, the significance and meaning of concepts like truth and knowledge were to be found in a logical analysis of language and in efforts to develop a theory of semantic rules linking concepts with observations. Wittgenstein's later work turns away from this concern with linking meaning of words to the syntactic and semantic properties of statements and propositions and toward an understanding of how the meaning of words arises within and is fixed by different linguistic practices.

The philosopher Peter Winch (1926–1967) linked the notion of language games to the notion of *Verstehen* and argued that understanding the meaning of language and action is possible only if one understands the different language games or social practices in which that language and action occur. Variations on this idea of how linguistic practices shape social reality are foundational to pragmaticist, phenomenological, constructionist, hermeneutic, and poststructural theories.

For example, a radical interpretation of the notion of language games leading to the view that all meanings are relative to some particular culture, way of life, group, or social practice is found in some versions of social constructionism. This view unfolds as follows: Taking their cue from Wittgenstein's notion of language games (as elaborated by Winch), some radical social constructionists begin with the premise that language is embedded in social practices or forms of life. They then argue that different language games or different forms of life are incommensurable. In other words, the rules that govern a particular form of life circumscribe and close off that form of life to others. Hence, it is only within and with reference to a particular form of life that the meaning of words and actions can be deciphered, described, and understood. Thus, standards for rationally evaluating beliefs are completely dependent on the particular language game or form of life in which those beliefs arise. No evaluation of beliefs *across* different forms of life is possible. Hence, this is epistemological relativism.

Another radical interpretation of the notion of language games called linguistic idealism—the notion that reality is nothing but the product of linguistic convention—is offered by some postmodernists and poststructuralists. John Patrick Diggins (*The Promise of Pragmatism: Modernism and the Crisis of Knowledge and Authority,* University of Chicago Press, 1994, p. 435) provides a brief and not particularly charitable summary of this view as

> the conviction that all human cognition is inescapably verbal or textual and consists of a web of unstable, dancing signifiers having no reference to a reality beyond the text; words full of sound and fury signifying not nothing but almost everything, as though the script were out of control; philosophers assuming they are looking for truth and waking up to realize they are only writing words about words, manipulating metaphors, alternating verbal images. (p. 435)

See also Language, Meaning.

KEY REFERENCES

Bernstein, R. J. *The Restructuring of Social and Political Theory.* Philadelphia: University of Pennsylvania Press, 1976.

Turner, S. R. *Sociological Explanation as Translation.* Cambridge, UK: Cambridge University Press, 1980.

Winch, P. *The Idea of a Social Science and Its Relation to Philosophy.* London: Routledge & Kegan Paul, 1958.

LAWLIKE GENERALIZATION   Lawlike does not mean almost a law; rather, the terms *lawlike, nomological,* or *nomothetic* are meant to distinguish generalizations that have the force of laws from those that are merely accidental. Generalizations that have lawlike force state what *must* be the case. I might claim 'All the books on the bookshelf in my office are published in the United States.' (A generalization because it is in the form 'All *X's* are *A's.*') That may in fact be true, but its truth is accidental; the statement is not a lawlike generalization because it does not possess the quality of unrestricted necessity.

See also Generalization.

KEY REFERENCE

Little, D. *Varieties of Social Explanation: An Introduction to the Philosophy of Social Science.* Boulder, CO: Westview Press, 1991.

LEBENSWELT   See **LIFEWORLD.**

LIFE-HISTORY METHODOLOGY   See **BIOGRAPHICAL RESEARCH.**

LIFEWORLD   The everyday world or the life world (*Lebenswelt*) is the intersubjective world of human experience and social action; it is the world of commonsense knowledge of everyday life. It is constituted by the thoughts and acts of individuals and the social expressions of those thoughts and acts (e.g., laws, institutions). The lifeworld (and its phenomena) is regarded as the primary object for study by the human sciences. Describing what the lifeworld consists of—that is, the structures of experience and the principles and concepts that give form and meaning to the lifeworld—has been the project of *phenomenology.* Edmund Husserl (1859–1938) claimed that the lifeworld was the basis for meaning in every science; in all natural and social science (as well as logic and mathematics) the lifeworld is presupposed and pregiven. Husserl's transcendental phenomenological philosophy sought to explain the existence and meaning of the lifeworld. He distinguished between the "natural attitude," characteristic of our being in the lifeworld—our everyday relatively unproblematic involvement with people, things, the world—and the "phenomenological attitude," the philosophical act of pure reflection in which we suspend, distance ourselves from, or bracket all the intentions, awareness, and convictions characteristic of the natural attitude. This posture Husserl called the transcendental epoché ("transcendental" meaning literally to get beyond or transcend the limits of ordinary experience). Husserl argued that by making the phenomenological reduction (bracketing)—moving back from the natural attitude to the phenomenological attitude—we are capable of recognizing the true nature and meaning of the lifeworld, its ultimate transcendental ground, which, in Husserl's view, was the transcendental ego (a quite complex notion in Husserl's philosophy).

Building on Husserl's work, but relinquishing somewhat the attachment to phenomenological psychology and transcendental philosophy, Alfred Schutz (1899–1956) developed a descriptive phenomenology of the lifeworld or a *phenomenological sociology*. Schutz analyzed the concepts of subjective meaning, action, experience, intentionality, behavior, and intersubjectivity and thereby sought to develop a theory that explained the lifeworld. (For a brief summary and critique of some of Schutz's major ideas as they relate to defining the aim of social inquiry, see R. J. Bernstein, *The Restructuring of Social and Political Theory,* Part III, University of Pennsylvania Press, 1976.)

Philosophical hermeneutics is also concerned with understanding the principles and organization of the lifeworld but from a somewhat different perspective. Rather than portray the structures or features of the lifeworld, philosophical hermeneutics is concerned with understanding how we are part of or engaged with that world and how conditions of our engagement (e.g., language, the nature and structures of communication) make interpreting that world an inescapable feature of our existence.

See also Action, Multiple Realities.

KEY REFERENCES

Husserl, E. *The Crisis of European Sciences and Transcendental Phenomenology,* D. Carr, trans. Evanston, IL: Northwestern University Press, 1970.

Schutz, A. *Collected Papers,* Vol. 1. M. Natanson, trans. The Hague, The Netherlands: Martinus Nijhoff, 1967.

Schutz, A. *The Phenomenology of the Social World,* G. Walsh and F. Lehnert, trans. Evanston, IL: Northwestern University Press, 1967.

LIMINALITY   *Limen* is the Latin word for *threshold*—that point, for example, in a doorway separating one room from another. Liminality, as often discussed by the social anthropologist Victor Turner (1920–1983), describes the cognitive and emotive state of being 'in-between,' neither here nor there. In means being between stages, on the margins, in an indeterminate state, occupying yet questioning one's own position. Turner argued that liminality occurs during changes in one's social status and/or psychological state, as, for example, during a rite of passage or while on a pilgrimage.

See also *Understanding*.

KEY REFERENCE

Turner, V. *Dramas, Fields, and Metaphors: Symbolic Action in Human Society.* Ithaca, NY: Cornell University Press, 1974.

LITERARY TURN (IN SOCIAL SCIENCE)   This phrase refers to the increasing interest in recent decades in examining the literary or rhetorical features of the texts produced by social inquirers. It does not simply point to a form of literary criticism concerned only with tropes, narrative strategies, and other textual devices, however. Rather, it reflects the assumption that writing is central to what social inquirers do both in the field and after, and that writing about others is part of the complex process of social construction and reconstruction of reality. The literary turn introduced the idea that socio-logical and anthropological texts are fiction—that is, made or crafted by the inquirer—and thus shaped by rhetorical, political, institutional, and discipli-nary conventions.

The examination of fieldwork texts as literature is intimately linked to the issue of ***representation***. It challenges naïve ***ethnographic realism*** and assumptions about transparency of representation and the immediacy and authenticity of field experience. Within the literary turn, the examination of written texts becomes a means of addressing questions about the methodology, epistemology, politics, authority, and ethics of the activity of social inquiry. Literary processes (e.g., metaphor, figuration, and narrative) at work in texts are explored to understand how they help constitute the inquirer-as-author and the human ***action*** and people he or she seeks to represent.

See also *Rhetoric, Text, Voice, Writing Strategies*.

KEY REFERENCES

Atkinson, P. *The Ethnographic Imagination: Textual Constructions of Reality.* London: Routledge, 1990.

Geertz, C. *Works and Lives: The Anthropologist as Author.* Stanford, CA: Stanford University Press, 1988.

Hunter, A., ed. *The Rhetoric of Social Research Understood and Believed.* New Brunswick, NJ: Rutgers University Press, 1990.

LITERATURE REVIEW   See REVIEW OF LITERATURE.

LIVED EXPERIENCE   See EXPERIENCE.

LOGICAL EMPIRICISM   This mid-twentieth-century more moderate version of *logical positivism* informs contemporary mainstream thinking in the philosophy of social science. It is represented in the work of Ernest Nagel (1901–1985), Hans Reichenbach (1891–1953), Rudolph Carnap (1891–1970), Carl Hempel (1905–1997), and to some extent Karl Popper (1902–1994) in *The Logic of Scientific Discovery* (1958). Three ideas central to this view are (1) the *covering-law model of explanation,* (2) the unity of sciences thesis, and (3) the distinction between the *context of discovery* and the *context of justification.* Logical empiricists hold that the aim of science is the development of theoretical explanations and that legitimate explanations, in turn, take the form of general (covering) laws; events to be explained are subsumed under covering laws. The controversy regarding what constitutes a legitimate scientific explanation and whether there can be laws in social science centers around the defense and critique of this central logical empiricist idea (see, for example, the collection of papers in Part II of *Readings in the Philosophy of Social Science,* M. M. Martin & L. C. McIntyre, eds., MIT Press, 1994). Logical empiricists also argue for the unity of the sciences, claiming that both natural and social sciences have the same aim and that there are no basic methodological differences between the two. They believe that philosophers like Wilhelm Dilthey (1833–1911), Max Weber (1864–1920), Alfred Schutz (1899–1956), Peter Winch (1926–1997), and others who claimed that there was a fundamental difference between explanation and understanding as goals of the natural and social sciences, respectively, were mistaken. In their view, the idea of pursuing an understanding of the 'meaning' of human action was a residue of metaphysical thinking. Finally, logical empiricists also draw a sharp line between the process involved in creating a theory or hypothesis (context of discovery) and the process required for testing that theory or hypothesis (context of justification). This distinction along with the **covering-law** model of explanation and the **naturalism** of logical empiricism are the foils for hermeneutic and phenomenological approaches to social inquiry. Despite a variety of criticisms of various features of this philosophy of science, the generalized picture of logical empiricism has become something of a vision of what the social sciences should be (see, for example, D. C. Phillips, *The Expanded Social Scientist's Bestiary,* Rowman & Littlefield, 2000).

See also Naturalism.

KEY REFERENCES

Brown, H. I. *Perception, Theory and Commitment: The New Philosophy of Science.* Chicago: University of Chicago Press, 1977.

Hempel, C. *Philosophy of Natural Science.* Englewood Cliffs, NJ: Prentice Hall, 1966.

Nagel, E. *The Structure of Science: Problems in the Logic of Scientific Explanation.* London: Routledge & Kegan Paul, 1961.

Reichenbach, H. *The Rise of Scientific Philosophy.* Berkeley: University of California Press, 1951.

LOGICAL POSITIVISM   From about 1922 to 1940, a group composed largely of philosophers and scientists that came to be known as the Vienna Circle developed a philosophy of science they called logical positivism. This philosophy enjoyed about a 30-year life before the weight of criticisms of these doctrines caused its internal collapse. It developed into a more moderate philosophy called *logical empiricism*. Logical positivism is a particular species of analytic or linguistic philosophy preoccupied with scientific philosophy; that is, it aimed to solve a special set of problems arising out of the activity and claims of the natural sciences. Its method was that of the analysis of scientific language—analyzing concepts, propositions, and scientific sentences in order to develop a transparent linguistic framework modeled on formal logic. It sought to discover the uniform logical structure of language and thus establish the foundation for all knowledge claims about the world.

From the positivist philosophy of Auguste Comte (1798–1857) and the *empiricism* of David Hume (1711–1776), the logical positivists appropriated the idea of a strong critique of *metaphysics* and a devotion to the value of empirical observations. From the analytic philosophers Ludwig Wittgenstein (1889–1951) (*Tractatus Logico-Philosophicus,* which first appeared in 1921), Bertrand Russell (1872–1970) (*Introduction to Mathematical Philosophy,* 1919), and Alfred North Whitehead (1861–1947) (coauthor with Russell of the three volume *Principia Mathematica,* 1910–1913), the logical positivists developed the idea of constructing a logically correct language that would readily distinguish between meaningful and meaningless scientific propositions. (Note, however, that Wittgenstein, Russell, and Whitehead were not positivists and rejected the scientistic, empiricist philosophy of the Vienna Circle.)

This philosophy rested on the central notion that there are only two legitimate forms of scientific inquiry that yield genuine knowledge: logical analysis and empirical research. Although there was not complete unanimity in the outlook of the group, generally they endorsed three central doctrines:

1. The verification theory of meaning: To be considered genuine, legitimate, and meaningful, a knowledge claim about the world must be capable of verification.

2. The doctrine of meaningful statements: Only two kinds of statements are of any value in scientific knowledge—the analytic statements of mathematics and logic, which are knowable a priori, and synthetic or contingent statements, which are knowable a posteriori based on verification through observation. Statements that are not capable of expression in either of these forms are not verifiable and, therefore, at best irrelevant to scientific knowledge and at worst meaningless. Hence, logical positivism was extremely hostile to theological and metaphysical speculation about the world. In fact, the logical positivists disdained the appellation 'positivists' because they felt that August Comte's philosophy of science was entirely too metaphysical.

3. A foundationalist epistemology: All justified belief ultimately rests on noninferential self-evident observations (protocol statements or observation statements).

See also Positivism.

KEY REFERENCES

Ayers, A. J., ed. *Logical Positivism.* New York: Free Press, 1959.
Friedman, M. *Reconsidering Logical Positivism.* Cambridge. UK: Cambridge University Press, 1999.

LOGOCENTRISM   See DECONSTRUCTIONISM.

M

MARGINAL NATIVE   See **PARTICIPANT OBSERVATION**.

MATERIALIST EXPLANATION   See **EXPLANATION**.

MEANING   A taken-for-granted assumption in qualitative inquiry is that it studies meaningful social *action*. What does it mean, however, to say that human or social action is meaningful or has meaning? Minimally, human action is considered meaningful in the sense that it cannot be adequately described in purely physical terms. Consider, for example, witnessing the identical physical movement of raising one's right hand above one's shoulder as performed by a woman on a busy city street as she steps to the curb; a third grader in a classroom; a witness stepping to the stand in a courtroom. In all three instances, the same physical phenomenon is observed, but in each instance, the meaning of the action is different. Moreover, the significance of the action cannot be adequately explained in terms of a behaviorist stimulus-response model. What comprises the meaning of this action (and more complicated social actions such as teaching, bargaining, trusting, worshiping, and so on) and how to understand that meaning is subject to a variety of different interpretations in the philosophical traditions that foreground qualitative inquiry.

The interpretivist tradition embraces two different views of what meaning is and how it is to be grasped or understood: First, the meaning of an action resides in the consciousness of the actor (her/his intentions, motivations, desires, attitudes, beliefs), and, hence, the inquirer must use some method of psychological reenactment (i.e., empathy) that facilitates tapping into the actor's own description of the action. The aim here is to understand the meaning of the action in terms of the actor's intentions. (This view of meaning is also operative in **conservative hermeneutics** where the aim is to understand the author's intended meaning.) Second, an action has meaning not by virtue of the actor's intention but because it is part of some larger web or system of actions. This web is variously interpreted as a system of action-guiding norms or action-constituting rules. Here the aim is to understand the intention of the act itself by locating it within some comprehensive scheme of communication or of institutionalized values and norms. In both of these views as defined in the interpretivist tradition, it is assumed that the meaning of action is fixed, finished, and complete and thus, in principle, determinable or discoverable by the inquirer.

The hermeneutic tradition (and this includes the different hermeneutic philosophies of Gadamer [1900–2002], Habermas, and Derrida [1930–2004]) introduces a different way of conceiving of meaning and the understanding of meaning. In this tradition, meaning resides neither in the intentions of the actor nor in the act itself. Meaning is undecidable, never fixed or complete, and exists only in 'reading' an action (or text) such that meaning is always meaning for someone. In Gadamer's hermeneutics, meaning occurs in the mediation or dialogue that occurs between the action (or text) to be understood and the interpreter in the context of the tradition in which the interpreter stands. Meaning thus is created or constructed each time one seeks to understand; hence, understanding meaning is never complete. The deconstructionist hermeneutics of Derrida shares this view of the incompleteness of meaning with one very important difference. For Gadamer, interpretation (understanding meaning) is a process of dialogue and listening in which the living word of conversation is privileged. In this process, the meaning of text, speech, or action is disclosed as it 'speaks' to the interpreter situated in her or his own tradition and cultural horizon. For Derrida, interpretation (understanding meaning) is also dialogic, but the dialogue privileges the sign (the 'word,' something that stands for something else) and reveals the irreducible equivocation, the continual breakup, and continual deferral (rather than disclosure) of meaning (what the sign stands for or is a sign of).

See also *Hermeneutic Method, Intentionalism, Interpretivism, Language.*

KEY REFERENCES

Collin, F. *Social Reality.* London: Routledge, 1997.
Fay, B. *Contemporary Philosophy of Social Science.* Oxford, UK: Blackwell, 1996.
Giddens, A. *New Rules of Sociological Method,* 2nd ed. Stanford, CA: Stanford University Press, 1993.
Habermas, J. *On the Logic of the Social Sciences,* S. W. Nicholsen & J. A. Stark, trans. Cambridge: MIT Press, 1988.
Outhwaite, W. *Understanding Social Life: The Method Called* Verstehen. London: Allen and Unwin, 1975.

MEANING REALISM   See INTENTIONALISM, OBJECTIVISM, REALISM.

MEDICAL SOCIOLOGY   This field, devoted to the study of individual and group behaviors with regard to health and illness, is one of the sites in which qualitative inquiries, particularly ethnographic studies, are often used.

KEY REFERENCES

Bloor, M. "The Ethnography of Health and Medicine," in P. Atkinson, A. Coffey, S. Delamont, J. Lofland, & L. Lofland, eds., *Handbook of Ethnography.* London: Sage, 2001.
Charmaz, K., & Olesen, V. "Ethnographic Research in Medical Sociology," *Sociological Methods and Research,* 1997, 25, 452–494.

MEMBER CHECK   Also called member or respondent validation, this is a sociological term for soliciting feedback from respondents on the inquirer's findings. It is often claimed to be an important procedure for corroborating or verifying findings or of assuring they are valid and meet the criterion of *confirmability*. However, many researchers see it as a problematic notion in several respects. First, on epistemic grounds, it is not entirely clear how the procedure actually helps establish the truth of findings. Suppose, for example, that a member check yields a difference of opinion between the inquirer and respondents, and that respondents disagree with some or all aspects of the inquirer's findings and/or interpretations. The inquirer must then do further checking to explore the nature of the disagreement. For example, are respondents disagreeing to protect something—do they actually accept that the findings are correct but do not wish them to be made public because the findings somehow cast respondents in a bad light or are unbalanced, slanted in favor of something negative or positive? Are respondents ambivalent or unconcerned because they have not actually taken the time to inspect the findings? Are respondents disagreeing because the inquirer made an error in interpretation (if so, what kind of error, how can it be remedied)? Hence, rather than being some sort of simple corroboration or act of validation by respondents, member checking seems but one more opportunity to gather data about the integrity of the inquirer's findings. Second, implementing member checking may be coupled with the assumption that researcher effects must be minimized. On this view, the researcher must guard against doing anything in the field that would influence respondents or change their behaviors or opinions. This, of course, assumes that the inquirer must stand apart from the world he or she studies. Thus, in doing member checking, the inquirer must somehow guard against introducing bias. However, member checking assumes a quite different character and meaning to the extent that the inquiry becomes a more participative and dialogical undertaking and less the monological activity of the lone fieldworker doing research *on* respondents. Third, member checking may be more of an ethical act than an epistemological one. In other words, it may simply be the civil thing to do for those who have given their time and access to their lives to give them the courtesy of knowing (or to honor their right to know) what the inquirer has to say about them. The consensus seems to be that member checking is not profitably viewed as either an act of validation or refutation but is simply another way of generating data and insight.

See also Triangulation, Validity.

KEY REFERENCES

Bloor, M. "Notes on Member Validation," in *Contemporary Field Research,* R. M. Emerson, ed. Prospect Heights, IL: Waveland Press, 1983.
Fielding, N. G., & Fielding, J. L. *Linking Data.* Newbury Park, CA: Sage, 1988.

MEMOING   This analytic procedure was suggested by Barney Glaser for explaining or elaborating on the coded categories that a fieldworker develops in analyzing data. Memos are conceptual in intent, vary in length, and are primarily written to oneself. The content of memos can include commentary on the meaning of a coded category, an explanation of a sense of pattern developing among categories, or a *description* of some specific aspect of a setting or phenomenon. Memos capture the thoughts of the inquirer while he or she is engaged in the process of analysis. Typically, the final analysis and interpretation are based on integration and analysis of memos.

See also Analyzing Qualitative Data.

KEY REFERENCES

Glaser, B. *Theoretical Sensitivity: Advances in the Methodology of Grounded Theory.* Mill Valley, CA: Sociology Press, 1978.

Miles, M., & Huberman, A. M. *Qualitative Data Analysis,* 2nd ed. Thousand Oaks, CA: Sage, 1994.

Strauss, A. *Qualitative Analysis for Social Scientists.* Cambridge, UK: Cambridge University Press, 1987.

METAETHNOGRAPHY   This is a term coined by George Noblit and R. Dwight Hare for the process of creating new interpretations from the synthesis of multiple field studies. Although this idea is something of a qualitative analog to the notion of statistical meta-analysis, the authors emphasize that metaethnographic inquiry is interpretive, not aggregative or analytical. They describe three strategies for analysis: reciprocal translation of one study into the terms of another; refutational synthesis—opposing the claims of two or more studies; and lines-of-argument synthesis in which the interpreter engages in something like grounded theorizing, combining parts of various studies into an integrated whole.

See also Cross-Case Analysis, Review of Literature.

KEY REFERENCE

Noblit, G., & Hare, R. D. *Meta-Ethnography: Synthesizing Qualitative Studies.* Newbury Park, CA: Sage, 1988.

METANARRATIVE   See GRAND NARRATIVE.

METAPHYSICS   This is the study of reality, of being, of the real nature of whatever is, of first principles. Sometimes called ontology (although some philosophers define ontology as a branch of metaphysics), it is concerned with understanding the kinds of things that constitute the world. For example, Platonism is a theory of metaphysical dualism: There is the world of matter—appearances, everyday life, the senses—and the world of mind—true realities, the objects of the intellect. Cartesian metaphysics posits a somewhat different mind-body dualism: Human beings are composed of the mental and the material. Much contemporary psychology assumes a metaphysical distinction between an inner mental life and outer physical behavior, although Descartes (1596–1650) never proposed the distinction in this way. *Idealism* is a metaphysics as well. One version of idealism holds that nothing exists but minds and their content, the experience of minds. Another version acknowledges that there are material things in the world as well as minds but seeks to reduce matter to mind by arguing that the universe is constituted by mind. Martin Heidegger's (1889–1976) metaphysics, central to the work of Hans-Georg Gadamer (1900–2002) and *philosophical hermeneutics,* aimed at understanding *Dasein* or human being in the world. Edmund Husserl's (1859–1938) phenomenology, a metaphysics concerned with the essential structures of conscious experience, strongly influenced Alfred Schutz (1899–1956), whose work in turn provides the philosophical basis for *phenomenological sociology* and *ethnomethodology.* The logical positivists were openly hostile to metaphysics—to any philosophical claims about reality, truth, or being. They argued that metaphysical statements were incapable of being judged as true or false and thus of no consequence for increasing scientific knowledge of the world. Thus, it is not incorrect to say that contemporary postpostivistic philosophy of human and social sciences is marked by a return of the metaphysical, if by that phrase we mean a renewed concern with the nature, constitution, and structure of being and social reality and how knowledge of same plays a role in our claims to know social reality.

KEY REFERENCE

Blackburn, S. "Metaphysics," in *The Blackwell Companion to Philosophy,* N. Bunnin & E. P. Tsui-James, eds. Oxford, UK: Blackwell, 1996.

METHOD   In a very general sense, method (or research methods) refers to the set of investigative procedures used within a particular field of study or discipline. This term encompasses a number of different connotations that are relevant to the practice of qualitative inquiry.

In the everyday, ordinary usage of the term in qualitative studies (and social inquiry more generally) *method* denotes a procedure, tool, or technique used by the inquirer to generate and analyze data. Typically, three classes or types of tools are used to generate qualitative data: ***interviewing*** (listening, talking, conversing, recording), ***observation*** (watching, videotaping), and ***document analysis*** (reading, photographing). Tools for analyzing qualitative data are equally varied and include displays, taxonomies, typologies, constant comparison, enumeration, analytic induction, content analysis, and univariate and bivariate statistical analyses. This cornucopia of methods available to qualitative inquirers does not simply point to eclecticism of method. Rather, it signals the fact that qualitative inquiry is not defined by a preoccupation with a particular method: There is no one method or set of methods that if adopted render a particular inquiry as precisely ***qualitative***.

Method is also conventionally understood in purely instrumental terms. In other words, as a tool, method contributes to the generation and growth of ***knowledge*** but is itself transparent or neutral, or at least the effects of a method on the object of understanding are determinable and controllable. In the conventional understanding of method, the question "How does this method *constitute* its object?" is considered irrelevant. This feature of method is the subject of considerable criticism in feminist and critical theory approaches to social understanding.

It is often said that qualitative inquiry eschews the use of the scientific method, but just what that claim means is not always clear. In the philosophy of science, it is generally acknowledged that there is no operational definition of what is commonly called scientific method. Rather, this term signals a broad approach to or logic of inquiry (also called the ***hypothetico-deductive method***) that includes the identification and clarification of problems, the formulation of tentative solutions, the practical or theoretical testing of these solutions, and the elimination of those solutions deemed not successful in solving the problem. Precisely how these activities are conducted varies widely given different research designs, research questions, tools, and so forth. There are many qualitative studies that follow this logic; there are others that object to the underlying assumptions of this logic, most notably the assumption that the logic is applicable to understanding social ***action***.

A modern, Cartesian, or Enlightenment conception of method also assumes a subject-object dichotomy. It begins from the belief that we should separate the mind (the subject, knower, consciousness) from the thing (that which is to be known, the object of consciousness). In this way of thinking, the function of method is to bracket **bias** or **prejudice** and keep the object of understanding at arm's length where it can be observed safely with disinterest and lack of involvement. Thus, it is not the subjectivity of the inquirer that produces knowledge but the method. Defenders of this idea argue that it is precisely because method functions in this way that we are able to acquire an objective, rational **explanation** of the way the world really is (i.e., the truth about the world) free of the predilections, eccentricities, prejudices, and characteristics of age, social location, race, class, gender, and ethnicity that define the inquirer. In other words, genuine, legitimate knowledge is limited to methodically self-conscious knowledge. This understanding of method is alive and well in some versions of **Verstehende sociology** and **phenomenological sociology**.

A variety of criticisms is aimed at undermining or overthrowing the central place that method occupies in a modern or Cartesian conception of what constitutes knowledge in human affairs. For example, defenders of **philosophical hermeneutics** model knowledge and understanding on practical reason, dialogue, and interpretation as fundamental activities of being human. They challenge the idea that understanding our social world is to be determined by method and that knowledge is the product of methodical consciousness. Likewise, many feminist epistemologies challenge the idea of method as requiring disengaged, detached objectivity. Postmodernists offer a more radical critique. Since, as Lyotard once noted, **postmodernism** sets out to change the meaning of the word *knowledge,* and it challenges the very idea of an inquirer as knowing subject, postmodernist approaches generally reject all claims that methods (or inquirers) produce knowledge. A postmodernist inquirer may employ a 'strategy' like deconstruction but never a method. These strategies are used to further the paradox of multiple meanings and to play with an infinite variety of interpretations.

See also *Knowledge, Hermeneutic Method, Methodology, Mixed Methods.*

KEY REFERENCES

Kaplan, A. *The Conduct of Inquiry.* New York: Harper & Row, 1964.
Phillips, D. C. *The Expanded Social Scientists Bestiary.* Lanham, MD: Rowman & Littlefield, 2000.
Tuana, N., ed. *Feminism & Science.* Bloomington: Indiana University Press, 1989.

METHODOLOGY This is a theory of how inquiry should proceed. It involves analysis of the assumptions, principles, and procedures in a particular approach to inquiry (that, in turn, governs the use of particular methods). Methodologies explicate and define (a) the kinds of problems that are worth investigating, (b) what comprises a researchable problem, testable hypothesis, and so on, (c) how to frame a problem in such a way that it can be investigated using particular designs and procedures, (d) how to understand what constitutes a legitimate and warranted explanation, (e) how to judge matters of generalizability, (f) how to select or develop appropriate means of generating data, and (g) how to develop the logic linking problem-data generation-analysis-argument.

Methodology is a particular social scientific discourse (a way of acting, thinking, and speaking) that occupies a middle ground between discussions of method (procedures, techniques) and discussions of issues in the philosophy of social science. This two-way relationship is displayed in Figure M.1. There is no direct, unbroken, logically necessary link between various positions on issues in the philosophy of social science, methodologies, and methods. For example, two researchers could each be committed to scientific realism and to the notion of disinterested social science but employ different methodologies (e.g., participant observation and quasi-experimentation). Likewise, a single methodology (e.g., life-history methodology or participant observation methodology) can be quite differently defined in interpretive ethnography, symbolic interactionism, critical social science, cultural studies, postmodern ethnography, and feminist inquiry, depending on a researcher's perspectives on critical issues in philosophy of social science (e.g., the nature of knowledge generated via that methodology; the meaning of 'experience' and 'subjectivity'; the meaning of 'culture'; the relationship of descriptive and normative concerns of social science; the ethical obligations of the inquirer).

Methods and methodology display a synergetic relationship: A particular method (or set of methods) is employed (and given meaning within) a methodology that defines the object of study and determines what comprises an adequate reconstruction of that object. This relationship is illustrated in Table M.1, which reveals how various kinds of qualitative data (textual data, transcripts, observations, etc.) are generated in different ways and acquire different meaning in light of different methodologies.

See also Method, Mixed Methods.

ISSUES

For example, causation, explanation, historicism, nomologicalism, subject-object relation, fact-value distinction, intentionalism, structure vs. agency, the nature of meaning, relation of self-other, value-neutrality, scientific realism, justification, theory of language.

METHODOLOGIES

For example, quasi-experimental/experimental methodology, survey research methodology, participant observation methodology, naturalistic inquiry, symbolic interactionism, ethnomethodology.

METHODS

For example, procedures for generating qualitative and quantitative data—structured and unstructured interviews, structured and unstructured observations, types of document analysis, psychometric and sociometric measures; procedures for analyzing data of various kinds—descriptive and inferential statistics, constant comparison method, coding, analytic induction, conversational analysis, narrative analysis.

Figure M.1   Interrelationships of Methods, Methodologies, and Issues in the Philosophy of Social Science

KEY REFERENCE

Kaplan, A. *The Conduct of Inquiry.* New York: Harper & Row, 1964.

METHODS OF TEXT ANALYSIS   See TEXTUAL ANALYSIS, METHODS OF

MICROETHNOGRAPHY   This is an approach to field study specifically concerned with exhaustive, fine-grained examination of either a very small unit within an organization, group, or culture (e.g., a particular classroom in a school); a specific activity within an organizational unit (e.g., how physicians

Table M.1   Illustration of Relationships Between Methodologies and Methods in
                  Qualitative Inquiry

Methodology	Methods Of Generating Qualitative Data	Object Of Understanding And Theorizing Reconstructed By Method
Social Phenomenological	Registering methods (e.g., audiotape and videotape transcribed documents); methods of contextual description	The social or everyday life (the lifeworld) understood from the perspective of interaction or the interaction order; the social accomplishment of reality
Ethnographic and Naturalistic	In-depth, ethnographic (semantic), and unstructured interviews; life-history interviews; participant observation	The social or everyday life (the lifeworld) understood from the actor's perspective, knowledge, experience, intentions, interpretations, etc.
Narrative and Interpretive Interactionist	'Active' and narrative interviews	The dialogic process of communication; the 'exchange process' and the joint construction of accounts of social life in conversation and reflection
Objectivist Hermeneutics	Exegesis; hermeneutic circle	Author's intended meaning of the text

NOTE: For the idea of this illustration, I am indebted to Dr. Bettina Dausein, of the Universität Bielefeld,.for a lecture given at the International Symposium on Lifelong Learning and Experience at Roskilde University, Denmark, August 1999.

communicate with elderly patients in an emergency room); or ordinary everyday conversation.

See also Ethnomethodology.

KEY REFERENCE

Spindler, G., ed. *Doing the Ethnography of Schooling: Educational Anthropology in Action.* New York: Holt, Rinehart & Winston, 1982.

MISUNDERSTANDING   See UNDERSTANDING.

MIXED METHODS   This is the notion of using multiple methods to generate and analyze different kinds of data in the same study—for example, combining a narrative analysis of in-depth interviews with a content analysis of
questionnaire responses, or conducting an ethnographic study alongside a
quasi-experimental study of the same social phenomenon. The notion has
received considerable attention in the field of social and educational program
evaluation, in which discussions unfold about mixing methods at both 'technical' levels (i.e., generating different kinds of data via different procedures)
and 'philosophical' and 'paradigmatic' levels.

Underlying the notion appears to be the pragmatic assumption that to
judge the value of an educational or social program or policy, an evaluator
ought to employ whatever methods will best generate evidence of the warranted assertability of the value of that program or policy. This is a relatively
noncontroversial assumption in a variety of social science research endeavors.
For example, it is not uncommon for an ethnographer who is investigating the
relationship of schools to their communities or one who is studying household
decision making regarding the allocation of educational resources to boys and
girls to engage in substantial periods of intense participant observation and
also to conduct a more structured household or community survey. It is also
not at all unusual for a social policy analyst to design a study to determine the
success of policy implementation that uses both measured variables and interviews with key participants involved in the implementation. In both cases, the
object of study is framed by a particular purpose and set of questions, and different kinds of evidence generated via multiple, or mixed, methods is deemed
relevant to addressing the purpose of the study and answering the questions.

Beyond this common understanding and practice of combining methods
and types of data, it is not readily apparent what 'mixing' so-called paradigms
or philosophies means or how that might be accomplished. Several preliminary questions must be answered: First, just what are the likely candidates for
'philosophies' or 'paradigms' and what does each entail? Second, what does it
mean to 'apply' that philosophy or paradigm to the study of some problem or
phenomenon? Third, what does the verb 'to mix' mean in this circumstance—
just what is it that is being mixed when applying different philosophical frameworks? Consider an example at the level of methodologies. For the sake of

argument, assume that ***ethnomethodology*** and ***naturalistic inquiry/ethnography*** are candidates for different 'paradigms.' What would it mean to 'mix' the ethnomethodologist's concern with understanding *how* social life is accomplished in talk-in-interaction with the interpretivist's concern with the meaning of social life or with understanding *what* is happening? Each defines the object of the study quite differently and employs different means to generate and analyze different kinds of data. Surely, each kind of study provides a different perspective on social life, but what would it mean to 'mix' these perspectives? Or consider, again, for the sake of argument, that ***philosophical hermeneutics*** and ***deconstructionism*** are candidates for 'philosophies,' and suppose they are 'applied' to the analysis of texts. It will become immediately apparent that they are not compatible because they make a host of different assumptions about what reading a text means and what such a reading yields. Both philosophies, however, share some central concerns—for example, the undecidability of the meaning of a text, and a strong criticism of method as the path to knowledge. Thus, just what it might mean to mix philosophies is not all that obvious.

Perhaps advocacy for the notion of mixed methods is an implicit endorsement of pluralism in social science. It might be a way of saying that our understanding of social life should not be driven by either/or thinking—for example, structure versus agency, historicism versus nomologicalism, and meaning versus cause. Rather, we should accept that different ways of framing and studying social phenomena yield different kinds of understandings. And these different understandings ought to be engaged with one another, not simply tolerated as different.

See also *Methodology, Paradigm, Pluralism.*

KEY REFERENCES

Brannen, J. "Working Qualitatively and Quantitatively," in C. Seale, G. Gobo, J. F. Gubrium, & D. Silverman, eds., *Qualitative Research Practice.* London: Sage, 2004.

Greene, J. C., & Caracelli, V. J., eds. *Advances in Mixed-Method Evaluation: The Challenges and Benefits of Integrating Diverse Paradigms.* New Directions for Evaluation No. 74. San Francisco: Jossey-Bass, 1997.

Tashakkori, A., & Teddlie, C., eds. *Handbook of Mixed Methods in Social and Behavioral Research.* Thousand Oaks, CA: Sage, 2003.

MODERNISM/MODERNITY   See POSTMODERNISM, PRAXIS, RATIONALISM.

MONOLOGICAL   See DIALOGISM, DIALOGUE.

MULTIPLE REALITIES   A central insight of the *interpretive turn* in the social and natural sciences is that the meaning of human action and language can only be grasped in relation to some specific context or frame of reference (see **INDEXICALITY**). For example, Thomas Kuhn (1922–1996) (*The Structure of Scientific Revolutions,* 2nd ed., University of Chicago Press, 1970) argued that paradigms were such a frame of reference in the natural sciences; Peter Winch (1926–1997) (*The Idea of a Social Science,* Routledge & Kegan Paul, 1958) held that social action can be understood only in the context of particular forms of life or *language games* (concepts he borrowed from Ludwig Wittgenstein's [1889–1951] philosophy). Another notion that shares this basic premise is multiple realities. Originating in the psychology of William James (1842–1910), a theory of multiple realities was developed by Alfred Schutz (1889–1956) as part of his phenomenology of the *lifeworld* or social world in which we live. Schutz used the idea of multiple realities or "finite provinces of meaning" to clarify the relationship between the reality of the world of everyday life and the world of scientific, theoretical contemplation. He explained that the paramount reality or primary world in which we live is the intersubjective world of daily life. It possesses a specific set of characteristics that mark its unique "cognitive style." For example, we do not doubt its existence; in it we experience a particular form of sociality; in it we have a specific time perspective, and so on. But we also live our lives in other worlds or finite provinces of meaning upon which, in Schutz's words, we "bestow the accent of reality." These include the world of dreams, art, religion, the play world of the child, the world of scientific contemplation, the world of the insane, and so on. Each of these provinces of meaning has its own "cognitive style," and as we alter attention from one finite province to another, we experience a "shock" of breaking through the "system of relevances" unique to one province of meaning to shift to the system of relevances unique to the other. Schutz emphasized that these different provinces of meaning were not literally different realities. He wrote,

> The finite provinces of meaning are not separated states of mental life in the sense that passing from one to another would require a transmigration of the soul. . . . They are merely names for different tensions in one and the same consciousness, and it is the same life, the mundane life, unbroken from birth to death, which is attended to in different modifications. (p. 232)

Turning to the finite province of meaning called scientific contemplation, Schutz explained that its distinctive cognitive style centered on the attitude of the "disinterested observer" who turns the world into an object of contemplation. This attitude, in turn, is indispensable to scientific theorizing about the world. The scientific attitude means that the scientist puts her or his bodily existence, subjectivity, social relationships, and so on in brackets so as to adopt an attitude of total disinterested contemplation. The scientist suspends the "cognitive style" and the concerns that dominate her or his everyday life. Thus, the same individual acting in the finite province of meaning of the everyday world adopts a radically different set of relevant concerns, attitudes, and interests when acting in the finite province of meaning of scientific contemplation.

KEY REFERENCE

Schutz, A. *Collected Papers,* Vol. 1. M. Natanson, trans. The Hague, The Netherlands: Martin Nijhoff, 1967.

N

NAÏVE REALISM See REALISM.

NARRATIVE Several senses of this term figure prominently in many versions of qualitative inquiry. Generally, the term refers to any spoken or written presentation, but it is primarily used in a more narrow sense to mean a form or genre of presentation organized in story form. Story, in turn, refers to a kind of writing that describes a sequence of actions or events with a plot (a beginning, middle, and end) arranged in temporal order. The term may be used to indicate a particular kind of data; for example, a narrative interview is specifically designed to elicit narrative data—an informant or respondent's story. Narrative data or stories can be of two kinds: A personal experience story relates the teller to some significant episode, event, or personal experience, and a personal history or the reconstruction of a life is a more encompassing and involved account. Narrative may also refer to a discourse form or form of research reporting that is distinct from an argumentative form. In an argument, a conclusion is compelled because of the form of the argument. Moreover, the argument form in research reporting is typically synchronic (focuses on a limited set of events in a specific time period). A story form for research reporting, however, is typically diachronic (dealing with a phenomenon as it changes over time). It contains surprises, coincidences, embellishments, and other rhetorical devices that draw the reader in and hold attention in a different manner.

See also *Narrative Inquiry*.

KEY REFERENCES

Polkinghorne, D. *Narrative Knowing and the Human Sciences.* Albany: SUNY Press, 1988.

Polkinghorne, D. "Reporting Qualitative Research as Practice," in *Representation and the Text: Re-framing the Narrative Voice,* W. G. Tierney & Y. S. Lincoln, eds. Albany: SUNY Press, 1997.

NARRATIVE ANALYSIS   This term refers to a variety of procedures for interpreting the narratives or stories generated in research. It includes formal/structural means of analysis (e.g., examining how a story is organized, how it is developed, and where it begins and ends), functional analyses of what a story is 'doing' or what is being told in the story (e.g., telling a moral tale, a cautionary tale, a success story, or a chronicle of trials and tribulations), and analyses of stories as a particular kind of oral performance.

See also Narrative Inquiry.

KEY REFERENCES

Coffey, A., & Atkinson, P. *Making Sense of Qualitative Data.* London: Sage, 1996.

Daiute, C., & Lightfoot, C., eds. *Narrative Analysis: Studying the Development of Individuals in Society.* Thousand Oaks, CA: Sage, 2004.

Mishler, E. G. "Models of Narrative Analysis," *Journal of Narrative and Life History,* 1995, 5(2), 87–123.

Polkinghorne, D. "Narrative Configuration in Qualitative Analysis," *Qualitative Studies in Education,* 1995, 8(1), 5–23.

Riessman, C. K. *Narrative Analysis.* Newbury Park, CA: Sage, 1993.

NARRATIVE CRITERIA   See VERISIMILITUDE.

NARRATIVE ETHICS   Also called virtue ethics, this approach to ethical reasoning emphasizes the connection between a substantive conception of human nature (i.e., a concept of the 'good' or purpose of human life) and its connection to personal identity and the virtues (excellences of character). It views morality as a telling and living of individual and collective stories in which conceptions of the purpose of human life and virtues are given intelligibility. The centrality of stories or narratives to this view of ethics emphasizes the moral order and unity of life and the moral self as integrated (moral identity and moral purpose are linked over time). Narrative ethics is highly critical of ethical theories that view morality in terms of a series of episodic decisions disconnected from identity and human purpose.

See also Ethics of Qualitative Inquiry.

KEY REFERENCES

MacIntyre, A. *After Virtue.* Notre Dame, IN: University of Notre Dame Press, 1981.
Newton, A. Z. *Narrative Ethics.* Cambridge, MA: Harvard University Press, 1995.

NARRATIVE EXPLANATION   (Also called narrative constructivism or historical constructivism) Narrative explanations are stories (historical narratives) constructed about past events that give an accounting of and an account for those events. There is a long-standing controversy in the discipline of history over whether constructing stories about past events actually *explains* the occurrence of those events. The debate unfolds between defenders of ***covering-law model of explanation*** applied to history, on the one hand, and proponents of a unique form of narrative understanding, on the other. Thus, the debate echoes the more general argument in the human sciences over whether explanation or understanding is its proper aim.

See also Historicism, Narrative Realism.

KEY REFERENCES

Hempel, C. "The Function of General Laws in History," *Journal of Philosophy,* 1942, 39, 35–48.
Mandelbaum, M. *The Anatomy of Historical Knowledge.* Baltimore, MD: Johns Hopkins University Press, 1977.
Mink, L. "The Autonomy of Historical Understanding," *History and Theory,* 1965, 5, 24–47.
Roth, P. "Narrative Explanations: The Case of History," *History and Theory,* 1988, 27, 1–13.

NARRATIVE INQUIRY   This is a broad term encompassing the interdisciplinary study of the activities involved in generating and analyzing stories of life experiences (e.g., life histories, narrative interviews, journals, diaries, memoirs, autobiographies, and biographies) and reporting that kind of research. Narrative inquiry or research also includes examination of the methodology and aim of research in the form of personal narrative and *autoethnography*.

KEY REFERENCES

Ellis, C., & Bochner, A, eds. *Composing Ethnography: Alternative Forms of Qualitative Writing.* Walnut Creek, CA: AltaMira Press, 1996.
Josselson, R., & Liebech, A., eds. *Interpreting Experience: The Narrative Study of Lives.* Thousand Oaks, CA: Sage, 1995.
Lieblich, A., Tuval-Mashiach, R., & Zilber, T. *Narrative Research: Reading, Analysis, Interpretation.* Thousand Oaks, CA: Sage, 1998.

NARRATIVE PSYCHOLOGY   Narrative has been proposed as particular cognitive function, way of thinking, or rationality. For example, Jerome Bruner (1986) has argued that there are two distinctive ways in which we order experience. The two are complementary but not reducible to one another: the paradigmatic or logico-scientific mode and the narrative mode. The former leads to the well-formed argument that seeks to convince us of its truth through "tight analysis, logical proof, sound argument, and empirical discovery guided by reasoned hypothesis"; the latter leads to good stories that seek to convince us of their lifelikeness. Each mode of thought has different criteria for evaluating its outcome. Bruner has written about the psychology of narrative thought, particularly how it is that we construct the world through narrative. Narrative psychology also includes examinations of how narratives are central to the construction of self-identity.

KEY REFERENCES

Bruner, J. *Acts of Meaning.* Cambridge, MA: Harvard University Press, 1990.
Bruner, J. *Actual Minds, Possible Worlds.* Cambridge, MA: Harvard University Press, 1986.
Murray, M. "Narrative Psychology," in J.A. Smith, ed., *Qualitative Psychology: A Practical Guide to Research Methods.* London: Sage, 2003.
Sarbin, T. *Narrative Psychology: The Storied Nature of Human Conduct.* New York: Praeger, 1986.

NARRATIVE REALISM   (Also called narrative ontology) This is a doctrine concerned with the storied nature of being or how narrative is the very 'lived' character of human existence. (*Narrative explanation,* on the other hand, is concerned with narrative as the 'told' character of existence.) The expression 'we lead storied lives' expresses this concern. There are many strands of thought entailed here, but generally narrative realism holds that narrative structures exist in the human world and not simply in the stories that people tell about that world. Narrative is regarded as a temporal structure inherent in our way of living and acting.

KEY REFERENCES

Carr, D. *Time, Narrative, and History.* Bloomington: Indiana University Press, 1986.
Ricoeur, P. *Time and Narrative,* 2 vols., K. McLaughlin and D. Pellauer, trans. Chicago: University of Chicago Press, 1984–1986.

NATIVE'S POINT OF VIEW   This is one of the methodological innovations marking the emergence in the 1920s of participant observation as the scientific approach of ethnography. Earlier interpreters'—missionaries, government administrators, traders, travelers, and the like—accounts of the native life of indigenous peoples generally failed to offer the perspective as well as the practices of the members of the group (i.e., 'the natives') themselves. By placing increased emphasis on powers of observation of events in daily life and on the collection of first-person, native, or insider accounts, the methodology of *participant observation* sought to establish a firmer scientific basis for anthropological understanding.

See also Emic/Etic, Ethnographic Naturalism, Other (The Other, Otherness).

KEY REFERENCE

Stocking, G. W., Jr., ed. *Observers Observed: Essays on Ethnographic Fieldwork.* Madison: University of Wisconsin Press, 1983.

NATURALISM   This is one of four basic approaches to the study of social phenomena (the others are *antinaturalism, critical social science,* and *pluralism*). The naturalist holds that the social or human sciences should approach the study of social phenomena with the same aim and methods as the natural sciences approach the study of natural (physical) phenomena (hence, the phrase "naturalistic interpretation of the social sciences"). In other words, the social sciences should have as their goals both prediction and causal, nomological *explanation* of human behavior. Naturalists like Karl Popper (1902–1994) and Ernest Nagel (1901–1985) admit that the search for lawlike explanations (or explanatory theory) in the social sciences may be more difficult due to the nature of the subject matter. Yet they insist that there are no fundamental differences in kind in the explanatory goals of the natural and social sciences. *See also Logical Empiricism.*

KEY REFERENCES

Bernstein, R. J. *The Restructuring of Social and Political Theory.* Philadelphia: University of Pennsylvania Press, 1976.

Little, D. *Varieties of Social Explanation.* Boulder, CO: Westview Press, 1991.

Phillips, D. C. *The Expanded Social Scientists Bestiary.* Lanham, MD: Rowman & Littlefield, 2000.

NATURALISTIC INQUIRY   In the social sciences literature, naturalistic inquiry is the name for a particular methodology that emphasizes understanding and portraying social *action* (i.e., the meaning, character, nature of social life) from the point of view of social actors. It emphasizes that this kind of understanding can be forthcoming only from first-hand, eyewitness accounts of 'being there.' It aims at faithful, authentic reproduction or representation of others' ways of life. Some notable examples of the use of this term include the following: In 1969, two psychologists, Edwin Willems and Harold Rausch, edited a collection of papers titled *Naturalistic Viewpoints in Psychology* in which they defined naturalistic inquiry as "the investigation of phenomena within and in relation to their *naturally occurring* contexts." In 1971, sociologist Norman Denzin published the paper "The Logic of Naturalistic Inquiry" in which he explained that the naturalist inquirer resists using methods that oversimplify the complexity of everyday life. In 1978, Egon Guba published the monograph *Toward a Methodology of Naturalistic Inquiry in Educational Evaluation* in which he identified the characteristics of naturalistic inquiry and compared it with what he called more conventional (experimental and quasi-experimental) inquiry. Several years later, Guba and Yvonna Lincoln published *Naturalistic Inquiry* (Sage, 1985) in which they contrasted postpositivist and naturalist paradigms on philosophical and methodological dimensions. (In a subsequent formulation of their approach to qualitative studies that appeared in *Fourth Generation Evaluation* [Sage, 1989], Guba and Lincoln renamed their approach constructivist.) What these various methodologies sharing the same name have in common is a commitment to studying human action in some setting that is not contrived, manipulated, or artificially fashioned by the inquirer; hence, the setting is said to be 'natural' or 'naturally occurring.'

Some confusion surrounding the term stems from the fact that in philosophy of social science, naturalism or naturalistic refers to efforts to define the aim of the social sciences as the same aim as the natural sciences (see ***naturalism***). One who rejects those efforts (i.e., rejects the naturalistic interpretation of the social sciences) is an *anti*naturalist. Thus, to the philosopher, those qualitative inquirers who call themselves naturalistic inquirers are actually *anti*naturalists. To put it more concretely, the philosopher might say that a better title for Guba and Lincoln's book is "Antinaturalistic Inquiry."

See also Ethnographic Naturalism.

KEY REFERENCE

Gubrium, J., & Holstein, J. *The New Language of Qualitative Method.* Oxford, UK: Blackwell, 1997.

NATURALISTIC INTERPRETATION OF THE SOCIAL SCIENCES See NATURALISM.

NATURAL SETTING   See ETHNOGRAPHIC NATURALISM, NATURALISTIC INQUIRY.

NATURWISSENSCHAFTEN A German term usually translated as natural sciences.

See also Science, Verstehen.

NEGATIVE CASE   An instance or case that refutes or challenges a developing hypothesis is called a negative case. This notion is central to the logic of testing hypotheses as explained in ***analytic induction***. The idea of using negative case analysis to establish the *credibility* of a researcher's conclusions has also been discussed as a key feature of *naturalistic inquiry*.

KEY REFERENCES

Fielding, N. G., ed. *Actions and Structure*. London: Sage, 1988.
Lincoln, Y. S., & Guba, E. G. *Naturalistic Inquiry*. Beverly Hills, CA: Sage, 1985.

NOMOTHETIC KNOWLEDGE Nomothetic knowledge comprises knowledge claims that have the character of a *law like generalization*. Compare to *idiographic interpretation*.

See also Covering-Law Model of Explanation, Explanation.

NONFOUNDATIONAL EPISTEMOLOGIES Literally, nonfoundational epistemologies are attempts to describe how knowledge is possible absent secure and certain foundations for knowledge claims. The leading version of nonfoundationalist epistemology is *coherentism*, which is the view that the justification of a belief involves an assessment of the degree of coherence of that belief within a system of beliefs. Nonfoundationalist epistemology stands in opposition to foundational epistemology, which claims that justification is a matter of relating a belief to some kind of foundational beliefs (i.e., beliefs which are fundamental, basic, or 'brute' and hence in need of no additional justification). For the foundationalist, justification is pictured like a building with foundational beliefs at the base and all other beliefs supported by that foundation. For the nonfoundationalist, justification is more like the picture of a raft in which each plank (i.e., belief) is supporting every other. Some beliefs (like some planks) can, over time, be found to be unreliable and are replaced without dismantling the entire raft. This latter image, also called Neurath's boat, was developed by the logical positivist Otto Neurath (1882–1945).

See also Foundationalist Epistemologies.

KEY REFERENCE

Grayling, A. C. "Epistemology," in *The Blackwell Companion to Philosophy*, N. Bunnin & E. P. Tsui-James, eds. Oxford, UK: Blackwell, 1996.

O

OBJECTIVISM   While often used as a synonym for *foundationalist epistemologies, objectivism* has other important connotations. First, it can be used as
another term for metaphysical (or ontological) realism—the doctrine that there
is an independently existing world of objective reality that has a determinate
nature that can be discovered. Second, it can be taken as equivalent to the epistemological doctrine of meaning realism—the view that human *action* is an
'object' in which meaning resides independently of consciousness and experience;
with the right methods, that meaning can be discovered (see *intentionalism*).
Third, it can refer to a belief in a particular metaphysical and epistemological
relation of subject to object. For example, Pierre Bourdieu (1930–2002) defined
objectivism as the "theoretical relation" to the world. In that relation, the social
world is "a spectacle offered to an observer who takes up a 'point of view' on the
action and who. . . proceeds as if it were intended solely for knowledge"
(p. 52). For Bourdieu, the important contrast is between the theoretical relation
to the world with its attendant attitude of objectification and a "practical relation" to the world. A similar view is discussed by Charles Taylor who criticizes
an epistemology that privileges disengagement and control and assumes that
one does not live in or through one's experience but treats experience itself as
an object (see *intentionality*). Finally, the term *objectivism* can designate a
complex set of interlocking beliefs about the nature of reality (metaphysical
realism), the manner in which that reality can be known and knowledge claims
justified (logical positivist or representationalist epistemology), the role of the
scientist (an axiology of disinterest), and the Enlightenment belief in the
unquestioned power (and authority) of science to shape society.

See also Objectivity.

KEY REFERENCES

Bernstein, R. J. *Beyond Objectivism and Relativism: Science, Hermeneutics, and Praxis*. Philadelphia: University of Pennsylvania Press, 1983.
Bourdieu, P. *Logic of Practice*. Stanford, CA: Stanford University Press, 1990.
Fay, B. *Contemporary Philosophy of Social Science*. Oxford, UK: Blackwell, 1996.

OBJECTIVIST HERMENEUTICS   See CONSERVATIVE HERMENEUTICS.

OBJECTIVITY   In everyday usage, objectivity often refers to *a property or quality of a claim* (an assertion or statement)—for example, a claim is objective if it is supported with reasons and evidence (or warrantable, supportable); *a characteristic of a person*—for example, the objective person is unbiased, unprejudiced; or *an aspect or characteristic of a process* or means by which a claim is warranted—for example, the enterprise of science is objective because the claims of scientists are subject to public scrutiny and intersubjective criticism.

In the literature on social science methodology and philosophy, there are several interrelated but distinct senses of this term all broadly related to the question of justifying a claim:

1. An absolute or ontological sense reflecting a belief in metaphysical realism: The objectivity of science refers to its ability to know things as they really are.

2. A disciplinary or critically intersubjective sense: Objectivity refers to the process of inquiry, the ability to reach consensus within some specialized disciplinary community through dialogue, debate, and reasoned argument.

3. A mechanical sense: Objectivity means following the rules or procedures because these are a check on subjectivity and restrain idiosyncrasy and personal judgment.

4. A moral-political sense: Objectivity is fairness and impartiality, the absence of self-interest or prejudice that distorts judgment.

Some criticisms originating in qualitative inquiry (and in all of social science more generally) are directed at the notion of objectivity as a regulative ideal for inquiry in the first sense noted above—that is, the belief in an ability to know things as they really are. Other kinds of criticisms are aimed at objectivity as a stance or posture from which an inquirer allegedly can view social life unencumbered by prejudices and personal characteristics. Still other kinds of criticisms, specifically those raised in feminist epistemologies, are often simultaneously political and epistemological, for example, putatively objective science has a sexist bias; a concern with scientific objectivity has imposed a hierarchical and controlling relationship on the researcher-researched pair; holding to objectivity as a regulative ideal has meant excluding personal, subjective knowledge from consideration as legitimate knowledge.

See also Bias, Objectivism, Subjectivity.

KEY REFERENCES

Fay, B. *Contemporary Philosophy of Social Science.* Oxford, UK: Blackwell, 1996.
Harding, S. *Whose Science? Whose Knowledge?* Ithaca, NY: Cornell University Press, 1991.
Megill, A., ed. *Rethinking Objectivity.* Durham, NC: Duke University Press, 1994.
Natter, W., Schatzki, T. R., & Jones, J. P., III, eds. *Objectivity and the Other.* New York: Guilford Press, 1995.
Rescher, N. *Objectivity: The Obligations of Impersonal Reason.* Notre Dame, IN: Notre Dame University Press, 1997.

OBSERVATION   Direct firsthand eyewitness accounts of everyday social action have always been regarded as essential to answering the classic fieldwork question "What's going on here?" Extended periods of observation in the field define both anthropological work dating from the 1920s and fieldwork sociology originating in the Chicago School tradition of the 1930s. Observation as a method of generating data about human experience is characterized by the following traits: (a) Events, actions, meanings, norms, and so on are viewed from the perspective of people being studied; (b) a premium is placed on attention to detail; (c) events and actions can be understood only when they are set within a particular social and historical context; (d) social action is regarded as processual and dynamic, not a set of discrete events; and (e) efforts are made by the observer to avoid premature imposition of theoretical notions on participants' perspectives, although some general theoretical framework initially shapes the making and interpretation of observations (e.g., symbolic interactionism, semiotic conception of culture, structural-functionalism, and ethnomethodology).

This view of observation as method and its underlying epistemological assumptions is subject to strong criticisms in postmodern and poststructural theories that, in part, reflect Dewey's (1859–1952) critique of the spectator theory of knowledge. Dewey argued that modernist conceptions of knowing regarded it as a passive recording of facts about the world, wherein the accuracy of knowing was to be judged as a matter of correspondence between our beliefs and those facts. Dewey viewed knowing as doing, as a constructive activity. Knowledge was not passive, but instrumental, in that it guided our dealings with the world we experience. The criterion that constituted knowledge was not correspondence, but warranted assertability.

Postmodern and poststructuralist approaches to qualitative inquiry radicalize Dewey's criticisms of the knower as a neutral spectator. They claim that observation is part of the 'gaze' of an 'ocular epistemology' that privileges visual representations and (wrongly) assumes a relatively seamless link between textual representations (videotapes, transcriptions of audiotapes, photographs) and the way the world really is. They maintain that experience itself is composed or constructed and hence never stable and determinate such that it can be grasped in visual representations. Representations are always textual reconstructions, not literal images. They argue that if knowledge is equated to visual perception (knowing through seeing), then (a) understanding is excluded because, unlike seeing, understanding is processual, changing, and dynamic and (b) the conscious knower or subject is excluded from the act of knowing, for he or she is simply looking in or looking at the experience of others—the one looking, not also the one who is being looked at. These criticisms thus make problematic both epistemological and political dimensions of the traditional conception of the participant-as-observer who is peripherally involved or only marginally participates in the scene where he or she studies. They invite examination of collaborative approaches to social inquiry that introduce the idea of active participation of the inquirer in the setting and sharing the role of researcher with participants.

See also Knowledge, Participant Observation.

KEY REFERENCES

Bryman, A. *Quantity and Quality in Social Research.* London: Unwin Hyman, 1988.
Denzin, N. K. *The Cinematic Society: The Voyeur's Gaze.* London: Sage, 1995.
Lonergan, B. "Consciousness and the Trinity," in W. J. Ong, ed., *Interfaces of the Word.* Ithaca, NY: Cornell University Press, 1977.

OCULAR EPISTEMOLOGY   See OBSERVATION.

ONTOLOGICAL HERMENEUTICS   See PHILOSOPHICAL HERMENEUTICS.

ONTOLOGY See METAPHYSICS.

ORAL HISTORY   This is a method of gathering and preserving historical information recorded through interviews with participants in past events and ways of life. Oral history aims to gain a more complete or unique understanding of the past as experienced both individually and collectively by soliciting memories, reminiscences, and testimony from specific informants or respondents.

See also Biographical Research, Biographical Turn, Interviewing, Types of.

KEY REFERENCES

Bornat, J. "Oral History," in C. Seale, G. Gobo, J. F. Gubrium, & D. Silverman, eds., *Qualitative Research Practice*. London: Sage, 2004.
Dunaway, D. K., & Baum, W. K., eds. *Oral History: An Interdisciplinary Anthology,* 2nd ed. Walnut Creek, CA: AltaMira Press,1996.
Perks, R., & Thomson, A., eds. *The Oral History Reader*. New York: Routledge, 2006.

OTHER (THE OTHER, OTHERNESS)   In a general sense, the goal of all forms of human inquiry is to understand 'the Other' (another person, tradition, history, ancestors, being, etc.). Anthropological and sociological studies, in particular, aim to understand other people and their language, culture, community, norms, values, beliefs, ways of life, traditions, and so on. Also, although the notions of 'same' and 'other' date to Plato's philosophy, it was not until the mid- to late twentieth century that scholars in anthropology and sociology, among other fields, began to engage in serious criticism of the interlocking epistemological, moral, and political dimensions of the posture through which inquirers of one culture studied another. Where once it was commonplace to read of studying the 'natives,' understanding the 'native's point of view,' or fears of 'going native' (losing one's supposed objective stance and becoming part of the very others one was attempting to study), it is now recognized that racist and colonialist assumptions often were embedded in such language. One of the strongest and oft-quoted contemporary statements of the colonizing and racist gaze of scholars was Edward Said's (1935–2003) *Orientalism,* in which he argued that orientalists (scholars of the East) represented the interests of old colonial powers in viewing the East as 'other'—foil and prey of the civilizing and, ultimately, triumphant West. Historical studies indicate that orientalism accompanied the rise and subsequent development of the Western nation-states from the sixteenth century onward, and contemporary studies further reveal how this kind of racism has been not only an academic disposition but also institutionalized in a variety of agencies and endeavors that promote Western education and economic and political growth and development to help the 'underdeveloped' other.

Overlapping, and in some ways intersecting with, this kind of moral-political reconsideration of what it means to study other peoples and their ways of life is the broad critique of Cartesian subject-centered reason and its accompanying will to mastery of situations and closure to alternatives that seems to characterize modernity. This critique informs a variety of positions including the following:

1. The 'decentering of the subject' characteristic of the ***poststructuralism*** of Jacques Derrida (1930–2004).

2. The shift from a monological method-driven conception of knowledge of others to the view that understanding others requires being prepared for the other to speak to us (thus treating the other as a being to be met, not an object to be viewed, tolerated, or disregarded) and recognizing that dialogue and conversation (not method) are the conditions under which understanding emerges. These views are elaborated in the ***philosophical hermeneutics*** of Hans-Georg Gadamer (1900–2002) as well as in Martin Buber's (1878–1965) I-Thou philosophy.

3. The concern with the primacy of the ethical over the ontological as found in the work of Paul Ricoeur (1913–2005) and Emmanuel Levinas (1906–1993) and elaborated in the postmodern ethics of Zygmunt Bauman. These positions on what it means to engage the other have, in turn, influenced scholarship in feminist thought, anthropology, gay and lesbian theory, post-colonial studies, multicultural studies, and other fields.

See also Ethnocentrism, Politics of Research, Understanding.

KEY REFERENCES

Bauman, Z. *Postmodern Ethics.* Oxford, UK: Blackwell, 1993.

Davis, C. *Levinas: An Introduction.* Notre Dame, IN: University of Notre Dame Press, 1996.

Di Leonardo, M., ed. *Gender at the Crossroads of Knowledge: Feminist Anthropology in the Postmodern Era.* Berkeley: University of California Press, 1991.

Friedman, M., ed. *Martin Buber and the Human Sciences.* Albany: SUNY Press, 1996.

Levinas, E. *Otherwise Than Being or Beyond Esse*nce. A. Lingis, trans. The Hague, The Netherlands: Martinus Nijhoff, 1981.

Ricoeur, P. *Oneself as Another.* K. Blamey, trans. Chicago: University of Chicago Press, 1992.

Said, E. *Orientalism.* London: Routledge & Kegan Paul, 1978.

P

PARADIGM   In Thomas Kuhn's (1922–1996) monograph *The Structure of Scientific Revolutions* (1962), the term *paradigm* played a significant role in his argument about the rationality of scientific inquiry. In the years following that publication (and its subsequent 1970 revision), it was particularly fashionable to talk about the qualitative versus quantitative 'paradigm debate' in the social sciences (although Kuhn's book did not discuss the social sciences). The term offered a convenient conceptual shorthand for pointing to apparently significant differences in methodologies. It was not always entirely clear, however, what the term actually meant in this context. Difficulty with the use of the term stemmed from Kuhn's own lack of conceptual clarity. Among the many uses of the term, he singled out two quite distinct definitions in responses to his critics. On the one hand, a paradigm refers to a type of cognitive framework—an exemplar or set of shared solutions to substantive problems used by a very well-defined, specific community of scientists (e.g., radio astronomers, protein chemists, and solid-state physicists) both to generate and to solve puzzles in their field. Kuhn argued that the essential activity of puzzle solving could be carried out only if the community of scientists shared these concrete exemplars, for scientists solved problems by modeling them on previous puzzle solutions. Using this definition, it is doubtful that social scientists have similar kinds of paradigms that guide their work. On the other hand, Kuhn also used the term to mean a disciplinary matrix—commitments, beliefs, values, methods, outlooks, and so forth shared across a discipline. This sense of paradigm as a worldview or general perspective is generally what social scientists appear to have in mind when they use the term. The following are critical issues: (a) What actually comprises different methodological paradigms or disciplinary matrices in social inquiry? What are the beliefs, assumptions, and values about the aim of social inquiry, self, society, human agency, method, and so forth shared by inquirers committed to postmodern versus interpretive ethnography, for example, or those committed to feminist theory or philosophical hermeneutics? (b) In what way do similar concerns and commitments cut across or overlap paradigms/disciplinary matrices that are often regarded as distinct? (c) How are these paradigms actually accomplished, enacted, or constituted socially and politically?

See also Methodology.

KEY REFERENCES

Guba, E. G., ed. *The Paradigm Dialog.* Newbury Park, CA: Sage, 1990.
Guba, E. G., & Lincoln, Y. S. "Competing Paradigms in Qualitative Research," in *Handbook of Qualitative Research,* N. K. Denzin & Y. S. Lincoln, eds. Thousand Oaks, CA: Sage, 1994.
Gutting, G. *Paradigms & Revolutions: Applications and Appraisals of Thomas Kuhn's Philosophy of Science.* Notre Dame, IN: University of Notre Dame Press, 1980.

PARADIGMATIC KNOWLEDGE CLAIM   This notion refers to a typical instance, specimen, archetype, model, or exemplary form of a knowledge claim. What is the exemplary form of a knowledge claim in social inquiry? In other words, what kind of knowledge does social inquiry aim to produce? These questions are explored by the feminist philosopher Lorraine Code. She argues that in a *logical empiricist* framework, a simple observational statement about an object—for example, 'the door is open,' 'that square object is red'—is regarded as paradigmatic and fundamental for what it means to know. More complex claims are built out of these simple observational statements. However, she contends that knowing other people is at least as worthy a candidate for paradigmatic status as is knowledge of objects. She maintains that the former kind of knowledge is qualitatively different from simple observational claims in the following ways: (a) It assumes a different subject-object relation; (b) these claims to know are open to negotiation between knower and 'known'; (c) the process of knowing other people requires constant learning—how to be with them, respond to them, act toward them; and (d) this kind of knowledge is never complete or finished—even if one knew all the facts about someone (or about one's self), that would not guarantee that one would know that person as she is.

The issue of what constitutes a specimen (paradigmatic) knowledge claim is important for conceiving of the various aims of qualitative inquiry. Forms of qualitative inquiry wedded to empiricist assumptions generally regard simple observational claims as most important. Code, however, argues for forms of feminist inquiry that take seriously the notion of knowing other people as defining what it means to seek knowledge. Approaches to qualitative inquiry that draw on *philosophical hermeneutics* echo a similar view in arguing for practical-moral knowledge or knowledge of *praxis*. Some social constructionists also hold this view. For example, John Shotter argues that social inquiry must shift its focus from efforts to understand objects to understanding human beings—from an interest in epistemology to an interest in practical hermeneutics. Practical hermeneutics, in turn, examines what Shotter variously refers to as knowledge in practice, knowledge held in common with others, or the kind of knowledge one has from within a situation, group, social institution, or society.

See also Epistemology, Knowledge.

KEY REFERENCES

Code, L. *What Can She Know? Feminist Theory and the Construction of Knowledge.* Ithaca, NY: Cornell University Press, 1991.
Shotter, J. *Conversational Realities.* London: Sage, 1993.
Taylor, C. "Gadamer on the Human Sciences," in R. Dostal, ed., *The Cambridge Companion to Gadamer.* Cambridge, UK: Cambridge University Press, 2002.

PARTICIPANT OBSERVATION   The notion of 'being there,' of witnessing social action firsthand, emerged as a professional scientific norm in cultural anthropology in the early twentieth century. As an *ethnographic method,* participant observation is a procedure for generating understanding of the ways of life of others. It requires that the researcher engage in some relatively prolonged period of engagement in a setting (e.g., community, group, or classroom), take some part in the daily activities of the people among whom he or she is studying, and reconstruct their activities through the processes of *inscription, transcription,* and *description* in *field notes* made on the spot or soon thereafter. More broadly conceived, participant observation is a methodology that assumes immersion in a setting (along with observation, reflection, and interpretation) is the best way to develop knowledge of others' ways of thinking and acting. It encompasses logistical, ethical, and political concerns involved in entering the world of those one studies, gaining their trust, developing empathy, and understanding their ways of talking about and acting in their world. Participant observation is also an epistemology, a way of knowing. It is a way of gaining access to the meaning of social action through either empathetic identification with those one is observing, through witnessing how the behaviors of actors acquire meaning through their connection to linguistic or cultural systems of meanings or forms of life, or both.

Participant observation is a means whereby the researcher becomes at least partially socialized into the group under study in order to understand the nature, purpose, and meaning of some social action that takes place there. It has been commonplace to insist that the participant observer adopt the stance of a marginal native or professional stranger. In this role, the fieldworker always maintains some respectful distance from those studied—cultivating empathy but never sympathy, rapport but never friendship, familiarity but never full identification (i.e., 'going native'). This critical distance is required for creating an objective account of what is being studied. Hence, the participant observer is advised always to maintain something like dual citizenship—having primary allegiance to an academic culture or disciplinary home while taking up temporary residence in the culture or group being studied.

Postmodern ethnography is characterized by a variety of criticisms of the foregoing account of participant observation as a methodology and epistemology. Criticisms are directed at (a) assumptions about the nature and purpose of researcher-actor interaction; (b) what counts as legitimate, credible, and authentic knowledge that allegedly results from firsthand, eyewitness accounts; (c) what the fieldworker is actually doing when he or she claims to be 'recording' observations of interactions and utterances and 'documenting' the lived realities of others; (d) what constitutes the *authority* of the participant observer; and so on. Other criticisms of participant observation are offered by feminist ethnographers who argue *for* closeness, friendship, and mutual identification with women being studied, and by participatory researchers who advocate for a form of research *with,* not *on,* the people being studied.

See also Ethnographic Naturalism, Ethnography, Intentionalism, Observation.

KEY REFERENCES

Atkinson, P., Coffey, A., & Delamont, S. *Key Themes in Qualitative Research.* Walnut Creek, CA: AltaMira Press, 2003. (Chapter on "Participant Observation and Interviewing")

Clifford, J. "On Ethnographic Authority," *Representations,* 1983, 1(2), 118–146.

Stocking, G., ed. *Observers Observed: Essays on Ethnographic Fieldwork.* Madison: University of Wisconsin Press, 1983.

PARTICIPATORY ACTION RESEARCH (PAR)   This is a broad designation for several kinds of *action research* that place a premium on the politics and power of knowledge production and use. Participatory action researchers typically work with groups and communities experiencing or subject to control, oppression, or colonization by a more dominant group or culture. Three characteristics appear to distinguish the forms of this practice from other forms of social inquiry: (1) its participatory character—cooperation and collaboration between the researcher(s) and other participants in problem definition, choice of methods, data analysis, and use of findings (Note: There are various ways of participating or collaborating including participants-as-researchers, participants networked to share knowledge, participants as problem formulators, researcher-as-colleague, and researcher-as-participant.); (2) its democratic impulse—PAR embodies democratic ideals or principles, but it is not necessarily a recipe for bringing about democratic change; (3) its objective of producing both useful knowledge and action as well as consciousness raising—empowering people through the process of constructing and using their own knowledge. PAR is also marked by tension surrounding the simultaneous realization of the aims of participant involvement, social improvement, and knowledge production. Some advocates of PAR disavow all efforts to produce general or theoretical knowledge and focus instead on the improvement of particular practices.

See also Collaborative Ethnography, Cooperative Inquiry.

KEY REFERENCES

Fals-Borda, O., & Rahman, M. A., eds. *Action and Knowledge: Breaking the Monopoly with Participatory Action Research.* New York: Intermediate Technology/ Apex, 1991.

Freire, P. *Pedagogy of the Oppressed.* New York: Herder & Herder, 1970.

McTaggart, R., ed. *Participatory Action Research: International Contexts and Consequences.* Albany: SUNY Press, 1997.

Reason, P. *Participation in Human Inquiry.* London: Sage, 1994.

Whyte, W. F., ed. *Participatory Action Research.* Newbury Park, CA: Sage, 1991.

PEER DEBRIEFING   In this procedure, a fieldworker confides in trusted and knowledgeable colleagues and uses them as a sounding board for one or more purposes. The fieldworker may wish to recount ethical or political dilemmas encountered in the field and solicit colleagues' reactions or simply have colleagues serve as good listeners. Peer debriefing can also involve sharing ideas about procedures and logistics in the field in order to get advice and to check the *dependability* of ways of proceeding, and it can involve sharing one's evolving attempts at describing and analyzing qualitative data in order to achieve some kind of consensual validation.

KEY REFERENCE

Lincoln, Y. S., & Guba, E. G. *Naturalistic Inquiry.* Beverly Hills, CA: Sage, 1985.

PERFORMANCE ETHNOGRAHY   See **PERFORMANCE STUDIES.**

PERFORMANCE/PERFORMATIVE/PERFORMATIVITY   These terms appear with increasing frequency in the extensive literature on qualitative inquiry—for example, the performance of identities, the performance (scripting, enactment) of research—and reflect several interrelated but distinct ideas.

1. In the 1960s, as part of a broad critique of behaviorist psychology, Erving Goffman (1922–1982) used the sociology of the theatre, the dramaturgical perspective, or *sociology of performance* to analyze social interactions and relations in public. (*See also play.*)

2. The term *performative* was used by the philosopher J. L. Austin (1911–1960) to refer to a written or spoken utterance that affects action. According to Austin, there is a class of utterances that do not describe, report, or merely say something; neither are they true or false. Rather, these kinds of utterances perform or are part of an action (the classic example used by Austin is the utterance "I do" spoken in a wedding ceremony). Austin's notion of a performative and, more broadly, his theory of how we accomplish things with language have been influential in *ethnomethodology, conversation analysis, deconstructionism,* some feminist scholarship, and poststructuralist theory.

3. *Performativity,* a term introduced by Lyotard (1924–1998), refers to the state of affairs that characterize modernity. Modernity values and desires

performativity (i.e., efficiency, completion, perfection, and measurement); consider, for example, the keen interest in performance management and performance assessment in virtually all aspects of social life (see *audit culture/society*). Performativity is a particular form of legitimation arising in modern capitalism and producing a bleak state of affairs that Lyotard called "a generalized computerization of society."

4. Used in a somewhat different sense, partially influenced by Austin's notion of a performative, *performativity* can also refer to the notion that language 'performs' (produces) identity. For example, Judith Butler argues that gender identity is not an attribute of self, but that one comes to be 'gendered' through a performative combination of sex, gender, sexual practice, and desire.

5. *Performance* often refers to an act or event. In the case of *performance texts* (experimental texts that are dialogical, multivoiced, etc.) or *performance art,* the term signals a different genre or form of telling, reporting, or portraying. As an event or act, a performance belies the notion of a 'real' experience or performance; performance texts or art are often ironic in that they undercut the meaning of a performance as complete, certain, perfect. Presence and reproduction, hallmarks of a 'real' performance, are replaced by experience and representation in a performance text. Performance texts in postmodern and feminist ethnography may also be viewed as a genre in which the formerly silenced are given *voice.*

6. The notion of a *performance aesthetic* evident in rhetorical strategies of both writing and performing reflects some of the notions discussed above. This is an aesthetic of no completion, no perfection, no complete realization or 'carrying out' of things. It emphasizes a serious playful mood. This, in turn, is related to the notion of a *performance ethic*—a way of relating to others that cautions against the dangers of taking *the other* for granted and of ways of understanding that close down rather than open up change and difference.

KEY REFERENCES

Austin, J. L. *How to Do Things with Words.* Oxford, UK: Oxford University Press, 1962.
Butler, J. *Excitable Speech: A Politics of the Performative.* New York: Routledge, 1997.
Denzin, N. K. *Interpretive Ethnography: Ethnographic Practices for the 21st Century.* Thousand Oaks, CA: Sage, 1997.
Denzin, N. K. "Performance Texts," in *Representation and the Text: Re-Framing the Narrative Voice,* W. G. Tierney & Y. S. Lincoln, eds. Albany: SUNY Press, 1997.

Lyotard, J.-F. *The Postmodern Condition: A Report on Knowledge*. Minneapolis: University of Minnesota Press, 1984.

Parker, A., & Sedgwick, E. K., eds. *Performativity & Performance*. New York: Routledge, 1995.

Turner, V. *The Anthropology of Performance*. New York: PAJ Publications, 1986.

PERFORMANCE STUDIES   Incorporating perspectives, theories, and concepts from anthropology, cultural studies, sociology, drama, art, and philosophy, and displaying influences from feminist theories, critical social science, and queer theory, performance studies is an academic field that critically examines performance and its relationships to representation, culture, politics, pedagogy, and texts (and other forms of expression). Performance ethnography is one genre of this broad field of study that also includes performance art, personal narrative, and drama.

KEY REFERENCES

Denzin, N. K. *Performance Ethnography*. Thousand Oaks, CA: Sage, 2003.

Madison, D. S., & Hamera, J., eds. *Handbook of Performance Studies*. Thousand Oaks, CA: Sage, 2005.

Turner, V. *The Anthropology of Performance*. New York: Performing Arts Journal Publication, 1986.

PHENOMENOLOGICAL SOCIOLOGY   This social theory aims to describe the structures of experience or the *lifeworld*. Its principal architect was Alfred Schutz (1899–1956), who built on the *phenomenology* of Edmund Husserl (1859–1938) to develop a phenomenological foundation for Weber's idea of meaningful social action. Schutz aimed to explain how it is that the lifeworld is actually produced and experienced by individuals. He sought to explain the essence of what he called the 'natural attitude'—the fact that we do not doubt the existence of the everyday world and its intersubjective, social character. Schutz argued that in order to effectively study the everyday world, the social inquirer must bracket or suspend one's taken-for-granted attitude toward its existence; the inquirer must assume the attitude of a disinterested observer. Schutz's work was an early influence in the development of Garfinkel's *ethnomethodology*.

See also Multiple Realities, Phenomenology, Verstehen.

KEY REFERENCES

Giddens, A. *New Rules of Sociological Method,* 2nd ed. Stanford, CA: Stanford University Press, 1993.

Schutz, A. *Collected Papers,* 3 vols. M. Natanson, ed. The Hague: Martinus Nijhoff, 1973.

Schutz, A. *The Phenomenology of a Social World.* Evanston, IL: Northwestern University Press, 1967.

PHENOMENOLOGY   This complex, multifaceted philosophy defies simple characterization because is not a single unified philosophical stand-point. It includes the transcendental phenomenology of Edmund Husserl (1859–1938), the existential forms of Maurice Merleau-Ponty (1908–1961) and Jean-Paul Sartre (1905–1980), and the hermeneutic phenomenology of Martin Heidegger (1889–1976). Generally speaking, phenomenologists reject scientific *realism* and the accompanying view that the empirical sciences have a privileged position in identifying and explaining features of a mind-independent world. Phenomenologists are opposed to the empiricist idea that genuine legitimate knowledge can be had only by rejecting the way we perceive the world of everyday life as 'mere appearance.' Hence, phenome-nologists insist on careful description of ordinary conscious experience of everyday life: the *lifeworld*—a description of 'things' (phenomena or the essential structures of consciousness) as one experiences them. These phe-nomena we experience include perception (hearing, seeing, etc.), believing, remembering, deciding, feeling, judging, evaluating, and all experiences of bodily action. Phenomenological descriptions of such things are possible only by turning from things to their meaning, from what is to the nature of what is. This turning away can be accomplished only by a certain phenomenological reduction or epoché that entails 'bracketing' or suspending what Husserl calls the "natural attitude." The natural attitude is the everyday assumption of the independent existence of what is perceived and thought about.

The two major variants of phenomenology influential in contemporary qualitative methodologies are the hermeneutic and the existential. The former, perhaps best known through the work of Hans-Georg Gadamer (1900–2002) and Paul Ricoeur (1913–2005), tends to focus on the collective or intersubjec-tive features of moral-political life as evident in a primary concern with issues of language and the nature and structure of communication. The latter variant is perhaps best known to social scientists through the work of the phenomenological sociologist Alfred Schutz (1899–1956)—a colleague of Husserl—who considerably influenced the social constructionist views of Peter Berger and Thomas Luckmann (*The Social Construction of Reality,* Anchor, 1967) and the development of **ethnomethodology** by Harold Garfinkel and Aaron Cicourel. This kind of phenomenology is more oriented toward describing the experience of everyday life as it is internalized in the subjective consciousness of individuals.

The use of the term *phenomenology* in contemporary versions of qualitative inquiry in North America tends to reflect a subjectivist, existentialist, and noncritical emphasis not present in the Continental tradition of phenomenology represented in the work of Husserl and Heidegger. The latter viewed the phenomenological project, so to speak, as an effort to get beneath or behind subjective experience to reveal the genuine, objective nature of things, and as a critique of both taken-for-granted meanings and subjectivism. Phenomenology, as it is commonly discussed in accounts of qualitative research, emphasizes just the opposite: It aims to identify and describe the subjective experiences of respondents. It is a matter of studying everyday experience from the point of view of the subject, and it shuns critical evaluation of forms of social life.

See also *Lifeworld, Phenomenological Sociology.*

KEY REFERENCES

Crotty, M. *The Foundations of Social Research.* London: Sage, 1998.
Hammond, M., Howarth, J., & Keat, R. *Understanding Phenomenology.* Oxford, UK: Blackwell, 1991.

PHILOSOPHICAL HERMENEUTICS Also called ontological **hermeneutics**, this is a philosophy of the humanities (or of the self-understanding of the humanities as historical sciences) attributable to Hans-Georg Gadamer (1900–2002), who built on the hermeneutic philosophy of Martin Heidegger (1889–1976) and drew on Aristotle's theory of practical knowledge. Because philosophical hermeneutics is not a methodology, and cannot be transformed into one without making it into something other than it is, its relevance for qualitative inquiry is not easily grasped. Moreover, the vast majority of approaches to qualitative inquiry are informed by thinking characteristic of the empirical sciences, not the humanities.

Gadamer was sharply critical of Dilthey's (1833–1911) view that hermeneutics was a *method* for generating knowledge in the human sciences. Philosophical hermeneutics is neither a method nor a methodology for obtaining knowledge and is not based on a traditional *subject-object relationship*. It aims to explicate a way of understanding (or a mode of experience in which we understand) through which truth is disclosed and communicated—truth that is not a matter of verification through methodical procedures of the empirical sciences. Understanding is an event or process that one participates in versus a process that is constructed by the knower (subject) to make sense of (discover the meaning of) an object (action, text, etc.).

Philosophical hermeneutics assumes that understanding an object (a *text,* a work of art, *human action,* another speaker, etc.) and interpreting it are essentially the same undertaking. Following Heidegger's lead, Gadamer argues that hermeneutics is ontological, universal, and conversational: It is ontological because 'understanding' is our very mode of being in the world, universal because understanding underlies all human activity, and conversational because the interpretation of an object is always a dialogical encounter—as interpreters we participate in, open ourselves to, share in, and listen to the claims that the object is making upon us. Understanding is always open and anticipatory; one never achieves a final, complete interpretation. This is so because we are always interpreting in light of 'prejudice' (or prejudgment, preconception) that comes from the tradition of which we are part. This tradition does not stand apart from our thought but constitutes the 'horizon' in which we do our thinking. Furthermore, language is the medium of all understanding in philosophical hermeneutics. Language is not understood as an instrument or tool, but an activity that, like play, reflects an intentionality and allows for both the constitution of meaning and the instability of meaning. Philosophical hermeneutics has also been characterized as a hermeneutics of trust because it reflects the belief that meaning or truth will be found through interpretation modeled on dialogue and conversation. It is thus often contrasted with *deconstructionism* or the *hermeneutics of suspicion*.

See also Experience, Hermeneutic Circle, Play, Praxis, Qualitative Inquiry.

KEY REFERENCES

Dostal, R. J., ed. *The Cambridge Companion to Gadamer.* Cambridge, UK: Cambridge University Press, 2002.

Gadamer, H.-G. *Truth and Method,* 2nd rev. ed., J. Weinsheimer & D. G. Marshall, trans. New York: Crossroad, 1989. (Originally published in German in 1960, first English translation 1975)

Risser, J. *Hermeneutics and the Voice of the Other: Re-reading Gadamer's Philosophical Hermeneutics.* Albany: SUNY Press, 1997.

PHOTO-ELICITATION, METHOD OF   In this method (also called photo-interviewing), photographs are integrated into the process of interviewing as a stimulus or means of evoking memories, understanding behaviors, examining perceptions, and so on. This is a strand of the broader field of *visual research methods.*

KEY REFERENCES

Collier, J., & Collier, M. *Visual Anthropology: Photography as Research Method.* Albuquerque: University of New Mexico Press, 1986.

Harper, D. "Meaning and Work: A Study in Photo-Elicitation," *International Journal of Visual Sociology,* 1984, 2(1), 20–43.

Huworth, R. "Photo-Interviewing for Research," *Social Research Update,* 2003, 40, 1–7.

PHRONESIS   See PRAXIS.

PLAY   As signifying a drama analogy, this notion relates broadly to the dramaturgical sociology of Erving Goffman (1922–1982) and his interest in studying actors in sociopolitical situations. Play as a metaphor for life or experience, however, is centrally important in both *philosophical hermeneutics* and *deconstructionism* as well. Both philosophies share the view that play is a kind of event, encounter, or movement that has no goal, that renews and repeats itself, and in which players (if they are truly playing) lose themselves. Play is not trivial but serious. But the seriousness belongs to the event itself, not the player, in the sense that the play itself is a kind of fascination with the world that takes over the player. Playing is a kind of being played. Thus, the primacy of the event (play) is emphasized over the conscious reflection and control of the player.

In the philosophical hermeneutics of Gadamer (1900–2002), play is a dialectic of transcendence and appropriation. On the one hand, as one gives oneself to play, one becomes fascinated with the world and loses oneself in the game or play. The play takes over determining possibilities and moving the player into the unknown. On the other hand, play affects a kind of self-discovery; it reveals possibilities to the player and thus is a kind of self-transformation. Being at play (or the event of play) is like being in a genuine conversation or dialogue with a text or with another person. Play is thus an analogy for the event of understanding. Both activities share the following features: There is a back-and-forth movement; each player or party to the conversation is exposed, vulnerable, and at risk; and in each event, one recognizes that other players or dialogue partners have something to say, and this requires not the subjectivity of a distanced onlooker but participation and involvement in the play or conversation. Gadamer argues that it is in this kind of encounter that a kind of disclosure takes place, a recognition of meaning (although this is not recognition as in recollecting an original meaning).

The deconstructionism of Jacques Derrida (1930–2004) makes use of this conceptualization of the metaphor of understanding as play, but with one important difference. Deconstructionism does not agree that meaning unfolds or is disclosed through play or that there can be such a thing as a continuity of meaning across encounters. For the deconstructionist, play reveals only the radically ambiguous nature of meaning, the continual play of indeterminate meanings.

See also Dialogue, Poststructuralism.

KEY REFERENCES

Gallagher, S. *Hermeneutics and Education*. Albany: SUNY Press, 1992.
Michelfelder, D. P., & Palmer, R. E., eds. *Dialogue and Deconstruction: The Gadamer-Derrida Exchange*. Albany: SUNY Press, 1989.

PLURALISM   This is one of four basic approaches to the study of social phenomena (the others are *antinaturalism, naturalism, critical social science*). Pluralists maintain that antinaturalistic and naturalistic approaches to the study of social life are complementary or compatible. They see no real difficulty with a social science that seeks both to explain human action and to interpret its meaning. A common view is that explanatory (naturalistic) and interpretive (antinaturalistic) approaches are compatible because each illuminates a different aspect of human *action* necessary for a complete understanding.

More broadly, pluralism is a type of reaction to the variety of traditions, philosophic orientations, methodologies, political perspectives, cultural views, values, and so on that characterize not simply the current scene in social science but life more generally. Bernstein (1991, pp. 335–336) argues that how one responds to this 'pluralization' can take several forms: (a) fragmenting pluralism—here one only communicates with one's own 'group' and sees no need to engage with others outside this small circle; (b) flabby pluralism—"where our borrowings from different orientations are little more than glib superficial poaching"; (c) polemical pluralism—here the existence of plural points of view does not signify a genuine willingness to listen and learn from others but becomes an "ideological weapon to advance one's own orientation"; (d) defensive pluralism—a form of tokenism where one pays lip service to the fact that others do their own thing, but we are already convinced that there is nothing to be learned from them; and (e) engaged fallibilist pluralism, which means

> taking our own fallibility seriously—resolving that however much we are committed to our own styles of thinking, we are willing to listen to others without denying or suppressing the otherness of the other. It means being vigilant against the dual temptations of simply dismissing what others are saying by falling back on one of those standard defensive ploys where we condemn it as obscure, wooly, or trivial, or thinking we can always easily translate what is alien into our own entrenched vocabularies. (pp. 335–336)

See also Mixed Methods.

KEY REFERENCES

Bernstein, R. J. *The New Constellation: The Ethical-Political Horizons of Modernity/ Postmodernity.* Cambridge, MA: MIT Press, 1991.
Braybrooke, D. *Philosophy of Social Science.* Englewood Cliffs, NJ: Prentice-Hall, 1987.
Fay, B. *Contemporary Philosophy of Social Science.* Oxford, UK: Blackwell, 1996.
Roth, P. *Meaning and Method in Social Science: A Case for Pluralism.* Ithaca, NY: Cornell University Press, 1987.

POIESIS   See PRAXIS.

POLITICS OF RESEARCH   Topics in the politics of qualitative inquiry include (a) examination of the political forces that operate *on* the enterprise of research from the outside, so to speak, to influence the choice of questions, topics, methods, and so on; (b) the micropolitics of relating to the people studied in field settings; (c) the sociopolitical stance of individual inquirers (including matters of advocacy, the politics of *representation, voice,* emancipatory aims of research, and so on); (d) the politics of identity and standpoint; (e) and the politics that act *through* the enterprise of inquiry. How these concerns are addressed depends, in large part, on how one conceives of the proper relationship between explanatory (descriptive) and normative (critical) interests of the social sciences.

Two long-standing political-ethical images of the inquirer based on the belief in value neutrality in social science are (1) the image of the liberal scholar who is committed to the ideal of knowledge for knowledge's sake and (2) the ideal of the disinterested social scientist who views her or his task as that of developing and testing empirical explanations of the social world and not changing that world. Scholars from a variety of philosophical persuasions maintain that value neutrality in the social sciences is an impossibility. They aim to restore (in a variety of ways) normative criticism to a proper place in social theorizing and, in so doing, seek ways to reunite theory and practice in research.

One way in which this kind of criticism of the politics and ethical aims of social research unfolds is through efforts to theorize the activity of social inquiry not simply in epistemological terms but as a kind of social agency. Hence, critics explore social inquiry as an economic, political, and social institution (practice) that accrues and exercises power to define the sociopolitical world. For example, Dorothy Smith (1990b, p. 2) identifies sociology as one of the "ruling apparatuses of society—those institutions of administration, management, and professional authority and of intellectual and cultural discourses which organize, regulate, lead, and direct capitalist societies." A similar view is expressed by the sociologist Zygmunt Bauman in his analysis of expertise in modern societies. Likewise, Charles Lindbloom argues that contemporary industrialized societies tend to be scientifically guided societies that look to the expertise of social scientists for social problem solving, social betterment, and guided social change.

Social scientists participate in the construction of ruling relations not by exercising social authority to command obedience or control decisions about policy but by virtue of the epistemological or cognitive authority that society invests in their discipline or profession. This role for social science in society leads to what Dorothy Smith calls a conceptual practice of power—a power to define the sociopolitical world through objectified knowledge. This power is exercised not simply in the scientific pronouncements (theories, claims) of social science professionals but also through the metaphysical commitments that are reflected in social scientific activity itself. In other words, social scientists do not simply teach us their scientific views, they also convey their beliefs about the sociopolitical world.

Scholars concerned with the ways in which politics act through the institution of social science often argue that traditional practice of social inquiry has been depoliticized: To depoliticize a practice of cognitive authority is to close the question of authority in favor of the experts, while to politicize the expertise of social science professionals is to open the question of cognitive authority to the critical scrutiny of society at large. Sandra Harding explains that the kind of politics that act less visibly and less consciously through the dominant institutional structures, priorities, practices, and languages of science paradoxically function as a kind of depoliticization. A depoliticized practice, in Harding's (1992, pp. 568–569) view, "certifies as value-neutral, normal, natural, and *not political at all* the existing scientific policies and practices through which powerful groups can gain the information and explanations that they need to advance their priorities."

See also Critical Theory, Disinterested Social Science, Ethics of Qualitative Inquiry, Fact-Value Distinction, Other (The Other, Otherness), (The) Problem of the Criterion, Standpoint Epsitemologies.

KEY REFERENCES

Ali, S., Campbell, K., Branley, D., & James, R. "Politics, Identities and Research," in C. Seale, ed., *Researching Society and Culture,* 2nd ed. London: Sage, 2004.

Atkinson, P., Coffey, A., & Delamont, S. *Key Themes in Qualitative Research.* Walnut Creek, CA: AltaMira Press, 2003. (Chapter 3: "Whose Side Are We On?")

Bauman, Z. *Intimations of Postmodernity.* London: Routledge, 1992.

Fuller, S. *Social Epistemology.* Bloomington: Indiana University Press, 1988.

Haan, N., Bellah, R. N., Rabinow, P., & Sullivan, W. M. *Social Science as Moral Inquiry.* New York: Columbia University Press, 1983.

Hammersley, M. *Taking Sides in Social Research: Essays on Partisanship and Bias.* London: Routledge, 2000.

Harding, S. "After the Neutrality Ideal: Science, Politics, and 'Strong Objectivity,'" *Social Research,* 1992, 59(3), 567–587.

Lindbloom, C. *Inquiry and Change.* New Haven, CT: Yale University Press, 1990.

Smith, D. *The Conceptual Practices of Power.* Boston: Northeastern University Press, 1990a.

Smith, D. *Texts, Facts, and Femininity: Exploring the Relations of Ruling.* New York: Routledge & Kegan Paul, 1990b.

POLYPHONY   See DIALOGISM.

POSITIVISM   This is a term coined by Auguste Comte (1798–1857) indicating a philosophy of strict empiricism—the only genuine or legitimate knowledge claims are those founded directly on experience. Comte sought to advance the project of 'positive knowledge' by distinguishing this kind of dependable empirical knowledge from claims made by theology and ***metaphysics.*** He divided history into three stages—the theological, the metaphysical, and the positive. In the last stage, metaphysical speculation is dissolved by science. He developed a unified hierarchical conception of the sciences and argued that the goal of science was prediction accomplished by identifying laws of succession. Sociology, in his view, should aim at identifying the laws that govern the development of society. The term is often used as shorthand for ***logical positivism,*** or more generally to designate any approach that applies ***scientific method*** to the study of human ***action.***

See also Empiricism, Logical Empiricism.

KEY REFERENCE

Hollis, M. *The Philosophy of Social Science: An Introduction.* Cambridge, UK: Cambridge University Press, 1994.

POSTEMPIRICISM   This is the name for a collection of ideas and arguments in the philosophy of science that followed the demise of the strict ***empiricism*** of ***logical positivism.*** Postempiricist philosophers include Karl Popper (1902–1994), W. V. O. Quine (1908–2000), Norwood Hanson (1925–1967), Imre Lakatos (1922–1974), Paul Feyerabend (1924–1994), Thomas Kuhn (1922–1996), Stephen Toulmin, and many others. Postempiricism is a ***nonfoundationalist epistemology*** that accepts fallibilism but does not relinquish the idea that evidence is necessary for judging the truth or falsity of

scientific claims. The central ideas of the postempiricist view are the following: (a) Data are not detachable from theory; (b) the language of science is irreducibly metaphorical and inexact; (c) meanings are not separate from facts but, in some sense, determine facts; (d) scientific theories can never be either conclusively verified nor conclusively refuted by data alone; and (e) science consists of research projects or programs structured by presuppositions about the nature of reality. Ironically, many contemporary defenders of qualitative approaches to inquiry do not attack this postempiricist epistemology but attack instead a long-since-abandoned strict empiricism.

See also Postpositivism, Theory-Observation Distinction.

KEY REFERENCES

Brown, H. I. *Perception, Theory and Commitment: The New Philosophy of Science.* Chicago: University of Chicago Press, 1977.
Hesse, M. *Revolutions and Reconstructions in the Philosophy of Science.* Bloomington: Indiana University Press, 1980.

POSTMODERN ETHNOGRAPHY   This term signifies the postmodern critique of ethnographic practices in both classical and *interpretive anthropology*. Postmodern ethnography criticizes classical ethnography for privileging participant observation, for its tendency to assume a smooth link between 'being there' and understanding the lived experience of others, and for its effort to develop seamless, comprehensive descriptions of common material culture and perspectives. Interpretive ethnography is criticized for privileging *thick description* and for assuming that the ethnographer's understanding can unproblematically reflect the viewpoint of the '*other.*' Central concerns in the postmodern ethnographic critique include the connections between authorship, *authority, representation,* and rhetoric and an effort to experiment with textual forms for ethnography that decenter the monologic voice of the ethnographer in favor of dialogic or polyphonic texts.

See also Ethnographic Realism, Participant Observation, Postmodernism.

KEY REFERENCES

Clifford, J., & Marcus, G. *Writing Culture: The Poetics and Politics of Ethnography.* Berkeley: University of California Press, 1986.

Denzin, N. K. *Interpretive Ethnography: Ethnographic Practices for the 21st Century.* Thousand Oaks, CA: Sage, 1997.

POSTMODERN FEMINISM   See FEMINIST EPISTEMOLOGIES.

POSTMODERNISM   Although this term and *poststructuralism* are often used interchangeably, postmodern theory or postmodernism is generally regarded as a more encompassing notion. The term originated as a description of a particular architectural style opposed to modernist architecture and eventually was applied to graphic arts, literature, and the contours of social and political life. Broadly conceived, postmodernism is an attitude toward the social world at the present stage of its historical development—more of a diagnosis than a theory. It is radically interdisciplinary in character and rejects conventional styles of academic discourse. Many scholars claim that it is characterized by its opposition to four central doctrines that form the core of the Enlightenment tradition: (1) the notion of a rational, autonomous subject; a self that has an essential human nature; (2) the notion of *foundationalist epistemology* (and foundationalist philosophy in general); (3) the notion of reason as a universal, a priori capacity of individuals; and (4) the belief in social and moral progress through the rational application of social scientific theories to the arts and social institutions (law, family, education, etc.). Postmodernism is also characterized by its distrust of and incredulity toward all 'totalizing' discourses or *metanarratives*—those large-scale or abstract theoretical frameworks that purportedly explain culture, society, and human agency. In place of these metaframeworks, postmodern theory endorses heterogeneity, difference, fragmentation, and indeterminacy.

Not all scholars associated with postmodern thought describe their work as postmodern or themselves as postmodernists. In fact, few scholars agree as to what exactly the term means except perhaps that it represents a reaction to, critique of, or departure from modernism to which the Enlightenment gave birth. But this definition is problematic as well for the following reasons: If modernity is a historical stage in the development of society, then modernism is a reaction to modernity. The historical period of modernity is characterized by faith in reason, representation, certainty, continuity of meaning, essentialism, foundationalism, and a commitment to abstraction, grand theorizing, rationalization, and instrumentality in thought and society. Modernism is characterized as a significant and varied critique of all of these notions in architecture, literature, art, philosophy, and so on. Yet none of the scholars and artists engaged in this critique would be labeled postmodernists. Hence, postmodernism cannot simply be a reaction to or antithesis of modernism. It must be characterized by something other than the kind of opposition that has been mounted from within modernity itself. One way in which this difference has been drawn is to argue that modernist critiques of modernity generally exhibited faith that the problems of modernity could be solved. In other words, critics of modernity believed that they could at once be both subversive and redemptive, both critical and utopian. While postmodernism shares many of the same criticisms as modernism, what distinguishes it is that postmodern critics completely relinquish all faith in the redemptive power of modernist thought.

See also *Crisis of Legitimation, Crisis of Representation, Grand Narrative, Grand Theory.*

KEY REFERENCES

Best, S., & Kellner, D. *Postmodern Theory.* New York: Guilford Press, 1991.

Crotty, M. *The Foundations of Social Research.* London: Sage, 1998.

Harvey, D. *The Condition of Postmodernity.* Oxford, UK: Blackwell, 1989.

Posnock, R. *The Trial of the Century: Henry James, William James, and the Challenge of Modernity.* Oxford, UK: Oxford University Press, 1991.

Rosenau, P. *Post-Modernism and the Social Sciences.* Princeton, NJ: Princeton University Press, 1992.

POSTMODERN SENSIBILITIES   In the context of qualitative inquiry, this phrase appears to have been introduced by Jaber Gubrium and James Holstein to refer to a collection of beliefs, perspectives, and stances influencing the way one thinks about the purpose and practice of qualitative research (specifically, the act of interviewing). These sensibilities include calling into question conventional criteria for research and the idea of a universally valid and disinterested knowledge, skepticism regarding the authority and legitimacy of social science, a belief in ***representation*** as more rhetorical than reportorial, and practicing a form of reflexive empiricism. While perhaps not all would agree with his characterization, Alford (1998) summarizes these sensibilities as follows:

Human beings are both emotional and intellectual selves, constantly constructing the world around us. The categories we use in that complex process of self-construction are embedded in standpoints derived from our social memberships and identities. The world is thus socially constructed by language, and language is constituted by cultural meanings negotiated by persons with identities shaped by their historical experiences and social location. Knowledge is historically contingent and shaped by human interests and social values, rather than external to us, completely objective, and eternal, as the extreme positivist view would have it. (pp. 2–3)

See also Postmodernism.

KEY REFERENCES

Alford, R. R. *The Craft of Inquiry.* New York: Oxford University Press, 1998.
Alvesson, M., & Sköldberg, K. *Reflexive Methodology: New Vistas for Qualitative Research.* London: Sage, 2000.
Gubrium, J. F., & Holstein, J. A. *The New Language of Qualitative Method.* New York: Oxford University Press, 1997.
Gubrium, J. F., & Holstein, J. A. "Postmodern Sensibilities," in J. F. Gubrium & J. A. Holstein, eds. *Postmodern Interviewing.* Thousand Oaks, CA: Sage, 2003.

POSTPOSITIVISM   This term is used in several ways in the literature. It can mean 'nonpositivism,' that is, any epistemology other than that of *positivism* or *logical positivism*. It can more narrowly refer to a less strict form of positivism, namely, *logical empiricism*. Also, it sometimes is used as a synonym for *postempiricism*.

KEY REFERENCES

Crotty, M. *The Foundations of Social Research.* London: Sage, 1998.
Phillips, D. C., & Burbules, N. C. *Postpositivism and Educational Research.* Lanham, MD: Rowman & Littlefield, 2000.

POSTSTRUCTURALISM   This is the general name for a critique of *structuralism* that arose largely in France in the early 1970s through the work of Georges Bataille (1897–1962), Jacques Derrida (1930–2004), Michel Foucault (1926–1984), Julia Kristeva, Jean-François Lyotard (1924–1998), Roland Barthes (1915–1980), and Jean Baudrillard, among others. Poststructuralism shares many of the same concerns of structuralism (e.g., it is resolutely antimetaphysical and antihumanist; it accepts the fact that language plays a central role in the constitution of subjectivity and social reality). However, whereas structuralism was informed by the constructive scientific vision of identifying both social and linguistic order, poststructuralism is resolutely *de*constructive in intent. Although there is considerable variation among the views of the cluster of scholars identified as poststructuralist, several central themes are identifiable: First is the decentering of the notion of an individual, self-aware condition of being a subject. Poststructuralists question the value and existence of the metaphysical notion of a human being or conscious subject as a datum. The 'I' is not immediately available to itself because it derives its identity only from its position in language or its involvement in various systems of signification. Hence, subjects, authors, and speakers are irrelevant to the interpretation of texts. Second is pantextualism—everything is a *text*—and all texts are interrelated, which makes for 'intertextuality.' Third, meaning is unstable, never fixed, never determined or determinable, never representational. Fourth, *deconstructionism* is a poststructuralist strategy for reading texts that unmasks the supposed 'truth' or meaning of text by undoing, reversing, and displacing taken-for-granted binary oppositions that structure texts (e.g., right over wrong, subject over object, reason over nature, men over women, speech over writing, reality over appearance).

See also Semiotics.

KEY REFERENCES

Culler, J. *On Deconstruction.* Ithaca, NY: Cornell University Press, 1982.
Giddens, A. "Structuralism, Post-structuralism, and the Production of Culture," in *Social Theory Today*, A. Giddens & J. H. Turner, eds. Stanford, CA: Stanford University Press, 1987.
Seidman, S. *Contested Knowledge: Social Theory in the Postmodern Era,* 2nd ed. Oxford, UK: Blackwell, 1998.

PRACTICAL RATIONALITY/REASON   See PRAXIS, RATIONALITY, TECHNICAL RATIONALITY.

PRACTICAL TURN   Sociology and philosophy, in recent years, have been home to a turn to the practical—that is, to a profound concern with the situated, concrete, embodied actions and meanings of social actors. A central assumption in this turn is that the primary category of human reality is practice, not social structures or systems, on the one hand, nor the collection and combination of separate individuals and their attributes, on the other. Practice refers to engaged action or activity organized around a shared practical understanding. Driving an automobile is a practice in this sense, as is vegetarianism, visiting friends for an evening of dinner and conversation, banking (e.g., cashing a check, withdrawing money from an ATM, depositing money into an account), greeting a stranger, and so on. The practical turn is a bit difficult to explain in an economical way because it takes up several sets of issues including the definitions of *practice, practical reasoning,* and *practical knowledge;* explications of a relational ontology; the importance of recovering practical knowledge as an antidote to technical rationality; the way in which practical knowledge (individual capacities for discernment, deliberation, and good judgment) is implicated in discussions of public, democratic participation in decision making; and how the cultivation of practical reason relates to matters of education and learning.

See also Atomism, Holism, Praxis.

KEY REFERENCES

Bourdieu, P. *Outline of a Theory of Practice.* R. Nice, trans. Cambridge, UK: Cambridge University Press, 1997.

Dunne, J., & Pendlebury, S. "Practical Reason," in N. Blake, P. Smeyers, R. Smith, & P. Standish, eds., *The Blackwell Guide to the Philosophy of Education.* Oxford, UK: Blackwell, 2003.

Schatzki, T., Knorr-Cetina, K., & von Savigny, E., eds. *The Practice Turn in Contemporary Theory.* London: Routledge, 2001.

Stern, D. G. "The Practical Turn," in S. P. Turner & P. A. Roth, eds., *The Blackwell Guide to the Philosophy of the Social Sciences.* Oxford, UK: Blackwell, 2003.

Toulmin, S. *Return to Reason.* Cambridge, MA: Harvard University Press, 2001.

PRACTICE   See PRAXIS.

PRAGMATISM   Perhaps the only uniquely American philosophy, pragmatism is best known through the work of William James (1842–1910), John Dewey (1859–1952), and Charles Sanders Peirce (1839–1914) and through its revival as neopragmatism in the works of Richard Rorty. There are many versions of pragmatism and some are significantly different (e.g., the pragmatism of Peirce and that of Rorty). Generally speaking, however, this philosophy views knowledge as an instrument or tool for organizing experience, and it is deeply concerned with the union of theory and practice. For qualitative inquiry, pragmatism or the pragmatic outlook is important for at least two reasons: (1) Pragmatism is a philosophical source of *symbolic interactionism* and the *Chicago School of Sociology*, and (2) the contemporary pragmatic outlook comprises a set of ideas that are often appealed to in defending qualitative inquiry as a viable option in the social sciences. Richard J. Bernstein (1991) identifies these substantive themes as (a) antifoundationalism; (b) a "thoroughgoing fallibilism where we realize that although we must begin any inquiry with prejudgments and can never call everything into question at once, nevertheless there is no belief or thesis—no matter how fundamental—that is not open to further interpretation and criticism"; (c) "the social character of the self and the need to cultivate a critical community of inquirers"; (d) an "awareness and sensitivity to radical contingency and chance that mark the universe, our inquiries, our lives"; and (e) the view that there can be no escape from the plurality of traditions, perspectives, and philosophic orientations.

See also Instrumentalism.

KEY REFERENCES

Bernstein, R. J. *The New Constellation: The Ethical-Political Horizons of Modernity/Postmodernity.* Cambridge: MIT Press, 1991.

Diggins, J. *The Promise of Pragmatism: Modernism and the Crisis of Knowledge and Authority.* Chicago: University of Chicago Press, 1994.

Joas, H. *Pragmatism and Social Theory.* Chicago: University of Chicago Press, 1993.

Mounce, H. O. *The Two Pragmatisms: From Peirce to Rorty.* New York: Routledge, 1997.

West, C. *The American Evasion of Philosophy: A Genealogy of Pragmatism.* Madison: University of Wisconsin Press, 1989.

PRAXIS   There is a long history of this notion in Marxism, existentialism, and pragmatism, but perhaps it is currently best known to qualitative inquirers as occupying a central place in the hermeneutic philosophies of Hans-Georg Gadamer (1900–2002) and Jürgen Habermas. To grasp the special meaning of this term, it may be useful to contrast it to the more common word *practice.*

Praxis is a term for a particular form of human activity that means something different than our common usage of the word *practice*. Practice typically means the domain of everyday activity (i.e., the world of the practitioner) in which theory is applied or used; practice is about action and doing (while theory is about knowledge and thinking). In the literature on action research, considerable criticism is directed at theory for being too 'academic' and abstract and hence distant from or irrelevant to practice in this sense. Consequently, considerable attention is paid to improving practice by designing ways of getting knowledge (theory) somehow better aligned with or connected to practice (i.e., by beginning an inquiry with practitioners' own knowledge, doing coresearch, etc.). This distinctly modernist notion of practice as the everyday work of practitioners that ought to be informed and hence improved or perfected by theory (i.e., knowledge generated through the application of method) is not what praxis means to either Gadamer or Habermas. In fact, it is precisely this connection between theory and practice that they find problematic. The source of this difference lies in efforts of Gadamer and Habermas to revitalize Aristotle's (*Nicomachean Ethics,* Book VI) scheme of knowledge and action that is based on a threefold distinction between theory (*episteme*) and two forms of practical knowledge (*techne* and *phronesis*). This distinction is summarized below:

- *Theory* as an activity arises in the life of contemplation; it is separate from the practical and productive life of the polis (the life of individuals in society; the realm of morality, ethics, political life, education, etc.). Theory yields knowledge of necessary and eternal truths (*episteme*); such knowledge is not possible in the polis because of its inherently changeable and uncertain nature.
- Two other forms/modes of activity are the *productive* (*poiesis*) and the *practical* (*praxis*):
  - PRODUCTIVE ACTIVITY (*POIESIS*): REQUISITE KNOWLEDGE IS *TECHNE*. This is a form of activity under the firm control of an objective, impersonal method. It is an activity that has to do with making or fabrication. It is craftsmanship—an activity designed to bring about and terminate in a product or result. The product/result is separable from the one who produces it; and the knowledge required for (or which governs) this activity is also separable from the user of that knowledge. It is a kind of activity in which one can decide to willfully

participate or not participate. This particular kind of activity is associated with a type of practical knowledge called *techne* ('technical knowledge'). This is the kind of knowledge possessed by an expert in a specialized craft—a person who understands the principles underlying the production of an object or state of affairs, for example, a house, a table, a safe journey, a state of being healthy. Moreover, this kind of knowledge fits smoothly into a means-end framework: The materials and tools (including method) of this kind of practical knowledge are means used by the maker to bring about the end product/result. Practical knowledge itself (*techne*) is a means to the achievement of the final product as the end of the activity.

o PRACTICAL ACTIVITY (*PRAXIS*): REQUISITE KNOWLEDGE IS *PHRONESIS*. This is a form of activity that has to do with the conduct of one's life and affairs as a member of society. It is about doing the right thing and doing it well in interactions with fellow humans. It is an activity that leaves no separably identifiable outcome as its product, hence the end (aim) of the activity (i.e., being a 'good' human being, teacher, doctor, lawyer, etc.) is realized in the very doing of the activity itself. This is the kind of activity from which one cannot 'rest'— unlike the practical activity of poiesis, it is not an activity that one can set aside at will. Joseph Dunne (1993) explains that praxis is a "type of human engagement that is embedded within a tradition of communally shared understandings and values, that remains vitally connected to peoples' life experience, that finds expression in their ordinary linguistic usage, and that, rather than being a means through which they achieve outcomes separate from themselves, is a kind of enactment through which they constitute themselves as persons in a historical community" (p. 176). The distinct mode of practical knowledge associated with praxis is *phronesis* ('practical wisdom'). This is neither a technical nor a cognitive capacity that one has at one's disposal, but rather is bound up with the kind of person that one is and is becoming. This kind of practical-moral knowledge characterizes a person who knows how to live well; it is acquired and deployed in one's actions with one's fellow human beings. It demands an intellectual and moral disposition toward right living and the pursuit of human good and hence a different form of reasoning and knowledge. This kind of knowledge is variously referred to as deliberative excellence, practical wisdom, or practical reason. Associated cognitive virtues are understanding, judgment, and interpretation. *Phronesis* is intimately concerned with the timely, the local, the particular, and the contingent (e.g., what should I do *now,* in *this* situation, given *these* circumstances, facing *this* particular person, at *this* time).

Both Gadamer and Habermas argue that modernity is characterized by an assimilation of theory and *episteme* to *poiesis* and *techne.* Modern science invented a new form of theoretical knowledge based on methods, completely displacing the notion of theory as a contemplative ideal with a new form of *techne.* Scientific theory is pursued with the attitude of the technician (i.e., within the form of activity that Aristotle would have called *poiesis*). In other words, technical control through the use of an impersonal method is the defining perspective, framework, and interest within which scientific theory is assembled. In modern science, the only kind of knowledge that counts as both as theory and as a source of production is that given by science—that is, knowledge based on method (this is a definition of **scientism**).

For both Gadamer and Habermas, an even more troubling and dangerous feature of modernity is the assimilation of *praxis* (the practical domain of personal and social affairs) into *techne.* Roughly, this is equivalent to treating every human situation where practical-moral judgment is required (e.g., in teaching, managing, providing health care or social services) as presenting a technical problem to be solved by the application of knowledge generated via method. They both seek to recover the centrality of praxis to our self-understanding.

Both Gadamer and Habermas draw on the Aristotelian conception of knowledge and action in order to restore a sense of *praxis* to our life in society, and both agree that **hermeneutics** (understanding) plays an intrinsic role in this recovery. In other words, practical life/practical reason is the medium in which understanding takes place. This is so because in *praxis,* we must continually understand/interpret each other's language in gestures and speech, and without the reliable background of such understanding, *praxis* would be impossible. Moreover, *praxis* is not external to understanding; that is, one does not first understand (by generating knowledge based on method) and then 'apply' that understanding to *praxis.* Rather, in the 'event' of understanding itself, there is already an element of *praxis* (action-oriented self-understanding). Thus, for Gadamer, as we come to a clearer view of the nature of understanding, we possess a more adequate conception of *praxis.*

For Gadamer, recovering Aristotle's notions of *phronesis* as a form of knowledge is a key to understanding what it means to 'do' hermeneutics. *Phronesis* is a model of the problems of hermeneutics—the model helps to destroy the notion that knowledge (understood as *techne*) has authority or sovereignty over being (*praxis*). In Gadamer's view, the kind of knowledge and understanding that characterizes *praxis* is not technical knowledge anchored in method, but *phronesis*. Understanding is an event that happens within a relationship of vulnerability to that which one seeks to understand. The interpreter surrenders to an interaction in which he/she is always at risk and always in a situation demanding situated reflection (see *play*).

Habermas develops a conception of *praxis* that is itself deeply informed by critique. Gadamer believes that the possibilities for restoring our sense of the centrality of critical moral-political judgment in daily life lie within the tradition of *praxis* itself. Habermas disagrees, arguing that *praxis* itself is distorted by ideology; thus, we must have a vantage point outside of tradition, outside of *praxis,* from which to develop a critique of *praxis.*

See also Critical Hermeneutics, Critical Theory, Philosophical Hermeneutics.

KEY REFERENCES

Bernstein, R. J. *Beyond Objectivism and Relativism.* Philadelphia: University of Pennsylvania Press, 1983.

Bernstein, R. J. *Praxis & Action,* new ed. Philadelphia: University of Pennsylvania Press, 1999.

Dunne, J. "Back to the Rough Ground: 'Phronesis' and 'Techne,'" in *Modern Philosophy* and in *Aristotle.* Notre Dame, IN: University of Notre Dame Press, 1993.

Gadamer, H.-G. *Reason in the Age of Science,* F. G. Lawrence, trans. Cambridge: MIT Press, 1981.

Habermas, J. *Knowledge and Human Interests,* J. J. Shapiro, trans. Boston: Beacon Press, 1971.

Habermas, J. *The Theory of Communicative Action,* Vol. 1, T. McCarthy, trans. Boston: Beacon Press, 1981.

Lobkowicz, N. *Theory and Practice: History of a Concept from Aristotle to Marx.* Notre Dame, IN: University of Notre Dame Press, 1967.

Polkinghorne, D. E. *Practice and the Human Sciences.* Albany: SUNY Press, 2004.

PREJUDICE   *See Bias, Philosophical Hermeneutics.*

(THE) PROBLEM OF THE CRITERION   The following is the problem of the criterion: How can we specify *what* we know without specifying *how* we know it, and vice versa? While there is no generally accepted resolution to this skeptical argument, the central project of *epistemology* remains the justification of knowledge claims—how are we to decide that any particular account or interpretation of the world is valid, genuine, legitimate, and true? Philosophers and methodologists have devoted much effort to specifying the appropriate *criteria* for making such an assessment.

The legitimization of social scientific inquiry has hinged on the fact that it is particularly preoccupied with means for developing and testing accounts of social phenomena for their accuracy or truth. The advent of *postmodernism* and *poststructuralism* in social thought has cast the project of epistemological justification, and hence the traditional grounds of authority for social science, into question. For some scholars, issues of epistemological criteria no longer matter; what does matter is political justification. For other scholars, the epistemological and the political are collapsed into an interlocking larger issue. Of course, social science has always had scholars who focused on the political nature of the enterprise. But within recent decades, concerns about the politics of method, hostility toward allegedly authoritative claims of *representation*, denials of the possibility of truth, and so forth have called into question the importance of the search for *epistemic criteria* in social science. For many social theorists, the central problem of social science is no longer one of developing the best criteria for establishing genuine knowledge but rather one of unmasking the values and politics of the enterprise of social inquiry that were hidden within the epistemological project.

See also Crisis of Representation, Politics of Research, Validity.

KEY REFERENCE

Smith, J. K. *After the Demise of Empiricism: The Problem of Judging Social and Educational Inquiry.* Norwood, NJ: Ablex, 1993.

PROPOSITIONAL KNOWLEDGE   On a relatively commonsense interpretation, propositions are sentences or statements that express in written or spoken language what we believe, doubt, affirm, or deny. (Of course, we express these dispositions in other ways as well.) Assertions, interpretations, evaluations, conclusions, findings, hypotheses and the like are familiar kinds of propositions or statements. Propositional knowledge is 'knowing that'—an assertion *that* something is so. It is a kind of knowledge distinguishable from 'knowing how'—knowledge of how to do something.

The phrase *propositional knowledge* is often used in the literature on qualitative inquiry in a way that connotes something more like abstract formal language. Logic is such a language—its grammar and interpretation are determined solely by rules defining its symbols. Propositional knowledge thus often means something like the expression of scientific knowledge claims in a formal mathematical calculus. (A propositional calculus employs symbols for variables in combination with logical operators also expressed in symbolic form, e.g., $p \supset q$ is read "if p then q" or "p implies q"; $p \equiv q$ is read "p is equivalent to q" or "p if and only if q.") The logical positivists argued that all genuine scientific knowledge should be capable of expression in this kind of formal language. They believed that by stating (and analyzing) claims about the world using the tools of formal logic, one could arrive at a way of expressing knowledge claims in propositions that were unambiguous, timeless, and expressive of unchanging relations. Qualitative inquiry in general opposes this view. Hence, when the phrase *propositional knowledge* is used in contrast to notions like tacit knowledge, experiential knowledge, practical knowledge, and so forth, it may be a way of expressing opposition to the idea that there is only one way to speak of what constitutes genuine, legitimate knowledge of the world.

See also *Language, Narrative Psychology, Tacit (Personal) Knowledge.*

KEY REFERENCE

Bunge, M. *Finding Philosophy in Social Science.* New Haven, CT: Yale University Press, 1996.

PURPOSIVE SAMPLING   See SAMPLING LOGIC.

Q

QUALITATIVE EVALUATION This is a broad designation for a variety of approaches to evaluating (i.e., determining the merit, worth, or significance of) social and educational programs, policies, projects, and technologies that make use of typically 'qualitative' methods for generating data (e.g., unstructured *interviewing, observation, document analysis*) and nonstatistical means of analyzing and interpreting those data. These approaches arose in the mid-1970s as a reaction to the dominance of randomized and quasi-experimental designs and the use of standardized measures of achievement as the primary means of evaluation. Included here are approaches known as case study evaluations, responsive evaluation, illuminative evaluation, and *naturalistic inquiry* or fourth-generation evaluation.

KEY REFERENCES

Guba, E., & Lincoln, Y. S. *Fourth Generation Evaluation.* Newbury Park, CA: Sage, 1989.
Patton, M. Q. *Qualitative Evaluation and Research Methods,* 2nd ed. Newbury Park, CA: Sage, 1990.
Reichardt, C. S., & Rallis, S. F., eds. *The Qualitative-Quantitative Debate: New Perspectives.* New Directions for Program Evaluation, No. 61. San Francisco: Jossey-Bass, 1994.

QUALITATIVE INQUIRY *Qualitative* is a not-so-descriptive adjective attached to the varieties of social inquiry that have their intellectual roots in *hermeneutics, phenomenological sociology,* and the *Verstehen* tradition. Many scholars use the phrase *qualitative inquiry* as a blanket designation for all forms of social inquiry that rely primarily on qualitative data (i.e., data in the form of words) including *ethnography, case study research, naturalistic inquiry, ethnomethodology, life-history methodology,* and *narrative inquiry*. To call a research activity *qualitative* inquiry may broadly mean that it aims at understanding the *meaning* of human *action*. Perhaps the clearest use of the adjective is to distinguish between qualitative data—nonnumeric data in the form of words—and quantitative data—numeric data. The term is also used, however, as a modifier for *method, methodology, research,* and *paradigm* and as a synonym for *nonexperimental* and *ethnographic*. Because the adjective is used in so many different ways, it does not clearly signal a particular meaning or denote a specific set of characteristics for qualitative research.

Often, the use of the term *qualitative* involves both implicit and explicit comparisons to some equally ambiguously used adjective, '*quantitative*'—as, for example, in the phrase "qualitative methods versus quantitative methods." Broadly speaking, qualitative methods are procedures including unstructured, open-ended interviews and participant observation that generate qualitative data, while so-called quantitative methods (e.g., structured questionnaires, psychometric measures, and tests) are means of generating quantitative data. However, one could easily generate qualitative data via an open-ended interview, transform those data into numbers, and analyze them by means of nonparametric statistics. Hence, what precisely comprises a so-called qualitative method is not all that clear.

Qualitative method or qualitative inquiry is also notoriously difficult to define precisely because, according to some scholars, it refers to a social movement that developed within universities beginning in the late 1960s in the Anglophone world, more so than a particular field of study. The movement began with the rediscovery and legitimation of ways of studying social life that were present, particularly in sociology and anthropology, long before that time. The movement has grown and expanded into an intellectual arena that embraces different methodologies and epistemologies, and oftentimes contradictory ideas about the purpose of engaging in qualitative inquiry.

Qualitative also denotes "of or relating to quality." A quality is an inherent or phenomenal property or essential characteristic of some thing (object or experience). There appears to be only one variety of qualitative inquiry that takes the definition of quality as its starting point. Elliot Eisner's explication of qualitative inquiry (e.g., *The Enlightened Eye,* Macmillan, 1991) begins from the point of view that inquiry is a matter of the perception of qualities of some object or event and an appraisal of their value. The work of Eisner and his students aims to define and illustrate an aesthetics that explains how qualitative aspects of the experiences and settings of teaching and learning are to be perceived, appreciated, interpreted, understood, and criticized. The metaphors he employs for capturing the dual features of his methodology are connoisseurship and criticism.

The idea that the experience of art is closer than that of science to the way of knowing characteristic of the *Geisteswissenschaften* (and, hence, at least some forms of qualitative inquiry) and that there is a kind of truth and knowledge available through art that cannot be obtained by scientific method is also a central idea in *philosophical hermeneutics*.

See also Frameworks for Qualitative Inquiry.

KEY REFERENCES

Alasuutari, P. "The Globalization of Qualitative Research," in C. Seale, G. Gobo, J. F. Gubrium, & D. Silverman, eds., *Qualitative Research Practice.* London: Sage, 2004.

Denzin, N. K., & Lincoln, Y. S., eds. *Handbook of Qualitative Research,* 2nd ed. Thousand Oaks, CA: Sage, 2000.

Richardson, J. T. E., ed. *Handbook of Qualitative Research Methods for Psychology and the Social Sciences.* Leicester, England: The British Psychological Society, 1996.

Schwandt, T. A. "Three Epistemological Stances for Qualitative Inquiry: Interpretivism, Hermeneutics, and Social Constructionism," in N. K. Denzin & Y. S. Lincoln, eds., *The Handbook of Qualitative Research,* 2nd ed. Thousand Oaks, CA: Sage, 2000.

Seale, C. F. *The Quality of Qualitative Research.* London: Sage, 1999.

QUALITATIVE MARKET RESEARCH This is a specific area of research making use of methods of in-depth interviewing, critical incident technique, and *focus groups* to generate and analyze information on customers' desires, behaviors, and evaluations of products and services as an aid in marketing decision making.

KEY REFERENCE

Mariampolski, H. *Qualitative Market Research: A Comprehensive Guide.* Thousand Oaks, CA: Sage, 2001.

QUALITATIVE NURSING RESEARCH   This phrase refers to the study of phenomena of interest to the practice of nursing using a variety of means commonly associated with qualitative inquiry, including case study research, interviewing, narrative inquiry, participant observation, discourse analysis, and phenomenological research.

KEY REFERENCES

Holloway, I., & Wheller, S. *Qualitative Research in Nursing,* 2nd ed. Oxford, UK: Blackwell, 2002.
Lattimer, J., ed. *Advanced Qualitative Research for Nursing.* Oxford, UK: Blackwell, 2003.
Morse, J. M., ed. *Qualitative Nursing Research.* Thousand Oaks, CA: Sage, 1990.

QUALITATIVE PSYCHOLOGY   This phrase broadly refers to the use of qualitative research methods (e.g., grounded theory, narrative inquiry, and conversation and discourse analysis) and the infusion of various epistemologies and methodologies foregrounding qualitative inquiry (e.g., phenomenology, existentialism, and hermeneutics) in the study of psychological phenomena.

See also Narrative Psychology.

KEY REFERENCES

Kopala, M., & Suzuki, L. A., eds. *Using Qualitative Methods in Psychology.* London: Sage, 1999.
Smith, J. A., ed. *Qualitative Psychology: A Practical Guide to Research Methods.* London: Sage, 2003.

QUANTIFICATION   See QUANTITATIVE.

QUANTITATIVE   This is an adjective indicating that something is expressible in terms of quantity (i.e., a definite amount or number). Thus, it is accurate to talk of quantitative measures and quantitative data. However, the term is often used as a synonym for any design (e.g., experimental and survey) or procedure (e.g., statistical) that relies principally on the use of quantitative data and then contrasted with 'qualitative' accordingly, yet so-called qualitative studies can and often do make use of quantitative data. Quantification is the activity or operation of expressing something as a quantity or amount, for example, in numbers, graphs, or formulas. Quantification or the reliance on quantitative data is a near ubiquitous phenomenon not simply in the sciences but in all aspects of the administration of social life.

See also Qualitative Inquiry.

KEY REFERENCE

Porter, T. *Trust in Numbers: The Pursuit of Objectivity in Science and Public Life.* Princeton, NJ: Princeton University Press, 1995.

R

———— ◆ ● ◆ ————

RADICAL HERMENEUTICS   See DECONSTRUCTIONISM.

RATIONALISM   This philosophical position is composed of many variations that generally hold that reason is the primary way we acquire knowledge.
Moderate rationalism is equivalent to faith in reason, a belief in the value of
critical discussion and valid argumentation. So-conceived, moderate rationalism is an essential aspect of modernity, for it is opposed to superstition, dogma,
and authoritarianism. It is the opposite of irrationalism—the view that it is
pointless to engage in rational discussion; rather, one must trust in feeling and
intuition. Modern cultural, social, scientific, technological, governmental, and
administrative practices all reflect trust in reason and, hence, a moderate rationalism. More extreme or radical rationalism (often associated with Descartes
[1596–1650], Kant [1724–1804], and Leibniz [1646–1716]) is equated with
faith in the ability of reason unaided by perception, experiment, or action. The
radical rationalist argues that minds have a priori structures or categories of
understanding that organize and give meaning to our sense experiences. Hence,
data are neither the primary source of knowledge nor the final arbiter of what
constitutes a legitimate knowledge claim.

   In the social sciences, rationalism is most often opposed to *empiricism*
that privileges sense experience as the basis for all knowledge. In the philosophy of social science, Karl Popper's (1902–1994) critical rationalism is a
strong critique of the strict empiricism of *logical positivism*. In practice,
contemporary natural and social science reflects a blend of rationalism and
empiricism, reason and observation.

KEY REFERENCES

Bunge, M. *Finding Philosophy in Social Science.* New Haven, CT: Yale University Press, 1996.
Hollis, M. *The Philosophy of Social Science: An Introduction.* Cambridge, UK: Cambridge University Press, 1994.

RATIONALITY   This is the state or characteristic of being reasonable. The question of what it means to behave rationally when faced with competing (different, contradictory) interpretations is a central issue in debates between *objectivism* and *relativism*. Objectivists typically argue that to resolve a dispute between competing interpretations, one must have a set of *criteria*. As Bernstein (1986) explains, they believe that

> if we cannot come up with universal fixed criteria to measure the plausibility of competing interpretations, then this means that we have no *rational* basis for distinguishing better and worse, more plausible or less plausible interpretations, whether these be interpretations of texts, actions, or historical epochs. (p. 358)

Their fear is that without such criteria, reasonable choice between competing interpretations is impossible, and the only alternative is relativism—all evaluation of competing interpretations becomes relative to some particular culture, society, theoretical framework, or conceptual scheme. What it means to behave rationally or reasonably in the face of competing claims thus appears to be framed in terms of an either/or choice: either objectivism (rational behavior) or relativism (irrational behavior).

There are at least two major alternative views, however. One is a strong skeptical view that holds that the objectivists' search for *foundational* criteria is not simply misguided, but dangerous. Strong skeptics argue that if being reasonable or rational means having foundational criteria, then the very idea of being rational requires deconstruction. They hold that search for criteria that can decisively resolve interpretive disputes encourages an intolerance of 'otherness,' ambiguity, and diversity of views. Thus, new strategies are required for circumventing or subverting that demand for answerability to reason through which, it is believed, power and control are exercised. The radical relativist seeks to make space in thought for that which is allegedly nonassimilable to reason, namely, diversity, heterogeneity, pluralism, and difference.

A second view is a more moderate skepticism that does not necessarily seek to deconstruct the idea of rationality but looks to recover a different kind of rationality. Moderate skeptics agree that we can never find a set of foundational criteria that can settle disputes over competing interpretations in an objective, impartial manner, because criteria themselves are always socially formulated, negotiated, interpreted, and applied. However, they claim that we need not, as a result, be suspicious of the very idea of rationality. Rather, we must recover the idea of practical rationality—that is, how in our practices we exercise a kind of contextually embedded and situationally sensitive practical judgment (see *praxis*) of the particular and support our comparative judgments with arguments and the appeal to good reasons. Bernstein (1983) holds that

> central to this new understanding is a dialogical model of rationality that stresses the practical, communal character of rationality in which there is choice, deliberation, interpretation, judicious weighing and application of criteria, and even rational disagreement about which criteria are relevant and most important. (p. 172)

KEY REFERENCES

Bernstein, R. J. *Beyond Objectivism and Relativism.* Philadelphia: University of Pennsylvania Press, 1983.

Bernstein, R. J. "What Is the Difference That Makes a Difference? Gadamer, Habermas, and Rorty," in *Hermeneutics and Modern Philosophy,* B. R. Wachterhauser, ed. Albany: SUNY Press, 1986.

Burbules, N. C. "Moving Beyond the Impasse," in *Constructivism in Education: Opinions and Second Opinions on Controversial Issues,* D. C. Phillips, ed. Ninety-ninth Yearbook of the National Society for the Study of Education. Chicago, IL: University of Chicago Press, 2000.

Smith, N. H. *Strong Hermeneutics: Contingency and Moral Identity.* London: Routledge, 1997.

Taylor, C. *Philosophical Arguments.* Cambridge, MA: Harvard University Press, 1995.

Toulmin, S. *Return to Reason.* Cambridge, MA: Harvard University Press, 2003.

REACTIVITY   This is a state of affairs that results from the use of any means to generate data that influence the respondents, participants, or subjects who provide the data. Reactivity is typically regarded as a threat to *validity* and something that can be prevented through the use of completely unobtrusive observation or measurement. However, the notion of reactivity is actually part of a more encompassing condition of all research that can never be eliminated, namely, that there are always effects of the audience and the context on what people say and do. Thus, rather than wrestle with the elimination of reactivity through finding the right, allegedly nonreactive procedure, a wiser choice is to recognize that all accounts produced by researchers must be interpreted within the context in which they were generated. Interpretations must examine, as carefully as possible, how the presence of the researcher, the context in which data were obtained, and so on shaped the data.

See also Reflexivity.

KEY REFERENCE

Hammersley, M., & Atkinson, P. *Ethnography: Principles in Practice.* London: Tavistock, 1983.

REALISM   Broadly conceived, this is the doctrine that there are real objects that exist independently of our knowledge of their existence. On a daily basis, most of us probably behave as garden-variety empirical realists—that is, we act as if the objects in the world (things, events, structures, people, meanings, etc.) exist as independent in some way from our experience with them. We also regard society, institutions, feelings, intelligence, poverty, disability, and so on as being just as real as the toes on our feet and the sun in the sky. However, more than this commonsense realism is often at stake in the literature on qualitative inquiry. Hence, it is important to distinguish several varieties of realism.

In terms of a theory of perception, *naïve (or direct) realism* denies the importance of a mental entity (an awareness *of* some object) that is interposed between the perceiver and the object. Direct realism claims that the external, independently existing physical object is directly perceived—the things in the world just are as they appear. This theory contrasts with *representative realism,* which argues that we do not directly perceive external objects, but rather we perceive the effects (images, ideas, impressions, etc.) that these objects have on us. These two theories are of considerable significance in the current debate about ***representation*** in contemporary qualitative inquiry, although one seldom sees an examination of the philosophical issues involved here in that literature.

Metaphysical realism is the doctrine that the world exists independently of consciousness. A related epistemological doctrine called ***meaning realism*** holds that meaning exists in objects (including human actions, events, etc.) independent of whether we as agents are aware of same. The distinction in these two forms of realism is important for understanding the philosophy of constructivism. The constructivist believes that meaning does not have an independent existence; meaning is not 'objective' in this sense, or simply 'out there' awaiting discovery. Rather, meaning comes into existence only through the engagement of knowers with the world. One could, without contradiction, quite readily accept metaphysical realism (there is a world of things, events, objects 'out there' whether I can conceive of them or not) and still be a constructivist when it comes to epistemology—that is, what those things, events, and so on mean. This is the kind of constructivism characteristic of the ***philosophical hermeneutics*** of Hans-Georg Gadamer and Charles Taylor. More radical versions of constructivism deny both metaphysical realism and meaning realism and hold that it is not simply what one makes of the world that is constructed, but that the world itself is constructed.

Scientific realism is the view that scientific theories refer to real features of the world, or the view that real things are just exactly as science takes them to be. 'Real' here refers to whatever it is in the universe (i.e., forces and structures) that causes the phenomena that we perceive with our senses. Scientific realism argues that what is 'real' is not necessarily only that which we can directly observe. To understand this idea, it may help to contrast it with the view of ***logical positivist.*** Logical positivists did not deny that there was a real world; they insisted that the world consists of observable particulars. However, they rejected any elements of realism in their ***epistemology*** (i.e., in their theory of what constituted a legitimate scientific explanation). The logical positivists believed that what is real is a world of discrete or particular events that are observable. These events actually exist whether we observe them or not. The interest of logical positivists into questions of reality stopped there, however. They argued that the only sure path to knowing this world was the experience of the senses. Thus, logical positivists were thoroughgoing empiricists. They believed that reality is that which can be observed and what we can observe is only the constant conjunction of events—some set of events is followed by the appearance of events of another kind. Explanations are thus simply a question of locating an event to be explained in (i.e., 'covering it' with) an observed regularity. For the logical positivist, there is nothing deeper, so to speak, to the notion of explanation than the proper logical arrangement of well-verified observations. The test of whether a theory is true or false is nothing more than a test of its success or failure at predicting events. Hence, there is no need to talk of whether theories *actually* refer to causes, forces, necessities, mechanisms, or any other such unobservable 'real' underlying entities. All such talk is metaphysical speculation and has no place in what constitutes genuine, legitimate scientific knowledge.

Scientific realism and logical positivism agree that there is a world of events 'out there' and that there are patterns or regularities of events that can be observed. However, scientific realists distinguish the empirical (that which we observe with our senses) from the real (the processes that generate the events we observe). Realism rejects logical positivist epistemology. It holds that to claim that one has genuine, scientific knowledge, it *is* important to decide whether theories are 'really' true or false (and not just valid by virtue of their ability to predict), whether something like a cause really exists, whether there really are things out there like electrons, gravity, force fields, society, social structures, and the like. Realists believe that a genuine scientific explanation must go beyond statements of observed regularities to get at the mechanisms, processes, structures, or whatever unobservable, real, underlying forces actually account for the regularities (constant conjunctions of events) that we observe.

Doctrines of this kind of scientific (or ontological) realism are met by strong opposition from varieties of *ontological relativism,* such as expressed by Richard Rorty. The latter views claim that the world is just what we take it to be according to our current interpretive practices. In other words, the truth of scientific theories is not a matter of determining whether they in fact mirror the real world. Rather, the meaning and truth of theories are matters decided within a particular conceptual scheme or language game—a particular habit of construing evidence according to some logic of inquiry that we have adopted that answers to our own ideas of what is good in the way of belief. This antirealist stance is characteristic not only of Rorty's neopragmatism but of much social *constructivism* as well.

See also Empiricism, Ethnographic Realism, Objectivism, Representation.

KEY REFERENCES

Bhaskar, R. *Reclaiming Reality: A Critical Introduction to Contemporary Philosophy.* London: Verso, 1989.

Crotty, M. *Foundations of Social Research.* London: Sage, 1998.

Outhwaite, W. *New Philosophies of Social Science: Realism, Hermeneutics and Critical Theory.* New York: St. Martin's, 1987.

Rorty, R. *Philosophy and the Mirror of Nature.* Princeton, NJ: Princeton University Press, 1979.

REALIST TALE   See ETHNOGRAPHIC REALISM.

RECIPROCITY   This is a kind of social behavior—a mutual give-and-take, an exchange of gifts or services—in which we routinely engage in social life but that is especially important in *field studies* where the researcher is accorded the privilege of access to the lives of those he or she studies. Paying respondents, informants, and participants and doing small favors like giving them a ride to work, picking up their dry cleaning, baby-sitting their children, buying them a meal, and so forth are reciprocal social acts that might be performed by a field researcher. Reciprocity is part of the larger ethical-political process of building trust, cultivating relationships, and demonstrating genuine interest in those whom one studies. Which of these kinds of activities to engage in or how far to take the act of reciprocity is a matter of ethical *judgment* regarding what is appropriate in the circumstances in question and hence requires practical wisdom.

See also Ethics of Qualitative Inquiry, Field Relations.

KEY REFERENCES

Johnson, J. M. *Doing Field Research.* New York: Free Press, 1975.

Wolcott, H. F. *The Art of Fieldwork.* Walnut Creek, CA: AltaMira, 1995.

REDUCTIONISM   This is the idea that we can (and ought to) replace one vocabulary (set of concepts or theory) with a second vocabulary (set of concepts or theory) that is more primary. Examples of attempts at reductionism include the logical positivists' bid to reduce the vocabulary of theory to the vocabulary of observation statements; logicism—the bid to reduce mathematics to logic; the reduction of psychology to neurology; the reduction of social science explanations to natural science explanations, especially those of physics or biology; and methodological individualism—reducing explanations about social reality to statements about individual human actions.

See also Holism.

KEY REFERENCE

Collin, F. *Social Reality.* London: Routledge, 1997.

REFLEXIVITY   Discussion of the meaning and consequences of reflexivity in the conduct and writing of qualitative inquiry is extensive. In *ethnomethodology*, reflexivity refers to the fact that all accounts (in speech and writing) are essentially not just *about* something but are also *doing* something. Written and spoken accounts do not simply represent some aspect of the world but are in some way involved in that world. This kind of (ontological) reflexivity is simply unavoidable.

The term *reflexivity* is also used in a methodological sense to refer to the process of critical self-reflection on one's biases, theoretical predispositions, preferences, and so forth. This kind of self-inspection can be salutary for any kind of inquiry, and fieldworkers are often encouraged to record and explore these evolving dispositions in personal notes in their *field journals*. Reflexivity in a methodological sense can also signal more than inspection of potential sources of bias and their control. It can point to the fact that the inquirer is part of the setting, context, and social phenomenon he or she seeks to understand. Hence, reflexivity can be a means for critically inspecting the entire research process including reflecting on the ways in which a fieldworker establishes a social network of informants and participants in a study; and for examining one's personal and theoretical commitments to see how they serve as resources for generating particular data, for behaving in particular ways vis-à-vis respondents and participants, and for developing particular interpretations. Reflexivity understood in this way is held to be a very important procedure for establishing the *validity* of accounts of social phenomena. This is particularly true for many critical researchers concerned with the criticism that their research can become nothing more than a self-serving ideology as well as for feminist researchers wary of duplicating androcentric perspectives and race and class bias in their investigations.

Reflexivity is also used in an ideological sense to signal various strategies for composition and writing that reflect specific theoretical, political, and intellectual agendas. This kind of reflexivity is characteristic of what are called 'messy texts'—forms of experimental writing that reject the 'finished' appearance of a *realist tale* written by a detached observer. They reflect an open-endedness, incompleteness, the full presence of the writer in the text, and the continual movement back and forth between description, interpretation, and multiple voices. Ethnopoetics and *autoethnography* are examples.

See also Bias, Representation.

KEY REFERENCES

Alvesson, M., & Sköldberg, K. *Reflexive Methodology: New Vistas for Qualitative Research.* London: Sage, 2000.

Denzin, N. K. *Interpretive Ethnography: Ethnographic Practices for the 21st Century.* Thousand Oaks, CA: Sage, 1997.

Marcus, G. E. "What Comes (Just) After 'Post?'" in *Handbook of Qualitative Research,* N. K. Denzin & Y. S. Lincoln, eds. Thousand Oaks, CA: Sage, 1994.

Potter, J. *Representing Reality: Discourse, Rhetoric and Social Construction.* London: Sage, 1996.

Sanjek, R. "On Ethnographic Validity," in *Fieldnotes: The Makings of Anthropology,* R. Sanjek, ed. Ithaca, NY: Cornell University Press, 1990.

RELATIVISM   In general, this is the doctrine that denies that there are universal truths. There are several interrelated senses of the term, however:

1. *Epistemological relativism* is a doctrine about our experience of or knowledge of the world. It is the belief that notions of rationality, truth, goodness, rightness, and reality can *only* be understood as relative to some specific theoretical framework, language game, conceptual scheme, set of social practices, or culture.

2. *Ontological relativism* is a doctrine about the nature of reality. It is the belief that reality *itself* is determined by our language or conceptual scheme.

3. *Descriptive cultural relativism* is a long-standing perspective in anthropology. This is the view that acceptable social practices (or the morality of such practices) differ from society to society or culture to culture—in other words, something like "Group A believes X; group B believes Y." However, cultural relativists (those who simply describe differing social practices) are not necessarily judgmental or ethical relativists.

4. An *ethical or judgmental relativist* holds that there are no universally valid moral principles, and hence would say that group A and B are both right.

5. *Cognitive relativism* is the belief that there are no universal truths about the world. In poststructuralist thought, this kind of relativism is often associated with universal perspectivalism and thus leads to radical *skepticism*. Universal perspectivalism is attributable to Friedrich Nietzsche (1844–1900), who argued for the interpretive and radically perspectival character of all knowing. He argued that there can be no such thing as absolute knowledge that transcends all perspectives; we must face the fact that there are only interpretations of interpretations. Hence, we can never know whether there is any such thing as valid knowledge. Richard Rorty, Nelson Goodman (1906–1998), and Hilary Putnam each offer contemporary versions of cognitive relativism that are (at least according to their authors) not simultaneously given to radical Nietzschean skepticism.

KEY REFERENCES

Bernstein, R. J. *Beyond Objectivism and Relativism.* Philadelphia: University of Pennsylvania Press, 1983.

Fay, B. *Contemporary Philosophy of Social Science.* Oxford, UK: Blackwell, 1996.

Goodman, N. *Ways of World Making.* Indianapolis, IN: Hackett, 1978.

Krausz, M., & Meiland, J., eds. *Relativism: Cognitive and Moral.* Notre Dame, IN: University of Notre Dame Press, 1982.

Putnam, H. *The Many Faces of Realism.* LaSalle, IL: Open Court, 1987.

Rorty, R. *Objectivity, Relativism and Truth: Philosophical Papers, Vol. 1.* Cambridge, UK: Cambridge University Press, 1991.

RELIABILITY   This is an *epistemic criterion* thought to be necessary but not sufficient for establishing the truth of an account or interpretation of a social phenomenon. An account is judged to be reliable if it is capable of being replicated by another inquirer. Traditionally, social scientists assume that while not all repeatable or replicable observations or accounts are necessarily valid, all valid accounts are (at least in principle) replicable. Opinion is divided among qualitative researchers over whether this criterion has any meaning whatsoever in judging the accuracy of fieldwork accounts. Some scholars emphasize the importance of repeatability of observations within a given study both diachronically (the stability of a fieldworker's observations across data drawn from different time periods) and synchronically (similar observations within the same time period across different methods, e.g., observation and interview). Others argue that reliability can and must be addressed in fieldwork by procedures such as using conventionalized methods for recording field notes and analyzing transcripts, as well as making interrater checks on coding and categorization procedures and results. Still others have called for establishing *dependability*—an analog to reliability—through careful documentation of procedures for generating and interpreting data. Reliability here is a matter of assembling dependable evidence, and the methods used to assemble this evidence matter. (Making a claim about the meaning of this evidence is a *validity* issue.) Finally, some argue that reliability in qualitative study is a fiction because no investigator can ever literally replicate another's fieldwork.

KEY REFERENCES

Kirk, J., & Miller, M. *Reliability and Validity in Qualitative Research.* Beverly Hills, CA: Sage, 1986.
Lincoln, Y. S., & Guba, E. G. *Naturalistic Inquiry.* Beverly Hills, CA: Sage, 1985.
Sanjek, R. "On Ethnographic Validity," in *Fieldnotes: The Makings of Anthropology,* R. Sanjek, ed. Ithaca, NY: Cornell University Press, 1990.
Silverman, D. *Interpreting Qualitative Data.* London: Sage, 1993.

REPRESENTATION Depicting, portraying, or describing social phenomena is a goal not simply of qualitative inquiry but of all forms of social science. Representation in its many forms—as resemblance, replication, repetition, description, and duplication—is central to the modernist project of understanding the world. Whether inquirers ought to claim that they 'represent' the social world in their studies and precisely what they are doing when they try to represent, however, is a matter of great dispute.

Naturalistic inquiry assumes the importance of faithful representation of the lifeworlds of those one studies. Few such inquirers any longer cling to *naïve realism* and argue that their accounts are a literal mirror or representation of an external reality; few, however, would also abandon the idea that their portrayals, depictions, or descriptions, although fictions (in the sense of invented or crafted), should not also be accurate. Many struggle with the idea of fallible representation—seeking to find ways to give evidence or good reasons for their accounts that represent social phenomena without claiming that those accounts are certain or beyond revision.

Many postmodernists find the idea of representation totally unacceptable. They claim that the practice of taking one thing for another assumes (a) the ability to reproduce and duplicate reality and (b) the ability to make the transfer without loss of content. For these postmodernists, there is no such thing as the 'original' of anything that stands in some relation of equivalence to its representation; there is only the endless play of different representations. Hence, they believe that representation assumes *objectivism* and that the goal of *deconstructionism* is to reveal the foolishness of all representational claims. Postmodern-inspired qualitative studies sharing this way of thinking often claim that they 'evoke' rather than 'represent.' Pauline Rosenau (1992) summarizes this radical postmodernist view:

> Representation is politically, socially, culturally, linguistically and epistemo-logically arbitrary. It signifies mastery. . . . It signals distortion; it assumes unconscious rules governing relationships. It concretizes, finalizes, and excludes complexity . . . [It] is fraudulent, perverse, artificial, mechanical, deceptive, incomplete, misleading, insufficient, wholly inadequate for the post-modern age. (pp. 94–95)

See also Authority, Crisis of Representation, Description, Ethnographic Realism, Experience.

KEY REFERENCES

Danto, A. C. *The Body/Body Problem.* Berkeley: University of California Press, 1999.
Denzin, N. K. *Images of Postmodern Society.* London: Sage, 1991.
Gubrium, J. F., & Holstein, J. A. *The New Language of Qualitative Method.* Oxford, UK: Oxford University Press, 1997.
Rosenau, P. *Post-Modernism and the Social Sciences.* Princeton, NJ: Princeton University Press, 1992.
Van Maanen, J., ed. *Representation in Ethnography.* Thousand Oaks, CA: Sage, 1995.

REPRESENTATIVENESS   See SAMPLING LOGIC.

RESEARCH AS ARGUMENT   It may be helpful to all researchers, and not simply those committed to some form of qualitative inquiry, to think of research not primarily as a set of techniques or methods for answering a question but as argument connecting theoretical claims, method, and empirical claims (derived from evidence).

See also Method; Research Design; Theory, Uses of.

KEY REFERENCES

Abbott, A. *Methods of Discovery: Heuristics for the Social Sciences.* New York: W. W. Norton, 2004.
Alford, R. R. *The Craft of Inquiry.* New York: Oxford University Press, 1998.

RESEARCH DESIGN   Designs or plans for conducting qualitative studies vary considerably; there are no prescribed designs as, for example, one might find in survey research, experimental, and quasi-experimental studies in the social sciences. However, that does not mean that qualitative researchers conduct studies without careful forethought and planning. Every qualitative study requires some combination of theoretical claims and empirical evidence to produce an argument that answers the research question or problem that the study examines. Jennifer Mason explains that, broadly speaking, all plans for qualitative studies require fashioning answers to three broad questions: (1) What is my research about? (i.e., What is the phenomenon to be investigated? What might constitute evidence of that phenomenon? Why is this phenomenon worth investigating?) (2) What is the strategy for linking research questions, methods, and evidence? (3) How will the proposed research take account of relevant ethical, political, and moral concerns?

See also Emergent Design, Sensitizing Concepts.

KEY REFERENCES

Alford, R. R. *The Craft of Inquiry.* New York: Oxford University Press, 1998.
Mason, J. *Qualitative Researching.* London: Sage, 1996.

RESPONDENT   See **ETHICS OF QUALITATIVE INQUIRY, INFORMANT.**

RESPONDENT VALIDATION   See MEMBER CHECK.

REVIEW OF LITERATURE   All reviews involve analyzing and synthesizing multiple studies for the purpose of demonstrating their collective relevance for solving some problem, for understanding some issue, for explaining some relationship, and so on. Reviewing is an interpretive undertaking insofar as it is an effort to make sense of these studies and to establish their meaning. A widely held view is that reviews are a means of collecting and organizing the results of previous studies so as to produce a composite of what we have already learned about a particular topic. This approach assumes that knowledge accumulates within a field, and hence understanding of some phenomenon can be built up piece by piece, brick by brick, eventually yielding something like a more complete, thorough, and, hence, trustworthy understanding, which, in turn, can be more confidently applied to solving a problem of a particular kind.

This traditional notion of the literature review view is based on a biomedical model of combining multiple single studies that address related or identical causal hypotheses in order to arrive at a valid generalization of a causal relationship. For example, we want to know the efficacy of treatment A (e.g., some particular pharmaceutical therapy) for condition X (some particular form of cancer), so we examine all single studies of this relationship seeking, by means of induction, to synthesize the individual findings into a general conclusion.

This way of reasoning is extended to social phenomena when we ask about the general conclusion that can be drawn from various single studies about, for example, the effects of homework on academic achievement, the effects of busing on school desegregation, the effects of site-based management on parent and student satisfaction with public schools, and so on. Procedures for these kinds of integrative research reviews and meta-analyses are well established. Moreover, although we often think of such reviews as employing mathematical techniques for comparing, synthesizing, and analyzing results of multiple studies, statistical techniques are not a necessary feature of such reviews. For example, we might imagine a review that examines multiple case studies of school disciplinary practices aiming to understand what social structures serve as prominent causes of this social action, or to understand what social rules, institutional practices and norms, and so on comprise the underlying 'grammar' that gives such practices their meaning. Judging the quality of all such reviews is a matter of determining whether the review in question clarifies and resolves inconsistencies in the various studies under consideration, and whether the synthesis is consistent, parsimonious, fruitful, useful, and so on. These, of course, are 'interpretive' criteria, themselves subject to changing definition.

Margaret Eisenhart (1998) argues for an alternative to this traditional conception of literature reviews. She holds that an interpretive review ought to be consistent with the spirit of interpretive scholarship. That scholarship, she states, is marked by (a) its power to disrupt conventional wisdom by revealing something surprising, startling, or new; (b) its commitment to demonstrating how the meaning of human action varies by sociocultural context; and (c) its goal of enlarging the universe of discourse, expanding our ways of understanding how we interpret ourselves to ourselves. Hence, she suggests that an interpretivist-oriented review ought to "offer surprising and enriching perspectives on meanings and circumstances"; it ought to "shake things up, break down boundaries, and cause thinking to expand" (p. 396). A review should be less like a synthesis or consolidation of existing studies that aims to settle an issue or understanding and more like a reexamination or reconsideration that unsettles or disturbs what we might take for granted as "already learned."

See also Metaethnography.

KEY REFERENCES

Eisenhart, M. "On the Subject on Interpretive Reviews," *Review of Educational Research,* 1998, 68(4), 391–399.

Strike, K., & Posner, G. "Epistemological Problems in Organizing Social Science Knowledge for Application," in *Knowledge Structure and Use,* S. Ward & L. Reed, eds. Philadelphia: Temple University Press, 1983a.

Strike, K., & Posner, G. "Types of Syntheses and their Criteria," in *Knowledge Structure and Use,* S. Ward & L. Reed, eds. Philadelphia: Temple University Press, 1983b.

RHETORIC   Rhetoric is the art or technique of persuasion, especially through language. In qualitative inquiry, significant attention is paid to research as an inherently rhetorical (and not merely reportorial) activity.

See also Authority, Crisis of Representation, Literary Turn (in Social Science), Writing Strategies.

KEY REFERENCES

Atkinson, P. *The Ethnographic Imagination: Textual Constructions of Reality.* London: Routledge, 1990.

Geertz, C. *Works and Lives: The Anthropologist as Author.* Stanford, CA: Stanford University Press, 1988.

S

SAMPLE SIZE See SAMPLING LOGIC.

SAMPLING LOGIC There are two general strategies or logics for selecting units (organizations, events, people, documents, locations, etc.) to study in qualitative work: an empirical or statistical strategy (also called probability sampling) and a theoretical or purposive strategy (also called nonprobability sampling). Both can be employed in the same study, although many qualitative studies rely on only the latter.

In the logic of sampling based on an *empirical or statistical strategy,* sample units are chosen based on their representativeness of some wider population of units. A population of units is defined and enumerated (also called a sampling frame), and a sample is chosen from within that population using a procedure that assures that all samples have an equal or known probability of being selected (i.e., a procedure for random selection). Statistical means are used to judge the probability that characteristics and patterns observed in the sample are reflected in the population. Ideal sample sizes are calculable (given a sampling frame) based on the confidence level at which one wishes to make a generalization—in other words, one can determine the actual sample size needed to achieve, for example, a 95% confidence level in generalizing the findings from the sample of a population of a given size.

In the logic of sampling based on a *theoretical or purposive strategy,* units are chosen not for their representativeness, but for their relevance to the research question, analytical framework, and explanation or account being developed in the research. Relevance may be a matter of choosing a unit(s) because there may be good reason to believe that 'what goes on there' is critical to understanding some process or concept, or to testing or elaborating some established theory. Relevance may also be a matter of choosing a unit, because on the basis of prior knowledge, it is known to be an extreme, typical, deviant, unique, or particularly revelatory unit for shedding light on the issues that the researcher is seeking to elaborate. Finally, relevance may be a matter of choosing multiple places, cases, or sites to facilitate comparisons either because these different units are likely to yield predictable contrasts in under-standing the definition of social action or because they are likely to show the same or similar definition of social action. In theoretical or purposeful sam-pling, ideal sample size is simply not quantifiable. The size of the sample depends entirely on the nature of the study and the research questions and con-cepts being investigated.

There are two critical issues in the logic of *theoretical* or *purposive sam-pling*. First is the explicit establishment (and explanation) of a relevant criterion (or criteria) on the basis of which the selection of units will be made. Failing to specify and explain this criterion results in sampling in an ad hoc, unspecifi-able, and convenient manner, making it impossible to explain why particular units were chosen for study (i.e., Why *these* people, *this* event, *this* organiza-tion?). Second is the use of a strategy for checking that the units one is using are not chosen simply because they support the developing account. The most common strategy employed here is **negative-case** (or deviant-case) analysis.

When a researcher is studying complex social action within a particular locale (an organization, classroom, social service agency, etc.), additional con-siderations arise regarding sampling *within* that locale or site (also called *sam-pling within the case*). Here, the researcher seeks assurances that what is being observed is usual or customary, something that typically goes on there (rather than something being staged for the benefit of the researcher). Thus, a researcher may develop a representational map of the site that creates a working picture of the temporal, ritual, and routine features of the persons, organizations, or social actions under study (N. Denzin. *The Research Act,* 3rd ed. Englewood Cliffs, NJ: Prentice-Hall, 1989). Representational maps also guide the selection of those specific events, activities, interactions, and so on that will be studied within the site. Imagine, for example, that a fieldworker has selected a court-room as a profitable place in which to study the way in which lawyers and judges frame the behavior of juveniles charged with a crime. Before forming conclusions about the kinds of frames employed in that site, the fieldworker would want to be sure that he or she observed on several different occasions in court (mornings, afternoons, weekends, Mondays, Fridays, etc.), over several different events (complicated and uncomplicated cases), and across several different types of plaintiffs (males and females, Caucasians, Hispanics, African Americans, etc.), and (if appropriate) several different kinds of lawyers and judges (experienced and inexperienced, male and female, etc.).

See also Cross-Case Analysis, Generalization.

KEY REFERENCES

Flick, U. *Introduction to Qualitative Research.* London: Sage, 1998.
Hammersley, M., & Atkinson, P. *Ethnography: Principles in Practice.* London: Tavistock, 1983.
Mason, J. *Qualitative Researching.* London: Sage, 1996.
Patton, M. Q. *Qualitative Evaluation and Research Methods,* 2nd ed. Newbury Park, CA: Sage, 1990.

SAMPLING, TYPES OF In an *empirical* or *statistical strategy* (also called probability sampling), samples are of three types—simple random sampling, more complex stratified sampling, and cluster sampling. A *theoretical* or *purposive strategy* (also called nonprobability sampling) usually employs either *maximum variation sampling*—selecting a wide range of cases or incidents to get variation on the concepts of interest, or *emblematic sampling*—choosing a case or incident because it is extreme or deviant, typical or average, or emerging or novel. A *convenience sample* may also be used—that is, a case is chosen simply because one was allowed access to that case.

KEY REFERENCES

Patton, M. Q. *Qualitative Evaluation and Research Methods,* 2nd ed. Newbury Park, CA: Sage, 1990.
Seale, C. F. *The Quality of Qualitative Research.* London: Sage, 1999.

SCIENCE One aspect of the contemporary (political) debate about the academic status of qualitative inquiry is whether it can properly be called a science. In this regard, it is worth noting that the German term for science (*Wissenschaft*) has a much broader sense than that associated with the English use of the term *science,* which is typically restricted to physics, chemistry, biology, and so forth.

Wissenschaft, however, is not narrowly limited to those forms of science that employ the empirical methods of observation and experimentation, but refers to any systematic, rational form of inquiry with rigorous and intersubjectively agreed-upon procedures for validation. *Wissenschaft* includes both the sciences of mathematics and logic and the hermeneutics and phenomenological disciplines concerned with the interpretation of meaning and the description of experience. The intellectual tradition encompassing all the methodological and epistemological concerns of the natural sciences is referred to as *Naturwissenschaften,* and that tradition sets them apart from the tradition of the human or social sciences, or *Geisteswissenschaften. **Naturalism*** is a defense of the former tradition, while ***antinaturalism*** defends the latter. Many poststructuralists would likely disavow any and all attempts to form something called a science of any kind, seeing such attempts as nothing more than linguistic inventions of totalizing, all-encompassing worldviews or metanarratives.

See also Explanation.

KEY REFERENCES

Outhwaite, W. *Understanding Social Life,* 2nd ed. London: Allen and Unwin, 1986.
Polkinghorne, D. *Methodology for the Human Sciences.* Albany: SUNY Press, 1983.

SCIENTIFIC METHOD   See METHOD.

SCIENTISM   The term may have originated with F. A. Hayek (1899–1992) (*The Counter-Revolution of Science: Studies in the Abuse of Reason,* 1955), who traced the idea to the French positivists Auguste Comte (1798–1857) and Henri Saint-Simon (1760–1825). In very general terms, twentieth-century Continental philosophy (e.g., phenomenology, existentialism, philosophical hermeneutics, critical theory, and poststructuralism) is characterized by its reaction to scientism. Jürgen Habermas provides the following succinct definition: "Scientism means science's belief in itself: that is, the conviction that we can no longer understand science as *one* form of possible knowledge, but rather must identify knowledge with science" (p. 4). In various ways, Continental philosophers have argued that the extension of scientific method and rationality (and the cognitive authority bestowed on same) beyond the subject matter of natural science to all aspects of social life has led to a narrowing of the public sphere, the transformation of moral-political issues into technical problems to be solved, a loss of personal identity, and the erosion of personal responsibility for decision making.

See also Praxis.

KEY REFERENCES

Cooper, D. E. "Modern European Philosophy," in N. Bunnin & E. P. Tsui-James, eds., *The Blackwell Companion to Philosophy.* Oxford, UK: Blackwell, 1996.

Habermas, J. *Knowledge and Human Interests,* J. J. Shapiro, trans. Boston: Beacon Press, 1971.

Ross, D. *The Origins of American Social Science.* Cambridge, UK: Cambridge University Press, 1991.

SEMIOTICS   Also called semiology, this is the theory of signs or the theory investigating the relationship between knowledge and signs. A *signifier* is an acoustic image of a spoken word as heard or read by a recipient of a vocal, written, or otherwise displayed message (e.g., the sound or image of the word 'dog'). The *signified* is the meaning called forth in the mind of the recipient resulting from the stimulation of the signifier (e.g., a four-legged short-haired creature with floppy ears, a tail, and that barks). A *sign* is a unity of signifier and signified. A sign is understood to be an entity or object that carries information—for example, a word, gesture, map, road sign, model, picture, or diagram. *Semiosis* is the symbolic activity (speaking, drawing, dancing, writing, etc.) or process of interpreting or producing meaningful signs; the activity of taking one thing as a sign of another thing.

The major original contributors to this theory were the Swiss linguist Ferdinand de Saussure (1857–1913) and the American philosopher Charles Sanders Peirce (1839–1914). Saussure's semiotic theory demonstrated that words do not derive their meaning from standing for things in the world; rather, they derive their meaning from sets of relationships and contrasts with other signs. Saussure argued that the proper object for linguistic investigation was *langue* (the shared set of structural properties or rules underlying language use). This focus on structure is what marks his theory as one of structural linguistics. Criticism and extensions of Saussure's work foreground French poststructuralist semiotic theory (e.g., Roland Barthes [1915–1980], Jacques Derrida [1930–2004], Michel Foucault [1926–1984], and Julia Kristeva).

See also Poststructuralism, Structuralism.

KEY REFERENCES

Barthes, R. *Mythologies.* London: Palladin, 1972.
Hawkes, T. *Structuralism and Semiotics.* London: Methuen, 1977.
Saussure, F. de. *Course in General Linguistics.* London: Peter Owen, 1960/1919.

SENSITIZING CONCEPTS   This term was coined by Herbert Blumer (1900–1987)—who also coined the term *symbolic interactionism*—to refer to the way in which symbolic interactionists (and now qualitative inquirers more generally) make use of concepts in their research. Sociopsychological concepts like family, victim, stress, stigma, and so forth are held loosely at the outset of a study; they are not given full operational definitions so that the inquirer might explore how the concept is manifest and given a particular meaning in the set of circumstances under investigation. Sensitizing concepts are not *emic* or indigenous concepts, but generated by the inquirer from existing studies and theory. They are used to provide a general sense of direction and reference for a study.

KEY REFERENCES

Blumer, H. *Symbolic Interactionism.* Englewood Cliffs, NJ: Prentice-Hall, 1969.
Van den Hoonaard, W. C. *Working with Sensitizing Concepts.* Thousand Oaks, CA: Sage, 1997.

SKEPTICISM   To be skeptical is to be doubtful. Moderate versions of skepticism doubt that there is knowledge of certain kinds—for example, rationalists are skeptical about the possibility of empirical knowledge. Radical skepticism is the belief that we can never know whether there is *any* knowledge (cognitive skepticism) or universally valid moral principles (ethical skepticism). A radical skeptical attitude characterizes the work of many postmodernist scholars who hold that there is no such thing as knowledge understood as justified belief.

See also Epistemology, Relativism.

KEY REFERENCE

Bohman, J. F. "Holism Without Skepticism: Contextualism and the Limits of Interpretation," in *The Interpretive Turn,* D. R. Hiley, J. F. Bohman, & R. Shusterman, eds. Ithaca, NY: Cornell University Press, 1991.

SOCIAL ANTHROPOLOGY   See CULTURAL ANTHROPOLOGY.

SOCIAL CONSTRUCTIONISM   See CONSTRUCTIVISM.

SOCIOLOGY OF SCIENTIFIC KNOWLEDGE (SSK)   Also spoken of as social studies of science, this is a broad label for a loose collection of scholars including those in the Strong Programme of the Edinburgh School (e.g., Barry Barnes, David Bloor), the Bath School (e.g., Harry Collins), and others including Steven Shapin, Simon Schaffer, Steve Woolgar, Bruno Latour, and Karin Knorr-Cetina, who conduct ethnographic studies of scientific practice (in, for example, the laboratories where scientists work). The work is broadly social constructivist in its orientation—it regards cognition as socially determined—although not all those affiliated with this kind of work use the term *constructivism.*

   Traditional sociology of science is concerned principally with the social conditions and norms that enable epistemic justification of scientific claims (or the generation of genuine [i.e., true] knowledge) and with the study of social and psychological factors that lead both to discoveries and to errors. SSK studies are more concerned with understanding how it is that scientific activity generates or constructs the facts about the physical world. Controversy surrounds these studies when they claim that it is not simply the facts about the world that are constructed but that physical reality itself is constructed through the activity of scientists.

KEY REFERENCES

Bloor, D. *Knowledge and Social Imagery,* 2nd ed. Chicago: University of Chicago Press, 1991.
Collins, H. M. *Changing Order: Replication and Induction in Scientific Practice.* London: Sage, 1985.

Knorr-Cetina, K. D., & Mulkay, M., eds. *Science Observed: Perspectives on the Social Study of Science.* London: Sage, 1983.

Pickering, A., ed. *Science as Practice and Culture.* Chicago: University of Chicago Press, 1992.

SPECTATOR THEORY OF KNOWLEDGE   See OBSERVATION.

STANDPOINT EPISTEMOLOGIES   These ways of knowing share the assumption that existing relations between politics and the production of knowledge in society are neither neutral nor necessarily as scientifically and socially progressive as social (legal, government, health, education, etc.) institutions and academic disciplines claim. They argue that the purportedly culturally and politically neutral conceptual frameworks of research disciplines (including their standards for objectivity and method) are not in fact neutral at all, but serve a society's dominant group's values and interests. One way to correct this state of affairs is to develop knowledge using standpoint methodology, which enables us to see the world from behind, beneath, or outside the dominant group's conceptual and material practice of power (see *politics of research*).

Standpoints are ways of thinking about the nature of knowledge that begin with the assumption that there is no universal, Archimedean vantage point (no 'view from nowhere') from which we can know the world. All efforts to know, and all knowledge, are socially situated. Various kinds of standpoint epistemologies (e.g., from the standpoint of women, gays, lesbians, people of color, and people experiencing colonial oppression) share the assumption that 'knowing' must begin in the experiences, interests, and values of some traditionally excluded group, for in that way, dominant knowledge claims can be effectively criticized and revised. Standpoint epistemologies are a means of deconstructing what has passed for knowledge, so as to expose its exclusions and dominant perspectives (e.g., masculinist, Eurocentric, racist, and straight). Standpoints are almost always linked to some liberatory, emancipatory, or critical aim.

A key issue for standpoint epistemologies is the consequence for knowledge of substituting 'views from everywhere' for the idea of a 'view from nowhere.' Influenced by postmodern thought, many scholars argue that all views (standpoints) are partial and incomplete, and it is impossible to imagine uniting them into a single complete or collective view of what knowledge is. Hence, knowing is always an act of living within limits and contradictions.

See also Politics of Research.

KEY REFERENCES

Asante, M. K. *The Afrocentric Idea.* Philadelphia: Temple University Press, 1987.

Collins, P. H. *Black Feminist Thought.* New York: Routledge, 1991.

Harding, S. "How Standpoint Methodology Informs Philosophy of Social Science," in S. P. Turner & P. A. Roth, eds., *The Blackwell Guide to the Philosophy of the Social Sciences.* Oxford, UK: Blackwell, 2003.

Harding, S. *Whose Science? Whose Knowledge?* Ithaca, NY: Cornell University Press, 1991.

Smith, D. E. *The Everyday World as Problematic.* Boston: Northeastern University Press, 1987.

STATISTICAL EXPLANATION This is a form of causal explanation in which evidence of statistical correlation is combined with knowledge of causal factors or mechanisms through which observed correlations evolve. These explanations differ from ***deductive-nomological explanations*** only to the extent that they imply probabilistic as opposed to deterministic claims. These kinds of explanations are rare but not completely unknown in qualitative studies. A weak analog to this idea is found in M. Miles and A. M. Huberman's *Qualitative Data Analysis* (2nd ed., Sage, 1994). There they describe various means for developing empirically supportable causal networks, causal models, and causal chains linking variables. While the associations between variables are not measured mathematically, the scheme reflects the underlying idea of establishing correlations among variables and developing a causal story explaining the mechanisms linking the variables into a network or chain.

See also Causal Analysis/Causality, Explanation.

KEY REFERENCE

Little, D. *Varieties of Social Explanation: An Introduction to the Philosophy of Social Science.* Boulder, CO: Westview Press, 1991.

STATISTICAL GENERALIZATION   Also called a statistical inference, this is a form of generalization based on drawing a sample from a class of things called a population. Statistical tests are then used to make an inference (an estimation of the likelihood) that what was found to be characteristic of the sample is true for the population as a whole.

See also Generalization, Sampling Logic.

KEY REFERENCE

Little, D. *Varieties of Social Explanation: An Introduction to the Philosophy of Social Science.* Boulder, CO: Westview Press, 1991.

STRUCTURALISM   This is both a way of thinking about the world and a methodology for investigating the world that is concerned with identifying and describing its underlying structures that cannot be observed but must be inferred. What exactly a structure is varies depending upon the discipline in which structures are discussed. For example, the underlying determinate structure may be economic as in the case of Marxism, a particular 'grammar' of language in the case of linguistics, a 'system' in system analysis, or gender relations in the case of some feminist structural analyses. Jean Piaget (1896–1980) provides a general definition of a structure as an arrangement of entities that are characterized by wholeness or internal coherence, dynamism and the capability of transforming or processing new material, and self-regulation (*Structuralism,* C. Maschler, trans. and ed., Routledge & Kegan Paul, 1971). Structuralist theories descended from the work of the Swiss linguist Ferdinand de Saussure (1857–1913) and the adaptation of Saussure's ideas for the analysis of language to the analysis of culture by the anthropologist Claude Lévi-Strauss in the 1960s. Roughly, Lévi-Strauss viewed aspects of cultural behavior—ceremonies, kinship relations, rites, totemic systems, marriage laws, myths, and so on—not as entities in their own right but as structures in the larger whole or system called culture. Taken together, these aspects form a kind of language of culture, and each aspect is a partial expression of the total language. The organization of culture becomes intelligible through an analysis of its relational structures in much the same way that the organization of a language is made clear by analyzing its grammar.

Structuralist thinking spread beyond the boundaries of linguistics and anthropology to influence other disciplines, including philosophy, literary theory, biology, physical anthropology, and political theory. Its central idea of widespread structural regularities across time and space and its commitment to forming a scientific basis for the study of the innate properties of human nature, human cognition, language, and sociocultural phenomena have found an appeal in these disciplines.

See also Functionalism, Poststructuralism.

KEY REFERENCES

Boyne, R. "Structuralism," in *The Blackwell Companion to Social Theory,* B. S. Turner, ed. Oxford, UK: Blackwell, 1996.
Giddens, A. "Structuralism, Post-structuralism and the Production of Culture," in *Social Theory Today,* A. Giddens & J. H. Turner, eds. Stanford, CA: Stanford University Press, 1987.

SUBJECT   This term has two meanings that are completely opposite. In social science research, the *subject* refers to the person being studied—that is, the research subject or the object of investigation. In philosophy of social science, the *subject* is the knower or inquirer who aims to understand or explain an object of knowledge. (*See Figure S.1 and* **Subject-object relationship***.*)

SUBJECTIVISM   There are two different senses of this term. First, it is a doctrine that holds that all judgments (e.g., claims, interpretations, and assertions) are *nothing but* reports of an individual speaker's feelings, attitudes, and beliefs, or that whatever one claims to be the case is nothing but a matter of personal opinion or taste. This understanding of subjectivism is compatible with ***relativism***—that is, the view that 'anything goes' or that any interpretation is as good as any other. Second, it is a doctrine that holds that subjectivity is the ultimate reality, so to speak. Edmund Husserl's (1859–1938) phenomenology of transcendental subjectivism is a well-known example. Husserl offered two kinds of arguments against the doctrine of ***realism:*** He attempted to show that there is no real world that is wholly independent of the 'subject' that knows or experiences that world, and that the knowing subject does not itself belong to the world that it knows or experiences—that is, this subject is the "transcendental Ego." This understanding of subjectivism is clearly not equivalent to relativism because Husserl sought to show that transcendental subjectivity was a *universal* truth.

See also Objectivism.

KEY REFERENCES

Bunge, M. *Finding Philosophy in Social Science.* New Haven, CT: Yale University Press, 1996.
Hammond, M., Howarth, J., & Keat, R. *Understanding Phenomenology.* Oxford, UK: Blackwell, 1991.

SUBJECTIVITY   From an epistemological point of view this notion has been discussed in terms of (a) the personal view of an individual, (b) an unwarranted or unsupported (or unwarrantable, insupportable) claim, and (c) a biased or prejudiced account. These three senses of the term are not necessarily equivalent. For example, just because a statement or claim is someone's personal view, it does not necessarily follow that it is unwarranted or biased. Thomas Kuhn (1922–1996) in *The Essential Tension* (University of Chicago Press, 1977) sought to distinguish the *judgmental* character of a choice, decision, or statement from its *subjective* character. He argued that there are some kinds of subjective choices that are simply matters of taste— for example, when one expresses "I like ice cream." When one is called upon to make a personal judgment, however, then one must give reasons that support that judgment. To be rational and reasonable in this case is to give reasons for one's judgment.

The term has also been used more broadly to refer to the notion of **lived experience** in its historical, political, and physical contexts. Here, the primary issues are the (subjective) experience of sense of self as evident, for example, in discussions of **reflexivity** and **emotion** in qualitative work.

Many postmodernists reject the language of subject and subjectivity altogether as being the trappings of modernity. They are postsubjective or champion the decline of subjectivity, which means that they aim to de-emphasize the subject as focus for analysis. They also seek to do away with the idea of a rational, unified subject as knower, arguing that there are multiple and contradictory subjectivities that are produced by discursive practices.

See also Intersubjectivity, Judgment, Objectivity, Subjectivism, Subject-Object *Relationship.*

KEY REFERENCES

Ellis, C., & Flaherty, M. G., eds. *Investigating Subjectivity.* Newbury Park, CA: Sage, 1992.

Rosenau, P. *Post-Modernism and the Social Sciences.* Princeton, NJ: Princeton University Press, 1992.

SUBJECT-OBJECT RELATIONSHIP   The conceptual distinction, dualism, or dichotomy of subjects (knower/thinkers) and objects (what they know or think about) is central to most all of Western philosophy. (Of course, subjects can themselves be objects of thought and knowledge as is assumed in the notion of *reflexivity.*)

The traditional way of understanding the subject-object (S-O) relationship characteristic of the philosophy of *naturalism,* and assumed in many varieties of qualitative inquiry, is depicted in Figure S.1. Considerable criticism of this portrayal is directed at the idea that it mistakenly regards a clear-cut separation of subject and object as a substantive (i.e., real) distinction (see the doctrine of *objectivism*). To regard the S-O relationship as a real distinction, the argument goes, is to believe that the subject stands fundamentally as independent of, apart from, or over and against objects of knowledge. Subjects stand alone as fully separate, self-defined entities; the state of being a subject (*'subjectivity'*) is characterized by its ability to have a purely theoretical, contemplative, rational, or intellectual grasp of objects (including both self and world). Furthermore, meaning resides in objects and is discoverable. To fully grasp (discover and extract) and to correctly represent that meaning, subjects must exercise their faculty or capacity to reason in a way free from the effects of standpoint, that is, independent of historical context, prejudices, tradition, and so on. Reason thus requires the correct use of *method* (whether Descartes' method of rational doubt or empirical method) because method is a device that helps prevent reason from being corrupted by prejudice, tradition, and so forth. Following the rules of method helps ensure the distancing of the object of study from the observer (subject or knower) thereby making objective knowledge possible. Critics call this portrayal of the *epistemology* and *ontology* of the S-O relationship a stance of disengagement. Disengagement is equivalent to objectification—that is, to objectify that which one seeks to understand is to treat it as separate from oneself.

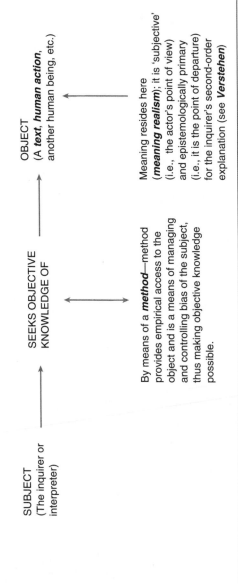

SUBJECT
(The inquirer or
interpreter)

SEEKS OBJECTIVE
KNOWLEDGE OF

OBJECT
(A *text*, *human action*,
another human being, etc.)

By means of a *method*—method
provides empirical access to the
object and is a means of managing
and controlling bias of the subject,
thus making objective knowledge
possible.

Meaning resides here
(*meaning realism*); it is 'subjective'
(i.e., the actor's point of view)
and epistemologically primary
(i.e., it is the point of departure)
for the inquirer's second-order
explanation (see *Verstehen*)

Figure S.1   The Traditional Model of the Subject-Object (S-O) Relationship Reflecting the Human Sciences Understood
Within Naturalism

Drawing on the intellectual traditions of phenomenology and philosophical hermeneutics, critics argue that the fundamental relationship of self to object (world) is actually one of engagement. (Compare Figure S.1 to Figure H.2.) As Gallagher (1992) explains, "the living human being understands the world as he [*sic*] finds himself already in it, not as an anemic egological entity eruditely confronting an opposing objective entity" (p. 45). Subjectivity is always already in the world, situated in relation to objects; subjects are always in dialogue, participating in making sense of self and world. Views of human agency as embodied, of self as dialogical, of meaning as constructed in interaction, of knowledge as something we participate in (versus something we acquire as individuals through cognitive mechanisms of input and processing), all follow from these criticisms of the disengaged S-O relationship.

See also Body, Dialogism, Hermeneutic Circle, Intentionality, Understanding.

KEY REFERENCES

Adorno, T. W., & Horkheimer, M. *Dialectic of Enlightenment,* J. Cumming, trans. New York: Herder & Herder, 1972.

Crotty, M. *The Foundations of Social Research.* London: Sage, 1998.

Gallagher, S. *Hermeneutics and Education.* Albany: SUNY Press, 1992.

Smith, M. J. *Social Science in Question.* London: Sage (in association with the Open University Press), 1998.

Taylor, C. *Philosophical Arguments.* Cambridge, MA: Harvard University Press, 1995.

SYMBOLIC INTERACTIONISM   This social psychological and sociological theory has it roots in American ***pragmatism***. Like all frameworks informing qualitative studies, this theory comes in a variety of forms and thus is difficult to summarize briefly. Many of the shared assumptions of this school of thought derive from the work of Herbert Blumer (1900–1987) (*Symbolic Interactionism: Perspective and Method,* Prentice-Hall, 1969) who, in turn, was influenced by the philosopher and social theorist George Herbert Mead (1863–1931). The Blumer-Mead version of symbolic interactionism rests on three premises. First, humans act toward the objects and people in their environment based on the meanings these objects and people have for them. Second, these meanings derive from the social interaction (communication, broadly understood) between and among individuals. Communication is symbolic because we communicate through language and other symbols and in communicating create significant symbols. Third, meanings are established and modified through an interpretive process undertaken by the individual actor. The influence of pragmatism on symbolic interactionism is evident in the latter's claim that humans are purposive agents who confront a world that must be interpreted rather than a world composed of a set of stimuli to which the individual must react. The meanings an actor forms in interpreting the world are instruments for guiding and forming action. Symbolic interactionism is thus characterized by its rejection of associationist or behaviorist psychologies. It also evinces a profound respect for the empirical world; to understand the process of meaning making, the inquirer must attend carefully to the overt behaviors, speech, and particular circumstances of behavior settings in which interaction takes place. The inquirer can understand human action only by first actively entering the setting or situation of the people being studied to see their particular definition of the situation, what they take into account, and how they interpret this information.

KEY REFERENCES

Denzin, N. K. *Symbolic Interactionism and Cultural Studies*. Oxford, UK: Blackwell, 1992.

Joas, H. "Symbolic Interactionism," in *Social Theory Today*, A. Giddens & J. H. Turner, eds. Stanford, CA: Stanford University Press, 1987.

Plummer, K., ed. "Symbolic Interactionism in the Twentieth Century: The Rise of Empirical Social Theory," in *The Blackwell Companion to Social Theory*, B. S. Turner, ed. Oxford, UK: Blackwell, 1996.

T

TACIT (PERSONAL) KNOWLEDGE   Tacit knowledge is having an awareness of certain things in a way that is quite different than focusing our attention on them. In contrast to explicit knowledge, in which a knower is self-aware of the state of having knowledge, tacit knowledge is implicit. It is genuine knowledge one can have without being self-consciously aware of having it. Yvonna Lincoln and Egon Guba have argued that the tacit knowledge of the field researcher as 'human instrument' plays a significant role in distinguishing the methods of *naturalistic inquiry* from the methods of conventional social inquiry. Tacit knowledge enables field researchers to be situationally responsive and to key into potentially important information. Lincoln and Guba claim that this kind of adaptability and flexibility of the 'human instrument' marks naturalistic inquiry as uniquely different from experimental and quasi-experimental inquiry that relied on paper-and-pencil instruments (i.e., questionnaires) and mechanical recording devices for data gathering.

Viewed more broadly, a defense of the importance (even necessity) of tacit or personal knowing in scientific inquiry plays a significant role in criticisms of *logical positivism* and *logical empiricism*. These philosophies sought to eliminate from science (or at least greatly minimize) tacit knowledge or, more broadly, any kind of knowing that would be regarded as personal *judgment* and appraisal. The chemist and philosopher Michael Polanyi (1891–1976) is generally credited with explaining why the ideal of scientific detachment is suspect and pointing out that the personal participation of the knower in all acts of knowing (including scientific knowing in the context of justification) is essential. Polanyi argued that the inevitable inclusion of personal, tacit assessments and judgments in all aspects of knowledge acquisition did not necessarily undermine the objectivity of science but rather called for an alternative analysis of scientific objectivity. Polanyi (Polanyi & Prosch, 1975) summarized his argument as follows:

> [T]he processes of knowing (and so also of science) in no way resemble an impersonal achievement of detached objectivity. They are rooted throughout (from our selection of a problem to the verification of a discovery) in personal acts of tacit integration. They are not grounded on explicit operations of logic. Scientific inquiry is accordingly a dynamic exercise of the imagination and is rooted in commitments and beliefs about the nature of things. It is a fiduciary act. It is far from skepticism itself. It depends upon firm beliefs. . . . Science is not thus the simon-pure crystal-clear fount of all reliable knowledge and coherence, as it has for so long been presumed to be. Its method is not that of *detachment* but rather of *involvement*. It rests, no less than our other ways of achieving meaning, upon various commitments which we personally share. (p. 63)

Other postempiricist philosophers of science incorporate this insight into their arguments about the rationality of science. Thus, it seems reasonable to say that tacit or personal knowing plays an important role in *all* forms of scientific investigation.

See also Propositional Knowledge, Weltanschauung.

KEY REFERENCES

Brown, H. *Perception, Theory and Commitment: The New Philosophy of Science.* Chicago: University of Chicago Press, 1977.

Lincoln, Y. S., & Guba, E. G. *Naturalistic Inquiry.* Beverly Hills, CA: Sage, 1985.

Polanyi, M. *Personal Knowledge: Towards a Post-Critical Philosophy.* Chicago: University of Chicago Press, 1958.

Polanyi, M., & Prosch, H. *Meaning.* Chicago: University of Chicago Press, 1975.

TECHNICAL RATIONALITY   This is both a kind of knowledge and a conception of reason or way of thinking that emerged in the Enlightenment. It places a premium on detachment and objectivity, replication of operations and findings, and *nomothetic knowledge,* in short, the features we attribute to the modern scientific outlook or attitude. Criticisms of the way in which calculative, impersonal scientific and technical rationality had come to dominate the social, economic, and political institutions (as well as the very concept of being human—i.e., social technologies of the self) of late-capitalist, mass societies figured prominently in the work of the *Frankfurt School,* notably the work of Theodor Adorno (1903–1969) and Max Horkheimer's (1895–1973) *Dialectic of Enlightenment* (London: Verso, 1979; first published in 1944) and Herbert Marcuse's (1898–1979) *One-Dimensional Man* (Boston: Beacon Press, 1964), as well as the work of Jürgen Habermas. Habermas, as well as Gadamer (1900–2002), argued that technical rationality increasingly overshadowed practical knowledge, judgment, or rationality, and in much of their work they have mounted a defense of the importance of the latter to human well-being and the survival of social life.

See also *Praxis, Use of Qualitative Inquiry.*

KEY REFERENCES

Dunne, J., & Pendlebury, S. "Practical Reason," in N. Blake, P. Smyers, R. Smith, & P. Standish, eds., *The Blackwell Guide to Philosophy of Education.* Oxford, UK: Blackwell, 2003.

Toulmin, S. *Return to Reason.* Cambridge, MA: Harvard University Press, 2001.

TELEOLOGY The Greek word *telos* means purpose or end, and teleology is the doctrine that human beings (and/or nature) have a basic purpose (what that purpose is and where that purpose comes from is debated among teleologists). If human beings have a telos, that means that they pursue that end or purpose as part of their nature or essence. A nonteleological view holds that purposes or ends are something that human beings impose on the world and themselves. Teleological explanation of human behavior is often contrasted with mechanistic explanation characteristic of *behaviorism;* the latter does not include references to final causes, ends-in-view, and the like but aims to explain behavior in terms of physiochemical processes or stimulus-response. In the philosophy of science, functional explanations found in biology and anthropology are often referred to as teleological because they explain the occurrence of an event or trait in terms of the purpose it serves (e.g., a biological trait is explained because it is useful to the organism's survival).

KEY REFERENCE

Taylor, C. *The Explanation of Behaviour.* London: Routledge & Kegan Paul, 1964.

TEXT   There are at least three related ways in which to think of the importance of the notion of text in qualitative work. The broadest conception is explained by Clifford Geertz, who asks, "What analogies do social scientists use to imagine what social life (the object of social inquiry) is like and how it can be best explained?" Traditionally, social science has looked to analogies drawn from the natural sciences to explain social life in terms of laws, forces, structures, and mechanisms. In approximately the past three decades, however, it has become increasingly popular for social theorists to borrow analogies from the humanities and, hence, to view and explain social *action* as if it were like moves by players in a game, performances by actors in a drama, and sentences in a text. Of these three kinds of analogies, the textual analogy is, as Geertz suggests, perhaps the most venturesome and least obvious. Geertz (1983) notes, however, that it is a potentially very powerful analogy not least because it refigures social explanation:

> To see social institutions, social customs, social changes as in some sense "readable" is to alter our whole sense of what [sociological and anthropological] interpretation is and shift it toward modes of thought more familiar to the translator, the exegete, or the iconographer than to the test giver, the factor analyst, or the pollster. (p. 31)

The second, more narrow or technical understanding of text is specifically related to the textual paradigm of *hermeneutics*. The phenomenon of the text—biblical, classical, legal, and so on—and the interrelated issues of interpretation, language, and meaning in understanding a text lie at the heart of what it means to do hermeneutics. Although the work of Martin Heidegger (1889–1976) and Hans-Georg Gadamer (1900–2002) established the notion of ontological hermeneutics—not simply a textual hermeneutics but a universal, *philosophical hermeneutics* that reveals that interpretation is an inescapable feature of human experience—the 'text' still serves as the paradigm for philosophical hermeneutics.

To be considered a viable framework for the social sciences, philosophical hermeneutics had to be extended to address the subject matter of the social sciences. This required an argument by analogy: Social action can be read like a written text. This argument is most clearly explained by Paul Ricoeur (1913–2005). Ricoeur accepted the premise that the object of social science was meaningful social action construed as a whole (see *contextualism*), and he proceeded to explain why (a) this object displayed some of the same features constitutive of a written text and (b) the methodology of hermeneutics employs similar procedures in understanding this object as in interpreting written texts. Charles Taylor also develops this analogy in his defense of hermeneutical social science. Ricoeur's and Taylor's arguments lend support to the broad textual analogy for social theorizing explained by Geertz.

Poststructuralists offer a third understanding of text. Following Jacques Derrida (1930–2004), they hold that *everything* (life experiences, events, relationships, activities, practices, cultural artifacts, and so forth) is a text. This radical extension of the textual paradigm is often referred to as *pantextualism, textualism,* or the primacy of language. In this view, texts have several characteristics: (a) Texts (textual accounts) do not refer transparently to the social world; (b) they are 'writerly' texts capable of, indeed requiring, rewriting in every encounter by a reader (vs. a traditional notion of 'readerly' texts destined for a passive reader and read for a specific message); (c) every text is related to every other text—this is known as **intertextuality** (which can also refer to the broad poststructuralist theme that issues and concerns once thought distinct to a discipline are now blended and intertwined across multiple disciplines and fields of thought); and (d) every text is open-ended and indeterminate and thus the site of an infinite number of interpretations.

See also Action, Crisis of Representation, Poststructuralism.

KEY REFERENCES

Barthes, R. "From Work to Text," in *Textual Strategies: Perspectives on Poststructuralist Criticism,* J. Harari, ed. Ithaca, NY: Cornell University Press, 1979.

Geertz, C. "Blurred Genres: The Refiguration of Social Thought," in C. Geertz, *Local Knowledge.* New York: Basic Books, 1983.

Ricoeur, P. "The Model of the Text: Meaningful Action Considered as a Text," in P. Ricoeur, *Hermeneutics and the Human Sciences,* J. B. Thompson, ed. and trans. Cambridge, UK: Cambridge University Press, 1981.

Taylor, C. "Interpretation and the Sciences of Man," in C. Taylor, *Philosophy and the Human Sciences: Philosophical Papers 2.* Cambridge, UK: Cambridge University, 1985. (Originally appeared in the *Review of Metaphysics,* 1971, 25, 3–51)

TEXTUAL ANALYSIS, METHODS OF   Researchers can regard a text itself as an object suitable for analysis. A text can consist of words or phrases (such as responses to structured interviews or questionnaires) or more lengthy segments (as found, for example, in narrative research, analysis of written documents, or in responses to open-ended and unstructured interviews). Methods for analyzing data in the form of texts vary along a continuum anchored on one end by methods that emphasize content or *what* was said and on the other end by methods that emphasize form or *how* something was said. Analysis of texts undertaken in **content analysis** and **objectivist hermeneutics** is primarily concerned with content. Analysis undertaken by ethnomethodological means focused on making sense of talk in interaction (**conversation analysis** and **discourse analysis**) is more concerned with form. **Narrative analysis** and the kind of analyses undertaken in **semiotics** generally are concerned with both form and content.

KEY REFERENCES

Bernard, H. R., & Ryan, G. W. "Qualitative and Quantitative Methods of Text Analysis," in *Handbook of Methods in Cultural Anthropology,* H. R. Bernard, ed. Walnut Creek, CA: AltaMira Press, 1998.

Coffey, A., & Atkinson, P. *Making Sense of Qualitative Data.* London: Sage, 1996.

Manning, P. *Semiotics and Fieldwork.* Newbury Park, CA: Sage, 1987.

Silverman, D. *Interpreting Qualitative Data: Strategies for Analyzing Talk, Text and Interaction.* London: Sage, 1993.

TEXTUAL EXPERIMENTATION   One outgrowth of the *crisis of representation* in social science research is the effort to experiment with new textual forms for ethnographic work, many of which are based on the belief that an ethnographic report can no longer literally represent matter-of-fact accounts of others' experiences. Performance texts, as well as ethnodrama, ethnopoetry, and *autoethnography,* are notable examples.

See also Performance Studies.

KEY REFERENCES

Bochner, A. P., & Ellis, C., eds. *Ethnographically Speaking: Autoethnography, Literature, and Aesthetics.* Walnut Creek, CA: AltaMira Press, 2002.

Ellis, C., & Bochner, A. P., eds. *Composing Ethnography: Alternative Forms of Qualitative Writing.* Walnut Creek, CA: AltaMira Press, 1996.

Richardson, L. "Poetic Representation of Interviews," in J. F. Gubrium & J. A. Holstein, eds., *Handbook of Interview Research.* Thousand Oaks, CA: Sage, 2002.

TEXTUALISM   See TEXT.

TEXTUALIZATION   See TRANSCRIPTION.

THEMATIC ANALYSIS   Also called qualitative thematic analysis and interpretive content analysis, this is a common general approach to analyzing qualitative data that does not rely on the specialized procedures of other means of analysis such as *grounded theory methodology, discourse analysis,* and semiotic analysis. In this exploratory approach, the analyst codes (marks or indexes) sections of a text (e.g., a transcript, field notes, and documents) according to whether they appear to contribute to emerging themes.

See also Analyzing Qualitative Date, Coding.

KEY REFERENCES

Patton, M. Q. *Qualitative Research & Evaluation Methods,* 3rd ed. Thousand Oaks, CA: Sage, 2002.
Seale, C. "Coding and Analysing Data," in C. Seale, ed., *Researching Society and Culture.* London: Sage, 2004.

THEORETICAL CANDOR   This is a procedure for establishing the *validity* of analysis and interpretation in ethnography. The disciplinary perspectives and formal theories held by the *fieldworker* determine the site, problems, and objectives brought to the *field* thereby giving ethnography a particular purpose and meaning. In other words, theory has an a priori function in shaping research questions, problems, and initial hypotheses. In addition, once fieldwork is under way, the fieldworker develops something like a local theory about people, places, interactions, and events that determine much of what is heard and seen. Theoretical candor means making both kinds of theoretical decisions explicit in writing an interpretive account.

KEY REFERENCE

Sanjek, R. "On Ethnographic Validity," in *Fieldnotes: The Makings of Anthropology,* R. Sanjek, ed. Ithaca, NY: Cornell University Press, 1990.

THEORETICAL GENERALIZATION   See GENERALIZATION.

THEORETICAL SAMPLING   See GROUNDED THEORY METHOD-OLOGY, SAMPLING LOGIC.

THEORETICAL SATURATION   See GROUNDED THEORY METHODOLOGY.

THEORY, TYPES OF   A formal understanding common in the natural and social sciences is that theory is a unified, systematic causal *explanation* of a diverse range of social phenomena. Theory of this kind is evaluated in terms of the familiar criteria of parsimony, completeness, predictive power, and scope. Examples from different social science disciplines include exchange theory, kinship theory, cognitive dissonance theory, and Keynesian economic theory. Although what constitutes an adequate causal explanatory account is a matter of some debate, there is general agreement among naturalists, some critical social scientists, and pluralists that developing theory, understood in this way, is the proper goal of the social sciences.

It is also commonplace, however, to speak of theory in a less formal way—that is, theory may be said to come in many shapes and sizes depending on levels of sophistication, organization, and comprehensiveness. At the simplest level, there are *theoretical ideas* or, more simply, *concepts* that function as analytical tools. Concepts point the inquirer in a general direction but do not give a very specific set of instructions for what to see. A step up the ladder of sophistication, one finds *theoretical orientations* or perspectives (e.g., functionalism, symbolic interactionism, behaviorism, phenomenology, hermeneutics, feminism, social constructionism, and poststructuralism). These, more or less, are social theories that explain the distinguishing features of social and cultural life, and, thus, they serve as approaches to identifying, framing, and solving problems, and understanding and explaining social reality. *Substantive theories,* however, are different than these theoretical frameworks because they are about some specific social or behavioral phenomenon—for example, a social constructionist theory of living with a particular cancer, a feminist theory of nursing work, or a behavioral theory of children's play. Substantive theories can develop into *formal theories;* the difference is one of the comprehensiveness or scope of their explanation. The former, more or less, hover low over the data, as Clifford Geertz once noted; the latter are more removed from the case at hand. For example, through comparative analyses, a substantive theory of a mental hospital as a total institution can be extended to a theory of all institutions exhibiting these central features, or a substantive theory of the deviant career of the drug dealer can be extended to a theory of all kinds of deviant careers.

See also Critical Theory, Grand Theory.

KEY REFERENCES

Bernstein, R. J. *The Restructuring of Social and Political Theory.* Philadelphia: University of Pennsylvania Press, 1976.
Calhoun, C. "Social Theory and the Public Sphere," in *The Blackwell Companion to Social Theory,* B. S. Turner, ed. Oxford, UK: Blackwell, 1996.
Silverman, D. "Research and Social Theory," in C. Seale, G. Gobo, J. F. Gubrium, & D. Silverman, eds., *Qualitative Research Practice.* London: Sage, 2004.

THEORY, USES OF   A widespread concern in the teaching and learning of qualitative inquiry is how to use theory in qualitative studies. In the *hypothetico-deductive method* of research, theories are the source of hypotheses that are then investigated, in effect, to test the theory. Many forms of qualitative research, however, do not abide by this way of thinking of research; thus, the issue of how to use theory becomes more complicated. Furthermore, many qualitative researchers do not enter a study with a well-defined theoretical perspective; they are more likely to have a set of concepts or ideas as the impetus for their research. Perhaps the most useful advice is to focus on how to theorize the data, or how to think theoretically with one's data. Alford (1998) argues that every research study is an argument seeking to answer both theoretical and empirical questions. The former include "Why did something happen? What explains this? Why did these events occur? What do they mean?" The latter direct the researcher to evidence that helps answer theoretical questions. Empirical questions include "What happened? What is going on here? What are the patterns here?" Alford (1998) claims that

> The most fruitful way to think of the research *process* is to constantly move
> back and forth from reflective musings about the larger implications of

concepts and theories to quite concrete, grounded analyses of observations, evidence, or data. I call this process of moving back and forth from the theoretical and the empirical *tracks of analysis,* in the course of following different leads in the research literature and in the evidence. . . . The theoretical and the empirical aspects of a problem are thus always in tension with one another. Abstract concepts never perfectly fit the complexity of reality. Evidence never contains its own explanation. (pp. 28–29)

Silverman (2004) takes a similar position, arguing that to theorize the data, one should consider (a) chronology (Is it possible to gather data over time to look at processes of change?), (b) context (How are the data one generates contextualized in a particular setting, social context, or process?), (c) comparison (Can the data be divided into different sets that can be compared, or can the data you have generated be compared to other relevant data?), (d) implications (How did what you find relate to issues that are broader than your specific research problem?), and (e) lateral thinking (Explore relations between ideas and concepts; do not erect strong boundaries between them.).

KEY REFERENCES

Alford, R. R. *The Craft of Inquiry.* New York: Oxford University Press, 1998.

Anfara, V. A., Jr., & Mertz, N. T., eds. *Theoretical Frameworks in Qualitative Research.* Thousand Oaks, CA: Sage, 2006.

Silverman, D. "Research and Social Theory," in C. Seale, G. Gobo, J. F. Gubrium, & D. Silverman, eds., *Qualitative Research Practice.* London: Sage, 2004.

THEORY-LADEN OBSERVATION   See THEORY-OBSERVATION DISTINCTION.

THEORY-OBSERVATION DISTINCTION   The philosophy of *logical positivism* drew a sharp distinction between theory (concepts) and observation and assigned epistemological priority to observation statements. In other words, knowledge was said to rest on a foundation of unambiguous observations. Concepts and theories were entirely dependent for their meaning on the particular observation statements into which they could be unpacked. Thus, the logical empiricist Herbert Feigl (1902–1988) argued in classic inductivist fashion that theoretical concepts grow out of the "soil" of observation: Theory is meaningful only and precisely because of an 'upward seepage' of meaning from observation statements to theoretical concepts.

This sharp theory-observation separation was strongly criticized by postempiricist philosophers of science, who held that considerations like *tacit knowledge,* prior theory, metaphysical commitments, and the like influenced both the making of observations and decisions about what constituted fact. They challenged the relative priority of observation statements over theoretical statements characteristic of the strict inductivist approach of logical positivism and attempted to restore theoretical considerations to an equal footing with observation statements in our picture of the development of scientific knowledge. They demonstrated that while theory does not necessarily determine fact, all observations are, in an important sense, theory laden. They also demonstrated that all theories are underdetermined by observation or evidence. In other words, there is no body of evidence (data) that can conclusively demonstrate the superiority of one theory over another. Theories can, in various ways, be made to fit the evidence (or, in some cases, to disregard the evidence as anomalous).

There is now general agreement in the philosophy of science that the formation, testing, and success of scientific theories is not solely an empirical matter; that is, it does not depend on an unshakable foundation of observations. Rather, there is some sort of dynamic interplay between theory (concept) and observations (evidence) in what constitutes genuine scientific knowledge.

The abandonment of a strict theory-observation distinction and the recognition that theoretical presuppositions (concepts, conceptual schemes, theoretical orientations, etc.) play an important role in observation and testing do not necessarily lead to a relativist epistemology. For naturalists, and many anti-naturalists, it simply means that there is no absolutely reliable foundation for knowledge, which the logical positivists hoped for. However, some scholars couple the dissolution of the hard-and-fast theory-observation distinction with a doctrine of radical conceptual difference to draw a relativist conclusion as follows: (a) All empirical evidence is theory laden,; that is, observation is dependent on a conceptual scheme; (b) every conceptual scheme is relative to some language and norms of a particular group, community, or culture of inquirers; (c) these conceptual schemes are incommensurable; and, hence, (d) all knowledge is relative to a conceptual scheme, and comparisons across conceptual schemes are not possible.

See also Description, Empiricism.

KEY REFERENCES

Feigl, H. "The 'Orthodox' View of Theories," in *Minnesota Studies in the Philosophy of Science IV,* M. Radner & S. Winokur, eds. Minneapolis: University of Minnesota Press, 1970.

Hesse, M. *Revolutions and Reconstructions in the Philosophy of Science.* Bloomington: Indiana University Press, 1980.

THEORY OF SIGNS   See SEMIOTICS.

THEORY-PRACTICE RELATIONSHIP   See PRAXIS, USE OF QUALITATIVE INQUIRY.

THICK DESCRIPTION   Following advice given by Clifford Geertz in his widely cited 1973 essay "Thick Description: Toward an Interpretive Theory of Culture," many qualitative inquirers emphasize the importance of 'thick' as opposed to 'thin' description. Yet it is not entirely clear just what thick description is. Most efforts to define it emphasize that thick description is not simply a matter of amassing relevant detail. Rather, to thickly describe social action is actually to begin to interpret it by recording the circumstances, meanings, intentions, strategies, motivations, and so on that characterize a particular episode. It is this interpretive characteristic of description rather than detail per se that makes it thick.

See also Contextualism, Inscription, Representation, Transcription.

KEY REFERENCE

Geertz, C. "Thick Description: Toward an Interpretive Theory of Culture," in C. Geertz, *The Interpretation of Cultures.* New York: Basic Books, 1973.

TRANSCRIPTION   Transcription is the act of recording and preparing a record of a respondent's own words, and it yields a written account—a text—of what a respondent or informant said in response to a fieldworker's query or what respondents said to one another in conversation. The transcription may result from retyped handwritten notes or audio recordings. When a fieldworker records a speech made by a respondent, a respondent's description of an event, a conversation between respondents, a series of answers to a set of interview questions, and so on, the fieldworker is preparing a transcription. James Clifford argued that when reports of fieldwork are based largely on texts produced through transcription, they may have the effect of breaking up the monological authority of the fieldworker-as-privileged-author or interpreter of human action. He and other scholars, however, caution that transcription is not some kind of innocent recording of the way things really are. For example, John Van Maanen (1988) explains that transcriptions (as well as all other forms of field notes) are mediated

> many times over—by the fieldworker's own standards of relevance for what is of interest; by the historically situated queries put to informants; by the norms current in the fieldworker's professional community for what is proper work; by the self-reflection demanded of both the fieldworker and the informant; by the intentional and unintentional ways a fieldworker or informant is misled; and by the fieldworker's mere presence on the scene as an observer and participant. (p. 95)

Van Maanen borrows from Paul Ricoeur (1913–2005) the term *textualization*—the process whereby 'unwritten' behavior, beliefs, traditions, and so on become fixed, discrete, particular kinds of data—to claim that it is only in textualized form that data yield to analysis. Hence, he concludes that "the process of analysis is not dependent on the events themselves [as recorded in allegedly innocent transcriptions], but on a second-order, textualized, fieldworker-dependent version of events" (p. 95).

See also Inscription, Interviewing Logic.

KEY REFERENCES

Clifford, J. "On Ethnographic Authority," *Representations,* 1983, 1(2), 118–146.
Van Maanen, J. *Tales of the Field.* Chicago: University of Chicago Press, 1988.

TRANSFERABILITY See **GENERALIZATION, TRUSTWORTHINESS CRITERIA.**

TRIANGULATION This is a procedure used to establish the fact that the criterion of *validity* has been met. The fieldworker makes inferences from data, claiming that a particular set of data supports a particular definition, theme, assertion, hypothesis, or claim. Triangulation is a means of checking the integrity of the inferences one draws. It can involve the use of multiple data sources, multiple investigators, multiple theoretical perspectives, and/or multiple methods. The central point of the procedure is to examine a conclusion (assertion, claim, etc.) from more than one vantage point. For example, to understand the nature of communication between geriatric patients and internists in an outpatient clinic, the fieldworker might compare data from early and late phases of fieldwork, from different patient-physician pairs, from different times in the temporal cycle of the encounter (taking the medical history: testing, diagnosis, prescribing a treatment plan, follow-up), and so forth. Also, data from observations of patient-physician interactions may be compared with data from interviews with each party, and so on.

The strategy of triangulation is often wedded to the assumption that data from different sources or methods must *necessarily* converge on or be aggregated to reveal the truth. In other words, so the arguments goes, triangulation is both possible and necessary because research is a process of discovery in which the genuine meaning residing within an action or event can be best uncovered by viewing it from different vantage points. Many researchers argue that because triangulation is typically wedded to this assumption of **meaning realism,** it is inappropriate for qualitative research. Others disagree. For example, Martyn Hammersley and Paul Atkinson (1983) believe that the notion can be salvaged and made serviceable, providing the advice that

> one not adopt a naively "optimistic" view that the aggregation of data from different sources will unproblematically add up to produce a more complete picture . . . *differences* between sets or types of data may be just as important and illuminating. . . . [W]hat is involved in triangulation is not just a matter of checking whether inferences are valid, but of discovering which inferences are valid. (pp. 199–200)

KEY REFERENCES

Denzin, N. K. *The Research Act,* 3rd ed. Englewood Cliffs, NJ: Prentice-Hall, 1989.
Hammersley, M., & Atkinson, P. *Ethnography: Principles in Practice.* London: Tavistock, 1983.
Mason, J. *Qualitative Researching.* London: Sage, 1996.
Seale, C. "Quality in Qualitative Research," *Qualitative Inquiry,* 1999, 5(1), 165–178.

TRUSTWORTHINESS CRITERIA Yvonna Lincoln and Egon Guba coined this term to refer to one set of *criteria* for judging the quality or goodness of qualitative inquiry. In *Naturalistic Inquiry* (1985), they described criteria (and associated procedures) that were more appropriate for judging the trustworthiness of naturalistic investigations than traditional epistemic criteria (e.g., internal and external validity) and procedures. Trustworthiness was defined as that quality of an investigation (and its findings) that made it noteworthy to audiences. They developed four criteria that served as the naturalistic inquirer's equivalents to conventional criteria. First, *credibility* (parallel to internal validity) addressed the issue of the inquirer providing assurances of the fit between respondents' views of their life ways and the inquirer's reconstruction and representation of same. Second, *transferability* (parallel to external validity) dealt with the issue of *generalization* in terms of case-to-case transfer. It concerned the inquirer's responsibility for providing readers with sufficient information on the case studied such that readers could establish the degree of similarity between the case studied and the case to which findings might be transferred. Third, *dependability* (parallel to reliability) focused on the process of the inquiry and the inquirer's responsibility for ensuring that the process was logical, traceable, and documented. Fourth, *confirmability* (parallel to objectivity) was concerned with establishing the fact that the data and interpretations of an inquiry were not merely figments of the inquirer's imagination. It called for linking assertions, findings, interpretations, and so on to the data themselves in readily discernible ways. For each of these criteria, Lincoln and Guba also specified a set of procedures that could be used to meet the criteria. For example, *auditing* was highlighted as a procedure useful for establishing both dependability and confirmability, and *member check* and *peer debriefing,* among other procedures, were defined as most appropriate for credibility.

In *Fourth Generation Evaluation* (1989), Guba and Lincoln reevaluated this initial set of criteria. They explained that trustworthiness criteria were parallel, quasi-foundational, and clearly intended to be analogs to conventional criteria. Furthermore, they held that trustworthiness criteria were principally methodological criteria and thereby largely ignored aspects of the inquiry concerned with the quality of outcome, product, and negotiation. Hence, they advanced a second set of criteria called *authenticity criteria,* arguing that this second set was better aligned with the constructivist epistemology that informed their definition of qualitative inquiry.

See also Validity.

KEY REFERENCES

Guba, E. G., & Lincoln, Y. S. *Fourth Generation Evaluation.* Newbury Park: Sage, 1989.
Lincoln, Y. S., & Guba, E. G. *Naturalistic Inquiry.* Beverly Hills, CA: Sage, 1985.

TRUTH   This is one of the most difficult of all philosophical topics, and controversies surrounding the nature of truth lie at the heart of both apologies for and criticisms of varieties of qualitative work. Moreover, truth is intimately related to questions of *meaning,* and establishing the nature of that relationship is also complicated and contested.

There is general agreement that *what* is true or what carries truth are statements, propositions, beliefs, and assertions, but *how* the truth of same is established is widely debated. Major theories of truth include the familiar *correspondence theory,* which holds that a statement is true or false depending on whether the content of a statement or belief accurately matches or represents some state of affairs in the world. (A companion theory called the picture theory of meaning holds that a statement is true or false depending on whether reality matches the picture represented by the belief.) A *consensus theory* of truth, as found, for example, in the work of Jürgen Habermas, holds that the truth of a statement is a matter of consensus on beliefs and values that responsible people would reach in an ideal speech situation (i.e., a situation free from the distortions of everyday communication). A *coherence theory* of truth judges the truth or falsity of a statement in terms of the degree to which it is coherent with a background of settled (agreed-on and warranted) beliefs. A *contextualist theory* of truth, as held by Richard Rorty, for example, claims that truth is not something about which there can ever be an important philosophical theory because truth is a just a term of agreement; a statement is justified or regarded as true relative to some particular community or culture of inquirers. Somewhat in line with Rorty's views, many social constructionists are agnostic with respect to the idea of whether truth is a property of the content of statements and focus instead on how telling the truth is socially accomplished or how in interactions people construct a description or statement as 'being true.' A *pragmatic theory* of truth, as held, for example, by John

Dewey (1859–1952), claims that truth of assertions is determined by whether they function well in making our way in understanding the world. Dewey argued that the term *truth* ought to be replaced by the notion of warranted assertability.

For Hans-Georg Gadamer (1900–2002), Charles Taylor, and others in the tradition of philosophical hermeneutics, truth (and meaning) is something that is *disclosed* in the relationship of interpreter to the object of interpretation. Generally speaking, truth is a property or content over which interpretations 'compete,' and the better (more perspicuous and perspicacious) account offers an epistemic gain over the account that is less so.

For Michel Foucault (1926–1984) and his followers, *truth* is not at all a term of appraisal as is the case in the previous definitions. Foucault argues that an inescapable relationship of power and knowledge characterizes self and society in which truth is something produced and reproduced in particular systems of domination. Some postmodernists, such as Lyotard (1924–1988), hold an even more radical notion of truth (which at times seems close to a contextualist theory)—namely, that a true statement is simply one that is 'good' to make given the relevant criteria accepted within one's social circle of interlocutors.

A good deal of the current criticism (and confusion) about the nature and meaning of truth comes from the fact that truth is often assumed to be a construct that principally acquires its meaning in the doctrine of *realism*. In other words, it is held that to call a statement true is to claim that it accurately accounts for and explains events that actually occur in the real world. Hence, criticisms of the notion of truth are often directed at an epistemology of *representation* and associated epistemic values such as accuracy. Some critics argue that the term *truth* has no meaning other than as a socially constructed term because there is no 'actual' meaning 'out there' in events, objects, and interactions. Others accept that meaning is constructed in interaction but do not find that idea incompatible with the notion of truth as a real content.

Truth is also traditionally related to the notion of *objectivity,* when the latter is understood in a substantive way—that is, when 'objective' refers to the semantic content of a statement. In other words, to claim that a statement is objective may be to claim that it is true (or aims at being true) because the content of the statement reflects accurately the way things really are. Hence, criticisms of the notion of truth may be directed more broadly at criticism of the notions of objectivity and *objectivism*.

See also Validity.

KEY REFERENCES

Abbinnett, R. *Truth and Social Science.* London: Sage, 1998.
Bunnin, N., & Tsui-James, E. P., eds. *The Blackwell Companion to Philosophy.* Oxford, UK: Blackwell, 1996.
Smith, N. H. *Strong Hermeneutics.* London: Routledge, 1997.

TYPOLOGIES ⎸A typology is a device for organizing qualitative data for analysis by means of categorizing events or people into qualitatively different ideal types that are abstractions distilled from empirical evidence. Émile Durkheim's (1857–1917) types of suicide and Max Weber's (1864–1920) types of authority are well-known examples of theoretically meaningful typifications. Typologies can be both indigenous and analyst constructed. The former rely on the terms used by people in a particular setting to make distinctions they regard as important (for example, consider the terms that high school students use to identify different subgroup members). The latter rely on terms chosen by the analyst to make explicit patterns that appear to exist (for example, homeless individuals may be typed as transitional, episodic, and chronic). Unlike the analytic device of ***careers,*** typologies do not imply a sense of progression or development.

See also Analyzing Qualitative Data, Coding.

KEY REFERENCES

Martindale, D. *The Nature and Types of Social Theory.* New York: Harper & Row, 1981.
Patton, M. Q. *Qualitative Research & Evaluation Methods,* 3rd ed. Thousand Oaks, CA: Sage, 2002.

U

---•◦•---

UNDERDETERMINATION OF THEORY BY DATA See **THEORY-OBSERVATION DISTINCTION.**

UNDERSTANDING To say that we understand what others are doing or saying or that we have an understanding of them is to claim something quite different than that we 'know.' To understand is literally to stand under, to grasp, to hear, get, catch, or comprehend the meaning of something. To know is to signal that one has engaged in conscious deliberation and can demonstrate, show, or clearly prove or support a claim.

In Anglo-American thought, at least, knowing and knowledge are more often than not associated with intellectual achievement, cognitive performance, or a special kind of mastery of subject matter—we say, "She really knows her stuff," for example. That understanding is an activity different than knowing is perhaps more evident in the German words for "understanding": *Verständis* means comprehension, insight, and appreciation; **Verstehen,** which we translate as "understanding," also means to have an appreciation for something, to comprehend it (*für etwas Verständis haben*). In German, a difference between knowing and understanding is expressed in the questions "*Woher weißt du das?*" ("How do you know that?") and "*Wie verstehen Sie das?*" ("What do you make of that?").

To claim that we can achieve an understanding means that we also acknowledge the risk that we might *misunderstand*—that is, fail to grasp, catch, hear, or comprehend the meaning of something; fail to actually 'make something' out of our observation and listening; or construct an understanding that isn't all in concert with the circumstances of the event or interlocutor we aim to understand. (At times, it appears that some approaches to qualitative inquiry that claim they are given to understanding as an aim fail to take seriously the possibility and risks of misunderstanding.)

Achieving an understanding of others or of the meaning of social *action* is often spoken of as the goal of the human sciences (versus *explanation* as the goal of the natural sciences). How understanding is accomplished, however, is a matter of some dispute. Some see understanding as an act of discovery or exegesis in which one extracts the meaning inherent in text or speech (see *Intentionalism, Subject-object relationship*). Others regard understanding as an act of cocreation in which understanding the meaning of text or speech (how a text or a person 'speaks' to the interpreter) is accomplished only through dialogue and a posture in which the interpreter genuinely risks her or his own prejudices (prior understandings) (see *Hermeneutic circle*).

For example, Gadamer (1900–2002) claims that when we seek to understand what others are doing and saying, we are always standing in a *liminal* space between familiarity and strangeness. He adds that we are "pulled up short" when we encounter situations and people that challenge our expectations and assumptions—those situations wherein answers to the question "What should I make of this?" are not easy to come by. Gadamer explains that we can make sense of these challenging encounters with others in three ways. The first is to try to discover the typical behavior of the other and to make predictions about others on the basis of experience. We thereby form what we call knowledge of human nature. Here, subjects (knowers) regard *the other* as an object in a free and uninvolved way in much the same way as they would any other object in their experiential field. This is the methodological attitude of the social sciences—the idea of disinterested theoretical contemplation of an object of understanding.

In a second way of understanding the other, the interpreter acknowledges the other as a person, but this understanding is a form of self-relatedness. Here, the interpreter claims to know the other from the other's point of view and even to understand the other better than she understands herself. To be sure, the interpreter understands the immediacy of the other's claim, but it is coopted from the standpoint of the interpreter. This can be understood as a form of sympathetic listening in which we interpret others in our own terms and refuse to risk our own prejudgments in the process. Gadamer notes that by claiming to know the other in this way, one robs her claims of their legitimacy, and he argues that charitable or welfare work often operates in this way.

A third way of understanding begins from the full acknowledgement that as interpreters, we are situated within a tradition. It is only from such a posture that an interpreter can experience the other truly as an other and not overlook her claim, but let her really say something to us. Gadamer (1989) states that "without such openness to one another there is no genuine human bond. Belonging together always means being able to listen to one another" (p. 361). Thus, it seems that it is only the interpreter who is awake to this living in between who can have new experiences and learn from them. Understanding requires an openness to experience, a willingness to engage in a *dialogue* with that which challenges one's self-understanding. To be in a dialogue requires that one listen to the other and simultaneously risk confusion and uncertainty both about oneself and about the other person one seeks to understand.

It is only in a dialogical engagement of this kind, in a genuine conversation, that understanding is possible. As Gadamer states, "the miracle of understanding is not a mysterious communion of souls, but sharing in a common meaning" (p. 292). That common meaning can arise only in a dialogue wherein one does not simply defend one's own beliefs or criticize what the other believes, but rather seeks to become clear about oneself, about one's own knowledge and ignorance. It is only if an engagement is a genuine conversation that one can engage in checking, amending, and perhaps abandoning one's own prejudices by exposing them to the contribution of the other.

See also Dialogue, Intentionalism, Meaning, Subject-Object Relationship.

KEY REFERENCES

Gadamer, H.-G. *Truth and Method,* 2nd rev. ed., J. Weinsheimer & D. G. Marshall, trans. New York: Crossroad, 1989.

Kerdeman, D. "Hermeneutics and Education: Understanding, Control, and Agency," *Educational Theory,* 1998, 48(2), 241–266.

Risser, J. *Hermeneutics and the Voice of the Other: Re-reading Gadamer's Philosophical Hermeneutics.* Albany: SUNY Press, 1997.

UNITY OF METHOD   See LOGICAL EMPIRICISM, NATURALISM.

UNITY OF SCIENCES   See LOGICAL EMPIRICISM, NATURALISM

UNOBTRUSIVE DATA These are data that are generated (and often accumulated) without the conscious intent of the researcher or the subjects (or respondents) to whom the data applies. In what remains a classic statement of the nature and use of these data, Webb et al. (1966) classified these data as physical traces (data that are 'found' such as artifacts and forensic evidence), archival records, private records, and contrived observations (e.g., covert observation such as watching the way people make eye contact on a public bus). Examples of the use of these data include using the wear of floor tiles in a museum indexed by the replacement rate of those tiles to determine the relative popularity of exhibits; recording the setting of car radio dials on cars brought in for service to estimate the share of the listening audience of various radio stations; analyzing transaction log data on computers in public libraries to determine the kinds of sites searched and Internet queries made by public users; and analyzing the contents of household garbage (called a *behavior trace study*) to determine food preferences and alcohol consumption. The analysis of unobtrusive data rarely stands alone given what are often considerable problems in inference making based on the data. Moreover, there are obvious ethical issues entailed in the generation and use of several of these kinds of data.

KEY REFERENCES

Sechrest, L., ed. *Unobtrusive Measurement Today.* San Francisco: Jossey-Bass, 1979.
Webb, E. J., Campbell, D. T., Schwartz, R. D., & Sechrest, L. *Unobtrusive Measures: Nonreactive Research in the Social Sciences.* Chicago: Rand McNally, 1966.

USE OF QUALITATIVE INQUIRY How one conceives of the use of qualitative inquiry is related to conceptions of the purpose or aim of such research. As traditionally conceived, the aim of social science is the development of empirical, explanatory *theory*. Particular cases are studied for the purpose of forming general theoretical knowledge; they are not interesting in their own right. Once we are in possession of theory, we can, over time, achieve intellectual and practical mastery of the social world (in much the same manner that possessing a body of empirical explanatory theory in the natural sciences facilitates mastery of the physical world). A particular relationship between theory and practice or action is assumed here: The way to change the social circumstances of education, health care, work life, and so forth is through the technical application of social scientific knowledge (especially knowledge of the probable consequences of different courses of action) to social problems. Hence, here the notion of the use of social inquiry is largely instrumental and reflects *technical rationality*. Instrumental use can take at least two forms: It can be direct application of a research finding to a problem, or it can be more indirect or 'enlightening,' helping practitioners of various kinds better understand or appreciate the scope and complexity of a problem and its various solutions.

Other notions of use are less technical or instrumental but are instead more educative. For example, research approaches informed directly or indirectly by *critical theory* assume that research ought to be a kind of cultural criticism—both a way of better understanding ourselves and our society and a way of changing or transforming the same. In the tradition of *philosophical hermeneutics*, the kind of understanding one acquires from interpreting a text, culture, speech, and so forth is not distinguished from 'use.' In other words, there are not two separate activities of (a) acquiring an understanding, and then (b) applying or using it. Rather, the understanding or knowledge that one acquires in interpretation is already a kind of action-oriented self-understanding—also called *rationality or practical reason* (this is a view of use shared by Habermas as well).

Another educative sense of use follows from the view that we study the particular case in order to train perception and increase the capacity for practical reasoning and deliberation in those many situations in life that are full of too many details, idiosyncrasies, and exceptional aspects to permit the application of general knowledge. In this conception of use, previous case studies are regarded as useful not to the extent that they make possible general theoretical knowledge but rather because they help develop the capacity to attend to the morally and politically relevant features of the case at hand and thereby enhance practical wisdom.

See also Generalization.

KEY REFERENCES

Denzin, N. K. "Interpretive Ethnography for the Next Century," *Journal of Contemporary Ethnography,* 1999, 28, 510–519.

Fay, B. *Critical Social Science.* Ithaca, NY: Cornell University Press, 1987.

Misgeld, D., & Nicholson, G., eds. *Hans-Georg Gadamer on Education, Poetry, and History: Applied Hermeneutics.* Albany: SUNY Press, 1992.

V

VALIDATION HERMENEUTICS   See **CONSERVATIVE HERMENEUTICS.**

VALIDITY   In ordinary usage, validity is a property of a statement, argument, or procedure. To call one of those things valid is to indicate that it is sound, cogent, well grounded, justifiable, or logically correct. Psychologically, validity means having confidence in one's statements or knowledge claims.

In social science, validity is one of the *criteria* that traditionally serve as a benchmark for inquiry. Validity is an epistemic criterion: To say that the findings of social scientific investigations are (or must be) valid is to argue that the findings are in fact (or must be) true and certain. Here, 'true' means that the findings accurately represent the phenomena to which they refer, and 'certain' means that the findings are backed by evidence—or warranted—and there are no good grounds for doubting the findings, or the evidence for the findings in question is stronger than the evidence for alternative findings.

There is much discomfort with and some outright rejection of this criterion among some social inquirers committed to constructivist, postmodernist, feminist, and pragmatic perspectives. Their objections are many and interrelated. A few of the more salient ones are singled out here. First, some criticisms are based on a rejection of naïve or direct *realism*—the idea that we can have direct, unmediated knowledge of the world. Critics of this kind argue that if truth means our ideas about the world must correspond to the way the world really is, and if validity is a test of this correspondence, then there can be no validity because there is no unmediated, observer-independent account of experience to which an account can mirror or correspond. Second, and in a related way, other critics reject the notion that we discover the truth about the world—that is, that the truth is somehow 'out there.' They hold that all accounts of the world are language bound. Thus, if there is such a thing as truth, it is arbitrary, and validity would be relative to some particular language system or worldview. Third, still other critics reject the association of validity with *objectivism*—the doctrine that there must be permanent, ahistorical benchmarks or foundations for judging the truth of claims. Any attempt to associate validity with objectivism is greeted at least with *skepticism*. One additional, even stronger objection to truth and validity comes from radical postmodernists who hold that the very idea of truth as essential to knowledge or as a goal of science is a modernist, Enlightenment value associated with order, rules, logic, rationality, and reason, all of which are considered suspect, at best, and oppressive, at worst.

What this all means is that there are at least four different perspectives from which to understand the notion of validity:

1. Fallibilism: The fallibilist might argue that assessing the validity of a claim is indeed a test of whether the claim accurately represents the social phenomena to which it refers. Yet the fallibilist would explain that no claim ever actually reproduces an independently existing meaning, and no claims (no matter how warranted) are ever absolutely certain. Defenders of this view hold that one can have good reasons for accepting an account as more or less valid (true or false), yet an account is always subject to error and revision. Martyn Hammersley, for example, argues that we judge the validity of an account by checking whether it is plausible; whether it is credible given the nature of the phenomenon being investigated, the circumstances of the research, and the characteristics of the researcher; and, if we doubt either plausibility or credibility, by inspecting the credibility of evidence offered in support of the claim. On this view, all procedures typically cited as means of establishing validity (e.g., *analytic induction* for testing hypotheses, *triangulation, member check,* providing fieldwork evidence, *theoretical candor,* etc.) are nothing more or less than fallible means of making a case for a plausible and credible account.

2. Contextualism: Here, the validity of an account is regarded as relative to the standards of a particular community at a particular place and time. What is considered 'valid' is judged in terms of the current consensus about words, concepts, standards, and so on in a given community of interpreters.

3. Radical relativism: The most radical of postmodernists would argue that it is meaningless to talk of a valid (i.e., true) account of the world; there are only different linguistically mediated social constructions. On this radical perspectivalist view, validity is an empty issue (not simply because the term itself is a social construction) because no single interpretation or account can be judged superior to any other. There is only the endless interplay of different interpretations.

4. Replacement or displacement of validity: The central argument here is that the traditional epistemological concern with validity cannot be decoupled from aesthetic/rhetorical criteria, on the one hand, and political agendas, on the other. Hence, the focus shifts from determining whether an account is true to how the account was developed in conversation between inquirer and participants, how it was crafted in writing by the writer of the account, and whether the account advances a social agenda or offers cultural criticism.

See also (The) Problem of the Criterion, Reflexivity.

KEY REFERENCES

Denzin, N. K. "Aesthetics and the Practices of Qualitative Inquiry," *Qualitative Inquiry,* 2000, 6(2), 256–265.
Hammersley, M. *Reading Ethnographic Research.* New York: Longman, 1990.
Kvale, S. "The Social Construction of Validity," *Qualitative Inquiry,* 1995, 1(1), 19–40.
Lather, P. "Fertile Obsession: Validity After Poststructuralism," *Sociological Quarterly,* 1993, 34(4), 673–693.
Maxwell, J. "Understanding and Validity in Qualitative Research," *Harvard Educational Review,* 1992, 62, 279–300.

VALUE-FREE SOCIAL SCIENCE   See DISINTERESTED SOCIAL SCIENCE, FACT-VALUE DISTINCTION.

VALUE NEUTRALITY   See DISINTERESTED SOCIAL SCIENCE, FACT-VALUE DISTINCTION, POLITICS OF RESEARCH.

VERIFICATION   This is the activity of determining whether a statement is true or accurate. To verify is to confirm, substantiate, or validate a claim. Thus, financial auditors verify and then attest to the fact that a client's claims about the value of inventory, cash balances, amounts of short- and long-term debt, and so forth are in fact what the client says they are.

In the philosophy of science, verification (also called the principle of verifiability or the verifiability criterion of meaning) has a somewhat more specific and technical meaning associated with *logical positivism*. In that philosophy, verification is a criterion for determining whether a statement is a suitable candidate for genuine scientific knowledge. Only those statements capable of verification—capable of being shown to be either true or false either by means of observation or logical reasoning—were considered cognitively meaningful. The logical positivists used this criterion to exclude all other statements (such as those in metaphysics, ethics, or theology) as meaningless when it comes to establishing genuine knowledge. Their goal was to establish a foundation for all knowledge claims in the bedrock of observation statements. A variety of critics of logical positivism demonstrated that the verifiability principle was an impossible criterion to maintain. Currently, in the philosophy of science, it is widely acknowledged that verification is not a viable strategy for substantiating a hypothesis or theory; more appropriate criteria are testability and falsifiability. In all of social science, it is also generally understood that talk of verifiability as a reliable and relatively foolproof process of validating a statement or claim (in a strict sense of conclusive confirmation or disconfirmation) is mistaken. At best, a researcher assembles an argument to substantiate the inference (conclusion) drawn from the data he or she has generated. Substantiation is a matter of demonstrating the likelihood (never the certainty) that the conclusion is correct, genuine, or true or, at least for the time being, not incorrect or false.

See also Evidence, Logical Positivism, Warranted Assertion.

KEY REFERENCES

Ayer, A. J. *Language, Truth and Logic*. London: Gollancz, 1936.
Creswell, J. W. *Qualitative Inquiry and Research Design*. Thousand Oaks, CA: Sage, 1998.

VERISIMILITUDE   The term originates in Karl Popper's (1902–1994) philosophy of science. Popper held that the goal of science is increasing verisimilitude, where verisimilitude meant an approximation toward or closeness to the truth about the way the world really is. He argued that we could compare scientific theories by looking at the relative amounts of truth or falsity contained within each theory. This proved to be an indefensible position, although the notion of verisimilitude has been salvaged in modified form by the philosopher of science W. H. Newton-Smith.

The term *verisimilitude,* as it appears in discussions about the methodologies of qualitative inquiry, is used in ways quite different from that intended by Popper. There are three overlapping definitions of the term, all dealing with a quality of the text:

1. Verisimilitude as a criterion (others include plausibility, internal coherence, and correspondence to readers' own experience) sometimes cited as important for judging narrative inquiry. A narrative account (referring either to the narratives generated from or by respondents or to the narrative report produced by the inquirer) is said to exhibit the quality of verisimilitude when it has the *appearance* of truth or reality. (Note here that what Popper meant by approximation to the truth is quite different than appearance of truth.)

2. Verisimilitude as a criterion for judging the evocative power or sense of authenticity of a textual portrayal: A style of writing that draws readers into the experiences of respondents in such a way that those experiences can be felt.

3. Verisimilitude as the relationship of a particular text to some agreed-on opinions or standards of a particular interpretive community. A particular text (e.g., book review, scholarly essay, speech to a scholarly society, or research report) has verisimilitude to the extent that it conforms to the conventions of its genre.

A related word in poetics is *vraisemblance,* which refers broadly to the plausibility of any text and encompasses the three senses of verisimilitude noted above.

As a criterion for **narrative inquiry,** verisimilitude, and related nonepistemic criteria, has met with some strong opposition by scholars who claim that just because a story or narrative is compelling, plausible, lifelike, seemingly authentic, and so on, it does not follow that it is necessarily true. These scholars argue that while not all stories or narrative accounts need be true—provocative, entertaining fiction has its place, for example—in cases in which it is claimed that the narrative is explanatory or knowledge-bearing, a judgment about whether the account is true or false does matter.

KEY REFERENCES

Culler, J. *Structuralist Poetics: Structuralism, Linguistics, and the Study of Literature.* Ithaca, NY: Cornell University Press, 1975.

Newton-Smith, W. H. *The Rationality of Science.* London: Routledge & Kegan Paul, 1968.

Phillips, D. C. *The Expanded Social Scientist's Bestiary.* Lanham, MD: Rowman & Littlefield, 2000.

VERSTEHEN This is a German term for ***understanding*** used to refer both to the aim of human sciences as well as their method. Reacting to the growing prominence of empiricist and positivist epistemologies in the late nineteenth and early twentieth centuries, the German philosopher and historian Wilhelm Dilthey (1833–1911) set out to establish the unique nature of historical and cultural knowledge. He argued that what fundamentally distinguished the natural sciences (***Naturwissenschaften***) from the human (mental) sciences (***Geisteswissenschaften***) was that the former aimed at developing causal explanations (***Erklärung***) from the outside, so to speak, through the use of general laws, whereas the latter aimed at understanding meaning (*Verstehen*) from the agent's or actor's point of view by grasping the subjective consciousness of action from the inside: "Nature we explain; psychic life we understand." Dilthey relied heavily on the analysis of inner, psychic experience as distinct from (but related to) outer experience of external nature. He emphasized that the social inquirer must engage in a psychological reenactment (*Nacherleben*) or imaginative reconstruction of the experience of human actors in order to understand human social life and history. Hence, his view of *Verstehen* had strong overtones of psychologism (the doctrine that reduces the objects of consciousness to mental states).

This distinction between the natural and human sciences, and the role and meaning of *Verstehen,* was further elaborated by neo-Kantian philosophers Wilhelm Windelband (1848–1915) and Heinrich Rickert (1863–1936), who objected to the psychologism inherent in Dilthey's view. Windelband argued that the natural sciences seek ***nomothetic knowledge*** (general laws), whereas the historical sciences seek to describe unique events (***idiographic*** knowledge). Unlike Dilthey, he held that there was no essential difference in the *objects* that the two sciences studied, only a difference in *method.* Any kind of object (e.g., mental events or physical objects) could be studied by means of both methods. Windelband claimed that positivism's error was in believing that every event must be viewed nomothetically. Rickert developed a connection between ideal or transcendent cultural values and historical events, arguing that it was only through grasping this connection that the meaning of historical events could be made clear. He used the term *Kulturwissenschaften*—cultural sciences—to signal a revision of Dilthey's focus on inner, psychic experience.

Max Weber's (1864–1920) efforts to establish an **interpretive sociology** (*Verstehende* sociology) predicated on an understanding of actors' perspectives of their social action was, in turn, indebted to the work of these predecessors. Weber distinguished two kinds of *Verstehen:* "direct observational understanding," in which the purpose or meaning of human **action** is immediately apparent, and "explanatory understanding," which required grasping the motivation for human behavior by placing the action in some intelligible, inclusive context of meaning. Weber argued that human action is both open to and requires interpretation in terms of the subjective meaning that actors attach to that action. Social scientific (causal) explanation of human action had to be predicated on this kind of understanding.

The phenomenological sociologist Alfred Schutz (1899–1956) sought to clear up the meaning of *Verstehen* by distinguishing three senses of the term:

1. As "the experiential form of common-sense knowledge of human affairs": *Verstehen,* in this definition, has nothing to do with introspection or the subjective states of human agents. Rather, it refers to the intersubjective character of the **lifeworld** and the complex processes by which human beings come to recognize their own actions and those of their fellow actors as meaningful.

2. As an epistemological problem: The central issue here is how *Verstehen* (as a kind of knowledge) is possible. Here, Schutz drew on Edmund Husserl's (1859–1938) considerable work on the concept of the lifeworld (*Lebenswelt*). Husserl had argued that the lifeworld was ontologically prior; all scientific, logical, and mathematical concepts originate in this lifeworld. The lifeworld is the grounds of all understanding.

3. As a method unique to the human sciences: Schutz argued that social reality has a specific meaning and relevance structure for human beings living, acting, and thinking within it. *Verstehen* thus refers to a first-order process by

which we all interpret the world. The interpretation of the world sought by the social scientist must begin by grasping this first-order understanding. The social scientist then fashions a second-order interpretation of that world by employing the constructs of the social sciences. *Verstehen* thus also means a second-order process, a special means of entry into the lifeworld, by which the social inquirer seeks to understand the first-order process.

Despite the efforts of Schutz and others to clarify what is meant by *Verstehen* or interpretive understanding, ***logical empiricists*** (e.g., Theodore Abel and Otto Neurath) seized on the tendency to equate the act of under-standing with grasping subjective, mental states. They argued that *Verstehen* defined as psychological empathy or getting inside other people's heads was interesting only as a heuristic device for generating objectively testable hypotheses. This logical empiricist formulation of *Verstehen* has persisted to the present day and continues to be refuted. For example, echoing Schutz, Charles Taylor, in his often-cited essay "Interpretation and the Sciences of Man" (*Review of Metaphysics*, 1971, 25, 3–51), argued that *Verstehen* has nothing to do with innerorganic or psychological states but with understanding intersubjective meanings constitutive of social life. These meanings, in turn, are not grasped via empathy but by means of a hermeneutic process. And in defending interpretive anthropology, Clifford Geertz found it necessary to explain ("'From the Native's Point of View': On the Nature of Anthropological Understanding," in *Local Knowledge*, Basic Books, 1983) that ethnographers cannot claim "some unique form of psychological closeness" with their subjects. He argued that interpretive understanding of the meaning of human action is forthcoming more from the act of looking over the shoulders of others:

> The trick is not to get yourself into some inner correspondence of spirit with your informants. Preferring, like the rest of us to call their souls their own, they are not going to be altogether keen about such an effort anyhow. The trick is to figure out what the devil they think they are up to. (p. 58)

Hans-Georg Gadamer (1900–2002) accepted Dilthey's idea that the oper-ation of *Verstehen* is profoundly different than explaining the events of nature, but he too rejected the view that understanding depends upon a psychological reenactment of the experiences of human actors. In *Truth and Method* (2nd rev. ed., Continuum, 1989), he argued "*Verstehen ist sprachgebunden*"

("Understanding is tied to language"). Language is the medium of intersubjectivity and the concrete expression of traditions that give human actions particular meaning. *Verstehen* is achieved by entering into a conversation or dialogue with those traditions.

Jürgen Habermas's theory of critical social science accepts the view that the historical-hermeneutic sciences aim at interpretive understanding or *Verstehen* serving the ***interest*** of clarifying the conditions for communication and intersubjectivity. These social sciences stand in contrast to the empirical-analytic sciences that aim at explanation in the interest of controlling and manipulating the social world. Habermas, however, argues that each kind of science, although not reducible to each other, makes the mistake of claiming it provides the fundamental knowledge of human action. He defends a third, more basic, emancipatory cognitive interest that permits the dialectical synthesis of the other two interests and forms the basis of his understanding of a critical social science.

See also Explanation, Understanding.

KEY REFERENCES

Outhwaite, W. *Understanding Social Life: The Method Called* Verstehen. London: George Allen & Unwin, 1975.
Schutz, A. *Collected Papers, Vol. 1,* M. Natanson, ed. and trans. The Hague: Martin Nojhoff, 1967.
Weber, M. "Basic Sociological Terms," in *Economy and Society,* G. Roth & C. Wittich. eds. New York: Bedminster, 1968.

VERSTEHENDE **SOCIOLOGY   See INTERPRETIVE SOCIOLOGY.**

VISUAL RESEARCH METHODS   This is a collection of methods and approaches for using visual materials or images (e.g., drawings, photographs, and videos) in social research both to produce and to represent knowledge. The visual materials in question may be produced by the researcher or found or produced by those the researcher studies. Included here are techniques of ***photo-elicitation***, ethnographic film making, video interviewing, photography as a means of participant observation, and so on. These methods are employed in a number of different methodological and theoretical perspectives including cultural studies, discourse analysis, psychoanalytic interpretation, semiotic analysis, as well as *content analysis*.

KEY REFERENCES

Hamilton, P., ed. *Visual Research Methods* (4 volumes). London: Sage, 2006.
Pink, S. *Doing Visual Ethnography: Images, Media, and Representation in Research.* London: Sage, 2001.
Rose, G. *Visual Methodologies.* London: Sage, 2001.

VOICE   Two overlapping senses of this term are important in contemporary qualitative inquiry: One stems from the *literary turn* in the social sciences and the other stems from feminist philosophy.

1. As part of the increasing interest in the literary analysis of social science texts, scholars imported conceptual tools from literary criticism and narratology (the study of the nature, form, and structure of narrative) into social science discourse. "Voice" is one of those concepts that have become particularly useful tools. It is the set of textual signs that characterize the narrator in a text. Identifying signs of first-person narratives or third-person narratives is part of this notion. Voice includes analysis of all aspects of a text that provide information about who the narrator is—who "speaks." The associations between voice, authority, and the representation of social (and natural) phenomena are a central concern in the literary turn in the social sciences. Experiments with multivoiced, dialogic, and polyphonic texts are, in part, efforts to break up or decenter the monological voice of authority of the lone fieldworker who writes as if he or she is transparently and unproblematically reproducing social reality in an ethnographic account.

2. The concern with the connection between who speaks, who is heard, and what is voiced or given a voice is central to much feminist scholarship (although whether there is a necessary connection between voice and feminist scholarship is debated). While this scholarship shares the concern with voice as defined in the literary turn (and, in many ways, feminist work actually leads the criticism of authorial voice here), it also addresses issues in the politics of voice—for example, how women's voices have been silenced by means of

various social practices (including methodologies of social inquiry); how critiques of these practices can be used to nurture women's voices and bring them to the fore; how women's voices have been absent from social science (and natural science) investigations; and so on.

See also Crisis of Representation, Standpoint Epistemologies.

KEY REFERENCES

Bakhtin, M. M. *Speech Genres and Other Late Essays.* V. W. McGee, trans.; C. Emerson & M. Holquest, eds. Austin: University of Texas Press, 1986.

Fine, M. *Disruptive Voices.* Ann Arbor: University of Michigan Press, 1992.

Genette, G. *Narrative Discourse: An Essay in Method.* Ithaca, NY: Cornell University Press, 1980.

Tierney, W. G., & Lincoln, Y. S., eds. *Representation and the Text: Re-Framing the Narrative Voice.* Albany: SUNY Press, 1997.

WARRANTED ASSERTION The American pragmatic philosopher John Dewey (1859–1952) was generally dissatisfied with calling the outcome of research "knowledge" because that term suggested that knowledge as knowledge is absolute, certain, definitive, and enduring. Dewey argued that knowledge is always provisional and always the result of concrete, situated inquiries. To capture this twofold characteristic, he called the outcome of inquiry *warranted assertion*. Warranted assertions are beliefs strongly supported enough in argument and evidence to be confidently acted upon.

See also *Fallibilism, Knowledge.*

KEY REFERENCE

Biesta, G. J. J., & Burbules, N. C. *Pragmatism and Educational Research.* Lanham, MD: Rowman & Littlefield, 2003.

WELTANSCHAUUNG This is the German term for "worldview" or "philosophy of life." The *Weltanschauung* analysts was a name given to several philosophers of science (including Stephen Toulmin, Thomas Kuhn, Norwood Hanson, and Paul Feyerabend, among others) who were highly critical of how logical positivist epistemology construed the rationality of science as completely free of issues of human judgment. In contrast, they claimed that scientific theorizing was dependent not only on empirical observations but also on the scientist's worldview or conceptual perspective, which determined which questions are worth investigating and which answers are acceptable.

KEY REFERENCE

Suppe, F., ed. *The Structure of Scientific Theories,* 2nd ed. Champaign: University of Illinois Press, 1977.

WRITING STRATEGIES   With the advent of the *literary turn* in the social sciences, the purpose(s) of and strategies for writing or composing an account of qualitative inquiry (or, more broadly, any social scientific account) have become contested. In addition to familiar, traditional advice on techniques for composing a research report, a new tradition is emerging for conceiving of the purpose, style, and ethics of writing. Perhaps the greatest difference in the two ways of thinking about writing centers on the way each conceives of the relationship between language and science. The former regards language as necessary to science; after all, scientists must clearly express themselves in writing. In this way of thinking, however, language is really not much more than a medium that the scientist employs, in more or less effective ways, to display the conclusions or findings resulting from a research practice. In contrast, the concerns about poetics and *rhetoric* characteristic of the new ways of writing are marked by a belief that science, like literature, is an activity *situated in* language. This means that scientists-authors now look to practices other than research (e.g., literature, creative arts, and introspection) for ideas on how both to model and to represent their activity of making sense of the world of others (to understand what others are doing and saying), and that scientists-authors more self-consciously and publicly display the fact that they are artisans engaging in the craft of composition. These ways of thinking about writing are discussed in various new genres, including *autoethnography*, ethnographic fiction, ethnographic poetry, ethnographic drama, and narratives about the writing process itself.

KEY REFERENCES

Becker, H. S. *Writing for Social Scientists: How to Start and Finish Your Thesis, Book, or Article.* Chicago: University of Chicago Press, 1986.

Ellis, C., & Bochner, A., eds. *Contemporary Ethnography: Alternative Forms of Qualitative Writing.* Walnut Creek, CA: AltaMira, 1996.

Richardson, L. *Writing Strategies: Reaching Diverse Audiences.* Newbury Park, CA: Sage, 1990.

Wolcott, H. *Writing Up Qualitative Research.* Newbury Park, CA: Sage, 1990.